Path to Nigerian Development

Edited by Okwudiba Nnoli

Path to Nigerian Development

Edited by Okwudiba Nnoli

Codesria, B.P. 3304, Dakar, Senegal.

Path to Nigerian Development was first published by
Codesria, B.P. 3304, Dakar, Senegal in March 1981.

ISBN 0 86232 021 6

Designed by Mayblin/Shaw
Copyedited by Lorne Larson
Typeset by Margaret Cole
Proofread by Lorne Larson
Cover design by Jacque Solomons
Printed in U.S.A.

Distributed by Codesria in conjunction with Zed Press,
57 Caledonian Road, London N1 9DN, U.K.

U.S. Distributor
Lawrence Hill and Co., 520 Riverside Avenue, Westport,
Conn. 06880, U.S.A.

Contents

Contributors

Okwudiba Nnoli is Professor of Political Science and Head of Department at the University of Nigeria, Nsukka. He is the author of *Self-reliance and Foreign Policy in Tanzania* and *Ethnic Politics in Nigeria.*

Bade Onimode is an economist with Ecoconsultants of Nigeria. He was formerly Senior Lecturer in the Department of Economics at the University of Ibadan. He is the co-author of *Economic Development of Nigeria: The Socialist Alternatives.*

Inyang A. Eteng is Senior Lecturer in the Department of Sociology and Anthropology at the University of Nigeria, Nsukka.

T. Uzodinma Nwala is Senior Lecturer in the Department of Philosophy at the University of Nigeria, Nsukka. He is the author of *Justice on Trial* and *Mbaise in Contemporary Nigeria.*

Preface

This book was sponsored by the Council for the Development of Economic and Social Research in Africa (CODESRIA), an inter-African institution based in Senegal. It is part of its overall program of providing indigenous African explanations of African problems and phenomena, through the activities of National Working Groups and Multinational Working Groups. The former, drawn from academicians from an individual African country, concentrates on problems and phenomena of particular importance in their society, and the latter is composed of intellectuals from diverse African nations, and focusses on a problem of general importance to the continent as a whole. Thus, the Nigerian National Working Group was set up in 1977 under the auspices of CODESRIA, with me as the co-ordinator.

The motive force for the sponsorship of this program together with the necessary working groups was the failure of the dominant mode of analysis of Nigerian and African problems to provide an adequate intellectual basis for the socio-economic and political emancipation of the African peoples. In spite of this failure, the tendency has been for most of the African scholars and foreign analysts of African problems to continue to employ the same academic framework which in the past has proved sterile. And there is very little indication that it will do better in the future. In fact, it has provided no reason to necessitate any belief that its disastrous performance in the past will not be repeated in the future. But since this framework is associated with the world view of the present foreign and local rulers of the African countries various patterns of rewards, such as academic promotions, have been used to entrench it in African universities and intellectual circles as the dominant and majoritarian viewpoint.

Nevertheless, its shortcomings have necessitated the search for possible alternative frameworks for explaining and ultimately changing the African reality for the better. The development of a different theoretical viewpoint, even if at this point in time it may represent a minoritarian position, will serve not only to illuminate African reality from an altogether different vantage point, but hopefully will force the adherents of the majoritarian framework to think more critically about their analytical tools and try to justify their continued use of them.

Therefore, the members of the Nigerian National Working Group have been chosen on the basis of their capacity to provide an alternative explanation for, and therefore basis for the transformation of, Nigerian reality. Unfortunately, a number of the scholars who were invited to participate in the group were unable to do so because of health and other personal reasons. However, since the group has a long-term perspective of its activities, I hope that these distinguished Nigerian academics will eventually bring their wealth of understanding of Nigerian affairs to the activities of the group in order to enrich its members and be enriched in the process. It is hoped that the group will act as a forum for the exchange and development of new ideas and information on how best to tackle Nigerian problems in a way that is not constrained by the straightjacket of the prevailing majoritarian framework.

Another objective of the group expressed by the production of this book is to provide an alternative set of reading materials for the students and staff of Nigerian universities and all those interested in understanding the realities of Nigerian life. In this respect a particular interest exists in exposing the shortcomings of the prevailing analyses, correcting these shortcomings through a more adequate explanation of Nigerian problems, and providing valuable insights into these problems by focussing on some issues and phenomena which the majoritarian framework is too timid or to incapable to deal with, but which greatly enrich the understanding of the problems of the country. Such an objective does not entertain the possibility of analytical sacred cows. All aspects of national life are to be exposed.

Finally, the activities of the group are and will be motivated solely by service to the upliftment of the vast majority of the Nigerian people, the toiling masses. Therefore, it is opposed to the maintenance of inherited privileges or the acquisition of new ones. All concepts, analytical perspectives, and choice of problems to be discussed must justify themselves by their capacity to serve the interests of the masses. This attitude shuns the view that knowledge can be sought for itself. Instead it is dedicated to showing how to go forward with the masses of Nigeria in explaining and, above all, changing their conditions for their own betterment. In the process it is hoped that the true elements of Nigerian patriotism will emerge. And it will not be a patriotism that serves foreign interests.

I wish hereby to thank all those who have made this book possible, particularly CODESRIA who helped financially and organizationally in setting it in motion, sustaining its momentum, and finally producing it. My thanks also go to all the contributors for their excellent contributions, and their willingness to stand up and be counted in this struggle of the Nigerian masses for a better life. In addition, I wish to thank all those who have helped with the reading of the various contributions for their useful comments, and the typists. Without all these various inputs this book, especially its present high standards, may not have been achieved.

Okwudiba Nnoli
University of Nigeria, Nsukka
January 1977

1. Introduction: The Intellectual Aspects of the Struggle for Nigerian Development

Okwudiba Nnoli

The Two Contending Paths to Development

Today, Nigeria is involved in the second phase of its struggle for national liberation. The first phase ended with the achievement of political independence in 1960. Now, instead of the path to national freedom, Nigerians must tread the path to national development. In a historically short period of time they must emancipate the vast majority of their population from the pervasive and high incidence of poverty, ignorance, disease, squalor, poor diet, and poor shelter. Life for the majority is intolerable. A people faced with such a deplorable situation may perish, stagnate, or devise new ways and means of improving it. Nigerians are not an exception. And as a virile and ambitious people, they will not accept the alternatives of extinction and stagnation. Under the circumstances, the potentialities of any path to national progress out of the present socio-economic morass are very crucial indeed.

What are the alternative paths to national development? Which is the correct path and why? These are the most critical questions facing Nigerians today. The contributors to this book address themselves to these issues. They contend that at the present historical juncture Nigeria is faced with two alternative paths to development: the capitalist and socialist paths. This reality reflects the historical development of the two dominant and competing camps of the world community, the socialist and capitalist camps, each of which is led by a superpower. It is daily emphasized and reinforced by the competitive activities of these camps in furtherance of one or the other path to development. The superpowers and the other major powers use their enormous economic, political, and military power and influence in the world to ensure that the other states follow one or the other of these paths, and often attempt to obstruct the adoption of their rival's pattern of development. Under the circumstances, and in view of the absence at this point in time of a viable and influential third path, Nigerian-type societies have been compelled to follow in one of these two paths.

The capitalist path is presumed to lead to the pattern of 'the good life' which has been attained by the advanced capitalist societies. Of course, these societies vary politically, economically, culturally, and militarily. Some are political democracies; others are or have been fascist dictatorships. They also differ in terms of the degree of public participation in economic life, and in their type and manner of expression of cultural values, symbols, and rituals. These differences arise from their diverse historical and environmental conditions, particularly their inherited level of production, the nature of their social system, political organization, structure of social consciousness, ideological and socio-pyschological orientations, the views of their ruling classes and various social groups, and the rivalry between the various groupings within their ruling circles.

However, they are all characterized by capitalism and the capitalist mode of production. This is a system determined not by the people's attitude to wealth, their spirit of enterprise, desire for gain, or the use of money to finance a series of exchange transactions in order to make profit, but by the way in which the means of production are owned, and the articulation of social relations between individuals and groups arising from the production process, particularly the manner in which work is organized and the surplus from production is distributed. Its central determining feature is the transformation of labour power of man into a commodity to be bought and sold in the market for gain, like any other object of exchange. It was the first system of production, and so far the only one in the history of humanity, to make labour power a marketable commodity. Its prerequisites are the separation of the actual producers of products from their means of production, the concentration of the latter in the hands of a class of people constituting only a minor section of society, and the consequent emergence of a class for whom the sale of labour power is the only source of livelihood. Therefore, a system such as that of pre-colonial Nigeria, dominated by independent peasant and handicraft production where the peasant and craftsman own their own implements of production and undertake the sale of their own products, is not a capitalist system. There is no divorce between ownership and the creation of the products of production. It is the purchase and sale of inanimate objects, not human labour power, that is of primary concern.

Similarly, the existence of trade, money-lending, and a specialized class of merchants or financiers, even if they are wealthy, does not suffice to constitute a capitalist society. Men of wealth, no matter how acquisitive, are not enough. Their wealth must be used to buy and yoke labour power to the creation of products in order for the system to be a capitalist one. Although the acquisitive mentality, desire for gain in monetary transactions, and the accumulation of wealth by individuals date back thousands of years, capitalism is no more than four hundred years old. It is governed by the private investment of capital in production by a class which makes its living solely from the returns on this investment; the domination of labour by this capital in the determination of what is to be produced (and by what means) and how it is to be distributed; and the expanded reproduction of this capital through profit maximization.[1]

The socialist path on the other hand is presumed to lead to the pattern of good life enjoyed by the advanced socialist societies, and that predicted by socialist theory. In spite of differences arising from their varied historical, economic, political, and cultural experiences, socialist societies all operate the socialist mode of production. This is a system of production in which there is a separation of the actual producers from their means of production; the concentration of the latter in the hands of the social collectivity as a whole, the state; values are produced not as commodities for exchange in the market but to satisfy basic needs and prevailing consumption habits; certainly labour power is not a commodity to be sold and bought for profit; and the interests of labour are superior to, and dominant over, those of capital in deciding what is produced, how it is produced, and how the products are distributed. It entails a radical change in the relations of production through the collective ownership and control of the means of production, and the collective appropriation of the surplus social product. 'The production relations are not changed so long as the private employer has merely been replaced by the employer-state, embodied in some all-powerful manager, technocrat, or bureaucrat. They are not changed until the various groups of workers start to have a real day-to-day (and not merely formal and juridical control) over the management of the enterprise, the working out and carrying through of the plans, and the social surplus product created within the enterprise.'[2]

The socialist mode of production also entails the abolition of the hierarchical structure of the enterprise and the social division of labour between those who accumulate and those who produce. It further implies the elimination of alienated labour carried out on other people's orders and for the benefit of others, and therefore mechanical and non-creative. It is antithetical to the private appropriation of the necessary product of production in the form of wages, of exchange, and of the selling of labour power for a money wage, and the appropriation of part of the social product in the form of individual consumer privileges. In a socialist society, labour is regarded as the means to the full development of all the faculties and potentialities of the individual, and as a conscious service by him to the society. This is incompatible with the concept of labour as a way of earning one's living or appropriating the goods and services that one needs.[3]

The nature of organization of some of the pre-colonial Nigerian societies is sometimes confused with socialism. This confusion arises essentially from the tendency to define socialism in terms of the contemporary but historically specific products of socialist reconstruction in such countries as the Soviet Union and China, rather than in terms of its essence as delineated above. Therefore, the principles of joint production, egalitarian distribution, and the universal obligation to work found in both the pre-colonial societies and the socialist states have become a basis for wrongly categorizing the former as socialist. But in the pre-colonial systems a proletariat had not emerged, because the divorce between the producer and his means of production usually purveyed by capitalism had not taken place. In the historical development of humankind the pre-colonial modes of production antedate capitalism while socialism postdates it. They are entirely different social phenomena based on different levels of production, productive forces, and production relations.

Is There a Third Path to Nigerian Development?

In the debate over the correct path of Nigerian development, some suggest the possibility of a third path different from the capitalist and socialist options. Elliot Berg contends that there is little likelihood of success along the road of socialist modernization in Africa. He lists impediments like the difficult climatic conditions, the ossified structure of the African community, and the lack of skilled workers. In his view the socialist economy, in which the state plays the leading role, is much more complicated and difficult to operate than the capitalist market system. It requires many more experts, and in places where private African entrepreneurs have displayed an ability for efficient action, it is unlikely that government functionaries would be able to carry out the work as successfully.[4] He suggests a mixed economy as the third and suitable alternative. The Constitution Drafting Committee (CDC) virtually plagiarized Berg's argument.[5] But all is very subjective in Berg's world. No objective reasons are given for his speculations and no scientific evidence for his assertions.

On the question of the efficacy of state enterprises the enemies of socialism who advocate a third path often point out that the Nigerian public institutions have not done as well as the private ones. But again this is an exceedingly subjective assessment. No objective criteria are provided for comparison. The lapses of some state enterprises are pointed out and compared with the achievements of the successful private businesses. Nothing is said of the lapses of the unsuccessful private ones or the achievements of the successful state enterprises, including the propping up of virtually all the private enterprises through public sector loans and contracts awarded to the latter, as well as the purchase of their products. We all know, however, that the private enterprises were largely responsible for the cement scandal which nearly ruined the Nigerian economy, the Lockheed scandal and the general corruption in the country arising from their institutionalization of the 10 per cent commission, the hoarding of goods, the accompanying inflation and scarcity of goods, the numerous uncompleted contracts, the badly executed contracts, piracy in Nigerian waters, and armed robbery. The private sector is unwilling to undertake activities in the national interest which are not very profitable. Nigerian businessmen undermine national economic independence through junior partnerships with foreign companies who export our wealth to their countries.

The Nigerian public sector is equated with a socialist sector by proponents of a third path. Its historical origin, character, and development which suggest otherwise are ignored. For example, during the colonial period foreign capitalists could not operate their profit-making enterprises without the support of other activities which did not yield profits. The enterprises which yielded profits were found in the import-export trade, banking, insurance, shipping, wholesale and retail trade, and tin and petroleum mining. But railways and roads were important for the profitability of these enterprises; so was the mining of coal to be used in running the railway system. Similarly, electricity, telephone, telegraph and postal services, the civil service, the army and police were also important. The colonial state intervened to provide these services using the taxes and productive resources obtained from the colonized.

This is the historical origin of the public sector in the Nigerian economy. It is a sector that is based on the inability of its enterprises to generate profit, yet it is essential for the operation of the profit-making private sector. Least of all, it services the interest of the vast majority of the population, but is paid for by their taxes and other resources. Therefore, it emerged and has persisted as an instrument for the exploitation of the majority in addition to their exploitation in the production process. And because it was only peripheral to the interests of the foreign capitalists, conditions of work in it, particularly the wages, were less attractive than in the private companies, with a consequent lowering of worker morale and productivity. These shortcomings are in turn used to discredit public ownership of economic activities.

Often the argument for a third path presents the public sector as a form of socialization of the economy. The socialist ideology argues that production cannot be in the interest of the workers unless it is transferred from private to public hands. But socialist thought also points out that public ownership is important only if it leads to workers' control of production, which in turn should lead to their control of the decisions of the production process, particularly how its surplus is distributed. Also socialist theory dictates that the public enterprises operate with rules, procedures, and an ethos which institutionalize the dominance of labour over capital. Obviously, the Nigerian public sector was not designed to meet these socialist criteria or to serve the interest of the workers, the toiling people. If it were, its relations of production would have favoured the dominance of labour over capital, its mode of production and distribution would reflect this dominance, and it would have been propelled more by the desire to satisfy the basic needs and traditional consumption habits of the masses than by the desire to service the activities of the foreign capitalists, their local agents, and the colonial state.

With the coming of independence, a retrograde change has occurred in the public sector. Most of its activities are now performed by private contractors. Public enterprises now hardly execute any of their projects with their own personnel. How then can the failure of their projects be blamed on them rather than the private contractors who execute them? Public enterprises merely retain the form but not the substance of their previous existence. Their failures are today the failures of the private sector.

Other apologists of capitalism and imperialism such as the American political scientists Zbigniew Brzezinski and Samuel Huntington argue that socialism is acquiring capitalist features, that in the age of scientific and

and technological revolution it is becoming more and more similar to modern capitalism. They also suggest that capitalism has changed its nature and has begun to resemble socialism. Therefore, there is a third way of social development lying somewhere between capitalism and socialism.[6] The appeal contained in these assertions is directed to the eclectic and pragmatic mind. Its main objectives, however, are to allow the imperialist monopolies unimpeded access into, and permit local and foreign capitalists to strengthen their hold on, the new states. To support these assertions, no care is taken is show how the relationship between capital and labour in the capitalist and socialist countries has changed.

Some of the Nigerian adherents of the above viewpoint see the mixed economy as the necessary third road. For them all systems are mixed; it is merely a matter of the degree of mix.[7] All discussion of the relations of production is banished. In Nigeria, however, the mixed economy seeks to promote the capitalist path to development. It is really a neo-colonial, peripheral, capitalist economy in which both the public and private sectors promote capitalism under the aegis of world imperialism. Similarly, it is a mistake to think of the welfare state, or 'welfarism, as a middle road. It is a form of capitalism in which the productive forces are highly developed and welfare services are widely distributed. Nevertheless, its relations of production and manner of appropriating the surplus from production are capitalist. Private and public capital organizes, dominates, and exploits labour. This is the case in Sweden, Denmark, and Norway and also in Britain and France. Nigeria must first build advanced capitalism in order to develop a welfare state. As is clear from the contributions in this book, it is this capacity to develop advanced capitalism that is rendered problematic by the nature of the neocolonial society.

Reactionaries in Nigeria want people to shun socialism and follow a third path. Since most of their ideas about socialism come second,third, and fourth-hand from metropolitan bourgeois intellectuals who hardly go into the depths of its methology, they approach it as if it is simply a body of conclusions, some of which may be accepted or rejected. They suggest a vague unique system which borrows eclectically from primitive communalism, feudalism, capitalism, and socialism. This attitude is most unscientific and unhealthy. Socialism is not simply this or that aspect of life. It is a whole world outlook, with its own philosophical base and its own method of identifying problems and solutions. It cannot be broken up and applied in bits.

Finally, some of these advocates oppose socialism on grounds of cultural nationalism. They are averse to an ideology that is conceived in 'a foreign political and social climate.'[8] The geographical origin of socialism becomes a major reason for rejecting it. They forget that socialism is equally foreign to all the socialist countries of the world with the exception of East Germany. The originators of its ideas, Marx and Engels, were Germans. Nevertheless, the Russians, Chinese, Cubans, Vietnamese, and other peoples widely divergent in their cultural backgrounds, have found it useful for uplifting themselves from what seemed like an incurable malaise of national humiliation, as well as poverty, ignorance, and disease. And they have not lost their specific cultural identities in the process.

Socialist theory is not mechanistic.[9] Subjective consciousness of the toiling majority is one of its vital ingredients. Therefore, consciousness is a principal factor in socialist change. It is affected by knowledge, self-awareness, and organized activity all tied together. These in turn are influenced by local cultural values, ethos, ethics, and norms, and the totality of the peoples' past history. Thus, local cultural values usually become an integral part of socialist change. For instance, the socialist leadership of Tanzania demands the traditional communal virtue of hard work, but no longer in a context where local exploitation is allowed. The articles in this book suggest that at this historical juncture in Nigeria the attainment of the goal of socialism requires first and foremost the liquidation of the imperialist monopolies, creating a progressive and internally integrated national economy on the basis of developing the state sector and overcoming the colonial legacy in the sphere of socio-economic relations. There is nothing in the pursuit of these objectives that is antithetical to the best in Nigerian traditional cultural values. The details of how to resolve these problems and how to harness cultural values to their resolution are tactical questions which can only be discussed usefully in the course of revolutionary practice.

The insistence on an African identity is a worthwhile corrective not only for bourgeois cultural imperialism, but also for the dogmatic beliefs of some socialists. The identification with the particularity of experience is essential for appreciating the universality of experience. But in many countries, African socialism has come to mean a system of relations which uses traditional African forms to preserve capitalism, imperialism, and inherited privileges. While the Nigerian neo-cultural nationalists denounce socialism as foreign, they ignore the foreign capitalist influences in the country. Our schools disseminate Western bourgeois social theories as if they are not foreign. Nigerian factories turn out beer,cigarettes, and Coca-Cola introduced from foreign capitalist lands. The economy is dominated by an import-export sector that is structurally tied to foreign capital. Top Nigerian businessmen are mostly junior partners of foreign capitalists, or are otherwise dependent on the latter for their livelihood. Foreign capitalists monopolize major contract jobs in the country. Our taste and consumption patterns are increasingly determined by the advertisements of multinational corporations and mass media based in foreign capitalist countries. To call for originality and authenticity in these areas of national life is to blame all our troubles on imperialism (apparently a bad thing), or to be unrealistic.

Two important questions confront the advocates of a third road based on an indigenous ideology. First, what ideology shall prevail in the interim before the advent of the new system? Second, is our history of colonial and neo-colonial capitalism irrelevant to our present and future existence, which this ideology must address itself to? To ignore the historical changes that have taken place and advocate the application of old solutions to new problems is to express an unwillingness to tackle the problems. The net effect is an endorsement of the prevailing system.

A similar effect is produced by the desire to avoid the question of ideology. The *ad hoc* 'pragmatic' solution of problems as they arise takes place within certain prevailing broad general rules of behaviour and conduct, and is guided by them. They suggest what the problems are and how they should be resolved. In Nigeria, it is this system of rules – not the problems it defines – which is problematic. An ideological solution and, therefore, commitment is thus inescapable. To be non-ideological is to support the present capitalist path.

The Epistemological Foundation of the Socialist Path

Thus, the search for a third road to development is both a reflection of the bankruptcy of the present capitalist path followed by Nigeria, and an attempt to forestall the adoption of the socialist path which has become increasingly popular with the growing impotence of the neo-colonial policies to solve the problems of the vast majority of the population. As the two contending ideologies continue to be pitted against each other, the struggle between their respective ideologies in the academic community has intensified. The small minority that advocates the socialist path has grown in number, strength, boldness, and confidence. This book constitutes one of their major challenges to their adversaries. Since an analytical perspective which suggests what the definition and the solutions of the problems of development are underlies each path to development, these academic skirmishes involve a struggle over the correct interpretation and solution of the development problems and policies of the country. Herein lies the strength of the various contributions in this book. Not only do they establish the relevance of the Marxist methodology, which underlies the socialist path, to the study of the Nigerian society, they also indicate that such a method of study can be a very useful instrument in the understanding and, therefore, transformation of the reality of Nigerian social, economic, political, and cultural life. These qualities are embodied in the nature of that methodology.

The common epistemological foundation of all the contributions is historical materialism, a non-metaphysical system of ideas. The non-Marxist bourgeois tradition of analysis of society from Plato to Hegel and beyond is metaphysical in character, presuming a certain imminent order in nature above society, which serves as an ideal toward which all societies must strive. Such an order does not vary in time and space, and therefore can be transposed from one historical epoch to another, and from one part of the globe to another. More importantly, those societies which approximate this order more closely are superior to the others, and in fact have a duty, if not a right, to spread their pattern of life to the rest of mankind. This kind of thinking lay behind Hegel's and the Nazi's concept of the master race, and the rationalizations of colonialism. Hence, the parliamentary system of government, the free enterprise economic system, freedom of the press, and individualism are advocated for all societies. This metaphysical character of the non-Marxist intellectual tradition is the basis for the foreign economic, cultural, ideological, and political domination of one society by another.

Historical materialism rejects this metaphysical and ahistorical conception of social life. It maintains, instead, that society is inseparable from men, even analytically. Social life begins with concrete human beings whose needs lead them to production. Therefore, there is no human order outside that created by the laws of social interaction, which manifest themselves only through human activity. As a scientific method, historical materialism considers the general aspects, tendencies, and laws of development of a society in order to elucidate the general laws governing the development of any human society. As these general laws of world history operate variously in different historical epochs and concrete human situations due to the changing and diverse needs of man, and the accompanying changes and diversity in his pattern of production, this method of analysis investigates in detail each concrete human condition in order to delineate the social laws applicable to it, and the kind of social order created by these laws. Such a methodology cannot be the intellectual basis for foreign cultural and ideological domination of one society by another. It must be oriented toward the local conditions.

The search for recurrent patterns, without which the laws of social development cannot be discerned, is carried on in the context of the analyses of particular societies, with the identification of these recurrent patterns being preceded by the observation of non-recurrent specific attributes. There is no substitute for the examination of particular conditions as a prelude to the delineation of recurrent phenomena. This confers particularity on the Marxist analytical perspective. The uniqueness of detail is as crucial to understanding as the recurrent pattern. Historical events present a unity of the recurrent and the unique. Both attributes are determined by examining concrete societies. No recurrent pattern or unique details identified in one society can be transposed to another automatically and mechanically. And they cannot be the object of abstract theorizing. Analytically, there are no superior or inferior societies. There is no approximation to the ideal pattern since no such pattern exists. The human activity of each society must be the beginning and end of analysis. Under these circumstances cultural domination is impossible. Imitation by one society of social processes in another is outlawed.

Lenin taught that owing to the existence of national differences, the unevenness in the levels of economic and cultural development, the character of traditions, and other features, the principles of scientific socialism should be applied in such a way as would 'correctly modify these principles in certain particulars, correctly adapt and apply them to national and national-state distinctions.'[10] In an address to the Second Congress of Communist Organisations of the East, he reiterated that 'relying upon the general theory and practice of communism, you must adapt yourselves to specific conditions such as do not exist in the European countries, you must be able to apply that theory and practice to conditions in which the bulk of the population are peasants, and in which the task is to wage a struggle against medieval survivals and not against capitalism.'[11]

In a similar emphasis on the study of specific concrete situations, Marx remarked, 'events strikingly analogous, but which take place in different historical environments, lead to entirely different results. Studying each of these evolutions separately and then comparing them, it is easy to find the key to understanding these phenomena, but this understanding can never be attained by utilizing a universal master key in the form of a general historico-philosophical theory.'[12] Engels stressed that the laws of the development of society do not have 'any reality, except as approximation, tendency, average, and not as immediate reality.'[13] In general, therefore, the question of what political, social, or economic measures demand greater time and effort, and the sequence of these measures themselves, must be decided according to the concrete situation in a country. The science of man is constantly progressing, not only because of the widening historical experience of mankind, but also because every concrete fundamental study based on a concrete method becomes a milestone in appraising this experience.

Also, historical materialism always considers the relation between social being and social consciousness. In this way it can explain the laws of history not as the effect of some mysterious forces directing the affairs of men, or the result of some fortuitous movement toward an ideal state of affairs, but as the effect of recurrent patterns manifesting themselves through men's concrete activity, through their struggle to attain specific goals which often have nothing in common with the general course of history but which nevertheless stand in organic relation to this course. Thus, historical materialism does not suffer from that ideological distortion characteristic of a metaphysical outlook, which is the basis for cultural domination.

In spite of this emphasis on the particular and the concrete, there is a universalistic aspect to Marxist methodology. The materialist conception of history formulated by Marx and Engels perceives human society as a highly complex phenomenon, comprising a maze of diverse relations and connections arising from man's activities. These human activities tend to vary from one society to another. These variations give an appearance of chaos and uniqueness of detail to the history of mankind. Yet historical materialism contends, and has been able to demonstrate, that there is a certain recurrent pattern in that history. Marx was able to apply the yardstick of recurrence to the history of mankind without sacrificing the details and concreteness of the particular situation. Hence, although world history has passed through stages of the primitive communal, slave, feudal, and capitalist modes of production and social formations to the socialist mode or production and social formation, the history of each society has not necessarily passed, and may not necessarily pass, through all these stages. The course of each must be examined concretely in order to be able to identify its pattern and direction of motion.

History and Local Conditions

The historical character of the Marxist methodology employed by all the contributors to this book compels them to take into account and address themselves to the concrete local condition, without wasting time on sterile abstractions. This is because the Marxist method is based on the view that history is not determined by ideas but by material production, and that history is not made by isolated political heroes and military leaders but by the masses, particularly the working people. Prior to Marx, sociologists and other social scientists examined, at best, only the ideological motives of human activity, usually neglecting the material circumstances, which they treated as a side issue unessential to history. The view that social activity and, therefore, history are the outcome of religious, political, legal, and other ideas was dominant. Even today, bourgeois social science assigns the primary role in history to individual personalities and non-human factors such as capital, technology, and know-how. But the materialist conception of history formulated by Marx and Engels believes that the masses, as the producers of all material and spiritual values available in society, are the makers of history.[14] This is a corollary of the Marxist belief in the production process as the primary, principal, and crucial dimension of the life of society and, therefore, of history. If the production of material goods is the basis of history, then the decisive role in history belongs to the actual producers of these goods, the masses.

This belief in the historical role of the masses has an important bearing on the question of the relevance of Marxist methodology in Nigerian-type societies. If individual personalities create history, then it is possible for the relevant individual to come from outside the society. By focussing on him, it may be possible to understand the history of the society without examining the local conditions. This is impossible if the focus of history is the masses. It is unrealistic to expect the masses to come from outside the local society and environment. We are therefore compelled to direct our attention toward the various local conditions associated with their lives. Thus, a detailed examination of local conditions as a basis for the understanding and transformation of the lives of the people is ensured.

Besides this role of history in ensuring local relevance, it is vitally important for understanding and changing reality. As Marx has observed: 'The first and most important of the inherent qualities of matter is motion, not only mechanical motion but still more impulse, vital life-spirit, tension, or . . . the throes of matter.'[15] Human society is constantly changing. To divorce this process of change from social analysis is to isolate the past from the present and the future, or to explain the past with little reference to the present and the future, or to predict or visualize the future without using the experiences of the past and the present. In such an analysis there is very little indication of movement and casuality. Explanation gives way to description and wishful thinking. Unlike the case in the natural sciences, a fact in the social sciences is a union of the past, the present, and the future. This organic link cannot realistically be broken, even for analytical purposes. No fact is useful to social knowledge unless it is characterized by this link. This is why Lenin warned doctrinaire Marxists that 'to ignore the changes which have taken place . . . and to continue advocating the old solutions given by Marxism would mean repeating the old conclusions by rote, without being able to use the Marxist method of research to analyze the new political situation.'[16]

Also, an historical perspective leads to a holistic and concrete focus and away from the atomization and abstraction of the subject matter characteristic of bourgeois social science. One can study every social phenomenon in isolation and stop at that. On the other hand, it is possible to study all social phenomena in their mutual relationship without examining any one of them in isolation. In both cases the study will be one-sided. The correct methodology is to study all social phenomena both in isolation and in their mutual relationship in time and space, which means to study a concrete situation dialectically.[17] The scientific dialectical method by which historical materialism investigates the life of society, considering it in the process of its continuous development, implies that historical materialism itself keeps developing as it draws its general conclusions from fresh concrete historical experience and the findings of the social sciences.[18]

An historical perspective forces the analyst to take into account 'not individual facts, but the sum total of facts, without a single exception, relating to the question under discussion. Otherwise there will be the inevitable, and fully justified, suspicion that the facts were selected or compiled arbitrarily, that instead of historical phenomena being presented in objective interconnection and interdependence and treated as a whole, we are presenting a 'subjective concoction'.'[19] As Lenin has aptly pointed out: 'Minor facts, if taken out of their entirety, out of their interconnection, if they are arbitrarily selected and torn out of context, are merely things for juggling, or even worse.'[20] Thus historical materialism is concerned with the unique details of concrete local conditions, enjoining the analyst to put such details into wider national, international, and historical contexts.

Furthermore, an historical approach focuses attention on the unity of the old and the new, often accounting for the emergence of the new from the old. Historical materialism conceptualizes social life as a dialectical phenomenon in which the new is conceived in the womb of the old, is given birth by the latter, and nurtured into maturity by it. On completing this, its historic role, the old may wither away, atrophy, or coexist with the new, but in a subservient position. Soon the new becomes the old and repeats the process. History moves on. The phenomenon cannot be fully understood outside this dialectical process between the old and the new because the process not only indicates the various forces which constitute the phenomenon but also the dynamics of their interaction. The unity of the past and the present is thus affirmed.

Underlying this dialectical process is man's role as a history-maker under conditions of his changing needs and goals. A citizen finds in his society full-formed social relations such as relations of production and a state structure. Although he may influence the circumstances he finds himself in, he cannot choose them. Therefore, the laws operating in society are as objective and independent of individual will as are the laws of nature. Yet there are some distinctions between the laws of nature and laws of society. The most important of these distinctions is that the laws of nature not only operate independently of human will and consciousness, but are altogether independent of men. For them, man might simply not exist. Of course, having knowledge of natural laws, man can often accelerate changes in natural conditions in a direction useful to society.

The situation is altogether different with the laws of society. Although they operate independently of man's will, they are always realized through men, through human activity. Therefore, history is entirely the product of human activity. History is made by men, but they have to make it in accordance with the objective circumstances prevailing during the lifetime of each generation, and not just as their fancy takes them, or according to some foreign or even local model. Therefore, human activity is the main condition necessary for the laws of history to operate. Human activity varies from society to society and from generation to generation. Thus the history of one society or generation cannot be transposed to another. Hence, on the question of the destiny of the countries of Asia and Africa, Engels aptly remarked that 'as to what social and political phases these countries will then have to pass through before they likewise arrive at socialist organisation, I think we today can advance only rather idle hypotheses . . .

Also, history must not be regarded as a fatalistic process whereby people carry out the one and only possible course of events dictated by historical necessity. Historical necessity manifests itself in different ways, and not necessarily at once. History is governed by laws, but the ways of history are not fatally determined. Historical choice is decided in the struggle of social forces, as a result of which one of the possible variants of historical development is determined. At times progressive forces may be defeated and reactionary forces may prevail temporarily. In the end, however, the forces of progress tend to get the upper hand.[21] This is the viewpoint of historical materialism. The ability of a given society to make history is not a divine gift, but a potentiality accumulated by the labour and the intellectual activity of the masses and individuals, together with their ability to search for the new and to struggle against obsolete institutions and notions.

Finally, the Marxist method of social analysis is characterized by the view that history is based not on ideas but on material production. Marx successfully argued that in order to be able to think man must first satisfy his material needs, particularly the needs for food, water, and shelter. Therefore, at the basis of history is the production of all those goods and services which go to satisfy man's material needs.[22] If material production thus provides the primary relationships in a society, then ideas have their origin in these relationships and perform certain functions for aspects of such relationships. In other words, ideas do not have an independent force of their own isolated or divorced from society in general and the society's production process in particular. They arise from society, are anchored in the production process, service the society and, therefore, must be understood within the local context. They cannot serve as an ideal imposed on local conditions which are then forced to conform to this ideal. Therefore, social, political, cultural, and religious relations organized on the basis of such ideas cannot be set above the society, or understood in isolation from the material basis of the society. Ultimately these relations derive their existence from, and serve the social production process of, the society.

The production of man's material needs varies from one society to another. This variation is the result of differences in the inherited level of production, the nature of the productive forces, and the character of the social relations of production that the members of the society enter into largely independently of their will. In the view of historical materialism these variations confer a certain particularity to societies, which are related to changes in social, political, and cultural relations, and which must be taken into account by the analyst. Thus, by its emphasis on material production as the basis of society and human history, Marxism emphasizes factors of the local conditions in the analysis of society.

The Usefulness of the Marxist Method

As will be amply illustrated by the contributions of this book, the application of Marxist methodology to the analysis of Nigerian-type societies is useful in various ways. Among other uses, it exposes as hollow the bourgeois assertion that Marxism is irrelevant to Africa because of the differences between Africa and Europe where the theory was developed. Mention has already been made of the different ways by which this method of analysis focuses on concrete conditions, including their unique details. It must be emphasized, however, that it is wrong to regard an analysis as concrete merely because it concerns a definite fact of reality. The study of facts must not be limited to their superficial descriptions. Such facts need to be explained to disclose the essence of the historical process of the reality under study. Explanations cannot be achieved outside a theory, and for Nigerian-type societies this theory must be one which enables the overall picture of the reality to emerge in the different forms of its evolution as engendered by colonialism and neo-colonialism.

Another aspect of the Marxist method which generates the accusation of irrelevance to African conditions concerns its perspective of class analysis. Many non-Marxist African intellectuals and politicians assert that Africa is devoid of classes. Therefore, according to their argument, since class analysis is the most important and fundamental aspect of Marxist theory, Marxism does not apply to Africa. There are two areas of ignorance and misconception in this argument. The one concerns what constitutes the fundamental unit of Marxist analysis, and the other relates to the nature and dynamics of classes and class struggle. The fundamental unit of Marxism is the production process, the mode of production. It is characterized by the productive forces or the instruments with which man carries on its productive activities, and the relations of production or the pattern of inter-human interaction established at the workplace. The bourgeois argument wrongly equates relations of production exclusively with class relations. But class relations are only a specific type of relations of production. There are other relations of production which are not class relations, such as the relations between the father, his wife, and children in the family production unit that characterized a number of pre-colonial Nigerian societies. For Marxism, the most fundamental element of analysis of social relations is the relationship of production, including, but not limited to, class relations. Therefore, all that is needed for it to be relevant in a situation is the existence of production, a universal phenomenon.

On the question of the existence or non-existence of classes, the matter can only be settled by empirical analysis of the type found in some of the contributions of this book. Nevertheless, the bourgeois argument makes the mistake of thinking of Nigerian-type societies as essentially the same as what they were during the pre-colonial period. It ignores the impact of peripheral capitalism purveyed by colonialism on the present system of social stratification in Africa. It neglects the vast and rapidly expanding literature on the emergence, persistence, and change of various classes in contemporary African societies.[23] In addition, such an argument wrongly attributes the same system of social stratification to all the pre-colonial Nigerian and other African social formations irrespective of their level of production, mode of production, and degree of social division of labour. Although there were various classless pre-colonial African systems, there were also many in which classes were highly developed. Examples include the Hausa-Fulani societies of northern Nigeria.

Furthermore, the bourgeois argument against the existence of classes in Africa stems in part from its false assumption of the absence of class struggle in Africa. One of the contributions specifically and empirically addresses itself to this question. There is a tendency to assume that class struggles are waged by the underprivileged classes against the ruling privileged classes. Although this is true, class struggle also means, and often means first of all, the struggle waged by the dominant privileged class, and the state acting on its behalf, against the subordinate underprivileged classes.[24] The former usually marshals a broad arsenal of ideology, law, physical repression, direct exploitation, devious schemes such as the infamous British policy of divide and rule, and the manipulation of ethnic sentiments and hostility against the latter. The ruling classes, for instance, determine what is to be learned in schools and how much is to be learned, who is to vote, what political parties are to be registered and how, whether the trade unions can participate in politics, whether there is a price and wage freeze and how this should be enforced, and which of the parties to violent strike confrontations should be brutalized by the police. These are as much instruments of the class struggle as the use of the strike action by workers.

The character of the class structure and the class struggles in Nigerian and other African societies cannot be expected to follow the classical lines found in Europe of the past and present. The class structure of the former has its roots not only in the capitalist mode of production as in Europe but also in colonial conquest and domination.[25] Part of the sociological dimension of the development of social forces in these societies must be viewed as a process of organizing the under-privileged classes from a conquered population, and consequently must examine closely the relations between the victor and vanquished in order to delineate those developments that are dictated not only by economic imperatives but also by strategic and tactical considerations of containment of the subject population. The consequences of this development for activities during the post-colonial period become crucial indeed.

The application of the Marxist methodology to the study of Nigerian problems is also useful because it compels a thorough critique of the prevailing bourgeois theoretical framework, thereby exposing its irrelevance to local conditions, and its essential service to the cause of imperialism. Because of its dominant position this bourgeois framework is usually uncritically accepted by its Nigerian practitioners, who hardly question its relevance to the African environment. Very often obsolete varieties of the framework continue to be current in Nigerian-type societies well after their abandonment in Western intellectual circles. As a corollary, the Marxist perspective is avoided as a plague because of the hostility toward it by Western academics, with no effort made to subject it to rigorous assessment to determine its relevance to African conditions. In this regard, the practitioners of the Marxist perspective enjoy an obvious advantage over their bourgeois adversaries. Like all the contributors to this volume most of them have been trained in the West and Nigeria and, therefore, have been socialized into the bourgeois academic tradition. Their present identification with Marxism implies a prior critique of the bourgeois system and its rejection as useless for understanding and above all transforming African reality. It also implies a critique of the Marxist system, its acceptance as useful in understanding African problems, and its acceptance as a superior method of social analysis. While the Marxists are very familiar with the literature of the bourgeois tradition, the bourgeois academics are not familiar at all with the literature of the Marxist tradition, but nevertheless reject it. Who has a closed mind academically?

The Marxist perspective provides guidelines for assessing the relevance and usefulness of scientific concepts and ideas in the sphere of social life. They must justify their existence by their capacity to illuminate the people's production system, changes in it, social forces associated with these changes, their ideas, and the social, economic, and political institutions built on the basis of these ideas. Above all, it asks illuminating questions about the major beneficiaries of the programs generated by scientific concepts. Such questions are not answered by the argument that all members of the society benefit. That is a truism. The important issue for analysis concerns the differential in the benefits accruing to the various segments of the society, because it determines the degree of their commitment to the application of the concepts. Marxist concepts are oriented toward programs which benefit the masses more than their minority exploiters and oppressors, while bourgeois concepts emphasize benefits skewed in the direction of the privileged minority.

Also, assertions of the bourgeois perspective remain unsubstantiated, indeed uninvestigated. For example, the model of development of Nigerian-type societies projected by that perspective is that of the West. Its essence is catching up with the West in terms of the number and quality of artifacts created in the advanced capitalist societies. But the validity of this model is hardly seriously studied or discussed. It is merely held as an article of faith. Therefore, the whole question of whether the supremacy of capital in production, the profit motive, and individualism are able to repeat their historic role in the radical transformation of productive forces in Europe is not even put on the agenda of academic research and study. The impact of the introduction of capitalist relations and productive forces by foreign conquest and domination on the possibility of development through capitalism is not discussed.

The Marxist method puts on the agenda for research and analysis the sacred cows of bourgeois analysis of development such as exploitation, oppression, inequality, and other forms of injustice. It makes it very difficult to continue to obscure the real nature of the economic and power relationships among Nigerians, and between them and the capitalist world with which they are linked. It removes the mask over foreign capitalist exploitation, manipulation, and domination of Nigeria, exposing the instruments and agencies, including their local counterparts, employed in these infamous policies. In the process it illuminates the basic elements of the true patriotism of Nigerian-type countries. Thus, Marxist methodology helps to remedy the poverty of scholarship of contemporary social science in and about Nigeria with respect to the intelligent and scientific study of the impact of foreign capital on the pattern of production in the country, the size of the market, the pattern of use of resources, the pattern of consumption, the multiplier and accelerator effects, the pattern of investment, and the innovation of technology.

Furthermore, Marxism vigorously counteracts the unscientific tendency to conceive of social reality in terms of objects of empirical observation. It enjoins analysts to probe beneath what people say they are doing, and what they seem to be doing, in order to discover the laws of human behaviour which are critical for the development of society. This injunction is particularly relevant in Nigeria where ethnicity has come to be perceived as the major problem and consequently most of the national energy is devoted to it, in spite of the fact that its objective role in the development of the country dictates a lesser emphasis. The more easily observable ethnic phenomenon assumes a greater priority than the less observable but more developmentally determining struggle among classes. The latter is even denied. The Marxist method helps to reorder this priority. The question is not whether or not Nigerians are ethnically conscious on most issues of social and economic life. They may well be. The critical question concerns the major determining factor in the historical march of a people. And the history of mankind demonstrates that development is associated with changes in class relations and other relations of production – as in the transformation from feudalism to capitalism in Europe and from capitalism to socialism in the Soviet Union – not in ethnic relations.

Finally, by its emphasis on the historic role of the masses in the process of development, the Marxist study calls attention to the intolerable living conditions of the Nigerian masses. This attention is vital not only in order to illuminate their problems, but also to prevent their utter neglect by the privileged classes which isolates them completely from the mainstream of world civilization. In fact, historical materialism enables a conception of development as a dialectical phenomenon in which the masses interact with their physical, biological, and human environments, transforming them for their own betterment and that of humanity at large. Development becomes the unending improvement in the actualization of the inherent capacity of the masses to live a better and more rewarding life. This concept of development enables us to examine all our relationships, internal and external, to see if they constitute an asset or an obstacle in the march of the masses toward self-emancipation from the shackles of their human and non-human environments,

Therefore, Marxism encourages research in the critical area of ownership of economic undertakings in industry, commerce, agriculture, and real estate – particularly the place of labour in these enterprises – to determine its impact on the life of the masses. In addition, it encourages the investigation of the continuity of the colonial economy into the post-colonial period and the role of foreign capital in the process, which bourgeois African scholarship has ignored, in order to expose its continuing deleterious consequences for the masses. Also, the Marxist method focuses on the class structure created by the activities of foreign capital during the colonial period, its continuation, expansion, and consolidation over the past decades of Nigerian independence, and the consequences of all these for the continued poverty and misery of the masses. The consequences of this class structure for the African nation's capacity for self-reliant socio-economic and political transformation can then be scientifically examined.

And in relation to social engineering, Marxism guides research into determining ways and means of strengthening the general political effort of the masses for development, through capturing their true aspirations, increasing their social, cultural, and political consciousness, and, therefore, acting as an effective instrument for their mobilization into a cohesive and purposeful movement aimed at liquidating the inherited and emerging obstacles to their collective self-emancipation. An immediate task in this regard concerns the recovery of their self-respect and self-confidence, factors which are critical for overcoming the obstacles of development. Marxism indicates with whom to go forward in analyzing and, above all, changing the Nigerian society.

References

1. Maurice Dobb, *Studies in the Development of Capitalism* (London: Routledge and Sons, 1963, rev. ed.), chapter 1; Richard C. Edwards, Michael Reich, and Thomas E. Weisskopf (eds.), *The Capitalist System* (Engelwood Cliffs, N.J.: Prentice-Hall, 1972).
2. Ernest Mandel, *Marxist Economic Theory* (London: Merlin, 1962), p.644.
3. *Ibid.*, p.654.
4. Elliot J. Berg, 'Socialism and Economic Development in Tropical Africa' in *The Quarterly Journal of Economics* (November 1964), pp. 549–73; Elliot J. Berg, 'Structural Transformation Versus Gradualism: Recent Economic Development in Ghana and the Ivory Coast' in Philip Foster and Aristide R. Zolberg (eds.), *Ghana and the Ivory Coast: Perspectives on Modernization* (Chicago: University of Chicago Press, 1971). Also see the critique of Berg by V. Solodovnikov and V. Bogoslovsky, *Non-Capitalist Development* (Moscow: Progress Publishers, 1975), pp. 14–17.
5. Federal Republic of Nigeria, *Report of the Constitution Drafting Committee Containing the Draft Constitution* (Lagos: Federal Ministry of Information, 1976), Volume I, p. xiii.
6. Zbigniew K. Brzezinski, 'The Soviet Political System: Transformation or Degeneration?' in Zbigniew K. Brzezinski (ed.), *Dilemmas of Change in Soviet Politics* (N.Y.: Columbia University Press, 1969); Z.K. Brzezinski, *Between Two Ages* (N.Y.: Viking Press, 1970); Samuel P. Huntington, *Order in Changing Societies* (New Haven: Yale University Press, 1968); S.P. Huntington, *Authoritarian Politics in Modern Society* (N.Y.: Basic Books, 1970); Zbigniew K. Brzezinski and Samuel P. Huntington, *Political Power: USA/USSR* (N.Y.: Penguin, 1977). Also see the critique of them by Solodovnikov and Bogoslovsky, *op. cit.*, pp. 15–17; and William Y. Elliot, *Education and Training in the Developing Countries: The Role of US Foreign Aid* (New York: Free Press, 1966), p.339.
7. Report of the Constitution Drafting Committee, *op. cit.*, p.xiii.
8. *Ibid.*, pp. xiii–xv.
9. V.I. Lenin, 'Left-Wing Communism – An Infantile Disorder' in V.I. Lenin, *Collected Works* (Moscow: Progressive Publishers, 1965), Vol. 31.
10. *Ibid.*, p.92.
11. V.I. Lenin, 'Second Congress of Communist Organizations of the East' in V.I. Lenin, *Collected Works* (Moscow: Progress Publishers, 1965), Vol. 30, pp.161–2.
12. Karl Marx in *Archives of Marx and Engels*, Vol. 1, pp.254–5.
13. Friedrich Engels to Karl Marx in Fredrich Engels, *Selected Correspondence* (Moscow: Progress Publishers, 1956), p. 563.

14. Lenina Ilitskaya, translation, *ABC of Dialectical and Historical Materialism* (Moscow: Progress Publishers, 1965), p.268.
15. Karl Marx and Fredrich Engels, *The Holy Family* (Moscow: Progress Publishers, 1956), p.172.
16. V.I. Lenin, 'The National Question in Our Programme' in V.I. Lenin, *Collected Works* (Moscow: Progress Publishers, 1965), Vol. 6, p.458.
17. R. Ulyanovsky and V. Pavlov, *Asian Dilemma: Theories and Critical Studies* (Moscow: Progress Publishers, 1973), p.10.
18. Lenina Ilitskaya, *op. cit.*, p.252.
19. Lenin, *Collected Works*, Vol. 23, pp.273–5.
20. *Ibid.*, p. 272.
21. Marx and Engels, *Selected Correspondence*, p.35.
22. Lenina Ilitskaya, *op. cit.*, pp.254-5.
23. See for example, Issa G. Shivji, *Class Struggle in Tanzania* (Dar es Salaam: Tanzania Publishing House, 1975); Issa G. Shivji, 'Peasants and Class Alliances' in *Review of African Political Economy*, 3 (May–October, 1975); Immanuel Wallerstein, 'Class and Class Conflict in Contemporary Africa', *Monthly Review*, 26, 9 (February 1975); Mamood Mamdani, *Politics and Class Formations in Uganda* (N.Y.: Monthly Review Press, 1976); Amilcar Cabral, *The Struggle in Guinea* (Cambridge, Mass.: Africa Research Group Reprint [n.d]); Colin Leys, *Underdevelopment in Kenya* (London: Heineman, 1975).
24. Benard Magubane, 'The Making of the South African Working Class 1875–1925' paper presented at the U.S. Social Science Research Council Conference on the Politics of the Common People in Africa in Mount Kisco, 28 November–1 December 1978, pp.32–33; Ralph Miliband, 'The Coup in Chile', *Socialist Register 1973* (London: Merlin Press, 1974), pp.453–4.
25. Benard Magubane, *op. cit.*, pp.5–9.

2. Development/ Underdevelopment: Is Nigeria Developing?

Okwudiba Nnoli

The Artifacts of Development

The widespread view, within and outside the country, that Nigeria is developing is ill-conceived and misguided. It is based on a notion of development that commits us to a wholesale imitation of others and, therefore, to a wholesale repudiation of our state of being.[1] The oft-stated goal is to catch up with the West. Such a goal permits us to want passionately goods and services which we cannot create for ourselves with the resources at our disposal, and it causes us to neglect our basic needs and local resources.[2] Obviously, this is not a healthy notion of development. It deepens our sense of inferiority. And, as Claude Ake has aptly pointed out: 'Even if catching up with the West were a legitimate goal, we do not help the achievement of this goal by cultivating our sense of inferiority and inadequacy.'[3]

In spite of their newly-found cultural nationalism, Nigerian academic, social, political, and military leaders still look at the development of their country in terms of seeking to achieve many of the conditions of good life in Western Europe, America, and Japan. These include industrialization. economic affluence, military hegemony, advanced technology, urbanization, and the parliamentary political process. The concept of development involved here is that of a checklist of artifacts.

The view of a developing country which these leaders share is one of a country that is increasingly acquiring more and more artifacts of the type found in the Western countries and Japan, and which are created by the financial and industrial leaders of these foreign countries. These foreign societies are regarded as developed; and they have a large number of cars, roads, hospitals, computers, television sets, radio sets, technicians, educated people, good houses, airways, iron and steel complexes, agricultural machinery, high-heeled shoes, lipsticks and other types of cosmetics, efficient managers, an advertising industry that exploits sex, trade fairs, and various other artifacts. The more of such items Nigeria can procure or produce within its territory, the closer it is presumed to come to the standard of the West and, therefore, the more developed it becomes. In other words, the narrower the gap between our country and the Western nations, the faster is our progress in the race to catch up with them and, therefore, the faster our country's development. Hence, an oversized army, a national airline and shipping line, superhighways, and various highly sophisticated institutions are the pride of the nation, and are given preference over basic necessities in the allocation of resources.

In fact, it may not even matter if these artifacts are procured from, or created here for us by, foreigners. It is considered only practical for them to provide the goods and services since we do not have the capacity to do so ourselves. And we need these products! Hence, there is the suggestion that the foreign multinational companies operating in Nigeria should be compelled by the government to grow more food for Nigerians.[4] But if we call in foreigners to rescue us, they end up providing us with only those goods and services whose supply they control. By so doing they are able to control us and manipulate our production process to suit their own interests. The inevitable consequence is our powerlessness to use our own resources to transform our internal and external environments in the ways we need and desire.

Among the Nigerians who hold this view of development, one asserts that: 'There is a strong belief that the Nigerian economy has passed the stage of economic take-off and reached that of self sustaining growth. Nigeria was one of the few African countries to realize that the survival of modern competitive capitalism as a philosophy of economic growth depends not so much on attacks on the economic systems of other countries as on the ability and the willingness of capitalism, guided by a proper national policy, to accept the increasing challenge facing it in a *rapidly developing country*.'[5] He further claims that: 'A purely subsistence economy a century ago has been transformed into a fairly sophisticated market economy.'[6] Both academicians and government officials view the major achievements of the 1962–68 development plan in terms of the successful completion of an oil refinery, the Nigerian Security and Mining Plant, a paper mill, a sugar mill, the Niger dam, the Niger bridge, some trunk roads and port extensions.

It is significant that the same view is held by the leading financial and industrial circles of Europe and America. They talk glibly about the dynamic nature of the Nigerian economy, its tremendous growth rate and the extensive changes taking place in the society. The economy was once said to be experiencing a boom which was transforming the life of the population. Such attitudes remind us of the praises showered on the nation and its leaders prior to the collapse of the First Republic. That collapse itself bore witness to the fact that the praises were not deserved, that the views of these foreign financial interests and their Nigerian academic spokesmen and political and military beneficiaries bear very little resemblance to the country's reality, particularly as far as the vast majority of the population is concerned.

It must be remembered that these foreign financial and industrial barons control the creation and marketing of these artifacts on which our development is purported to depend. Through this control and our peculiar colonial heritage they determine and dominate our production process in a manner that was never experienced by the Western nations or Japan in their respective histories. Obviously, therefore, by sponsoring a concept of development tied to these artifacts which they supply, they can continue to make profits in our country. They can have no interest in promoting a view of life in which Nigerians would control the creation and marketing of these artifacts. This would severely limit their profits and power. More important, they can have no interests in sponsoring a concept of development based on artifacts that they cannot create, market or control. In fact, in a world community where every country is competing for power and scarce resources to promote its interests, the foreign companies have no interest in providing us with more artifacts or power relative to their own countries because this would diminish their countries' bargaining strength. In any case, the advanced Western countries are not remaining still socio-economically. Their financial and industrial barons create new artifacts continually. Under the circumstances, an attempt to catch up with them in terms of the number and quality of artifacts we procure from them, or which they create in our society, will be an unending process with no prospects of Nigeria ever catching up. The country would be frozen at the social category of a developing nation.

This clear relationship between such a concept of development and foreign interests underlines the ideological character of that concept. It benefits certain countries, groups and individuals more than others and, therefore, rationalizes the interests of these, its major beneficiaries. The selective nature of the artifacts which are portrayed as reflecting development further exposes this ideological character. Only those artifacts that have shown some improvement over time are mentioned. Those areas where the conditions have worsened are conveniently ignored. But Nigerians are very much aware of the deteriorating situation of the drinking water supply, food production, and the major social services, particularly electricity supply, postal and telephone services, and air transport. Inflation is clearly uncontrollable; corruption has become more widespread and blatant. Port congestion, the shortages of housing, drugs and petrol, the hoarding of essential goods, worsening traffic conditions, increased traffic accidents and deaths, declining educational standards, loss of university autonomy, examination leakages, indiscipline at all levels of society, and an increase in strikes are fast becoming part of our life-style. The villages are decaying without the cities getting better, foreign reserves have dwindled causing severe foreign exchange problems, the crime rate is increasing and its character becoming more and more dangerous, and the prospects of democracy previously dangled before our eyes have turned into a plea for democracy under the burden of military dictatorship and the denial of political rights to all.

The proponents of the developing-country viewpoint leave us with no guidelines for assigning relative weights to improvements in some areas of life and the worsening of conditions in some other areas to enable us to decide whether Nigeria is really developing or not. What of other differences that are not associated with the number, type and quality of artifacts between the developed Western countries and Nigeria? Unlike the Western societies and Japan at any period in their histories, Nigeria exhibits the following characteristics:

(1) A divorce between our local resources and those (essentially foreign) that go into the production of the artifacts usually associated with development. As a result we are alienated from our bio-physical environment and are unable to creatively transform it for our own benefit and progress.

(2) A divorce between those development-oriented artifacts that we procure and create for our consumption and the basic needs of our people. Although these artifacts are predominantly luxuries they have taken precedence over our basic needs for food, water, housing materials and clothing that our people can easily afford. Again the result is alienation from our production process which adversely affects the capacity of our people to be committed to the national task of mobilizing mass energy for development.

(3) A system of export that is not based on the sale of surpluses of goods that are consumed first and foremost by the masses of our people. In many cases the export sector has been developed first and foremost for external consumption, with the local consumption, where it exists, assuming a secondary interest.

(4) Our capacity to procure or create the desired artifacts is practically totally dependent on external trade with very little input from internal interaction. Consequently, the nation is dependent for its progress on external conditions that it knows much less about and which it cannot control or manipulate. As the people thus lose mental contact with the totality of their production process they are alienated from it and lose interest in it. Production suffers and with it social progress.

(5) The centre of technological and sociocultural innovation related to the creation of existing and future development-oriented artifacts does not exist in the country. The research units of the foreign companies operating in Nigeria are located outside the nation in foreign countries. It is there that the task of creating new artifacts is carried on. Nigeria's role is confined to the menial and non-creative one of marketing or duplicating the new artifact in the local area. Under the circumstances Nigerians cannot acquire the capacity to create new artifacts not previously developed abroad. Our capacity for innovative transformation is, therefore, stunted.

(6) Other-centredness rather than self-centredness in outlook and behaviour. Foreign values, usually rationalized by the myth of international standards, become the guiding principles of behavior. Our people who have acquired development artifacts learn more and first about the Western countries than about the domestic situation, prefer to spend their holidays abroad, value their foreign business contacts more than their domestic equivalent, prefer to study abroad, use foreign personnel and businesses to perform local tasks, bank their money in foreign countries, emigrate there for higher paying and more rewarding jobs, and seek political asylum there whenever possible. With so much attention and energy devoted to external interaction, much less attention than is needed is left for reorganizing domestic resources

and capabilities, and harnessing them to the developing effort.

(7) There is an absence of an independent and creative ruling class of the type that brought the industrial revolution to the Western countries and Japan. The ruling class consists of a mixture of the various segments of the petty bourgeoisie, notably the intellectuals, professionals, bureaucrats, and military officials, and the comprador elements who participate in the import, export and wholesale trade, as well as the emerging small and dependent bourgeoisie of the commercial and industrial variant. All these groups are characterized by a dependent role in the production process, and an orientation toward consumption and the distribution of the products of production rather than toward productive investment and the creation of the products of production. It is a selfish, corrupt, and unpatriotic group of people whose major ambition is to achieve a parasitic existence in the society and enjoy conspicuous consumption. They are incapable of moving the country forward to progress.

(8) A high rate of migration from the rural to the urban areas that is in no way related to the increased productivity of agriculture in the rural areas and therefore the economic irrelevance of the migrants there. Hence, not only have the rural areas been decaying, the conditions of the cities have been worsening because of their inability to handle this large influx of migrants. The overall quality of life of the population has been deteriorating and with it their capacity for self and national transformation.

(9) A socio-economic compartmentalization of the nation arising from the economic activities of the foreign companies and the administrative and political organizations of the colonial era. There are hardly any salient economic exchanges generated by foreign capital linking the various regions of the country. Instead, salient economic exchanges exist between each area and the advanced capitalist societies of Europe and America. The weakness of national socio-political cohesion is a reflection of this fact. It is a source of micro-nationalism.

(10) External participation in the domestic activities of Nigeria by foreigners, which is not reciprocated by a similar Nigerian participation in their domestic affairs. There are no Nigerian companies doing large-scale business in the Western countries and Japan similar to the foreign firms of these nations in Nigeria. Such a situation breeds an inferiority complex on the part of Nigerians which militates against the development effort.

(11) The absence of any organic link arising from indigenous technology between agriculture and industry.

(12) The pervasiveness of a client mentality. There exists a psychological inability to comprehend the ability of the people as a whole to take the reins of their own development in their hands and to master the intricacies of modern technology, organization, and management. The result is a pervasive feeling of powerlessness of Nigerians to transform their society in a way they deem fit. They must depend for their salvation on foreign economic, political and, when necessary, military support;

(13) The incapacity of Nigeria to engage significantly in direct economic relationships with countries other than those of the West and Japan. This restriction of other external influences on the nation severely limits the scope of the national development effort through its limitation of possible external resources and developmental experiences.

As a social phenomenon this ideological motive for the Western concept of development has a history. During the earliest period of colonialism the colonialists portrayed the pre-colonial cultures of Nigeria as ahistorical, primitive and barbarous, dominated by intertribal wars, human sacrifice, and cannibalism, and lacking in any developed system of ethics or humane principles of conduct. This colonial ideology derided the intelligence of the Nigerian and denied his capacity to undertake any civilized activity. Such a Eurocentric devaluation of Nigerian cultures was accompanied by a corresponding glorification of the European way of life. Their unconditional condemnation was attended by the unconditional affirmation of the colonizer's world view. This racist myth was necessary in order to ensure foreign domination of local production and administration at minimal costs and with the least possible amount of coercion. By distorting, disfiguring and maligning the past of the colonized it hoped to alienate them from that past as well as from their traditional society, causing them to reject both and making it easy for them to accept life in the new colonial situation.

The social groups which made up the early colonial bureaucratic and administrative infrastructure, the foreign companies, and the missionaries were united in thinking of themselves as being assigned the special role of bringing civilization, justice, education and increased welfare to the colonized, primitive Nigerians, who had never enjoyed any of these benefits before and whom they considered as subhuman and inferior. Their mission was to civilize the natives, to raise them up from their primitive conditions to the vision of an ideal colony taken, naturally, from the way of life of the colonizer.

With the rise and increasing militancy of African nationalism which proclaimed the existence of viable pre-colonial African cultures and their historical contributions to ethics, education, science, philosophy and architecture, and which threatened the colonial order, the colonialists were forced to concede the existence of viable and humane cultures with sophisticated systems of politics and administration in pre-colonial Nigeria. Colonial ideology shifted its emphasis to the superiority and inferiority of cultures. An hierarchy of cultures was presumed in which the European culture was placed at the apex. The similarity of the local culture to the European counterpart became a basis for its status and position in this Eurocentric system of stratification.

Later, African cultural nationalism began to reject the superiority of white culture and to assert the merit, if not the superiority, of the African way of life. At the same time the emergence of the Union of Soviet Socialist Republics to a position of world power, and the extension of the socialist system to Eastern Europe and China, threatened the hegemony of the world capitalist system and inaugurated a period of intense ideological competition between the socialist and capitalist worlds. Under the new circumstances the colonialists were forced into further concessions. In the face of the fiercely internationalistic and universalistic claims of the socialist ideology, colonial racism saw its interest as lying in the promotion of the concept of cultural relativity. There were no longer any universally superior cultures. Each must be assessed within the context of its own environment. The colonialists and neo-colonialists began to project a vague, amorphous, ahistorical and largely subjective vision of an indigenous Nigerian way of life which must be protected from foreign ideology, usually limited to socialism.

Nevertheless, the colonial objective of enticing Nigerians to imitate, wholesale, the European way of life remained. It was argued that cultural relativity does not necessarily imply the absence of value judgements regarding the efficacy of the various cultures or the degree to which they have maximized social welfare in their respective environments. In this frame of mind the concept of development emerged as another but respectable way of capturing the content of the now discredited concept of the hierarchy of cultures. Always based on a dichotómous world, it was initially conceived in terms of a world divided into the developed and the underdeveloped countries. But it was soon realized that the concept of underdevelopment implied an inherent incapacity to attain development and was therefore objectionable to Third World nationalists. A more acceptable way of saying the same thing had to be found. Nigerian-type societies are not underdeveloped. They are developing. Reminiscent of the concept of the hierarchy of cultures in which the Euro-American culture is at the apex, development became the transformation of the lower-ranked societies into the type at the apex, the Western societies. The colonial and neo-colonial system of politics, economics and education has rested on an unchanging evolutionary theory which upholds Western civilization as the superior culture and justifies the civilizing mission of Westerners, the *sine qua non* during the colonial period of French direct administration, British indirect rule, and massive Western capital investment.

These illusory shifts in colonial and neo-colonial ideology have created confusion and ambivalence in the minds of Nigerian leaders who have stepped into the shoes of their erstwhile colonial mentors. On the one hand, they have continued to wage a relentless struggle against the remnants of colonial racism by demonstrating (via FESTAC, for example) the existence of viable pre-colonial Nigerian cultures and their contribution to humanity. In this way they hope to emancipate their people from a colonially-inherited inferiority complex. But on the other hand they continue to encourage the aspirations of the country towards achieving the artifacts of the Western world. By so doing, however, they in effect acknowledge the unworthiness of their people and the superiority of the European way of life. Their acceptance of the Western concept of development reflects and tends to reinforce their belief in the inferiority of Nigerians relative to their former colonizers.

A Critique of the Western Model of Development

Thus the West is the model for Nigerian development. But as a guide for the self-reliant and self-sustained transformation of the Nigerian society this model has been a disastrous failure. During the colonial period it identified the low level of national income and savings as the major obstacle to Nigerian development. With the exploitation of petroleum in the late 1950s and 1960s, as well as the vastly increased importance of this mineral as a revenue-earner following the oil boom of the 1973–1976 period, one would have expected this obstacle to have been eliminated. Nevertheless, the lot of the vast majority of Nigerians has remained deplorable. Statistics on the growth rate of the economy and the foreign reserves issued by successive praise-seeking regimes, and the illusions of an oil boom and a 'dynamic economy' spread by the foreign and local beneficiaries of the deteriorating economic conditions of the poor majority, have failed to whitewash the persistent underdevelopment of the country.

Modern technology and middle-level technical manpower, mechanization of agriculture, and 'executive capacity' are now held forth as the key to national development. Consequently, our young men and women are shipped in large numbers to foreign countries for technological training. But the prospects here again are not encouraging.[8] A recent United Nations report on the technological progress of Nigerian-type countries points out that they are trapped in the first of the three phases which characterized the technological history of the Western world and Japan.[9] This is because the policies of the kind they pursue are addressed to the symptoms rather than the underlying causes of their technological underdevelopment. Government expenditures and policies on science and technology merely create the form but not the substance of a local capability.[10] Their actions do not significantly affect the enormous bargaining power of the foreign multinational firms in such a way as to break their monopoly over technological innovation.[11]

As regards social and political development in Nigeria, the model is in a state of severe crisis. For the numerous social and political ills of the country its proponents either blame ethnicity, some assumed inherent Nigerian trait, or throw up their arms in total surrender and mount the pulpit to sermonize and moralize. Hence, the national drive against military coups, corruption and indiscipline has emphasized the pulpit and moral exhortations.

The only guideline provided by the model for the solution of the ethnic problem was faith in the evolutionary process by which increased functional differentiation would create new and cross-cutting bases for association. On the contrary, after nearly eighty years of so-called modernization, ethnicity has not only persisted but intensified.[12] It is now suggested in some circles that the ethnic problem has come to stay. All that can be done is to minimize its negative consequences by accommodating ethnic interests through the creation of states which accord to all ethnic groups a meaningful role in national life. The acceptance of this defeatist view is reflected in the creation of states, the search for an adequate formula for allocating revenues to them, and the injunction that the recruitment of political personnel and the distribution of amenities should reflect the 'federal character' of the country.[13] But the nation has witnessed the proliferation of states from two to three, four, twelve, and presently nineteen without any end in sight to the problem.

The hopes of national stability raised by the model have proved to be an illusion. They have been replaced by the realities of military coups, a disastrous civil war, and violent eruptions of workers' and peasants' frustrations. For example, in 1946 there were 16 labour disputes resulting in 10 strikes, but in 1949 a total of 70 disputes erupted giving rise to 36 strikes. The respective figures for successive years were: 1950, 82 disputes and 26 strikes; 1952, 59 disputes and 39 strikes; 1953, 54 disputes and 34 strikes; 1957, 137 disputes and 52 strikes; and 1959, 115 disputes and 54 strikes.[14] And the situation has been worsening. Also the political situation has deteriorated as the country moved from civil to military rule. Rather than creating and strengthening the direct links between the masses and their rulers the military leaders have returned to the system of indirect rule through powerful chiefs, some of whom have been deliberately created. Workers' associations have been emasculated and barred from politics.

Theoretically, the Western model for Nigerian development is clearly bankrupt. First, the bourgeois theory of development is based on a method characterized by a checklist of factors whose connecting links are at best tenuous. Development is dissected into the economic, social and political aspects. Economic development concentrates primarily on economic growth as reflected by the increases in the gross domestic product, industrialization, capital formation, welfare services, the development of the infrastructure such as roads, electricity and railways, and increased economic efficiency. Social development emphasizes the institutionalization of Western social norms and behaviour patterns. It involves the transformation of the extended family, primitive tribe, and the traditional sector of a 'dual society' whose structures, values and social attitudes impede economic change and social mobility. It also involves the cultivation of a high degree of achievement motivation which is necessary for profound changes in social stratification, urbanization, and economic development. The goal is to transform the particularistic features of the societies and economies of the colonies and neocolonies into those of the developed economies, which are presumed to have universalist values.

Political development focuses on political stability and the institutionalization of political goals and the means for achieving them. It is sometimes equated with increased differentiation and specialization of political structures and increased secularization of political culture. The modern political system is defined as one in which specialized political structures such as political parties and bureaucracies emerge and perform functionally distinct roles. At other times political development is associated with increased centralization of power in the state and the weakening of traditional authority, and increased popular participation in the political process. Sometimes it is also seen as the increase in the various capabilities of the system to solve such problems as the extraction and distribution of resources and the regulation and integration of the society, or the increase in the capacity of the system to perform certain functions, notably socialization, interest articulation, interest aggregation, political communication, rule-making, rule application and adjudication.

The obvious question regarding the relationship between these various aspects of development remains unanswered. It becomes obscured by the concepts of modernization and nation-building which profess to integrate them but which end up by merely giving us another checklist of characteristics. One is left only with faith in the fact that these atomized components of development are somehow linked. We are made to understand that they are mutually interrelated, but now how. This is because the methodology involved ignores an approach in which the explanatory variables are fully integrated, one with the other, as well as in time and space.

Second, the bourgeois theory of development divorces philosophy from socio-economic and political action. It is not guided by any notion of what ought to be. This is justified in the name of pragmatism and realism. Therefore, it does not question the existence of a particular fundamental structure or institution in the society but merely seeks to understand what it does and how best it can do it.[15] But to ignore what ought to be is to ignore a very important aspect of social reality. The underlying implication is that the prevailing system ought to continue. This is the ideology of the ruling class. The emphasis on law and order takes precedence over the demands for justice. This is the obvious hallmark of reaction and of a reactionary regime.

Third, history is divorced from social analysis or is marginal to it in this approach. Existing structures, attitudes, functions and interrelationships in society are examined in isolation from their past. Or the past is explained with little reference to the present and the future. Hence, proponents of the Western model of development merely abstract the various characteristics of Western societies, ignore the historical contexts within which these traits had developed, and counterpose them to the pre-colonial, colonial and neo-colonial societies of Nigeria, irrespective of differences in their levels of production, productive forces, relations of production, type and quality of leadership, the form and content of the government, and their values, norms, symbolic attributes and ethical standards, and how these had developed historically. In such analyses there is very little indication of movement and casuality. When history is made part of analyses it merely projects a linear view of development which assumes that the capitalist path followed by the Western countries and Japan is the only possible and most desirable path to increased welfare and well-being. Nigerian-type societies, it is argued, must pass through the various stages previously traversed by these developed countries. There is no room for the comparative analysis of histories as a basis for learning from the historical experiences of other nations. But the importance of history in social analysis lies in the fact that no social phenomenon is comprehensible and useful unless it is characterized by a union of its past, present, and future. The present cannot be understood outside the past and visions of the future. And the future cannot be planned for without understanding how it is emerging from, and related to, the present and the past.

Fourth, the Western model suffers from crude empiricism. Its single-minded devotion to quantification and the statistically manipulable obscure and mystify rather than clarify the process of development. Data on the gross domestic product (GDP), capital formation, rate of urbanization, and the rate of population growth assume great significance as indicators of development, essentially because they can be quantified. In this analytical world of figures, graphs, equations, and statistical notations, the role of man and the effects of the progress of development on him are completely obscured. All qualitative data such as injustice, exploitation and oppression are banned from the realm of analysis. Hence, a high premium is placed on the rate of growth of the GDP and industrialization and hardly any on whether this is the result of foreign or Nigerian creativity, who benefits from this growth (foreigners, the rich or the poor), and the consequences for the capacity of Nigerians themselves to manipulate their own environment. The most dramatic form of human intervention in the development process, notably revolutions, cannot be entertained by analysis. Man loses himself in a mass of data. What alienation! Under the circumstances mystification replaces explanation and ideology conquers science. But reality cannot be understood. It cannot, therefore, be transformed, which is what development is all about.

Fifth, and finally, the model suffers from the worst form of economic determinism. This is a logical consequence of the emphasis on quantification. Mathematical and statistical analyses have attained their highest degree of sophistication in the field of economics and economic development. The fields of social and political development have been less amenable to quantification and, therefore, have not received as much attention. It is assumed that when economic take-off is achieved, somehow the other aspects of development become transformed as well. How this will come about is hardly explained. And the various cases of economic growth without social and political development are not explained systematically and scientifically. In fact, from the perspective of the model, the practical battle for development is the battle for economic growth. Such a myopic view of development is hardly realistic in view of the totality of the phenomenon that is involved.

Even then there are serious questions regarding the viability of the process of economic development suggested for Nigeria by the model. After about eighty years of trying this process it has not yet solved the problems of poverty and low productivity of food and labour that have plagued the country for generations. And there is no vision whatsoever of when and how success would be achieved. Nevertheless, Nigerian leaders have uncritically accepted and are daily disseminating ideas about economic development which emanate from this model.

At the level of production, one such idea is that the investment of private capital is the engine of development and therefore superior to other factors of production. This false notion has been so successfully disseminated within the country that is now virtually an article of faith in development circles, in spite of the lack of any scientific or empirical basis. Logically, capital is clearly the product of human labour. It has no other basis for existence. And a creation cannot be more important than its creator. Human labour is, therefore, superior to capital. Empirically, the capitalist mode of production in which capital assumes priority over labour and the other factors of production is a relatively recent phenomenon. Before it, development had taken place. No one denies this. What then was the engine of development? Definitely not capital!

Quite apart from the problems related to logic and history, there is the whole moral question of what relative weight to attach to human and non-human factors. It is immoral to equate man's humanity, labour, with an inanimate object such as capital. While it is possible to assign monetary value to inanimate objects it is not possible to do so to man's humanity, especially in comparison with inanimate objects. Humanity has an inestimable and incomparable value. The evil of slavery lies in its violation of this precept.

The idea of the supremacy of capital over the other factors of production served the interests of the foreign financial and industrial oligarchies that organized production in Nigeria during the colonial times and are controlling it today. In fact, capital is the main factor of production that these oligarchies bring to the production process. The local input is essentially labour. Therefore, if in the relationship between capital and labour it is accepted that capital is superior because it is the engine of development, then several corollaries follow. First, in the distribution of the surplus from production the investors of capital should get more than those who put in their labour. In other words, the foreigner should be rewarded more highly than the Nigerian. This is clearly unpatriotic.

Second, a need is created for capital. During the pre-petroleum days this capital could only come from abroad. Even today, such capital has continued to come from foreign countries. Revenue from petroleum yields money income, not capital. Money income becomes capital when it yokes labour in production. In Nigeria, the financial and industrial oligarchies of Europe, America and Japan have continued to monopolize the capacity to do this. Our oil wealth which they receive as income and profit is turned into capital in production within and outside the country.

We have been made to feel that we need capital to develop or, in fact, to carry out any significant production. Therefore, we have been filled with the passion for capital. But this passion can now only be fulfilled in a significant way by foreigners. The inevitable consequence is our dependence on them. Its obvious concomitants are imitation, an inferiority complex, subordination, manipulation, loss of human dignity, and the inability to overcome the liabilities of underdevelopment. The more foreign countries can intensify our passion for capital that they control, the more they are able to control us and manipulate our behaviour. This is what dependence is all about.

Third, the uncritical acceptance of the superiority of capital over labour makes it difficult for Nigerians to see the extent, immorality and injustice of foreign exploitation that prevails in the relationship between inanimate foreign capital and local human labour. Instead, they want to join the foreigners in the exploitation of their compatriots. This creates divisions in the struggle of the local population against imperialist exploitation. Such divisiveness is inimical to development. It militates against the solidarity of the people in tackling the difficulties and challenges of social transformation. In this way the belief in capital as an engine of development is an ideological rationalization for, as well as an ideological mask over, foreign exploitation, manipulation and domination of the country, which obscures the real nature of the economic and power relationships among Nigerians and between them and the capitalist world of Europe, America and Japan with which they are very closely linked.

Similarly, the dissemination of the idea of the profit motive as an indispensable incentive for increased productivity is unpatriotic. Intrinsically associated with this notion is the tendency to produce for purposes of profit. Foreign capital is, therefore, permitted, even encouraged, to engage in local production that bears no relation to the basic needs of the vast majority of the population. It can engage in the production of crops that are not consumed in the country. Its technology is developed and its market organized to the neglect of local needs and habitual consumption habits. 'Productive activity bears no relation to real human needs. Everyone exploits greed to satisfy greed. And we are obliged to exploit greed in ways which stimulate greed.'[16]

Under the domination of the profit motive foreign capital organizes a local economy which is import-export oriented and enters the world market well before the local, regional and national markets have been developed. With respect to the dominant economic activities, the country produces what it does not consume and consumes what it does not produce. There is an irrepressible divorce between the pattern of resource use and local consumption as well as between the pattern of consumption and local needs.[17] Local production is organized to satisfy foreign economic needs while the local market serves the interests of foreign producers located within and outside Nigeria. This situation is clearly unpatriotic and intolerable.

In another respect, the acceptance of the profit motive is unpatriotic because it enables foreigners to cart away surplus value from our country. Supported by the notion that foreign capital is superior to local labour, foreigners appropriate an unusually and unduly large share of the products of local production. They are permitted to repatriate much of this surplus to their home countries on the grounds that it would encourage them to invest more in the local economy. In this manner the country has lost and continues to lose a lot of its wealth.

In fact, the foreign investors are being encouraged to invest in the nation through various incentives which allow them to repatriate more profits than usual. Quite apart from the income drain which this repatriation engenders, it adversely affects economic development in another significant way. Such repatriated funds are invested in the country of origin of the foreign investor rather than in Nigeria. Consequently, it gives rise to new production abroad rather than within the country. This hampers the geometric progression of production in Nigeria.

Also, the single-minded pursuit of profit by foreign capital has a negative impact on Nigerian unity. Its activities are externally oriented rather than being internally oriented toward the integration of the various ethnic homelands. In search of profits, the foreign firms organize their activities only in areas of gainful exploitation of local resources: the Ibadan-Lagos metropolitan area, the Kano-Kaduna-Zaria-Jos complex, and the Port Harcourt-Aba-Enugu-Onitsha axis. But these centers have remained economically isolated one from the other while being integrated with economic activities in Western Europe, America and Japan. A consequence of this false, disarticulated and non-cohesive national economy is that it can be broken up into micro-economies without serious danger to the various regional economic activities. The area interested in the export-import activities has no need of the rest of the country, which may indeed seem a burden upon it. It may, therefore, contemplate establishing a micro-independence. Secessionist sentiments are an ever present potential threat to national unity.

Another consequence is the creation of socio-economic imbalances among the various ethnic homelands of Nigeria. Foreign capital has a tendency to marginalize people, areas, and economic sectors that do not yield adequate profit. It organizes its activities without any regard whatever for geographical balance in the location of its socio-economic projects. Therefore, those ethnic homelands where they were located in order to maximize profits have experienced an earlier and higher rate of Westernization than other areas. This lack of concern by foreign capital for an all-round balance in the economic growth of the country is the historical origin and basis of the contemporary imbalance in the socio-economic achievements of the various ethnic homelands and groups. It is a source of stress in the social fabric of the nation.

Another value foisted on Nigeria by the financial and industrial barons of Europe, and unpatriotically disseminated by Nigerian leaders, is materialistic individualism. It was non-existent in the pre-colonial Nigerian societies where priority was given to the interests of the society, age group, or obligation to the ruler. Even the famed Hausa merchants who operated throughout West Africa and braved the hazards of the trans-Saharan trade subordinated their individualism and desire for monetary gain to the demands of clientage, the need to get ahead in society through climbing the social apron strings of the Emirs. Today, however, this alien value has become so deeply internalized by Nigerians that they now see it as inherent in the human character. But in Nigeria it serves first and last the economic interests of the Western and increasingly Japanese economic oligarchies and their Nigerian beneficiaries. Materialistic individualism is essential for the activities of foreign capital. Its acceptance facilitates the release of the labour power of the population from the restraints imposed on it by social ties.

One effect of its acceptance has been the social atomization of the hitherto cohesive Nigerian societies. Cohesive social ties have become permanently countered in colonial and neo-colonial societies by the disruptive forces of materialistic individualism. Everyone remains nearer to himself. Identification with a group has become only a partial one. Egotistic motives remain the most powerful motives and are only somewhat mitigated by group solidarity. The weakness of national identity is a consequence. And so are the social ills such as corruption and indiscipline. Social consciousness and a social conscience are stunted.

Most important of all, the supremacy of capital in production, the profit motive, and materialistic individualism are unable to repeat their historic role in Europe. There, they contributed significantly to the radical transformation of the productive forces. In Nigeria, they are impotent because they are motivated from outside the country and can only spread capitalist production to the extent allowed by an international division of labour in which the local area remains passive. The spread of capitalist production is denied any tendency of its own to destroy pre-capitalist forms of production and become exclusive. This restriction enables the foreign owners of capital to guarantee for themselves high rates of surplus value which are not stable but rising, unbridled extraction of absolute surplus value, and the irreversible plunder of natural resources.[18]

The peasantry is brought under direct domination of capital but on terms which freeze it at that social category, preventing it from transformation into the higher category of proletariat. The peasant gets only, or less than, the value of the reproduction of his labour power, equivalent to a wage. He is not paid the full minimum wage received by the agricultural proletariat such as those in state farms and plantations. The foreign financial and industrial oligarchies do not even pay ground rent for the peasants' land. But the peasant is reproduced as a peasant. He is impoverished and exploited on the basis of his own land, and the peasantry is literally frozen in the stagnant social category of peasantry. A local, independent and creative Nigerian bourgeoisie is even aborted by the activities of foreign capital. Only client capitalists dependent on the foreign economic barons emerge.[19]

Man as the Centrepiece of Development

On the contrary, development is neither catching up with the advanced countries nor the procurement of artifacts. Under certain conditions the artifacts emanate from the development process and reflect it. But the artifacts are not development itself and in certain cases may have no relationship whatever with that process. They reflect development only when they are the end-product of the efforts of the population to apply their creative energy to transformation of the local physical, biological and sociocultural environments. This is the situation in the advanced Western and Eastern countries. They cease to mirror development when they are provided by foreigners. In the latter case the local population is merely acquiring the products of others' development. This has been the experience of Nigeria.

Development is a dialectical phenomenon in which the individual and society interact with their physical, biological, and interhuman environments transforming them for their own betterment and that of humanity at large and being transformed in the process. The lessons learned and experiences acquired in this process are passed on to future generations, enabling them to improve their capacities to make further valuable changes in their interhuman relations and their ability to transform nature. Development is first and foremost a phenomenon associated with changes in man's humanity and creative energies, not in things. It is the unending improvement in the capacity of the individual and society to control and manipulate the forces of nature as well as themselves and other individuals and societies for their own benefit and that of humanity at large. It is a process of actualizing man's inherent capacity to live a better and more rewarding life. It implies increasing skill and capacity to do things, greater freedom, self-confidence, creativity, self-discipline, responsibility, and material well-being. Some of these attributes, particularly the moral categories, are not amenable to quantification. They can only be assessed qualitatively.

All peoples have shown a capacity for independently increasing their ability to live a more satisfactory life than before. The only major difference lies in the rate of this development. Therefore, there is nothing in the process of development which suggests that Westernization or its euphemistic variant, modernization, should be uncritically accepted. In fact, the distinction between developed and underdeveloped or developing societies is untenable because every society is still struggling to fully realize its potential creativity and probably never will. This is a progressive process that probably has no end.

The goal of the process at any particular time is circumscribed by the obstacles in the way of realizing this potential. It varies from society to society depending on their inherited level of production, the nature of their productive forces, the nature of the relations of production that they have established, the prevailing pattern of social and cultural relations, the quality and creativity of the leadership and the hostility or benignness of the physical environment and the neighbouring societies. In other words, the meaning of development is integrally related to the process of eliminating the obstacles in the way of a people to transform their physical, biological and socio-economic environments for the benefit of all of them. It depends on what these obstacles are. And they vary from time to time and from place to place.

Indeed, there is no nation that has achieved a complete mastery of all the obstacles in its path to social bliss, and there may never be. As old challenges have been overcome, new and sometimes more intractable ones have emerged. Therefore, development connotes training in the art of using local resources and creative human energy in problem-solving rather than a wholesale imitation of the path to a good life that some societies have achieved. From this viewpoint it is then possible for a people to accept that they are not all that they ought to be without feeling inferior to other peoples. This perspective enables us to examine all our relationships, including those with the Western powers, to see if they constitute an obstacle or an asset in our march toward our emancipation from the shackles of our human and non-human environments. We may have to disengage from the advanced capitalist societies instead of co-operating so closely with them as we now do.

Development refers to man's progressive qualitative and continued self-improvement. Since man extends and reproduces himself socially through labour, he improves himself economically, socially and culturally through the co-operative use of his labour with others in the transformation of his immediate physical and human environment. It is in this way that he is able to tame the wilderness and build very complex structures, organizations, and institutions for his own welfare. Therefore, development or man's qualitative self-improvement occurs when his labour conditions improve. Such an improvement varies directly with the elimination of all human and non-human impediments to the creative application of human labour. These impediments arise either from the hostility of the physical and biological environments, or from the hostility of the inter-human environment, the existing domestic and international pattern of social, economic and cultural relations. Both exert their impact through their consequences for the alienation of labour. Alienated labour loses its self-liberating and self-extending qualities.

In general there are two aspects to the alienation of labour. The one is psychological, the other material. At the psychological level, labour has a liberating impact because of the 'hurrah effect' arising from the creative and disciplined realization of the mental picture of the end-product of labour. Therefore, labour alienation arises when the worker, in his place of work, is divorced from continuous contact with the mental image of the end-product of production at all stages in the production process. This arises essentially as a result of the increasing division of labour in the production process generated by growth in production. It may also, as in the case of Nigeria, arise from an externally-imposed international division in which the basic needs and habitual consumption patterns are not the basis for significant capital investment, local resources are not the primary and major basis for economic transformation, and foreigners do most of the creative jobs. Under the circumstances, the creativity of human labour is dampened, adversely affecting the quality of the human population.

A good development policy must, therefore, find a way of ameliorating, if not totally eliminating, this kind of alienation of labour. Such a policy must attempt to involve the worker actively in the organization of the production process, at the same time as he is the executor of one or more productive functions in conjunction with others, co-operates with others to use the means of production and dispose of the products of labour, and is responsible for the work of the production collective and, ultimately, of the entire national economy. All these enable him to maintain mental contact with all aspects of the production process up to and including the end-product and its distribution. This democratic participation at the place of work, which is made possible by the elevation of workers to the status of proprietors of the economy, stimulates them to great creativity, awakens their latent energy and desire to work to the utmost of their ability, increases the productivity of labour, exploits material resources and working time optimally, and in general improves the production process.

Moreover, the worker, conscious of himself as co-proprietor strives not only to improve his own labour input, he is also deeply concerned that comrades work well too. He actively combats all manifestations of negligence, inefficiency and violations of discipline by those who do not yet have the necessary sense of responsibility. As a true proprietor, the worker, along with other workers, carries out a search for unexploited ways to raise productivity in order to improve the results of common labour. In other words, he takes part in the management of production.

This situation contrasts sharply with that in Nigerian-type production enterprises. Here the worker's zeal stems from the desire not to lose his job, to earn more, and from fear of punishment by management. There are no motives of a higher order expressing the awareness of social interest. And as many studies of Western sociologists themselves have shown, given the monopoly control of industry, the hired worker's personal initiative runs up against the bureaucratic organization of labour in which goals, forms, and methods of activity are categorically and rigidly prescribed. The worker loses all sense of initiative and creativity because his productive activities are in no way clearly and meaningfully connected in his mind with the general results of production or his basic needs and habitual consumption pattern. Work is for him only a source of wages, not the extension of his social self, the meaning of social life.

At the material level, adequate compensation for the creative efforts of labour provides a good measure of satisfaction and makes it possible for man to improve his labour power. Materially, therefore, the alienation of labour arises when the worker is denied an adequate material compensation for his contribution to the end-product of production. It also results from poor health, ignorance and in general the hostility of the physical and biological environment that reduces the productivity of the worker's labour and consequently his material reward. Today most of the problems in this regard are caused by the private ownership of the means of production and the accompanying disproportionate distribution of surplus values in favour of the owners of the means of production, usually a minority of the population. The workers are exploited. They are not paid wages commensurate with their labour in the production process. They are not paid wages commensuate with their human dignity since this is devalued in comparison with capital, the means of production. And funds which could be used in the public interest to provide social, health and other welfare services that improve man's capacities are diverted to the luxury consumption of the privileged, minority propertied class. The exploited worker becomes alienated and cannot maximize his productive power.

Thus an adequate development policy must address itself to the reorganization of the system of material incentives in favour of the broad majority of the working population. In a major way, this may be accomplished by the abolition of the private ownership of the means of production and with it the abolition of the exploitation inherent in the Nigerian-type system of production. In addition, a large part of the national surplus should be devoted to socially useful consumption such as full employment, health, education, social insurance, pensions, child and mother care, and leisure, which should be provided generously and free, or at minimal costs. Such measures help the worker to improve his creative labour.

The theory of the Western model of development argues that such social progress runs counter to economic growth because an attempt to divert funds from the rich to these social services for the majority tends to reduce the potential accumulation fund for investment. This is a sterile argument, and the history of many societies explodes this myth. In fact, the bulk of the incomes of the propertied classes in Nigerian-type societies, especially of the trading, usurious, finance and banking bourgeoisie, landowners, feudal and semifeudal elements, is utilized for non-productive consumption, enabling the upper classes to live in luxury at the level of ultra-modern Western standards. What is not thus consumed is hoarded in foreign banks. It is this pattern of life that sharply reduces the potential accumulation funds for investment.

At this historical juncture in Nigeria's existence, what are the major obstacles in its path to a self-generated and self-sustained creating transformation of its labour power and, hence, quality of life? In answering this question it should first be pointed out that self-confidence is crucial for overcoming challenges. It prevents one from being subjectively overwhelmed by the magnitude of the problem, thereby demoralizing one and sapping one's will to succeed. Such self-confidence is incompatible with a state of acute and pervasive alienation. In Nigeria, the most significant and fundamental obstacle to development is the lack of self-confidence of the individual and society arising from the colonial and neo-colonial system of production, as well as the accompanying socio-cultural and political relations. It leads to labour alienation.

The Nigerian operates within the context of a complex national and international division of labour which thoroughly alienates him. The society created on the basis of this division of labour dominates him but has no meaning for him in terms of the satisfaction of his material and psychological needs and his traditional consumption habits. It does not even use his local resources. At the psychological level the individual and his society feel powerless to influence events around them. As a result of the international division of labour imposed from outside during the colonial period and continued ever since, albeit with minor changes, Nigeria is assigned a passive and menial role. Initially it was to produce raw materials and import manufactured consumer goods and capital equipment. Its total perspective of the world production process is confined to this role, and it is not a creative role.

The country produces cocoa, groundnuts, tin, petroleum, and other raw materials which it does not consume, or only part of which it consumes. It sells them to the advanced capitalist nations. But it does not participate in and does not control in any way the transformation of these raw materials into manufactured goods in the latter countries. The question of influencing the prices attached to them, which it pays when they are imported into the country, cannot, therefore, arise. Nigeria plays a rather mechanical and partial role in the process relative to the advanced capitalist societies whose financial and industrial oligarchies participate both in the extraction of these raw materials in the local area and their transformation in the metropolitan factories. This enforced mechanical participation in world production creates alienation at the psychological level.

Similarly, in the foreign-owned factories, in the plantations, and even in the local peasant cash crop farms the individual's role is a mechanical one divorced from the meaning of his efforts in terms of the total production process in which he is involved, and in relation to his needs, habitual consumption patterns, the overall use of local resources, the mental contact with the vision of the end-products of the total production process from the beginning of production to the time that prices are attached to them. The inevitable consequence is alienation.

The same effect is produced by a political process in which the vast majority are the object rather than the subject of governance. During the civilian era their political role was confined to a mechanical one of periodically casting votes for parliamentary representatives in whose selection they played no part whatever. Under the military interregnum their role degenerated into one of mere obedience to innumerable and carelessly thought-out decrees from the government. Under both regimes their direct influence on government was forestalled by the institutionalization of chieftaincy. The chiefs assumed the role of liaison officers between the people and the government. This system of indirect rule assumes the powerlessness of the masses to take the reins of their own affairs in their own hands, and is used to deny them any political power. Consequently, the people cannot maintain any meaningful mental contact with the end-product of the political process from the beginning to the end, or with the totality of the political process. Their place and role in this totality remains inexplicable to them. Again the result is alienation.

At the material level alienation also prevails. Within Nigeria such alienation arises from the tendency of economic rewards to concentrate near the economic and political seat of power. Those furthest from this seat, the vast majority of the working population, are virtually ignored. The distribution of rewards in favour of the privileged classes prevails over the interest of the poor majority. Hence, super-highways, oceanliners, and a national airline take precedence over basic staple foods, clean water and preventive medicine. All efforts to reorder the priorities and, therefore, the pattern of reward have been successfully resisted by the privileged classes. At the international level, Nigeria's participation in the material reward system of the world capitalist order creates national alienation. Most of the wealth of this system is appropriated by the advanced capitalist societies. All attempts through the UNCTAD conferences to change significantly this pattern of incentives have so far failed. The major beneficiaries use the power of the system which they control to block any changes that threaten to erode their power and interests, even when such changes are in the interest of the underprivileged countries.

The persistence of these sources of alienation and the absence of an effective program for eliminating them suggest that Nigeria is not developing as we have been and are being made to believe. Obviously, the complex national and international division of labour that integrates the country into the world capitalist system has persisted and is being reinforced. It is the result of the activities of the Euro-American and Japanese financial and industrial oligarchies. And these activities have increased in both absolute and relative terms.

As is clear from the non-direct involvement of these oligarchies in cocoa, palm oil and groundnut production, the relevant effect does not need their direct participation in productive enterprises. What is important is that they control the production process by influencing what is produced, how it is produced, when it is produced, for whom it is produced, and when and how it is marketed. This point is particularly relevant because of the impression being created that the indigenization of productive enterprises would lead to local control of the economy. The foreign oligarchies can still ensure the necessary control of local production even though the enterprises are owned by Nigerians. They can do this by controlling the terms of the international division of labour, technology and, therefore, the various inputs into the local enterprises, access to the world market, business ethos, and bargaining processes between the local and foreign businesses. All these are possible provided that the country is integrated into the world capitalist system.

Only a complete break with the Euro-American and Japanese economic barons, a disengagement from the world capitalist system, can launch Nigeria on to the path of development. Until the foreign control of the local production process is eliminated, the nation cannot create the preconditions for being a developing country. Disengagement must lead to a national and an international division of labour which is controlled from within the country. This will lead to the local control of production and innovative technology, and prepare the ground for the abolition of that alienation that arises from the external manipulation of the production process. It will also enable the centre of creativity to be transferred to the country.

The lessons of the Nigerian civil wars are illuminating here. As a result of the federal blockade, the control over local production by the foreign enterprises was ended in the Biafran enclave. This enforced disengagement stimulated the creativity and imagination of the population, taxing their innovative mentality to the fullest in the production of their basic needs and means of survival. It afforded them an opportunity of enjoying a genuine sense of achievement. They knew why they engaged in production and in what role, and could visualize the end-product of the total production and its contribution to the society.

In addition, disengagement will attack the roots of our colonial mentality and inferiority complex caused by the initial racist myth with which the colonialists, missionaries, and foreign firms rationalized their domination of local production and socio-political relations, and which sustained that domination. With the elimination of the domination over production it becomes easier to overcome the myth of inferiority which rationalized it. A consequence will be the recovery of our self-respect and self-confidence, factors which are critical for overcoming the obstacles to development. In order to develop we need to work much harder, think much harder, and make other sacrifices. The difficulties may seem overwhelming. Under the circumstances we will need as much courage, stamina, self-respect and self-confidence as we can muster.

Therefore, the task of Nigerian leaders interested in guiding the country's national development must begin with the provision of valuable insights into how to effect this disengagement. It must correctly identify the major forces in favour of the break and those opposed to it, their relative strengths, how to shift the balance of forces in favour of disengagement, problems attendant on the successful accomplishment of the task, how to overcome these problems, and the relationship between the process of disengagement and the elimination of the other obstacles to development such as the alienation emanating from the internal pattern of distribution of material rewards.

The practical role of Nigerian leaders in this general political effort is to capture the true aspirations of the Nigerian masses and the other anti-imperialist forces, increase their social, cultural and political consciousness, and therefore act as an effective instrument for their mobilization into a cohesive and purposeful movement aimed at the liquidation of the inherited colonial and the present neo-colonial structures that sustain the activities of the foreign financial and industrial oligarchies. The immediate goal must be to enhance the economic, political and cultural power of the Nigerian masses against the interests of the foreign capitalist monopolies and their local agents and allies.

The task that is called for is a revolutionary one. Therefore, in the course of performing it Nigerian leaders must be motivated by the desire to learn with and from the masses. They must share in the struggle of the masses against their wretched existential conditions. This process of learning from the people is significant. The leader who wishes to contribute to the process of development that entails disengagement cannot derive his ideas and support from those same structures and institutions that he seeks to eliminate He must seek intellectual inspiration and ideas from the very people he wishes to serve and who objectively stand in sharp contradiction to the forces opposed to disengagement and, therefore, national development. What is required of the Nigerian leaders, first and foremost, is the abnegation or abdication of their class interests. Otherwise, they would remain incapable of understanding the march of their people to development as well as the direction of that march and would, therefore, be unable to contribute valuable insights to world civilization based on the Nigerian experience.

The Disservice of Nigerian Social Science: A Concluding Note

Unfortunately, Nigerian social science is incapable of preparing present and future leaders for this revolutionary task of development. Its origin, character, ethos and motivational interests are antithetical to any revolutionary transformation of the society. It emerged as part of colonial education, which caused it to be closely tied to the fundamental socio-economic and political interests and methods of that order. That education was primarily mercenary in character, tied to the availability of employment in the new order. It was not concerned with understanding the reality of social relations sufficiently to provide a basis for changing that reality for the betterment of the vast majority of the population. Neither was it conceived to prepare the individual to live effectively in his immediate physical and human environment and to transform it for his own good and the good of society. Nor was it interested in relating the needs of the vast majority of Nigerians to resources in their local area and the means available there for satisfying them. Its *raison d'etre* was the consolidation and advancement of the economic, social, cultural and political interests of the colonialists and neo-colonialists.

Inescapably, therefore, Nigerian social science espoused theories and disseminated ideas that were favourable or at least not inimical to the interests of the colonial ruling class, the financial and industrial oligarchies of Britain and the other European countries. Its theoretical framework was preoccupied with understanding the process of social change in order to prevent it from abolishing structures that protected the interests of these oligarchies for profit maximization and capital accumulation. Its central task was to rationalize and, if necessary, mystify rather than combat the fundamental structures of colonialism. It was essentially conservative in character. These attributes have been carried into the present neo-colonial period. Its dominant ethos has continued to emphasize the reform of and adaption to rather than liberation from the inherited colonial structures. It cannot function to the detriment of the fundamental structures of colonialism and neo-colonialism. Often, it masks this lack of objectivity under the cloak of being realistic, of 'facing the realities'. Science gives way to an ideology of the status quo.

It is frequently forgotten that what theories and concepts prevail in the academic community are not solely of academic or scientific interest. They usually have an ideological and political character. Social science is an integral aspect of and contributes to official policy. It serves ideological and political purposes not so much through the articulation of its ideological premises, analysis of specific data, or specific action recommendations, but more importantly by providing analytic frameworks and methods of handling data which suggest favourable ways in which individuals and groups may perceive, pose, interpret and solve problems. It does this through theorizing and the set of ideas it disseminates in the society.[20]

Hence, Nigerian social science analyses of colonial Nigeria avoid the fundamental issues of colonial oppression and exploitation under the aegis of foreign capital and the resultant distorted economic and social structures of the country. There is hardly an intelligent study of the effects of foreign capital on the pattern of production in the country, the size of the market, the pattern of use of resources, the pattern of consumption, the multiplier effect, the accelerator effect, the pattern of investment, and the innovation of technology. There have been very few rigorous analyses of the basic nature of the economic structure of the country during the neo-colonial era, and very little of the determining role of foreign capital in Nigerian life.

Hardly any significant research deals with the critical area of ownership of economic undertakings in industry, commerce, agriculture, and real estate, particularly the place of labour in these enterprises. The continuity of the colonial economies into the neo-colonial society and the role of foreign capital in the process is equally ignored. The class structure that was advertently or inadvertently created by the activities of foreign capital during the colonial period, its continuation, expansion and consolidation over the past nineteen years have not been examined scientifically. The consequences of this structure for the nation's capacity for self-reliant socio-economic transformation, and for the direction of social movement, are conveniently forgotten. In the examination of the relationship between colonialism and the foreign domination of the nation no attempt is made to trace the roles of an international division of labour controlled from outside the country, the external orientation of the economy, its high propensity to import, and foreign control of technology and access to markets, all of which arise from the purveyance of foreign capital by imperialism.

Any view that suggests the superiority of labour over capital in the production process is suppressed. Similarly, analyses which suggest that oppression and exploitation are associated with capitalist relations of production are dismissed as 'ideological', prejudiced, inappropriate, overflogged and even unprofessional. Hence, Nigerian social science is fundamentally and irrationally opposed to a Marxist approach to social analysis. Indeed, most of its teaching and reference materials originate from France, Britain, and America and are 'therefore soaking with official and widely shared anti-socialist and anti-communist ideology.'[21] Often the Marxist theory is dismissed as foreign. This is done in the name of patriotism, but such patriotic ideals are not allowed to intrude when an essentially foreign capital is extolled above an essentially Nigerian labour. It is a patriotism that serves the interests of foreign capital.

In other words, Nigerian social scientists have not been able to emancipate themselves from the shackles of the colonial world view. They are still disturbed by the inferiority complex promoted by this view and wish to transcend it. But they are trapped. They are unwilling and in fact, by training, incapable of questioning the pattern of production foisted on the country by the economic oligarchies of Europe, rationalized by the racist myth, and which the colonial and neo-colonial socio-cultural and political relations complement. They do not ask and cannot adequately answer the question: production of what, by whom, for whom, in whose interest, and why? They confine their analyses to superstructural relations divorced from the mode of production. They cannot see the relationship between the production process and the pattern of social, cultural and political relations. They are, therefore, unable to join the revolutionary struggle for the creation of a better society.

Similarly, they invest ideas with an origin and a function independent of the mode of production. Hence, their ideas about socio-economic and political organizations are essentially abstractions that have no economic content. They fail to realize that in Europe, when values such as freedom, equality and fraternity were first popularized, the capitalist classes had already gained dominance over their local economies and were arguing for these principles to enable them to dominate the political processes as well. The ideas rationalized their economic domination. In Nigeria they have been divorced from the local control of the economy. Thus, emphasis is placed on the study of Westernization, modernization, institution building, elite formation, the traditional structure of pre-colonial Nigeria or economic growth, colonialism and neo-colonialism that contains no fundamental analysis of the relations of production. It is this inability to integrate the analysis of the infrastructure and the superstructure of society which lies at the heart of the contradiction between the desire to extol the pre-colonial way of life on the one hand and the acceptance of Western Europe as the model of development on the other.

In addition, much of social science activity in Nigeria is motivated first and foremost by the desire to advance the social scientist's career. Primary concern is less with the subject of study – the material condition, needs and potential of the vast majority of Nigerians – than with marginal and innocuous problems of the inherited colonial activities that qualify him as an academic expert.[22] The emphasis placed on research and the number of publications (and their quality as determined by Euro-American academicians) as criteria for the academic promotion of social scientists in Nigerian universities encourages this concern and has become a strong pressure for academic conformity to the status quo. It is also reinforced by limited job opportunities, low salaries and discriminatory evaluation of qualifications. The pattern of recruitment of the social scientists, their assessment for promotions, their curricula, and their role in the power structure of the universities are organized in such a way as to weed out those fundamentally opposed to the activities of foreign capital and the world view of the financial oligarchies of Europe and America.

In any case Nigerian social scientists trained during the colonial and neo-colonial times are closely tied to the community of Western social scientists. Often they are products of metropolitan universities or proteges of metropolitan teachers in Nigerian universities, and have acquired from them their world view, manner of defining their academic problems, the method and techniques of analyzing them, and where and how to secure funding for their research. Inevitably their initial academic contacts were made at these universities.

Also, foreign governmental agencies, major corporations, their charitable foundations, and reactionary ideologies represented by some metropolitan social scientists have been major influences in shaping the direction, ideological content and funding of the research of Nigerian social scientists.[23] But any Nigerian who shapes his method and tool of analysis to collect such foreign support would not be looked upon favourably if he asks questions which are fundamentally damaging to the interests of foreign capital, even though such questions may be crucial for an understanding of the society. Moreover, such imperialist financing creates a situation whereby the centre of gravity for the acquisition of knowledge about Nigeria is located outside the country itself. It also militates against the growth of an independent center of creativity within the country.[24]

Thus Nigerian social science has rendered a disservice to the cause of Nigerian development. In its present form it is incapable of providing intellectual leadership and an adequate theory for the revolutionary tasks required by that process, Therefore, the necessary revolutionary transformation of Nigerian society must include the radicalization of Nigerian social science. It must be compelled to re-dedicate itself to the only justification for its existence, the greater welfare of the vast majority of the Nigerian population. The latter are quagmired in existential conditions that are destructive of human dignity and, therefore, intolerable. Under the circumstances the restructured and radicalized social science cannot afford to espouse the virtues of being realistic. Only a discipline that is clearly idealistic can give hope of a better future to the teeming and suffering poor of our country. And today this hope is vitally needed to generate the momentum for development.

References

1. Claude Ake, 'Development of What, for What and By Whom?' A paper presented at a conference on development strategies organized by the Dag Hammerskjold Foundation in Arusha Tanzania, September 1972.
2. *Ibid*.
3. *Ibid*., p. 4.
4. This suggestion was strongly argued in a conference paper later made public by Dr. Bolaji Akinyemi, the Director General of the Nigerian Institute of International Affairs.
5. R.O. Ekundare, *An Economic History of Nigeria* (London: Methuen, 1974), p.400. Emphasis is mine.
6. *Ibid*., p.383.

7. Frantz Fanon, *The Wretched of the Earth* (N.Y.: Grove Press, 1966), pp.169–72.
8. Norman Girvan, 'Technology: A New White Magic for Africa,' *Africa Development*, 2, 2 (1977), pp.5–7.
9. United Nations Economic Commission for Latin America, 'Technical Progress and Socio-Economic Development of Latin America,' ST-CEPAL 53-L.2 (1974), pp.26–28 referred to in *Ibid*. Phase I, technological importation, was followed by Phase II, modification and adaptation of the imported technology, and Phase III, mutual technological interchange with other countries.
10. *Ibid*.
11. Stephen Hymer, 'The Multinational Corporation and the Law of Uneven Development' in J.N. Bhagwati (ed.), *Economics and World Order* (N.Y.: Free Press, 1972), pp.113–40.
12. Okwudiba Nnoli, *Ethnic Politics in Nigeria* (Enugu: Fourth Dimension, 1978).
13. Federal Republic of Nigeria, *Report of the Constitution Drafting Committee Containing the Draft Constitution* (Lagos: Federal Ministry of Information, 1976), Vol. I, pp.viii–x.
14. R.O. Ekundare, *An Economic History of Nigeria* (London: Methuen, 1974) pp.371–3.
15. Emmanuel Wallerstein, 'Dependence in An Interdependent World: The Limited Possibilities of Transformation Within the Capitalist World Economy,' *African Studies Review*, 17, 1 (April 1974), p.2.
16. Claude Ake, *op. cit.*, p.20.
17. Clive Thomas, *Dependence and Transformation* (N.Y.: Monthly Review, 1974), pp.58–70.
18. Samir Amin, 'Capitalism, State Collectivism, and Socialism', *Monthly Review*, 29, 2 (July 1977), p.30.
19. See chapter 11 in this volume.
20. A renowned American social scientist, Klaus Knorr, is reported to have underlined this relationship between theory and official policy. See The African Research Group, *African Studies in America – The Extended Family* (Cambridge, Mass.: Africa Research Group, 1970), p.8.
21. *Ibid*., p. 61.
22. See A.U. Obeng, 'Social Research and National Development in Nigeria: Notes of A Nonparticipant Observer', a paper presented at the Conference on Social Research and National Development in Nigeria held at Ibadan, 28 September–4 October 1975.
23. Johan Galtung, 'Scientific Colonialism', in Africa Research Group, *op. cit.*, p.61.
24. *Ibid*.

3. Myths and Fallacies in Nigerian Development

Inyang Eteng

Myths and Fallacies

As irrepressible contradictions in the world capitalist system continue to leave disastrous tell-tales in the latter's trail, foreign and local intellectuals and consultants within the system have simultaneously intensified their efforts to flood Nigerian society with capitalist and neo-colonialist myths and fallacies brandished as well-tested and proven theories of development appropriate for the country. The sale of such pseudo-theories is, however, being increasingly recognized by the Nigerian radical left as one of the most subtle and exceptionally dangerous mechanisms by which neo-colonialism and capitalist imperialism intensify their stranglehold over the Nigerian political economy.

For reasons that will become clearer in the course of the discussion, past and present governments of the Federation and their development planners and implementers have gullibly ingested these pseudo-theories, and have consistently proceeded to tailor all national 'development' plans to the imperatives of monopoly capitalism. With the Third National Development Plan, the general mood of confusion, resignation and apathy which currently pervades the country strongly indicates that Nigeria has reached a development impasse.

From ideational and functional viewpoints, a myth is a traditional story or presentation of ostensibly historical events serving to unfold part or all of a people's *Weltanschauung*, their beliefs and practices.[1] However, from a scientific viewpoint, it denotes a phenomenon having an imaginary or unverifiable existence, an ill-founded belief held uncritically by an interested group. Similarly a fallacy is an argument which fails to satisfy conditions of correct inference. It is essentially an unscientific and baseless mode of explicating reality.

From a strictly scientific and objective standpoint, therefore, myths and fallacies are non-anchorable in empirically verifiable conditions of the existential world. Even where they directly or tangentially refer to the concrete world of reality, detectable epistemological strategies employed by their invokers in explicating this world are essentially speculative and, therefore, deficient. As false and erroneous ideas, they tend generally to be instrumentally employed by a dominant, superordinate class or group to deceive, mislead, delude and mystify, and in a Marxian sense, to implant false consciousness in the minds of members of an exploited and alienated subordinate group who are correspondingly forced to falsify and fragment their reality in time and space. In this context, myths and fallacies fall within the categories of dogma, doctrinaire and false ideology in their most pejorative, propagandist and constraining sense. In the hands of the capitalist exploiter, myths and fallacies constitute ideological and normative instruments of exploitation and mental control.

Some of these myths and fallacies have over the years been unobtrusively smuggled into Nigeria in the form of popular development models or 'scientifically-bounded' prescriptions aimed at resolving the nagging and the presumably insoluble problems of underdevelopment. They include several 'development' modes subsumed in what may be regarded as the 'Grand Liberal-Bourgeois Development Paradigm' against which Andre Gunder Frank and the New Left have unleashed a deserved and unmitigated critique.[2] Others, which to all intents and purposes appear as pseudo-scientific formulations expoused by ebullient but basically irrelevant Africanists, have been aptly described in another context as 'Blaming-The-Victim' and 'The Noble Savage' perspectives to Third World development.[3] The first abandons the lingering racial and biological interpretations of underdevelopment for a substitute model whose explanation of underdevelopment focuses primarily on malignant stresses imposed by the victim's environment, especially the presumed deleterious impact of the victim's autochtonous institutional arrangements. The second facetiously proclaims the African savage as an *homo sapiens economicus* and eulogizes him for his newly-discovered rational orientation to the money market. Based on different assumptions and rationalizations, both approaches perceive the African producer as noble only to the extent of his exploitability. Such erroneous theses about development in Latin America have been exposed by Rodolfo Stavenhagen,[4] Andre Gunder Frank and others.[5]

The fallacies considered below are some of the major propositions deducible from Nigeria's preferred 'mixed economy' approach to national development. It will be consistently argued that in so far as 'mixed economy' is a new semantic fabrication for monopoly capitalism in Africa, all propositions derived from this development paradigm are ahistorical, empirically untenable and programmatically irrelevant as far as authentic development in Nigeria is concerned.

Quest For A Nigerian Development Model

The clamor for ideological articulation is a relatively new element in the country's national development planning. This new trend has graphically sharpened the analytical and practical distinction between the ideological underpinning of a given development plan and its enunciated objectives. The mixed economy approach to national development recently proposed by the Nigerian Constitution Drafting Committee (CDC), therefore, constitutes a vantage point for an intelligent appraisal of the current status of the Nigerian political economy in general, and the question of development or underdevelopment within this matrix in particular. The mixed economy formula as recommended by the CDC indeed reflects the historical accumulation, as well as the current intellectual rallying point, of Nigeria's colonial and post-independence 'development' experiences, more so with respect to (a) conceptualization, planning and execution of self-initiated National Development Plans (1962–68, 1970–74 and 1975–80), and (b) some of the major assumptions (philosophical, ideological or otherwise) which undergird Nigeria's national development performances thus far.

It is apparently against this background that the terms of reference of the Nigerian Constitution Drafting Committee assume a special historical significance: the said Committee was mandated by the Federal Military Government to determine and recommend, among other things, 'constitutional provisions for protecting the people and the resources of this country [Nigeria] from foreign domination', and to ascertain 'the most suitable arrangements to ensure co-ordination of economic activities of the federation and the states, and to promote economic development of all parts of Nigeria'.[6]

Notwithstanding the apparent ambivalent interpretations to which the foregoing terms of reference are easily subject, they however indicate some half-hearted recognition of probable domination of the country's economy by foreign interests from which Nigerians ought to be securely protected. The terms of reference are also clearly appreciative of the nagging problem of co-ordinating disparate but structurally and dialectically linked enclaves of the national economy, which have unmindfully been dichotomized into either the 'public' and 'private sectors', the 'barter' and the 'money' economies, the 'rural' and the 'urban' enclaves, or the agricultural and the industrial -manufacturing sectors.

Realistic options open to the Drafting Committee would have, in the circumstances, included an acceptance of the incontrovertible reality of the pervasive dominance of world monopoly capital over the Nigerian political economy, with a view to providing an unbiased and detailed historical account of the nature of this foreign economic domination, leading to the proposal of a theoretically, empirically and programmatically sound blueprint essentially aimed at rescuing the entire country from its present development predicament. However, contrary to the recommendation of a sub-committee of the CDC for a socialist alternative to the present national development processes in Nigeria, a majority of the CDC members opted for the 'mixed economy' approach, a concept carefully chosen to mask the reality of past and present capitalist predations in the country.

The fallacies underlying this choice must, however, be exposed and in Andre Gunder Frank's words, the leviathan must be disrobed. But first, let us present a summary of the arguments of proponents of the 'mixed economy' and related 'co-operative federalism' approaches as reflections of the search for a national ideology.

The Mixed Economy Perspective

The argument which accepts the traditionality of the mixed economy production mode in Nigeria is central to a partial but critical understanding of the *raison d'etre* of the intense commitment of the country's bourgeoisie to the prevailing consumptionist capitalist system. This 'indigenousness' thesis is the most capricious and, indeed, the most ostentatiously flaunted by the mixed economy ideologues. Since other fallacies and myths are corrollaries of this main proposition, the essence of its entire argument needs to be succintly outlined.

In Section 3.7-2, Volume I, of the Draft Constitution,[7] a majority of the CDC (all members of the bourgeoisie and petty bourgeoisie drawn mainly from the medical and legal professions, political elites of the First Republic, compradorial businessmen, conservative academics, and retired public servants) argued elaborately to the effect that:

(1) Traditionally, Nigeria's ideology is and has always been a mixed economy one; hence, there are no compelling reasons for abandoning this native ideology in favour of one conceived and fabricated in a foreign political and social climate.

(2) The Constitution under a mixed economy approach generates a high degree of operational flexibility of the state apparatus, which consequently enables a popularly elected government to pursue policies which have been put and explained to the electorate.

(3) In point of fact, the traditional Nigerian economy is 'socialist' in certain areas while permitting individual incentive and private ownership in other areas. In other words, the native mixed economy ideology is a delicately balanced synthesis of capitalism and 'socialism'.[8]

(4) With respect to national development, a sharp distinction must be established between the ultimate goals of the state and the stages through which the country must pass in order to effectively attain these goals. It is, therefore, mistaken and, indeed, dangerous for the Nigerian leadership to make sonorous proclamations which ultimately may create a revolution of rising expectations among the masses with revolutionary consequences in the event of non-attainment or delayed realization of these unreasonable goals.[9]

(5) It stands to reason, therefore, that the most pragmatic and feasible goal of the state is basically to seek to enhance the welfare of the individual by providing more jobs and better educational, housing and health facilities, thus raising the general standard of living of the people.[10]

(6) This highly pragmatic goal is more readily attainable through a faster growth in the economy under a system of private investment and individual entrepreneurship than is possible given other modes of production. However, an outstanding ideological implication suggested by the history of Western

and Eastern Europe is that the twin goals of rapid development and extreme forms of income equalization cannot be pursued and achieved simultaneously. It, therefore, logically follows that since Nigeria is basically geared toward the attainment of rapid growth rates in the economy, existing inequalities in income and other opportunities must, at best, receive only secondary attention by the state during the initial development stages.[11]

(7) Socialism is not only foreign to Nigeria, it also relies wholly and entirely on paid bureaucrats of the state alone, while capitalism (and hence a mixed economy) depends on private entrepreneurs. But even if Nigeria opts for socialism, she does not have, and certainly cannot produce, hundreds of thousands of bureaucrats technically trained and politically indoctrinated over time by the state to ensure rapid development according to the logic of 'one hundred percent public ownership'.[12]

(8) Socialism is additionally rejected since in the two essential things that mean most for the comfort of the ordinary Nigerian citizen, namely, agriculture to produce food and housing to provide adequate shelter, the record of socialist economies is not as good as their achievements in heavy industries, and certainly inferior compared to the achievement of Western and other societies which allow for a large measure of individual initiative in economic achievements.

(9) In sum, it will be best for Nigeria that every sector of society comes under the mixed economy system in which the public sector plays a large and leading role, is able to determine basic prices and to mitigate the harsher effects of private competition, but at the same time allows room for private initiative.

It is clear from the foregoing summary that the mixed economy proponents pitched the presumed 'traditionality' of this capitalist mode of production against the equally presumed 'foreignness' of socialism, the assumed operational flexibility of the system against socialist bureaucratism, the proclaimed pragmatism of this economic system against presumed socialist utopianism and idealism, and, finally, the pro-welfarist orientation of a mixed economy against assumed anti-welfarist inclination of socialism. More importantly, the proponents consistently maintained that the most critical single factor accounting for these differences which portray the superiority of capitalism and, hence, a mixed economy, is the allowance is provided for individual initiative and private accumulation of wealth.

Co-operative Federalism

The Nigerian 'lumpen-bourgeois' advocates of the country's present distributive political economy are by no means a solid homogeneous group. Here and there one can detect some evidence of marginal disagreements and skirmishes over questions of 'equitable' resource distribution among themselves as prime beneficiaries of the system, and over the extent of state franchise that should be permitted in the running of the nation's economy presently controlled by the so-called 'private sector', a euphemism for foreign enterprises. Accordingly, an apparent disenchantment with some aspects of the mixed economy proposal was registered by an indeterminate minority of the CDC members, who suggested an 'alternative approach' to socio-economic development known as Co-operative Federalism. This system makes the following arguments:

(1) A social system is maintained by a certain acceptable value system and institutionalized arrangements that help realize these values. Thus, the constitutional proposals acceptable to the generality of members of the Drafting Committee essentially embody such fundamental values as wide sharing of political powers; abhorrence of concentration of power in a few hands, no matter the group; acceptance of open participatory decision-making processes; freedom of individuals to pursue freely-chosen vocations, including guaranteed freedoms of geographical mobility, of residence and of religious association.

(2) It is, therefore, inconsistent to adopt an economic system which will produce institutions incongruent with the foregoing political values, for this will lead to instability.

(3) What is more, control by the state of 'major sectors' adopted by the 'mixed economy' proponents only aims to transfer control of other sectors of the economy from multinational corporations to dominant party elites.

(4) Since the stability of a political system is maintained by economic institutions congruent with it, Nigeria should, therefore, opt for an economic system that inhibits the concentration of economic power in a few hands or groups, that guarantees the growth of a large population of moderately wealthy people with no extremes of poverty and wealth, and that permits an open participatory economy in which both public and private enterprises will co-operate in harnessing the productive forces of the Republic of Nigeria.

Judging from the muddled and contradictory logic, especially the confusion regarding the nature of causality between economy, polity and the general normative system of society adduced by the co-operative federalists, all of whom eventually endorsed the Draft Constitution in its entirety, it is pertinent to note that no fundamental distinction exists, either at the theoretical or policy level, between a mixed economy and co-operative federalism. Both formulations are predicated on the 'public' and 'private' sectoral dichotomy, the consistency of interests of both sectors, the possibility of humanizing capitalism, and the primacy of individual capital accumulation under free enterprise. Co-operative federalism is thus easily dismissed as another flimsy and superficial modification of the more inclusive mixed economy proposal. The main issue is basically a choice between capitalism and socialism, not between capitalism and a Nigerian variant of it. The latter by itself does not constitute an articulate ideology.

Let us now proceed to examine a few of the central fallacies subsumed in the mixed economy approach to national development in Nigeria. Included in this discussion are (a) the fallacy regarding ideology generally as the substructure of society and the economy as epiphenomenal; (b) the fallacy concerning the mixed economy as a traditional Nigerian ideology; (d) the fallacy which misconstrues the mixed economy as a universal development mode; and (d) the fallacy regarding the mixed economy as the most pragmatic development strategy in Nigerian circumstances.

Ideology as Substructure: The Hegelian Revival

The Nigerian ruling class and its legitimizing petty bourgeoisie are consistent and unequivocal in regarding the mixed economy, co-operative federalism, and other capitalist variants as ideologies. They grievously err, however, in confusing a given mode of production, specifically referring to a given organization and process of production and attendant social relations of production, with its supportive ideology. It is, nonetheless, an abiding Marxian legacy to analytically differentiate between the two, and to properly view ideology, and the entire normative system of society of which ideology constitutes a significant element, as epiphenomenal and, hence, derived from the imperatives of the ongoing mode of production, not the opposite as Hegal contended. This distinction, the nature of the causal relationship between the two, and indeed whether or not Nigeria has or ought to have an ideology, are some of the main topics of elitist debate in the country since the inception of the Murtala regime, debate which has intensified the search for an appropriate ideology for Nigeria. Yet the confusion between ideology as a system of ideas and the productive base which it mirrors has persisted.

Part of the main problem lies in the uncritical acceptance by the Nigerian bourgeoisie of the Hegelian fallacy which consistently regards a society's normative system as its base rather than the superstructural derivative of its mode of production. Typical of this position is the co-operative federalist assumption that 'any social system is maintained by a certain accepted value system and the institutional arrangements that help to realize those values', and that 'it is inconsistent that we should adopt an economic system that will result in institutions that are incongruent with the political values expressed above', for 'that will be an invitation to instability.' Even when the co-operative federalists correctly argued in another vein that 'the stability of a political system is maintained by the economic institutions congruent with it', it is obvious that for the most part that they and their mixed economy counterparts regard Nigeria's ontological system as its fundamental and most enduring substratum, while her economy is treated as merely epiphenomenal and, therefore, must be organized in such a way that it is operationally consistent with the existing ideological base as expressed in its political institution.

This endemic misconception of the nature of the logical link between ideology and the objective productive-distributive conditions of the Nigeria society is further illustrated by Lt. General Obasanjo's rhetorical question addressed to the National Workshop on Planning Strategy for the 1980s. He asked, 'should we not in our own interest, and in the interest of humanity, hark back to our own traditions of esprit de corps and communalism, and build an economy and a society that emanates from our genuis?'. To this poser he provided an answer when he declared that the choice is clear, although the task of building a society by Nigerians out of Nigerian culture and traditions will surely challenge Nigeria's collective intellect. Yet, for the Nigerian Head of State, Nigeria's 'trading post economy' and its vulgar materialism hardly constituted the existential reference point in the envisaged transformation.

For some intelligent observers, to have ever mooted the idea of 'communalism' was indeed a remarkable shift in orientation for the Nigerian military regimes that hitherto vouched to be completely dissociated with any ideology whatever. However, the crusade in search of a traditional ideology, led by the Nigerian Head of State who superintended a satellite capitalist economy, made this persistent misplacement and misinterpretation of the place of ideology in national development more critical than ever.

In his frequently cited Jaji speech of 12 September 1977, Lt. General Obasanjo again attempted an appraisal of the 'causes' of the present seemingly incurable ills of the Nigerian society. His typical liberal-bourgeois concern with the normative, the ethical, the psychological, and clinically pathological independence of their structural and historical antecedents was clearly indicated in this speech when he posited that '. . . the major cause of most of the ills of [Nigerian] society . . . is the sandy and shaky substratum on which we have tried to build the society through the colonial days by discarding the good part of our traditional society.'[13]

It is patently obvious from the foregoing statement that the non-material aspects of Nigeria's culture and traditions are made coterminous with the basic sub-structure of society. By this thesis, the confrontation between colonial mercantilism (and neo-colonial monopoly capitalism) and the African social order is essentially reduced to a mere confrontation between antagonistic ontological systems. By the same token, African victims of predatory capitalism are castigated for their wrong choice of foreign culture. From this standpoint, pre-colonial Africa is basically viewed as an ontological, not an economic, system. By implication, to set Nigeria on a more progressive development course, her system of values must be drastically altered.

This unwarranted functionalist fixation on moral laxity and indiscipline as 'causes' of Nigeria's underdevelopment is further illustrated in another speech by Lt. General Obasanjo in which he insisted that 'with the human and national resources available within the country, what was now needed to build a truly great nation were dedication and discipline.'[14] Here, once again, the Nigerian pro-capitalist distributive economy is taken as given, while the only crucial explanatory variable in the development praxis is the degree of ritualistic conformity to the prevailing normative system superimposed by the country's ruling class. Yet, this purely Parsonian solution is basically gratuitous since it was recognized in the same speech that 'we [Nigerians] cannot afford to build a nation in which a handful of people exclusively own and control means of production to the perpetual detriment of the majority'.

However, it is clear that proposed solutions to Nigeria's prevailing underdevelopment have been anything but efficacious, since the main problem has scarcely been located within its appropriate historical and structural matrix.[15] Let it be stressed, nonetheless, that it is fallacious to blame the present unacceptable condition of grinding poverty for the majority and booming wealth for a few on lack of dedication and indiscipline, for these are direct behavioural correlates of the country's prevailing capitalism and its contingent lopsided distribution of power and other resources and opportunities.

Indeed, the Nigerian reality clearly suggests that those who should be properly characterized as undisciplined, rapacious, unproductive, roguish, licentious and morally bankrupt, primarily include most members of the Nigerian lumpen-bourgeoisie and petty bourgeoisie, not the toiling masses whose labour power sustains this parasitic class. These unsavoury behavioural manifestations currently detected among the masses are clear evidence of progressive 'massification' of the generality of the Nigerian citizentry into the dominant materialistic culture established and ordained by the Nigerian leading bourgeoisie. The Nigerian masses, it must be emphasized, are not the originators of these obnoxious behavioural aberrations against which their initiators are pretentiously raving. Recent probes of official corruption in Nigeria strongly indicate that while top government officials cart away the substantial loot, their bureaucratic underlings only pick the crumbs. This point will be further considered later.

The Mixed Economy: Indigenous to Nigeria?

The 'traditionality' thesis can be dented on at least two grounds, namely its lack of historical content and its defilement of the intellectual requirement of structural and holistic analysis, from which its empirical untenability and policy ineffectiveness can easily be inferred. In this section the ahistoricity of this fallacy will be examined.

Typical of the 'traditionality' argument, aside from Lt. General Obasanjo's crusade for the revival of Africa's presumed traditional 'esprit de corps and communalism', is Dr. Nnamdi Azikiwe's anthropological misinterpretation of Africa's pre-colonial economy when he suggested that: 'We have discovered that the economy of our ancestors was communal in nature but was based on landed property. They traded by barter or by means of some form of exchange. This shows that they believed in private ownership and enterprise as well as the profit motive.'[16]

First, this thesis is completely ahistorical, if by 'tradition' it is implied that the mixed economy mode of production has been with Nigeria over the millenia. There is no intellectually justifiable reason for confusing Nigeria's pre-capitalist subsistence economies with the pro-capitalist satellite economy of modern Nigeria. It should have been obvious before now that all 'traditional' economies of the multilingual nationalities that were later amalgamated in 1914 under the British flag have had long histories, having themselves resulted from several centuries of dialectical transformations. These pre-colonial subsistence economies operated with observable variations with respect to the level of technological development, organization of production, social relations of production, types of goods and services produced, distribution and consumption patterns, and derived and supportive ideological system. But a point needs re-emphasis, namely: these pre-capitalist economies never constituted the original 'state of nature' by which these ethno-linguistic nationalities were identified. When did 'traditional' Africa begin? And what is the present justification for regarding contemporary Nigeria merely as an anthropological atavism?

Second, even when for the sake of argument the 'traditionality' concept is applied to the predominant mode of production of the totality of pre-colonial continental Africa, the argument is still as untenable as ever. Current evidence, though limited and rudimentary as it is, also convincingly indicates that pre-colonial African states, at least before colonial conquests, operated economies varied in their organizational structure and processes, as well as in their political and cosmological systems derived from their productive mechanisms.[17]

The band, for example, of Stone Age Nigeria, which subsisted on hunting and gathering and was virtually limited to a local community of small size and low population density, tended generally to organize its rudimentary polity and social relations around informal leadership, egalitarian distribution and intensive exchange of reciprocities. Similarly, the clan, frequently multi-local and approximating several acephalous, authochthonous Igbo sub-groups that emerged from the neolithic agrarian revolution, tended to organize extensive shifting agriculture within relatively small communities of low density whose equally rudimentary political organization was developed around informal leadership, egalitarianism and reciprocal exchanges.

On the other hand, a chiefdom, basically multi-local in form, consisting of large communities of moderate density that subsisted on extensive and intensive agriculture and herding, showed evidence of highly-specialized political functionaries, highly-crystallized class distinctions, and mechanisms for redistribution of rewards and opportunities. Similarly, the state (such as that of Oyo, Benin or Abuja), which was clearly multi-local and often involved an entire language group, generally rested on a subsistence economy based primarily on intensive agriculture, herding and inter-state commerce. The ancient state also operated a highly-developed political organization manned by highly-specialized political and other functionaries distributed among several large and densely-populated cities and towns with distinct estates or classes, relationships among which were considerably mediated by a highly-developed market exchange mechanism as well as clearly-defined patron-client resource networks.

In no sense, it must be emphasized, did these subsistence economies exhibit characteristics of the consumptionist, capitalist prototype now prevailing in modern Nigeria. Even the more mature of the ancient kingdoms of Africa – Zimbabwe, Ghana, Mali, Songhai – in the peak of their glories could not by any stretch of historical or sociological imagination be described in capitalist terms, notwithstanding their varying capacities for inter-state trade, commerce, and diplomacy, and regardless of their marked feudalistic systems of inequalities and obvious social contradictions and brutalities. In their general profiles and detailed characteristics, these pre-colonial economies were essentially subsistent, not capitalist. Their general scale of operation was comparatively small, their technologies rudimentary and simple, and their markets were similarly relatively underdeveloped, and never operated to mediate between social and administrative sub-divisions of the group, community or state, nor between producers and consumers, and certainly were never intended as the chief determinant of the division of productive labour nor the values of exchangeable goods and services.

Additionally, in these subsistence economies, a majority of producers were never drastically separated from ownership and control of the means of production, which were generally lodged in the family, the lineage and/or the community as significant units of production. Although parcels of communal land were and are still worked on an individual basis, distribution of these crucial means of production was conditioned by the level of available technology and the supply of labour and other productive techniques, especially in so far as alienation of communal land and other productive means was religiously sanctioned with obvious economic implications. Existing inequalities were also frequently diffused by other ascriptive considerations and by well-established norms of reciprocities which were stringently enforced.

To generate and augment available technologies and productive skills, socialization processes in these economies were geared toward the reproduction of adult skills and specialities, which were often lodged in occupational guilds and lineages, and which were directed toward the production of adults with multi-faceted productive skills, so that an individual was simultaneously a farmer, a fisherman, a hunter, a weaver and a wine-tapper. Above all, production which created less-intensive 'eco-crisis' than are presently experienced in all capitalist societies, was directly aimed at the satisfaction of *subsistence needs*, never directed for mass production of wastes nor for conspicuous consumption.

To designate these pre-colonial economies as 'capitalist' simply because there existed some kind of exchange in some kind of market based on some kind of medium of exchange is, therefore, to portray gross and inexcusable ignorance of the nature of the capitalist system. Most curiously, by denying history generally, and Nigerian history in particular, the Nigerian mixed economy proponents, by implication, deny the thorough-going and celebrated history of capitalist penetration, conquest and consolidation in the country. Even more crucially, the Nigerian ruling class and its supporters tend to feign ignorance of the major capitalist dynamics implicated with the very historical evolution of Nigeria as a country, dating back to the fifteenth century. And, by denying Nigeria's history in its totality, this parasitic bourgeoisie thus demonstrates a staggering inability to explain the very processes that brought them into existence, the sources of their power, and the implications and consequences of their dependent and client status *vis-a-vis* foreign monopoly capitalists.

This functionalist fixation on a presumed static Nigerian social order is unwarranted. It virtually smacks of intellectual myopia, if not downright fraudulence; more so since in their omniscience as the dominant theorists, planners, executors and evaluators of the nation's development plans, this ruling class ought to have realized that a true social development epistemology must inescapably demonstrate the historical and dialectical links between the past, present and future of Nigeria's development processes, noting their strengths and weaknesses, and their implications and consequences for the majority of Nigeria's producing population.

From a historical point of view, therefore, the 'traditionality' thesis must be rejected outright, especially when examined against the backdrop of the following underdevelopment-prone events associated with the historical evolution of Nigeria: early mercantilist explorations sponsored by Liverpool merchant adventurers which presaged initial coastal plunders by Europeans; the four hundred gory years of African enslavement which historically provided the economic foundations of both the Carribbean and Latin American plantation systems and the Industrial Revolution;[18] the subsequent 1884–5 balkanization and colonization of Africa under which process Nigeria came to be a British colony; the capitalist-inspired wars of 1914–18 and 1939–45 in which Nigerians under British tutelage were deployed as cannon fodder against the military might of Germany and her allies; the protracted liberation and independence struggles that invariably laid the foundations of post-independence, ethno-regional politics and the present post-civil war inter-state acrimony; the recent civil war itself (1967–70) inspired by capitalist oil politics and prosecuted on behalf of monopoly capitalism and the Nigerian lumpen-bourgeoisie; the current unrestrained dominance and predations of multinational corporations over the 'commanding heights' of the Nigerian economy; and the recent Nigerian-initiated, but wholly wasteful, FESTAC '77 and similar romantic and narcissistic cultural jamborees involving black peoples of the continent and the diaspora whose cultural past Nigeria concedes was ravaged and destroyed by Western capitalism.[19]

The list is virtually interminable. However, the fact that the past and present ruling classes and their supporting academics have consistently endorsed the prevailing capitalist system, and have even facetiously proclaimed it as an indigenous mode of production against all historical and contemporaneous evidence, is indeed an intriguing research problem. In sum, the 'traditionality' thesis and the ahistorical interpretation it calls forth tend to suggest the following testable proposition: *People who truncate and distort their history tend to live in a world of fantasies which they verbalize in fallacies*. The Nigerian bourgeois, mixed economy adherents are wilfully truncating and distorting the country's history, itself part of an unmistakable history of capitalist development in Africa. The current maddening chaos consequent upon their lumpen-bourgeois planning since independence is now being explained away in empty rationalizations and pseudo-theories. But try as hard as they can, the squalid Nigerian reality belies these untenable propositions.

The Mixed Economy: A Universal Mode of Production

A corollary of the 'traditionality' postulate is the myth that all world economies past and present, capitalist and socialist, subsistent and industrialized, are essentially mixed, meaning that they are all variations of public and private sectoral combinations in one form or another, no matter the ideology and regardless of the particular mode of production and distribution. More particularly, it is argued that both the American post-industrial free enterprise system and the Soviet directed, central-planning economy also reflect peculiar mixtures of both public and private sectors. Thus assumed, the universality of the mixed economy as the most pragmatic and widely accepted development strand is presumably substantiated. If the mixed economy works for all major industrialized nations of the East and the West, the argument goes, it can also work for Nigeria.

In the raging confusion and mass agitation in present-day Nigeria, now popularly caricatured among a wide spectrum of the citizenry as a 'country where nothing works,'[20] vague and contradictory interpretations of the mixed economy concept is currently being peddled by ideologues among whom are pro-government businessmen and bourgeois academics, some of whom are loquaciously masquerading as self-styled frontline 'socialists.' This public mis-education stunt is continuing with scarcely any clear analyses of concrete examples of specific mixed economies in operation for purposes of illustrating for the benefit of Nigerians exactly the nature of the structural matrix generated by the mix. In their vituperative, anti-socialist sloganeering, only vague and ambiguous hints are provided by the protagonists.

The functionalist 'universalism' fallacy derives, in part, from an absence of any systematic attempt at a holistic analysis of the present Nigerian political economy on the part of mixed economy proponents. Yet it ought to be borne in mind that a social event is best understood not only in terms of the historical dialectics that shape it but also by the dynamics of the widest structural matrix within which the event is subsumed.

However, the concept of 'mutually reinforcing and logically consistent sectors' tends generally to undergird the mixed economy advocacy. For example, in ambivalent reference to either Nigeria's pre-capitalist or colonial economy, Boeke's 'social dualism'[21] and Higgin's 'technological dualism',[22] each of which has long been discarded by serious Third World development analysts, are often invoked by the proponents. According to Boeke, underdeveloped economies generally consist of two relatively distinct sectors, each apparently subject to its own peculiar theory and mode of production, distribution, and consumption.[23] Boeke's 'social dualism' is essentially the consequence of the penetration into, and subsequent domination of, the 'traditional' pre-colonial economy by monopoly capital. However, in Nigeria, British colonialism *integrated* the disparate ethnolinguistic groups now constituting it as a satellite into the world monopoly capitalist hegemony, but *not* as an exclusive production system as Boeke suggests. The Nigerian traditionalists on the other hand view both the 'barter-exchange' and the 'communal' aspects of Nigeria's pre-capitalist economy as historically contemporaneous and, hence, structurally linked within the subsistence economies. The 'public' and 'private' sectoral mix in the current Nigerian economy is, thus, regarded as the modern projection of the socialist and capitalist homologues subsumed in the traditional economy.

The traditionalists among members of the Constitutional Drafting Committee are equally ambiguous regarding the proper structuring of the present Nigerian political economy. Their ambiguity is clearly demonstrated in the statement that 'in point of fact the Nigerian economy is "socialist" in certain areas of the economy whilst in other areas individual initiative and ownership is permissible', and that 'Nigeria has never hesitated to assume full ownership or control of sectors of the economy whenever it is necessary in the national interest to do so.'[24] These pretentious claims to altruism by members of the CDC on behalf of the exploited Nigerian productive class must, however, be immediately countered. First, the encouragement and protection of individual ownership and 'initiative' in the private sector, essentially dominated by foreign private enterprises, properly dates from the era of the colonial subjugation of Africa. The implication that these capitalist practices are traditional simply because they are 'Nigerian' is fallacious and untenable. The public and private sector distinction is merely verbal, for in practice the public sector serves while the private sector benefits.

Second, the CDC's reference to 'Nigerians' as *always* encouraging and protecting individual property ownership and control is basically a propaganda gimmick. It provides a false impression of decentralized systems of economic and political decision-making in colonial and post-independence Nigeria under both civilian and military regimes. In a country where coercive governments, whether superimposed by colonial conquest, by the ballot, or by the bullet, have persistently veered between tempered depotism and neo-fascism, any reference, however tangential, to mass participation of the Nigerian producers in economic and political decision-making affecting their destiny is, indeed, a bland falsification of Nigeria's social history. At least Lt. General Obasanjo recently conceded that all national development plans have consistently been made from above, with scarcely any attempt to incorporate the producing masses at the grassroots. Yet on the particular occasion when this comment was made, the Head of State was unmistakingly addressing a group of businessmen and petty bourgeois academicians who assembled under the aegis of the National Institute for Social and Economic Research (another institutional creation of the national ruling class) to deliberate on development planning strategies for the 1980s without a single member of the Nigerian proletariat and peasant producers.[25]

Third, by projecting the pre-capitalist, subsistence economy on Nigeria's modern pro-capitalist mode of production, and by deliberately assuming a capitalist-socialist synthesis within this economy, the traditionalists consequently talk glibly about the mutual benefits which the private and public sectors apparently derive from each other. Dr. Pius Okigbo, one of the most committed bourgeois economists in the country, and the Director General of a lucrative consultancy firm whose major clients include the federal and state governments, summarized this view when he indicated as follows: 'Since no system is pure and simple, in practice, there are mixed economies in which some public wants are satisfied with private goods and some private wants are satisfied with public goods. This in my view is the most workable and constructive definition of a mixed economy.'[26] The legendary tendency among the bourgeoisie to dabble in semantic subterfuges is easily portrayed in the above statement. Here the real interests of the Nigerian state functionaries as a class instrument of monopoly capitalist exploitation are cleverly hidden in the abstract concepts of 'public wants' and 'public goods', while the material interests of foreign and indigenous entrepreneurs are equally camouflaged in similar abstractions called 'private wants' and 'private goods'. And, to further provide an impression of the 'public' sector as actually controlling the 'commanding heights' of the national economy, Dr. Okigbo indicated that 'as of now about 40 to 45 per cent of the gross domestic product of Nigeria is produced directly by the public sector', and that 'about 49 per cent of the expenditure on the product is accounted for by the public authorities', while 'over 62 per cent of aggregate investment is made by the public authorities'.[27] To the unwary easily mesmerized by sectoral percentage distributions, these figures look ostensibly impressive.

On careful reflection, however, one wonders what is so impressive about nearly 60 per cent of the gross domestic product of the so-called 'leading' African sovereign state and self-styled champion of African liberation being predominantly controlled by foreigners. Also, the fact that Nigeria records over 62 per cent aggregate investment is scarcely anything to gloat over. It is composed largely of capital equipment generally imported from Western capitalist countries, and in partnership with neo-colonialist foreign interests whose metropolitan decisions she does not control and for whom she provides enormous capital and other resources through equity shares, cheap 'domesticated' labour and virtually free socio-economic infrastructures (electricity, water, transportation and communication, and political and military legitimation).

Indeed, Okigbo's carefully chosen figures generally hide the fact that a huge share of the investments is basically in non-capital generating, import-substitution industries concentrated in the Lagos-West-North axis essentially to take full advantage of available resources (particularly cheap labour) and maximum government protection against foreign competition. These figures also provide no hints regarding the dismal structure of Nigeria's foreign trade, nor the extent of profits annually made by multinational corporations which dominate the so-called private sector. Indeed, the enormity of these profits does not justify the official claim that Nigeria's consignment of the private sector to these rapacious multinationals is basically guided by national interests as generally defined, except in the vulgarized sense in which foreign enterprises incorporated in Nigeria, such as UAC of Nigeria Ltd., are usually accorded indigenous status by the benefitting national compradors. They are usually Nigerian in terms of profit-making, but foreign with respect to decision-making, control of the country's resources and resource networks, and expropriation of surpluses generated within the country.

Fourth, critics of Nigeria's distributive-consumptionist capitalism are consistently reminded of other atavistic survivals of 'traditional African socialism', which include, among other things, the continued exchange of customary, non-economic and non-quantifiable reciprocities outside modern market contexts among Nigerian rural residents and their supposedly non-detribalized urban counterparts; the lingering impact of the kin-group, the extended family, and the local community on various aspects of the social life of Nigerians, regardless of their place of residence; and the presumed communalistic ethos seemingly expressed in rural community self-help 'development' efforts, in co-operative movements, in religious brotherliness, and even in the commitment of Nigerians to their respective states, local government areas and village communities. These and other instances are supposed to constitute a normative rationale for government's control of the public sector on behalf of Nigerians still imbued with traditional socialist sentiments.

Fifth, the 'public sector' concept itself has taken several twists. When hard-pressed by mounting evidence of unspeakable incompetence, staggering corruption, and fraudulence among the public officials who man Nigeria's public corporations and other parastatals, the 'mixed economists' generally tend to confuse state capitalism with scientific socialism. Oblivious of the fact that public corporations in Nigeria, as elsewhere in the capitalist world, are basically capitalist in spirit, structure and operation, public bureaucrats and government appointees who man these bodies usually turn around to blame their gross inefficiency and general sloppy performance on presumed excessive bureaucratism and the denial of individual initiative by the public sector, generally but wrongly regarded as coterminous with the socialist component of the economy. However, as the recent purges of corrupt officials have shown, Nigerian public enterprises and the incompetent, 'ten/twenty per cent commission bureaucrats' who run them, cannot transcend the national pro-capitalist 'mixed economy' mode of production which both produces and nurtures them. A corrupt, free-for-all capitalist system cannot produce honest public officials.

At other times, the American post-Second World War anti-trust campaigns ineffectively aimed at regulating and controlling monopolistic and oligopolistic practices of national giant corporations which dominated weapons, automobile and communications industries, are normally cited as a universal justification for believing that the public sector can possibly control and regulate the private sector of the national economy. Sometimes inspiration is drawn from Galbraith's recent whimsical proposal which aims to infuse 'three socialisms' into the 'planning sector' of the American post-industrial economy.[28]

Others who now claim to be sympathetic to 'anti-Marxist socialism', just to be part of the socialist wind of change currently sweeping across the country, are also citing varieties of state capitalism with varying degrees of worker-peasant participation, such as West German co-determination, French tripartite administration of nationalized enterprises, the Yugoslav worker-participation system, and the Israeli *Histadrut* or producers' co-operatives. Yet as Blumberg has shown, with the exception of some encouraging results from the Yugoslav and Israeli experiences, these utopian experiments are total failures.[29] And having also learnt nothing from the dramatically disappointing results of the Mokwa Resettlement project[30] and from the Eastern and Western Nigerian farm settlement schemes of recent times,[31] the Nigerian 'non-Marxist socialists' are now eulogizing the recent extension of 5 to 10 per cent equity participation to Nigerian low-income workers serving multinational corporations under the revised indigenization policy of 1977 as a major revolutionary breakthrough in increased control of the national economy by Nigerians.[32]

Six, one other interpretation of the mixed economy concept also gaining ground is the claim that the Nigerian political economy as presently constituted provides enough room for future governments in the country to build either a capitalist or a socialist economy as may be chosen by the people. One of the most horrendous illustrations of this position is provided by Chief Rotimi Williams, an illustrious Nigerian legal luminary, a leading defense counsel in recent cases of currency smuggling involving some Nigerian business tycoons and their foreign co-conspirators, and chairman of the recent National Constitution Drafting Committee. In his celebrated and well-received defense of the present economic system on the floor of the Constituent Assembly, he likened capitalism and socialism to the right foot and the left foot respectively of a man. Since, according to him, a normal human being moves on both feet, it is only constructive and natural for Nigeria to operate an economy with a balanced admixture of capitalism and socialism.[33] This is sheer reductionism.

When all is considered, the obvious contradictions immanent in the mixed economy proposition are unmistaken. In one vein, the Constitution Drafting Committee emphatically rejected 'socialism' as a totally foreign fabrication, and yet in another vein the same Committee indicated, again unequivocally, that in actuality socialism and capitalism are intrinsic aspects of Nigeria's traditional economy. This is a contradiction *par excellence*, coming as it does from the cream of the Nigerian intellectual and professional bourgeoisie whose doubtful selection by the military regime as the country's best constitution makers have since earned them the satirical accolade, 'the 50 wise men'. However, no matter the level of abstraction, scientific socialism and capitalism are mutually exclusive categories; their synthesis into either a mixed economy or a neo-welfarism is, therefore, a historical impossibility.

The Mixed Economy: A Pragmatic Development Strategy?

Pragmatism connotes realism, the best and the most practical in the circumstances. When Nigerian mixed economy proponents employ this term, they often mean more than that; they generally invoke the spectre of maximum national advantage derived from the capitalist mode of production. Having clung tenaciously to the tenets of the traditional bourgeois development paradigm against which Third World scholars have launched relentless attacks,[34] the Nigerian squandering capitalists, whom Lt. General Obasanjo recently called 'commission agents',[35] now facetiously present themselves to the world simultaneously as champions of African liberation and as unabashed promoters of monopoly capitalism and neo-colonialism in Africa.

Since the end of the Nigerian civil war, no day passed without a national daily carrying news of at least one event in connection with Nigeria's partnership with the same foreign capitalists whose collaborators were butchering Africans in Zimbabwe, Mozambique, Botswana, Namibia and South Africa. State governors and their economic advisers are outdoing one another placatingly inviting foreign investors into their respective states. Federal and state economic commissioners are having a field-day in conferences and ceremonies marking the launching of one new industry or the other, and sermonizing on the great profits that await those foreign and indigenous entrepreneurs who are willing to avail themselves of Nigeria's 'traditional hospitality' and her economic open-door policy.[36] Trade missions from almost every known industrial country of Europe, Asia and the America have been stampeding to win some sizeable part of the Nigerian market.[37] All these are occurring at a time when the so-called North-South Dialogue on the New International Economic Order is known to have completely floundered, to the discomfiture of black Africa. The impression is being created that the mixed economy, a new fangled Rostowianism[38] which consolidates Nigeria's direct contact with Western Atlantic powers, is the best thing that has and can ever happen to the country.

But Nigeria is basically a satellite of the metropolitan capitalist system, and like all satellites her multilateral integration into this system increases her underdevelopment, not development. Samir Amin's theoretical contribution to African development literature clearly underscores Nigeria's client position in relation to monopoly capital.[39] Amin presents a four-sector model of development which posits 'a fundamental difference between . . . capitalist accumulation and . . . economic and social development characteristic of a self-centered system and that of a peripheral system'. This fundamental and crucial difference between the two economies within the capitalist fold is diagrammed below.

According to this formulation, sectors 2 and 4 basically represent the essential features of the self-centered advanced economies, while sectors 1 and 3 represent those of the peripheral, dependent economies of the Third World countries. According to this model, which captures the historical and contemporary Nigerian reality, the country's client economy came into being consequent upon demands imposed on it by a self-centered British economy, and later by the economies of other centres within the capitalist Atlantic Community. Operating primarily as the supplier of cheap raw commodities and as consumer of costly foreign goods and services, the Nigerian peripheral economy mainly serves the needs of a small sector of the population, thereby practically leaving the country's producing masses out of the mainstream of the so-called national development and modernization.

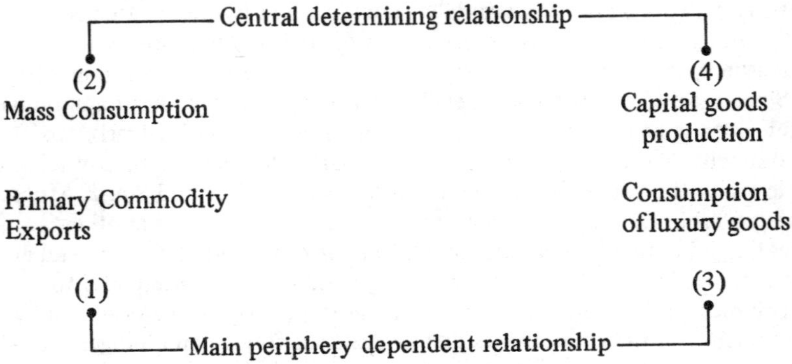

The mixed economy path to development may be the most pragmatic from the standpoint of the national ruling class and its legitimizing bourgeois academics. This is understandable, especially by reason of their historical incapacity to deal with the monopoly capitalist leviathan, and because of the benefit they derive from their invidious roles as multinational corporation commission agents. There is, however, no deterministic law which indicates that their whims and caprices and those of their foreign mentors should ever constitute the basic determinants of Nigeria's national development approach and its underlying philosophy and ideology.

The deleterious effects of the ongoing capitalist system now euphemized as the 'mixed economy' are glaring to most Nigerians. Generally, the emerging trends do not smack of authentic national development. For instance, the incursion of the capitalist mode of production unleashed insatiable and coerced land acquisition processes by the colonial government which was subsequently intensified by the national bourgeoisie and the ruling class,[40] leading to tragic depletion of arable land hitherto owned communally. This profit-motivated land acquisition also led to an increased incidence of land litigation with attendant peasant indebtedness and frequent loss of land aided by the colonial legal system.[41] As commercialization processes intensified, and as land came to assume special value as a capitalist factor of production, the promotion of export crop production was encouraged to the utter neglect of the production of local staples, a serious problem still nagging Nigeria today. By commercializing almost every mechanism of the traditional exchange of reciprocities,[42] the people's customary bases of social cohesion were seriously undermined, thus further rendering them easily subject to the colonialist exploitative 'divide and rule' strategy.

Polly Hill and Sara Berry have independently observed, though scarcely with any reference to its serious development implications and consequences, that the capitalist mode of production also led to the intensification of the processes of peasantization in the country.[43] Other equally serious writers have also noted the dialectical contradictions between rural and urban centres, between mental and manual labour, between agricultural and the industrial-manufacturing-commercial service sectors, and between the so-called 'public' and 'private' sectors consequent upon the penetration of capitalism into the country's indigenous subsistent economies.

Overall, the Nigerian capitalist economy is ostensibly growing. But like all satellite economies, it is growing without developing. As a 'trading post' economy, multinational corporations are having a field day 'wheeling and dealing', while their national bourgeois and petty bourgeois agents are busy arranging government contracts for building and construction, for shipping, for wholesale trading and for forwarding. As one state governor is dissipating his energy eulogizing the unregulated increase in the number of vehicles in the country as evidence of development, another in the national capital, Lagos, is racking his brains trying to solve the capital's near-insoluble traffic chaos. And as one Corrupt Practices Investigation Panel is submitting its report, another is being freshly commissioned to investigate new waves of corruption in another government ministry or parastatal.

Amidst urban squalor and rural poverty, Nigerian governments are either reclaiming marshy lands or acquiring new ones from cowed natives for 'urban development'and for redistribution to foreign firms and their local agents. In the land of urban squalor and rural poverty,where rural and urban taps scarcely run, where public utilities never serve the public, where amputees and other roving social rejects abound, and where common table salt and various local staples have intermittently become very scarce commodities, national governments have obdurately been erecting plush hotels and holiday resorts without the people's mandate. And in the land of urban squalor and grinding rural poverty, where materialism in its most vulgarized form now claims the total allegiance of most Nigerians as *the* fundamental religion, a recently commissioned workshop on development strategies of the 1980s has once again returned the verdict, against all evidence, in favour of the 'mixed economy' as *the* only path to authentic Nigerian development. That is not being pragmatic.

Conclusion

The mixed economy proposition provides a handy fulcrum for examining Nigeria's development or underdevelopment experience in both theory and practice since colonial times. As the newest euphemism for neo-colonialist monopoly capitalism, the mixed economy formula is grounded in fallacies, myths and pseudo-theories which are consistently pandered about as scientific truths, not only by traditional western bourgeois scholars, but even more tragically by their petty bourgeois mouthpieces among government officials and academics in Nigeria. In the possession of the national ruling class, myths and fallacies about the mixed economy approach recently advocated for Nigeria are generally intended to whitewash the social reality of the exploited and dehumanized masses of the country. Therefore, on both theoretical and policy grounds this proposal must be rejected.

In short, by confusing an ideology with the structural base from which it derives, by denying the history of capitalist development in Nigeria, and by further mislocating the present Nigerian peripheral economy outside of the world capitalist hegemony within which it is a dependent subset, the mixed economy advocates are bound to misinterpret the historical functions of the country's satellite economy and their specific historical roles in it. Oblivious of the overt plight of the masses, the ruling class has accordingly found it more profitable to team up with multinational corporations to squander the nation's wealth. And, learning nothing from history, they are riding roughshod over the land, emboldened by their deterministic presumption that scientific socialism in Nigeria is a historical impossibility.

This discussion is by no means exhaustive. It is, however, undertaken to show how the country's military regimes, which gloated over their capacity to execute national development plans with no clearly-articulated ideology, have deliberately and consistently subscribed to the capitalist-materialist doctrine of free enterprise and individual property ownership, to the massive exploitation of Nigerians by foreign and local interests. This essay also shows how unpopular regimes forcibly foisted upon the masses, beyond creating special incentives for their members and for their petty bourgeois legitimizers, also subscribe to fallacies aimed at creating a false consciousness in the minds of the exploited Nigerian producers.

However, the majority of Nigerians are under no illusions regarding the state of the nation's political economy, who controls it, who are the prime beneficiaries, and what functions specific classes play in this economy. Beyond military edicts and high-sounding official proclamations lies the reality of the Nigerian 'trading post' economy. The people know that taps do not run; that there are frequent black-outs; that mails crawl at a snail's pace; that local staples are intermittently in short supply; that house rents are astronomically high and are still increasing despite the much publicized rent edicts; that Nigeria basically operates silent telephones; that Lagos and other state captitals stink like a twelfth-century European moat; that there is a staggering rate of 'butchery' on Nigerian roads; and that frustrated youths are increasingly becoming criminal desperadoes irrespective of frequent public executions of armed criminals; that there is heedless squandering and unmitigated corruption at the highest levels of society, the shedding of official crocodile tears over public indiscipline notwithstanding; and that national development plans, essentially ill-motivated, ill-conceived and inefficiently executed, only serve the interests of foreigners and their Nigerian comprador stooges. The people know how the system operates. It is in order to increase this awareness, and to engender co-ordinated political actions against the system, that this essay is essentially written.

Capitalist fallacies and myths tend to die hard, but they are not indestructible. Left unchallenged, they constitute dangerous rationalizations subsumed in monopoly capitalist blueprints deliberately intended to mystify the exploited Nigerian producing masses. These myths and fallacies deftly smuggled into the country through various capitalist-controlled mass media must be consistently exposed, not only for the enlightenment of Nigerians, but more importantly to ensure that appropriate political actions are undertaken to structurally transform Nigeria's current satellite economy for the benefit of the country's producing population and Nigerian posterity.

References

1. Arden R. King, 'Myth', in Julius Gould and William L. Kolb (eds.), *A Dictionary of the Social Sciences* (London: Tavistock Publications, 1964), p.450; and *Webster's Seventh New Collegiate Dictionary* (Springfield: Merriam, 1965), p.300.
2. A. Gunder Frank, *Capitalism and Underdevelopment in Latin America: Historical Studies of Chile and Brazil* (New York: Monthly Review Press, 1967) and 'Sociology of Development and Underdevelopment of Sociology', *Catalyst*, 3 (1967), pp.1–67; Walter Rodney, *How Europe Underdeveloped Africa* (Dar es Salaam: Tanzania Publishing House, 1972); A. Chinweizu, *The West and the Rest of Us: White Predators, Black Slavers, and the African Elite* (New York: Random House, 1975); Ola Oni and Bade Onimode, *Economic Development of Nigeria: The Socialist Alternative* (Ibadan: Nigerian Academy of Arts, Science and Technology, 1975); and Ikenna Nzimiro, *Classes and Class Struggles In Nigeria* (New York: Monthly Review Press, forthcoming).
3. Inya A. Eteng, *Elements of Agrarian Capitalism in Western Nigeria: Burdens and Benefit*, Chapter 3; work in progress.
4. Rodolfo Stavenhagen, 'Seven Fallacies about Latin America', in James Petras and Maurice Zeitlin (eds.), *Latin America: 'Reform or Revolution'* (Greenwich, Conn.: Fawcett, 1968), pp.13–31.
5. Andre G. Frank, *Capitalism and Underdevelopment in Latin America* (New York: Monthly Review Press, 1967) and *Latin America, Underdevelopment or Revolution* (New York, Monthly Review Press, 1969).
6. *Reports of the Constitution Drafting Committee*, Vol. II, Sub-Committee on the Economy, Finance and Division of Powers; Terms of Reference Nos. 1 & 4, p.30 (Lagos: Federal Ministry of Information, 1976).
7. *Report of the Constitution Drafting Committee* containing the Draft Vol. I, Section 3.7–2, p.xiii (Lagos: Federal Ministry of Information, 1976).
8. The ambivalence of members of the Constitution Drafting Committee is reflected here when they put socialism in inverted commas, at the same time indicating that it is an important aspect of Nigeria's traditional economic system.
9. The CDC's position is similar to Spencerian and Durkheimian social policy recommendations for dealing with the problems of poverty resulting from industrialization in nineteenth-century Europe. Both

Spencer (British) and Durkheim (French) proposed, from different perspectives, moral education for socializing the poor people into accepting their lot in life. For both classical thinkers, government's responsibilities should not include the provision of welfare services to the people. The CDC's position is rather incomprehensible, considering that the members had earlier argued that government's primary function was the improvement of the people's standard of living through welfarism.

10. Government's welfarist concern, especially with respect to the provision of food and shelter for the people, unfortunately reduces the exploited Nigerian majority to the level of the lower organism whose major concern is the satisfaction of basic physiological needs (*a la* Maslow). Man, however, does not live by bread alone; he also needs self-recognition and opportunities for self-actualization. The provision of food, clothes and shelter, often regarded as a pragmatic but never-honoured policy, is usually a means of government's escape into self-abnegation from its responsibilities to the people.
11. 'Growth' and 'stage' theorists from Western Atlantic countries strongly hold the view that economic growth and equitable distribution of incomes and other resources are generally incompatible. Indeed, inequalities in income distribution are often deliberately advocated as precondition for economic growth. See for example, Bert F. Hoselitz, *Sociological Factors in Economic Development* (Glencoe: The Free Press, 1960); W.W. Rostow, *The Stages of Economic Growth: A non-Communist Manifesto* (Cambridge: Cambridge University Press, 1962); and a rebuttal of Rostow's formulation by Irina M. Osadchaya, 'Rostow's Theory of Economic Growth', *The Soviet Review*, 3,3 (1962), pp.49–58.
12. The CDC members couched development problems associated with the socialist approach to national development in hyperbole in order to deliberately portray socialism as an unworkable system. The members also demonstrated a pathetic ignorance of the distinction between socialist collective decision-making and capitalist managerial decision-making when they deterministically associated socialism with bureaucratic rigidities. Yet a majority of Nigerians are agreed that bureaucratic red tape is one of the greatest banes of Nigerian work organizations, particularly in the so-called public sector.
13. For Lt. General Obasanjo's celebrated Jaji speech entitled 'Our country Lacks Discipline', see *New Nigerian*, 19 September 1977, pp.8, 9 and 11. Some articulate Nigerians, however, took issue with the Nigerian Head of State on the question of who are really undisciplined, civilians or the military. Quoting specific cases of military post-war vandalism in Nigeria, Dr. Chuba Okadigbo notes, 'As the Nigerian Observer editorial of Tuesday, September 27, 1977 notes, we have had 'the Ugep incident (in which 1,006 houses were burnt), the Ekpe melee, the Agege fracas, the Kalakuta show, and the Shawdam affair, in which the much condemned Amachree treatment of the Gowon regime was meted to another journalist.' Excluding the brutal killing of a young medical officer [Dr. Okoro] by drunken soldiers in 1976, Dr. Okadigbo concluded that 'the Enugu hay-wire of Abakpa Nike infamy brings the sum total of

dangerous military/civilian clashes to six'. This number is an underestimate, for several cases of military rampages have gone unreported as the natural state of affairs in Nigeria. See *Daily Star*, 4 October 1977, p.13 on the question of military discipline in school; Editor-in-Chief's comment: 'Leadership and Followership – (Who is Guilty!)', *Newbreed*, August, 1977, pp.5–6, and Editorial Comment, *Daily Star*, 22 December 1977, p.3, which gave several instances of killings and destruction of property by soldiers, whereupon the Editor pleaded that the soldiers should be demobilized.

14. Lt. General O. Obasanjo on what it takes to develop Nigeria, see *Weekly Star*, 21 January 1977, p.1.
15. The preoccupation of the Nigerian ruling class with superstructural (normative) solutions include the FESTAC '77 cultural jamboree; programs such as the local government 'reforms' and contingent reactivation of traditional chieftaincies; sponsorship of mini-Festacs in the name of cultural revivalism, and the 'Sharia preoccupation' in the present constitution-making exercise; the so-called Great Purges; and the so-called government's 'low-profile' – all of which the former Head of State himself admitted (in his previously referred Jaji Speech) have been ineffective in curbing indiscipline among Nigerians, hence his call for a traditional ideology reflecting the Nigerian genius.
16. Nnamdi Azikiwe, 'Re-orientation of Nigerian Ideologies', *Weekly Star*, 2 January 1977, pp.12–13.
17. For reflections on tribal and peasant economies in Africa, see George Dalton, 'Traditional Production in Primitive African Economies', *Quarterly Journal of Economies*, 76 (1972), pp.360–78; L.H. Samuels (ed.), *African Studies In Income and Wealth* (Chicago: Quadrangle Books, 1963); Audrey Richards, *Land, Labour and Diet in Northern Rhodesia* (London: Oxford University Press, 1939); Paul Bohannan and George Dalton, (eds.), *Markets In Africa* (Evanston, III.: Northwestern University Press, 1962); Paul Bohannan and Laura Bohannan, *Tiv Economy* (Evanston, III.: Northwestern University Press, 1968); Polly Hill, *Migrant Cocoa Farmers of Southern Ghana* (Cambridge: Cambridge University Press, 1963).
18. Eric Williams, *Capitalism and Slavery* (London: Andre Deutsch, 1966).
19. The Federal Military Government of Nigeria has kept sealed lips over the total cost of FESTAC '77, a gigantic cultural revival program involving all African countries and Black peoples of the Diaspora. Professor Awojobi recently speculated in a Television Draft Constitution debate that over ₦700 million was involved, even when the bulk of the Nigerian masses know next to nothing about the way this huge sum was disbursed. Just as all expenditures on similar programmes are never published, so the salaries of the military personnel are kept top secret. Pressured by public opinion the Federal Military Government has recently announced that it spent a total of ₦142 million on FESTAC '77. This amount has been hotly disputed by a *New Nigerian* editorial.
20. Usman Zahradeen, 'Nothing Works – Oh, What a Country', *New Nigerian*, 11 January 1978, p.4. In utter disgust with present conditions in the country, Zahradeen advocated the following verse as part of the Nigerian Anthem:

Nigeria we hail thee,
Where no tap flows,
Where no light burns,
No telephone rings,
No traffic light works,
No train leaves on time,
No airplane arrives on schedule,
Where no student stays in class,
No official stays on seat,
Where no drinks are available,
No tea, no coffee on the shelves.

He concluded that 'I don't think we (present generation of Nigerians) are witnessing civilization.' Many Nigerians would wholeheartedly agree.

21. J.H. Boeke, *Economies and Economic Policy of Dual Societies* (New York, 1953), pp.3–5, reprinted in Gerald M. Meier (ed.), *Leading Issues in Economic Development*, 2nd ed. (Oxford University Press, 1970), pp.126–8.
22. Benjamin Higgin, *Economic Development*, rev. ed. (New York, 1968), pp.17–20, 296–305, See also Meier, *op. cit.*, pp.143–6.
23. J.H. Boeke, 'Social Dualism', in Meier, *op. cit.*, p.128.
24. *Report of the Constitution Drafting Committee containing the Draft Constitution, Vol. 1* (Lagos: Federal Ministry of Information, 1976), p. xiii.
25. For a full text of the opening address by the then Head of State, Lt. General O. Obasanjo, read on his behalf by the Governor of Oyo State, Brigadier David Jemibewon, at the National Workshop on Planning Strategy for the 1980s, held at the University of Ibadan, Ibadan on 2 January 1978, see *Daily Times* 11 January 1978, p.33 under the caption, 'Let's Turn to Agriculture, Technology'.
26. Pius Okigbo, 'A Re-examination of the Legislative Lists in Draft,' *New Nigerian*', 11 January 1978, pp.3, 7, 9, and 11. This text contains Okigbo's defense of the present satellite capitalism in Nigeria.
27. *Ibid*, p. 3.
28. John K. Galbraith, "The Public Purpose of Economies", *Dialogue* 6,4 (1973), pp.52–63. *Dialogue*, an American quarterly journal of opinion and analysis on current intellectual and cultural subjects, has been engaging in what properly amounts to benign salesmanship for multinational corporations. Reading between the lines, it is obvious that these apparently hardnosed (intellectual) 'analyses' of multinational corporations operations are intended to temper the growing Third World criticism against, as well as justified apprehensions of, these foreign enterprises for their corrupting and exploitative tendencies, in order to convince Third World countries of the potentials of these MNCs in serving the social purposes of the underdeveloped world. Typical of these subtle articles are: Peter F. Drucker, 'Managing Complex Organization', *Dialogue*, 7,2 (1974), pp.78–88; Raymond Vernon, 'Multinationals and Social Benefits', *Dialogue*, 7,1 (1974), pp.65–72, Walter Mondale, 'Toward International Economic Security', *Dialogue*, 8,1 (1975), pp. 3–13, and Samuel Pisar, 'Nationalism and the Multinational Corporation', *Dialogue*, 6,2 (1973), pp.64–70. Typical of the corrupting and

manipulative influence of multinational corporations is the recent ITT (Nigeria) escapade when its Nigerian representative Chief Abiola, reminiscent of ITT's Chile connexion in the death of Allende and the toppling of its government, brazenly distributed table calculators to members of the Constitutent Assembly as a gesture of goodwill. This scandalous act, which the Federal Military Government has apparently endorsed by its taciturnity, also received the blessings of arch-capitalists such as Kayode Lamina in his 'I back Chief Abiola', *Daily Times*, 3 February 1978, p.13.

29. Paul Blumberg, *Industrial Democracy: The Sociology of Participation* (London: Constable, 1968), pp.1–13. Blumberg argued that these experiments were doomed to failure essentially because the substantive decision-making from above had not involved the workers yet, and because decisions were still made by owners of capital.
30. K.D.S. Baldwin, *The Niger Agricultural Project* (Oxford: Blackwell, 1957). The Mokwa scheme in Northern Nigeria, a land resettlement project which aimed at mechanical farming patterned after the highly successful Gezira Scheme in the Sudan, was a total failure due to the inadequacy of technical experimentation and preliminary feasibility studies to test the adaptability of the Gezira mechanics to local conditions. Other factors included acute labour shortages, non-availability of appropriate machinery, confinement of settlers to oversized farms, and lack of proper motivation on the part of settlers.
31. On Eastern Nigerian Farm Settlement Scheme, see Barry Floyd and Monica Adinde, 'Farm Settlements in Eastern Nigeria: A Geographical Appraisal', *Economic Geography*, 43,3 (July 1967) pp. 189–205. On Western Nigerian Settlement Scheme, see Werner Roider, *Farm Settlement for Economic Development: Western Nigerian Case* (Munich: Weltforum-Verlag, 1971).
32. *Nigeria's Indigenization Policy: Proceedings of the 1974 Symposium Organized by the Nigerian Economic Society On the Subject Indigenization: What have we Achieved?* (The Nigerian Economic Society, 1974). For an appraisal of revisions of previous Indigenization Decrees see Akitunde Asalu, 'People's Capitalism: An Appraisal of the Nigeria Enterprises Promotion Decree', *Business Times*, 22 February 1977, pp. 3 and 5. Note that this policy, which aims at the promotion of the Nigerian capitalists as appendages of multinational corporations, is even designated 'People's Capitalism'.
33. One often hears similar reductionist comparisons as when the Nigerian bourgeoisie boldfacedly argues that God never created all human beings equal since all human fingers are never equal.
34. See note 2, as well as Kwame Nkrumah, *Neo-Colonialism: The Last Stage of Imperialism* (N.Y.: International Publishers, 1966).
35. Articulate Nigerians who see similar speeches by the Head of State, by state governors, and by government officials as mere rhetoric are no longer persuaded by whatever exhortations are contained in them. For example, Ahmed Abubaker, noting the recent contradiction between Nigeria's pretentiously radical foreign policy in Africa and the suffocating domestic conditions, asked 'What About the Home Front?' in *New Nigerian*, 18 November 1977, p.4. Similarly, Mohammed A. Kano in

New Nigerian, 25 October 1977, p.4 purposely asked a rhetorical question, 'Apartheid in Nigeria?' knowing fully well that the Nigerian judicial system discriminates against the poor generally. For Lt. General O. Obasanjo's speech on Nigeria's 'trading post' economy, which is full of brilliant insights but completely devoid of any concrete solution, see *Daily Times*, 11 January 1978, p.32, and Babatunde Jose Jr., 'Of Commission Agents and Industrial Barons', *Daily Times* 9 February 1978, p.3. Again, like every Nigerian liberal, the author still hopes that Nigerian businessmen and 'industrialists' will one day rise to their responsibilities to develop the nation – a hallucinatory expectation indeed.

36. In general, Nigerian planners still place high premium on diffusionism as the most preferred development mode. Accordingly, one of the most accepted open-door development strategies is contract awards through Tenders Boards of government ministries. Hence the following examples: Nigerian government signs ₦10 million pact for transformers, *Business Times*, 6 December 1977, pp.1, 32; Ondo State government awards ₦5.8 million contract to Alhaji W.O. Lawal and Sons Ltd. and Metalwood Engineering Ltd. for ₦3.1 million, *Business Times*, 6 December 1977, p.3; Nigerian Government signs contract for ₦400 million for a second iron and steel plant to be cited at Ovbian and Aladja, near Warri, with Gutehoffnung-Shette Sterkrade AG., *Business Times*, 11 October 1977, p.24; and Federal Government contract for telephone exchange installations amounting to ₦734.3 million for telephone switching, ₦810.9 million for transmission, ₦742.5 million on external lines plant, ₦91.4 million on subscribers instruments, and ₦30m on power plants during the Third National Development Plan period, *Business Times*, 1 November 1977, p.1.

37. For example, in March 1976 alone five trade missions from Western capitalist countries were in Nigeria: (1) Scottish Council Development and Industry trade mission (14–28 March 1976); (2) Reyrolle Parsons International (14–28 March 1976); (3) A British firm responsible for the two manual pedal organs in Yaba's Christ Apostolic Church (10 March 1976); (4) A group of 15 American corporation executives on a tour arranged by Overseas Private Investment Corperation (OPIC), a United State government agency which aids American overseas businessmen (23–27 March 1976), and a large industrial delegate with representatives from various ministries led by the Swedish Minister of Trade, Mr. Carl Lidbom (13–20 March 1976).

38. Rostow, *op. cit*. The mixed economy proposition is virtually the same old integrationist model of capitalist development in a new guise. For a critique of this policy being forced on Third World countries by Kissinger and Moyniham during UNCTAD IV and subsequent UN Seventh Session debates, see Geoffrey Barraclough, 'The Haves and Have-nots', *The New York Review of Books*, 23, 8 (13 May 1976), pp.31–41.

39. Samir Amin, 'Accumulation and Development: A Theoretical Model', *Review of African Political Economy*, 1, (August–November 1974).

40. See L.T. Chubb, *Ibo Land Tenure* (Ibadan University Press, 1961), pp. 27–32. More than 10 cases of such land acquisition by the petty bourgeoisie who had served the colonial administration were cited by this one-time colonial official; Peter Lloyd, *Yoruba Land Law* (Oxford

University Press, 1962); and N. Fadipe, *Sociology of the Yoruba* (Ibadan University Press, 1970).

41. Lloyd, *op. cit.*, pp.239–42 and 308–24; V. Dreissen, 'Cocoa Farming in Ife Division', *Journal of African Modern Studies*, 16, 2 (1976), pp.43–51; and 'Patterns of Landholding and Land Distribution in the Ife Division of Western Nigeria', *Africa*, 41, (1971).
42. For examples of the commercialization of traditional Yoruba *tito* (land fee and *isakolo* (produce rent), see Lloyd, *op. cit.*, pp.209–276 and chapters 11 and 12.
43. On typical peasant classes in Nigeria, see Martin Igbozurike, *Problem-Generating Structures in Nigeria's Rural Development* (Uppsala: Scandinavian Institute of African Studies, 1976), pp.44–5, and Ikenna Nzimiro, 'Capitalism in Nigerian Rural Societies', *Pan-African Journal of Social Studies*, (Nsukka, forthcoming).

4. Imperialism and Nigerian Development

Bade Onimode

> In contrast with the surging growth of the countries in the socialist camp and the development taking place, albeit much more slowly, in the majority of the capitalist countries, is the unquestionable fact that a large proportion of the so-called underdeveloped countries are in total stagnation, and that in some of them rate of economic growth is lower than that of population increase.
> These characteristics are not fortuitous; they correspond strictly to the nature of the capitalist system in full expansion, which transfers to the dependent countries the most abusive and barefaced forms of exploitation. It must be clearly understood that the only way to solve the questions now besetting mankind is to eliminate completely the exploitation of dependent countries by developed capitalist countries, with all the consequences that this implies. (Che Guevara, 1964).

Introduction

It may require some justification for linking imperialism and Nigerian development. Why should we expect any connection at all between them and, if one exists, what has it been? The answers hinge on the theoretical nature of imperialism and development, the specific character of imperialism in Nigeria, and the co-existence of imperialist activities with development struggles in the country.

At the theoretical level, it has been recognized that imperialism as the highest stage of capitalism has been a major mechanism for the development of the advanced capitalist countries and the underdevelopment of the Third World.[1] This means that for industrialised capitalist countries, sustained economic development in the periphery is incompatible with the international capitalist system. Hence, to the ruling classes of North America, Western Europe and Japan, the drive for development in the satellite countries appears profoundly subversive of the prevailing system of international domination; therefore, it has to be 'blocked, bribed or broken' in order to preserve the exploitative capitalist system. Moreover, the specific character of imperialism in Nigeria, which has involved slavery, colonialism and contemporary neo-colonialism, means that the historical and current underdevelopment of the country could not be explained or understood without an explicit analysis of imperialism in the whole process. This is particularly true since both the imperialist domination of Nigeria and the underdevelopment of the country are total processes involving all facets of national life. Finally, both processes have historically co-existed. The transformation from pre-capitalist to a predominantly capitalist mode of production in Nigeria occurred under colonialism, and the struggle for national development since independence has been taking place under neo-colonialism.

However, it must be emphasized that the investigation of imperialism and Nigerian development cannot be a static matter of bourgeois cost-benefit analysis, for the simple fact that both phenomena are fundamentally dialectical processes. To attempt to balance the costs and benefits of imperialism in Nigeria is, therefore, methodologically wrong and unscientific. It is this methodological error that has rendered bourgeois social science, which is itself an integral part of imperialism, such a manifestly epistemological barrier both to the understanding and to the liquidation of imperialism. What is required is a consistent dialectical analysis to unravel and demystify the essentially historical and social character of imperialism and development, which involves some strategic but non-quantifiable features.

This essay analyses the political economy of imperialism and development to underline their critical mechanisms, and then explores the nature of imperialism and development in Nigeria before 'flag' independence. The exercise is to provide a historical basis for understanding later developments in the relevant relationships. The contemporary phase of imperialism which emerged in 1960 is then examined with respect to the persistent underdevelopment of the country.

The Political Economy of Imperialism and Development

To present an analysis of imperialism and development in Nigeria in its proper perspective, it is necessary to make preliminary theoretical statements about the nature of both phenomena. Besides clarifying the approach adopted here, this should be useful for focusing the discussion on critical questions and eliminating the unnecessary confusion and ideological distortions that have beclouded the role of imperialism in the country and the Third World generally.

The political economy of imperialism necessarily has to start with the ideological distortions of bourgeois scholars. Some of these insist either that imperialism is just a relationship of dominance between two countries based on unequal power or, more vaguely, that it is the collective heritage of the 'dim past' of mankind attributable to psychological and other non-economic phenomena.[2] These denials of the specifically materialist Marxist theory of imperialism are designed to obscure its class and exploitative character in order to invalidate its revolutionary implications. The pathetic failure of such mystifications is best revealed by the increasing revolutionary struggles against imperialism. This is, perhaps, the best confirmation of the validity of the materialist position first elaborated by Marx and Lenin.[3] They demonstrated that imperialism in its mature form corresponds to the highest stage of the development of capitalism, the stage of monopoly capitalism, which emerged in Western Europe during the eighteenth century, especially after the Industrial Revolution. The propelling forces were the financial oligarchy corresponding to the upper stratum of the bourgeois class. Their objectives were the expansion of capitalist accumulation to avert the tendencies towards under-consumption and surplus capital.

Three broad phases of imperialist expansion can thus be distinguished. The first corresponded to open plunder, enslavement and savage colonization of the mercantilist type. This started with the rivalry among the Western European powers during the so-called 'age of discovery'. Thus, they said Mungo Park 'discovered' the River Niger which Africans had been utilizing for centuries before he was born. The second more pervasive and tenacious phase is identified with a new form of capital export to underdeveloped countries, which underlines the exploitative role of imperialist financial capital from the mid-nineteenth to the early twentieth centuries. (This phase has been carefully documented for Britain by Caincross.[4]) The third phase corresponded to the post-independent era in the Third World after the Second World War, when the giant multinational corporations became the basic units of imperialism in its neo-colonial stage.[5] This phase corresponded to the new character of the upper strata of the ruling classes of imperialist countries, which was now identified with industrial capitalists sitting over giant corporations. This has been the dominant character of imperialism in Nigeria since nominal independence in 1960, and elsewhere since about 1945. In all its phases, the appropriation of foreign economic surplus by the ruling classes of the imperialist countries for their development has been an unchanging objective of imperialism; it has always been an exploitative phenomenon.

In terms of historical materialism, the development process is identified fundamentally with class struggle. This arises when the development of the productive forces of society become fettered by the prevailing social relations of production. The dialectical conflict is a signal that the existing mode of production has outlived its usefulness. The conflict is resolved through the revolutionary destruction of the existing relations of production, the overthrow of the system of law, politics, education, etc. (i.e. the superstructure) based on the old mode of production, and the birth of a new social order.[6]

This means that the development process is characterized by two critical features. First, there is the struggle of opposing classes in which a ruling class tries to perpetuate a decadent *status quo* that the underprivileged classes militantly struggle to supersede. Second, a new social order is the objective of a development process.[7] This involves the structural transformation of the old social system; its economic, social and political institutions are changed with the application of new patterns of thought and work, more productive technology and new inputs. This means that the development process is infinitely more than the bourgeois 'growth-number game' centred around GDP: it is not a mere increase in income, whether national or per capita income, as preached by some bourgeois economists.[8]

In the context of the history of the world during the age of imperialism, the relationship between it and development has been direct and symmetrical for the imperialist countries and perverse for 'the wretched of the earth', the Third World. This is, perhaps, the most eloquent testimony to the fundamentally materialist and exploitative character of imperialism. It has generated phenomenal development in Western Europe, North America and Japan during all its phases, while it has produced and sustained incredible underdevelopment in the Third World.[9]

Given its basically exploitative motives of appropriating the national economic surplus of one country for increased capitalist accumulation in another, imperialism must enrich the latter by its impoverishment of the former. This is precisely why the ruling classes of imperialist countries are so vehemently opposed to the development of the Third World: they know that it cannot occur without the termination of their domination and brutal exploitation of these countries. And they know that they cannot afford this because it will spell their doom and the death knell of their unjust international capitalist system. This is why their intellectual apologists must distort and mystify the cause of underdevelopment in the Third World, the nature of development itself, and the requirements for it. Concurrently, the imperialist ruling classes have been doing everything possible to prevent real development in these countries while mounting massive propaganda about their so-called commitment to development in such deceptive stunts as 'the development decade', 'partners in progress', and 'development aid', all of which imply their exact antonyms. These myths and the underdevelopment of the Third World have been aided by the bourgeoisie of these countries in a framework of collaboration with imperialist ruling classes for common exploitative gains. This is also precisely why countries like Nigeria in the orbit of the international capitalist system must not view the imperatives for their national development in terms of exploitative 'aid', trade, foreign investment and similar imperialist mechanisms. Rather, they need a revolutionary proletarian ideology addressed urgently to the liquidation of imperialist domination of their economies for the achievement of national economic independence as the resolution of their lingering national question.

Imperialism and Development Before Independence

Two phases of imperialism are identifiable in Nigeria before 1960. These are the pre-colonial (or pre-1860 period) and the colonial (or 1860–1960 era). The impact of imperialism on Nigerian development dates back to the pre-colonial era because in that period imperialism impinged on Nigeria[10] and this had developmental implications. The pre-colonial activities of imperialists in this period consisted of slavery and the so-called 'legitimate trade'.

Walter Rodney states that from the arrival of the Portuguese in West Africa, shortly before the middle of the fifteenth century, they started seizing Africans and taking them to work as slaves in Europe, especially in Portugal and Spain.[11] The countries raided included Senegal, Liberia, the Ivory Coast, Ghana and Nigeria. From the time of their arrival to the eighteenth century, the Portuguese, Spaniards, Dutch, British, French and Danes carried away some twelve million Africans.[12] The Americans joined the slave trade later than the Europeans. Before abolition, these imperialists had established 'factories' or 'barracoons' on the Atlantic Coast (in Christianburg, Cape Coast Castle, Axim and Elmina on the Gold Coast, with the first being at Arguin in Mauretania in 1448) where they stored their manufactured goods and African 'commodities', which included gold for exchange.

This slave trade was clearly a form of large-scale export of potential economic surplus from Nigeria and other African countries. The labour-power of the slaves carried away represented so much unpaid labour or exploitation. Moreover, since slavery represented not just forced labour but the appropriation of the human person as another person's property, this savage form of exploitation included the appropriation of the potential surplus of the unborn. This is the sense in which the black population in the USA, the Caribbean and Latin America have all been *colonized*. The actual disruption of production during the slave raids and the resulting depopulation of Nigeria and other African countries from the slave trade disrupted production relations and crippled the domestic labour force of these countries; these contributed to the loss of potential surplus. Both losses (the gain to the imperialists and the loss to the Africans) constituted vital components of the surplus which could have been used for capital accumulation by Nigeria. Consequently, the slave trade was a source of underdevelopment in Nigeria during the pre-colonial and early colonial periods.

In spite of the cultural-ideological mystifications of the hired apologists of imperialism who rationalize colonialism – in terms of a 'civilizing mission', stamping out slavery, establishment of 'legitimate trade', introducing technology, developing exports and enabling colonial territories to develop – the general economic, political, social and moral bankruptcy of colonialism is now indisputable. In Nigeria the specific role of colonialism in the underdevelopment of the country can be analysed with respect to its dominant motives and mechanisms as well as the effects of these on specific sectors of the economy.

As revealed by the general analysis of colonialism and the specific activities of British colonialists in Nigeria, the motives for colonizing the country included the search for a cheap and steady supply of raw materials for British factories, market expansion for the mass production of manufactured goods, outlets for surplus capital, and employment of idle labour.[13] The raw materials sought included cotton for British textile factories, rubber for tyres and other products, palm oil and kernel for soap and margarine, groundnuts for manufactured oil, hides and skins for leather products, timber for furniture, as well as tin, coal, etc. These became the objects of intense production and export which were rationalized in terms of Nigeria's so-called comparative advantage in primary production.[14]

Nigeria's large internal market was also needed for dumping British textiles, machinery, equipment and various consumer goods. Export of capital was also important to sustain the rate of profit and expand capitalist accumulation in Britain. The wilful plunder of Nigeria's economic surplus was another motive. This took the form of taxes, Marketing Board surpluses, profits of British colonial enterprises, and others.[15] Moreover, the colonial state and economy were manned largely by the British: this constituted employment opportunities for the British labour force.[16] Political and cultural domination, like the imposition of English language, dress, education, religion and law, were not goals in themselves but means of integrating Nigeria into Britain to facilitate exploitation. Moreover, the means of cultural domination like English books, other educational materials, and the 'coat-and-tie' were British-produced and so they increased the opportunities for colonial exploitation through trade.

Thus, the mechanisms of colonialism in Nigeria centred around the colonial state and economy. They included military conquest and political coercion through British monopoly of the colonial state apparatus, the manipulation of this political power for unequal trade,[17] capital import, cultural penetration through Christianity and colonial education, as well as the dissemination of the British 'illusion of the colonial epoch'. The functioning of these mechanisms and their impact on Nigerian development are, perhaps, best revealed by investigating the effects of the colonial era in Nigerian history on the means of production and relations of production. Since these constitute the mode of production and the objects of development, it will be necessary to examine the effects of colonialism on various facets of the socio-economic system.

First, the colonial state apparatus was used for centralizing Nigeria's economic surplus in the colonial state, or in the hands of the British bourgeoisie in Nigeria. This was done through the imposition and collection of taxes, canalization of agricultural surplus into Marketing Board surpluses, the control of banking through the West African Currency Board (which was a kind of Central Bank for West Africa whose transactions were regulated by the Bank of England), the monopoly of commercial banking and appropriation of profits by British enterprises such as the United African Company (UAC), John Holt, and G.B. Ollivant. These surpluses were systematically transferred to Britain for capitalist accumulation there and de-capitalization in Nigeria.

Second, Nigeria's import-export trade was monopolized by the British in the context of bilateral integration of the country with the British economy. Thus, the export commodities discussed above were those required by the British economy. Sources of cheap raw materials and a market for dumping manufactures were thus important in the balkanization of Africa by imperialists. Nigeria's primary products were exported by the British in

British ships and sold to other British subjects at prices determined by the British. Similarly, Nigeria's imports such as textiles, food, beverages and drinks as well as other consumer goods, railway stock, vehicles and equipment were produced by the British, shipped in British ships, and sold by the British in Nigeria at prices dictated by them to their 'subjects'. The cycle was complete. Given the underlying colonial motive of exploitation, there is hardly any need to demonstrate the gross perverse effect of this so-called 'trade' on Nigerian development. These effects were particularly devastating after the Great Depression (1929–33) and during the World Wars. The terms of trade, balance of trade and balance of payments in this trade were persistently unfavourable to Nigeria, except in brief interludes like the immediate post-Second World War era (see Table 1). The direction of trade was mainly to Britain, as other imperialist countries were excluded from the trade.

Table 1
Nigeria's Colonial Foreign Trade, 1950–60

Year	*Terms of Trade*	*Balance of Trade (£ million)*
1950	110	35.44
1951	121	44.35
1952	119	20.33
1953	116	19.93
1954	133	44.33
1955	104	– 4.49
1956	97	–22.75
1957	96	–31.18
1958	100	–38.40
1959	106	–18.63
1960	104	–57.73

Sources: United Nations: *African Statistics (Economic African Bulletin for Africa* (June 1962); Central Bank of Nigeria, *Economic and Financial Review*, 15, 1 (June 1977).

To facilitate this exploitative export trade, mining,[18] and agriculture were commercialized as the export enclaves of the colonial economy. Nigerian peasants were encouraged through minimal prices and infrastructural incentives to cultivate so-called 'cash-crops' like cocoa, palm oil and kernel, rubber, groundnuts and cotton, which were the raw materials required for British factories. The scramble for Africa after 1880 was directly related to this need for cheap primary products. Food production was largely ignored and its labour supply seriously depleted by the increasing withdrawal of peasants into wage labour.

The consequences on Nigerian agriculture were predictable: it lost any internal stimulus for development. Indeed, the naked exposure of the country's agriculture to the vagaries of the imperialist market may well be one of the most permanent damages of British colonialism to Nigerian development: it has insured the stagnation, or even degeneration, of Nigerian agriculture to this day, with the real threat that the country may be unable to feed its own population.[19] With the neglect of agriculture in domestic and foreign investment allocations, low income elasticity of demand for its products by the rest of the economy, its stagnant and neglected technology together with poor price incentives, agriculture, which harboured between 70–80 per cent of the country's population, was one of the worst hit by colonialism. Its peasant producers, who were impoverished by multiple taxation, broken by colonial police and court repression, and submerged in a 'culture of silence' through illiteracy, were undoubtedly among the most brutally exploited by the savage colonialism of Britain.

Colonial industry was virtually proscribed. The very logic of the colonial system pointed to this. Since Britain was in Nigeria partly to seek an outlet for her own manufactured goods in order to stave off under-consumption, falling profit and depression at home, industrial development in Nigeria would obstruct that motive. Hence, as a *deliberate* policy, manufacturing was actively prevented in Nigeria as in other colonies. Only first-stage agricultural processing to reduce the volume and weight of exports like cotton, groundnuts and palm oil was allowed, and this was monopolized by British commercial enterprises like John Holt and UAC. Such processing consisted of cotton ginning as well as groundnut and palm oil extraction. Consequently, by 1962/63, manufacturing and processing accounted for barely 3.6 per cent of GDP.[20]

The financial sector was also monopolized by British finance capital. Commercial banking[21] was dominated by Britain's Barclays Bank and the Bank of British West Africa (incorporated in 1894 and now called Standard Bank). By 1959, foreign banks accounted for about 70 per cent of total time and savings deposits in the country, while insurance was controlled by New Africa Insurance (1955), Guinea (1958) and West African Provincial (1958). These banks and insurance companies were not even incorporated in Nigeria[22]; they were mere branches of their British parent companies. Together, these financial institutions constituted the main conduits for the export of Nigeria's surplus to Britain. In their operations they discriminated against Nigerians by giving the bulk of their loans and advances to expatriates; they required greater collateral security from Nigerians than from expatriates and engaged in ruinous competition against indigenous financial institutions.[23]

The physical and social infrastructural base of the colonial economy was very fragile and export-oriented. There were only two rail lines running north to south and connecting the hinterland to the sea for the evacuation of exports and the distribution of imports to the hinterland. Their construction created a huge demand for British railway machinery and equipment in the early twentieth century. Roads were few and designed to link the main administrative, commercial and export-production centres. There were two main ports in Lagos and Port Harcourt with few berths, while two small airports in Lagos and Kano linked the country with Britain. Nigerian Airways was essentially a subsidiary of Britain's B.O.A.C.[24]

Social infrastructure included a University College of London University, which was established at Ibadan in 1948 to cater for a population of about 30 million. This elitist college was supported by a few elitist secondary schools and slightly more primary schools. It was not until 1952, after regional governments run by Nigerians were established, that the number of educational institutions increased. But even then, the literacy rate was around 10 per cent by 1960.[25] Health facilities were few and far between with limited hospitals catering mainly for Europeans in overt discrimination against Africans. Pipe-born water and electricity were concentrated in a few urban centres. Most of these social infrastructure were not established until after the Second World War when Nigerian soldiers returning home after fighting for the British teamed up with students from abroad who had been taught 'liberty, equality and fraternity' and 'self-determination', and wanted to apply these slogans at home.

It was also after the Second World War that the British launched their 'Ten-Year Plan of Development and Welfare for Nigeria, 1946 to 1956', which was essentially a framework for colonial budgeting and ensuring financial accountability rather than development. It was a token to bribe the increasingly militant nationalist movement.[26] Its main thrust was the development of infrastructure but, even here, the capital programme was a gross underinvestment – total development expenditure from 1946 to 1956 was only £55 million, an annual average of £5.5 million for a population of about 30 million.[27]

Neo-Colonialism and Underdevelopment in Nigeria

> With the development of large capitalist monopolies in the leading capitalist countries, the capitalists of those countries lost interest in developmental investment in the less-developed countries because such investment threatened their established monopolistic positions. Consequently, investment in underdeveloped countries of capital from the highly-developed countries acquired a specific character. It went chiefly into the exploitation of natural resources to be utilised as raw materials by the industries of the developed countries; and into developing food production in the underdeveloped countries to feed the population of the developed capitalist countries. It also went into developing the economic infrastructure . . . needed to maintain economic relations with the underdeveloped countries.
>
> The profits which were made by foreign capital . . . were exported back to the countries where the capital came from. Or if used for investment . . . they were not used for industrial investment on any major scale, which, as we know from experience, is the real dynamic factor of modern

> economic development.
> Furthermore . . . the great Capitalist powers supported the feudal elements in the underdeveloped countries as an instrument for maintaining their economic and political influence. This provides another obstacle to the economic development of these countries. . .[28]

In Nigeria, the British carefully cultivated a domestic petty bourgeoisie consisting of chiefs, businessmen, lawyers, doctors, engineers, labour leaders, military and police officers before flag independence in 1960. It was to this elitist class that they handed over political power while retaining, with other imperialists, their economic domination of the country during the neo-colonial phase of imperialism in Nigeria, which has persisted since 1960 to this day. The fragile legitimacy and narrow economic base of the bureaucratic bourgeoisie or ruling group within this Nigerian petty bourgeois class, therefore, subordinated it to the foreign bourgeoisie on whose countries (especially Britain) Nigeria has now come to depend. Moreover, both the Nigerian and foreign capitalists have been sharing a common objective in the exploitation of the rest of the country. Consequently, close collaboration has developed between them for the perpetuation of the dependent status of Nigeria's neo-colonial economy.[29]

The critical nature of this dependence and associated exploitation has been documented.[30] To dramatize the dependence, a Nigerian member of parliament had been quoted as saying, 'when we speak of the industrialization of the country, what we really mean is foreign capital'. However, unlike the colonial period, Nigeria was no longer dependent on Britain alone but on the whole international capitalist system. Imperialism in Nigeria changed from a bilateral to a multilateral basis. Other imperialist countries, especially the U.S.A. and Japan, have been seriously challenging British hegemony in this country in a framework of multilateral integration of the country into world capitalism. The mechanisms for this, as for colonialism, include import-export trade, foreign investment, foreign 'aid' and cultural penetration. In particular, the giant multinational corporations have emerged through the vehicle of foreign investment as the dominant agents of neo-colonialism. Their sectoral activities provide an indication of the impact of neo-colonialism in Nigeria.[31]

Imperialist domination of various sectors of Nigeria's neo-colonial capitalist economy is, perhaps, most serious in the petroleum sector, which has been the most important sector since 1970. The major multinational oligopolies in this sector are depicted in Table 2. By 1976 these multinational corporations were producing the quantities listed in Table 3. Consequently, these multinational corporations have been appropriating most of the surplus from this sector and correspondingly de-capitalizing the economy.

In the industrial sector which has been growing most rapidly since 1960, imperialist monopoly capital is also dominant. Table 4 shows the distribution of foreign industrial investment by capital and consumer goods, and regions in 1964. Some of the multinational corporations that generate these invest-

Table 2
Yearly Output of Oil Companies Operating in Nigeria (bbls.)

Year	*Shell-BP*	*Gulf*	*Safrap*	*Mobil*	*Agip*	*Texaco*
1960	6,367,187					
1961	16,801,896					
1962	24,623,691					
1963	27,913,479					
1964	43,996,895					
1965	89,686,968					
1966	129,517,558	18,614,763	4,295,845			
1967	89,205,664	19,988,489	7,327,021			
1968	15,915,867	35,991,227	–			
1969	129,338,895	67,866,087	–			
1970	288,827,680	84,571,143	–	19,787,820	1,776,493	867,784
1971	404,286,571	101,128,848	8,598,469	26,430,407	14,061,624	3,796,852
1972	442,195,656	119,101,841	20,230,287	60,953,145	19,101,052	3,701,130
1976[a]	1,250,783	289,123	–	221,930	182,692	35,873

Note: 1976 output is in barrels per day
Sources: O. Oni and B. Onimode (1975) *Economic Development of Nigeria: The Socialist Alternative.* (Ibadan: Nigerian Academy of Arts, Societies & Technology). p.27; T. Turner 'Notes on the Nigerian Oil Industry', (Mimeo, 1975/76), pp. 1–2.

ments within the UAC, Lonrho and Unilever groups have over fifty subsidiaries.

Neo-colonial finance capital still dominates the financial sector. Table 5 shows the relative shares of foreign and indigenous banks in deposits as well as loans and advances. Moreover, there are still some nineteen major foreign insurance companies operating in the country.[32] Together, these financial institutions have been channelling the country's economic surplus overseas, financing expatriate enterprises in the country, and restricting local resource mobilization for national development.

Table 3
Nigeria – Output of Major Oil Companies, 1976

Company	*Barrels Per Day*
Shell-BP (British)	1,250,783
Gulf (American)	289,123
Mobil (American)	221,930
Agip/Phillips (Italian)	182,692
Elf (French)	75,532
Texaco	35,873
Ashland	11,471

Source: Terisa Turner, 'Notes on the Nigerian Oil Industry' (mimeo, 1975/76).

In the distributive sector, imperialist multinational corporations dominate the import trade in cars, trucks, electrical appliances, textiles and various consumer goods as well as plant and equipment. Some of the most important of these companies include UAC, John Holt, Union Trading Company (UTC), CFAO, and R.T. Briscoe. They control wholesale distribution of these commodities through a network of warehouses all over the country. The domestic distribution of the products of many local manufacturing subsidiaries like Nigeria Tobacco Company (NTC), Nigeria cement companies and textile factories is also handled by these multinationals.

In other sectors of the economy, the British Amalgamated Tin Mines are still prominent in tin mining, while civil engineering construction, which has boomed since 1970, is dominated by a West German-Italian-French oligopoly led by Julius Berger: the others include Dumex, Strabag, Stirling, Guffanti and Cappa and Dalberto. Together, these multinationals have handled contracts of at least ₦1 billion since 1970. Shipping is dominated by Britain's West African Lines, which accounts for some 60 per cent of total traffic by origin or destination; the government's Nigerian National Shipping Line established in 1961 barely accounts for 10 per cent of the traffic. Air transport is controlled by multinational corporations like British Caledonian,

Table 4
Foreign Industrial Investment in Nigeria, 1964

Sectoral Distribution	*Total Investment (₦ million)*	*As % of Regional Investment*	*As % of National Investment*	*As % of Respective National Investment*
Total Federation				
Industrial Goods*	162.8	–	56.9	–
Consumer Goods	123.2	–	43.1	–
Total	286.0	–	100.0	–
Federal Territory				
Industrial Goods	23.8	40.6	8.2	14.6
Consumer Goods	34.8	49.4	12.3	28.2
Total	58.6	90.0	20.3	–
Western Region				
Industrial Goods	25.2	45.6	8.9	15.4
Consumer Goods	30.0	54.4	10.4	24.4
Total	55.2	100.0	19.3	–
Eastern Region				
Industrial Goods	72.0	81.0	25.2	44.2
Consumer Goods	17.0	19.0	5.9	13.8
Total	89.0	100.0	31.1	–
Northern Region				
Industrial Goods	26.0	38.0	9.1	16.0
Consumer Goods	41.4	62.0	14.5	33.6
Total	67.4	100.0	23.6	–

Mid-Western Region				
Industrial Goods	15.8	100.0	5.5	9.8
Consumer Goods	–	–	–	–
Total	15.8	100.0	5.5	–

(*) Industrial goods include processed raw materials such as rubber, vegetable oils, refined petroleum products, saw-timber, smelted tin, aluminium sheets, cement and all other goods destined to be used as inputs by other manufacturers.
Sources: O. Teriba & M.O. Kayode, *Industrial Development in Nigeria: Patterns, Problems and Prospects* (Ibadan University Press 1975), p.155.

Table 5
Deposits and Loans of Nigerian Commercial Banks at 31 December 1975 (₦)

Operation	*Total All Banks*	*Total Expatriate Banks*	*Total Indigenous Banks*	*% Share of Expatriate Banks*
Current a/c Deposits	1,266,819	863,230	403,589	68.14
Savings a/c Deposits	521,306	376,836	144,470	72.28
Time Deposits	1,051,050	713,415	337,635	67.87
Total Deposits	2,839,175	1,953,481	885,694	68.80
Loan & Advances	1,475,613	1,049,159	–	71.09

Source: Central Bank of Nigeria, Lagos, 1975

Pan-Am, Lufthansa, Sabena, Alitalia and Swissair. In road haulage virtually all oil tankers for petrol haulage throughout the country were foreign-owned until 1973. In agriculture and forestry the major joint ventures between Nigerian governments and foreign multinationals include the African Timber and Plywood Company, Mushin Estates, Tate and Lyle, Savannah Sugar, Swiss-Nigerian Wood Industries and South-Eastern State Rubber plantations.

Table 6
Sources of Share Capital in Nigerian Registered Business Enterprises

Value of Shares (£)	*Number*			*Percentage*		
	Nigerian	*Expatriate*	*Total*	*Nigerian*	*Expatriate*	*Total*
1	146	113	259	56.4	43.6	100.0
1 – 1,000	267	418	683	39.0	61.1	100.0
1,001 – 5,000	182	193	375	48.5	51.5	100.0
5,001 – 10,000	62	124	186	33.3	66.7	100.0
10,001 – 20,000	46	82	128	35.9	64.1	100.0
20,001 – 50,000	47	128	175	27.9	73.2	100.0
50,001 – 100,000	28	80	108	25.9	74.1	100.0
Above 100,000	43	120	168	26.4	73.6	100.0
Total	821	1,258	2,079	39.5	60.4	100.0

Source: O. Teriba *et al*, 'Some Aspects of Ownership and Control Structure of Business Enterprise in a Developing Economy: The Nigerian Case', *Nigerian Journal of Economic and Social Studies*, 14, 1 (1972).

The share of expatriates in total share-capital is shown in Table 6: it shows that the bigger the capital investment, the greater the neo-colonial share, which varies between 51 and 74 per cent for shares of over ₦2,000. National economic planning since 1962 has not terminated this foreign grip on the economy because it has itself accepted the neo-colonial economy.[33]

Neo-Colonialism and Indigenization

Indigenization has been the collective national response to this pattern of stifling foreign domination and exploitation. The indigenization decrees of 1972 and 1976[34] have listed 22 and 17 enterprises respectively for total ownership by Nigerians, as well as 33 (1972) and 19 (1976) for 40 per cent and, later, 60 per cent equity participation by Nigerians. All other enterprises not included in the above are to have 40 per cent equity participation.

Besides the ineffective enforcement of the 1972 decree[35], indigenization has concentrated largely on small-scale Levantine enterprises and precluded total takeover of the oligopoly firms in the vital sectors of the economy. Moreover, indigenization through individual Nigerian purchase of enterprises or shares has inequitably given undue advantage to the rich and powerful members of the petty bourgeoisie with easy access to credit from the state-owned Nigerian Bank for Commerce and Industry, which financed much of the transactions together with other state and imperialist banks. Finally, equity participation by individuals does not really ensure effective control of foreign enterprises. It was probably not meant to do that. Consequently, indigenization has been a petty bourgeois compromise between patriotism and puppetism, which has at best strengthened the economic base of the petty bourgeoisie without seriously challenging the neo-colonial underdevelopment of the country.

Conclusion

This exploration into the role of imperialism in Nigeria's development leads to three main conclusions. First, British colonialism effectively blocked Nigeria's development for a critical period of one century through its colossal export of national economic surplus, proscription of manufacturing, stagnation of agriculture, unequal exchange in exports and imports, systematic denial of credit, neglect of education, and general distortion of the colonial economy in a perverse bilateral integration with the British capitalist system. Forced transition from a pre-capitalist to capitalist mode of production was about the only real development under colonialism.

Second, the collective consequences of colonialism constituted an effective foundation for the persistent underdevelopment of the country from the colonial period to the present. In particular, the cultivation of a Nigerian petty bourgeoisie under colonialism and the collaboration of this and the comprador elite with the imperialist bourgeoisie for the mutual beneficial exploitation of the country has intensified the contradictions of neo-colonial capitalist underdevelopment since flag independence. The seeds of this perversion were sown during the nationalist struggle, which was so obsessed with state power and its material benefits that it predictably failed to elaborate any developmental ideology. The persistence of stifling neo-colonial domination and exploitation, in spite of years of economic planning and recent indigenization, indicates the national irrelevance of the ruling Nigerian petty bourgeoisie to the resolution of the dialectically inseparable problems of neo-colonialism and underdevelopment in the country.

Third, as the working class has been engaging in class struggles since flag independence against the domestic and foreign capitalists for the liquidation of underdevelopment, the real hope for genuine development in the country must be identified with this underprivileged class. How soon they will imbibe the anti-imperialist ideology for the socialist transformation of the country remains to be seen. It, however, depends much on how long the petty bourgeoisie can maintain the *status quo* with its neo-colonial allies in the face of the mounting contradictions of underdevelopment in Nigeria and the world.

References

1. See P.A. Baran, *The Political Economy of Growth* (London: Monthly Review Press, 1967); and Samir Amin, *Accumulation on a World Scale: A Critique of the Theory of Underdevelopment* (London: Monthly Review Press, 1974).
2. For a detailed discussion of these bourgeois distortions of imperialism, see D.W. Nabudere, 'Imperialism in the contemporary world', paper presented to the 12th Annual Social Sciences Conference of the East African Universities, 20–22 December 1976.
3. J.A. Hobson, *Imperialism* (London: Allen and Unwin, 1902); V.I. Lenin, *Imperialism: The Highest Stage of Capitalism* (Moscow: Progress Publishers, 1970).
4. A.K. Cairncross, *Home and Foreign Investment, 1870–1913* (Cambridge: Cambridge University Press, 1953).
5. See Kwame Nkrumah, *Neocolonialism – The Last Stage of Imperialism* (London: Panaf, 1971).
6. A. Spirkin and O. Yakhot, *The Basic Principles of Dialectical and Historical Materialism* (Moscow: Progress Publishers, 1974), chapter 7.
7. Baran, *op. cit.*, chapter 1.
8. See Benjamin Higgins, *Economic Development: Principles and Policies* (London: Constable, 1959), chapter 1; Ragnar Nurkse, *Problems of capital formation in underdeveloped countries* (London: Oxford University Press, 1953); A.C. Hirschman, *The Strategy of Economic Development* (New York, 1955); W.A. Lewis, *Development Planning* (New York: Harper and Row, 1966).
9. For the elaboration of this imperialist asymetry, see Amin, *op. cit.*
10. Though the Nigerian State did not exist then, the territory and population that now constitute this country were affected by the imperialist activities on the coast of West Africa.
11. See Walter Rodney, *West Africa and the Atlantic Slave Trade* (Nairobi: East African Publishing House, 1967); Eric Williams, *Capitalism and Slavery* (London: Andre Deutsch, 1964).
12. Rodney, *op. cit.*, p. 6.
13. For detailed discussion of the exploitative motives of colonialism, see H. Brunschwig (1966) *French Colonialism 1871–1914: Myths and Realities* (London, 1966); L.H. Gann and P. Duignan (eds.), *Colonialism in Africa, 1870–1960*, 5 Vols. (Cambridge: Cambridge University Press, 1969–75); V. Perlo, *The Empire of High Finance* (New York: International Publishers, 1957).
14. See W. Smith, *Slaves and Palm Oil, Economic Transition and Politics on the Western Slave Coast, 1870–94* (Chicago, 1968).
15. For some accounts of these see K.O. Dike, *Trade and Politics in the Niger Delta, 1830–85* (Oxford: Clarendon Press, 1956); M. Crowder, *The Story of Nigeria* (London: Allen and Unwin, 1962).
16. For the role of colonialism on African underdevelopment, see Rodney

17. See A. Emmanuel, *Unequal Exchange: A Study in the Imperialism of Trade* (London: Monthly Review Press, 1972).
18. The only significant mining operations were tin, which was monopolized by Britain's Amalgamated Tin Mines, and coal mined at Enugu by the Coal Corporation.
19. See G.K. Helleiner, *Peasant Agriculture, Government and Economic Growth in Nigeria* (Homewood, Ill.: Richard D. Irwin, 1966).
20. *Second National Development Plan, 1962–68.* (Lagos: Federal Ministry of Information), p.51, table 4.
21. See W.T. Newlyn and D.C. Rowan, *Money and Banking in British Colonial Africa.* (Cambridge: Cambridge University Press, 1954).
22. Until 1968, during the civil war, foreign enterprises in Nigeria were not incorporated in the country.
23. See Newlyn and Rowan, *op. cit.*
24. In 1941 and 1946, total inward cargo through Kano and Lagos was 1.3 and 2.6 tons respectively, while the outward tonnage was 2.0 and 4.6 respectively. See Ola Oni and Bade Onimode, *Economic Development of Nigeria: The Socialist Alternative* (Ibadan: Nigerian Academy of Arts, Science and Technology, 1975). pp. 9, 163.
25. See B. Onimode, 'Approaches to the Measurement of Education's contribution to Growth', *Manpower Journal*, 11, 3 (1975), p. 45.
26. Between 1946 and 1950, the Zikists, a militant youth wing of the NCNC, were demanding revolutionary change in the country. See R.L. Sklar, *Nigerian Political Parties* (Princeton, N.J: Princeton University Press, 1963), chapter 11.
27. See I.P. Schatz, 'The Influence of Planning on Development: The Nigerian Experience', *Social Research*, 3, 1 (1960).
28. O. Lange, *Economic Development, Planning, and International Co-operation* (London: Monthly Review Press, 1963), pp. 10–11.
29. A.G. Frank, *Lumpen-Bourgeoisie and Lumpen-Development* (London: Monthly Review Press, 1974).
30. See Oni and Onimode, *op. cit.*, chapters 2 and 3.
31. *Ibid.*, chapter 2.
32. Apart from the three colonial companies, the 16 others are British India General, Crusader, Law Union & Rock, Mercury, NEL Life Assurance, N.E.M., Royal Exchange Assurance, Sun, Lion of Africa, New India Assurance, New Nigeria, United Nigerias, United Nigeria Life.
33. For the elaboration of this point, See Oni and Onimode, *op. cit.*, chapter 4.
34. See Nigerian Enterprises Promotion Board, *Nigerian Enterprises Promotion Decree* (Lagos, 1972) and *Federal Military Government's Views on the Report of the Industrial Enterprises Panel* (Lagos: Federal Ministry of Information 1976).
35. See *Federal Military Government's Views on the Report of the Industrial Enterprises Panel*, p.4. It shows that by 30 June 1975, only about 33 per cent of the enterprises affected by the 1972 decree were confirmed to have complied. It also states that: 'The enterprises exempted from the Decree, many of them on questionable grounds, numbered 81'.

5. A Short History of Nigerian Underdevelopment

Okwudiba Nnoli

Science versus Propaganda in the Origin of Underdevelopment

History is a living phenomenon. Like all living forms, it unites the past with the present and the future. Therefore, its living characteristics are displayed by historical analysis when the latter identifies a pressing contemporary problem, traces the pattern of its emergence from the past, thereby exposing causality and movement in its transformation, and thus indicating its direction of development in the future. Unfortunately, history departments in Nigerian universities deal with dead history. Past events, situations and personalities are studied as if for their own sake, and links between these and contemporary problems are at best tenuous. (This approach is typical of tribal history.) When some links are provided between past and present events, they are purely mechanical. What is usually presented is a series of events and factors strewn together in a chain-like formation. The only important link in the chain is time. Causality is submerged in a mass of data or is at best subjective and ephemeral. The future is hardly ever made part of the discussion. Of course, in the absence of causality and movement in analysis, the link with the future is impossible. History becomes a dead phenomenon, a study of the dead. Consequently, propaganda displaces scientific historical insights, or subjectivism reigns.

One area where propaganda and subjectivism prevail over science is in the study of the historical origins of Nigerian underdevelopment. The impression that has been created and is daily being reinforced is that the contemporary underdevelopment of Nigeria is a direct inheritance from the pre-colonial underdevelopment of the area. But this is left at the level of an assertion. Our history departments make no attempt whatsoever to prove or disprove it. They just reproduce it. The argument usually employed in this propaganda is often implicit: that the pre-colonial conditions have continued to be reproduced. Three obvious questions come to mind. Is this argument correct? If it is, why is it that after over eighty years of colonialism and neo-colonialism, these conditions have persisted? What forces are reproducing them and why? In order to be able to answer the first question adequately, it is necessary to explain pre-colonial underdevelopment, how it emerged, and what social forces perpetuated its existence. Thereafter, it becomes easier to assess whether or not those social conditions and forces which reproduced it in the past are still present today and whether or not they have the capacity to play the same role as they did in the past.

Contrary to the impressions usually conveyed by bourgeois and petty bourgeois historians and social scientists, the pre-colonial societies of Nigeria were not static systems. Without implying any linearity in their history, it is clear that over the past centuries, these societies have increasingly become more complex through sometimes evolutionary, and other times revolutionary, occurrences. Changes in their techniques of production, level of production, migrations, and patterns of contact with other societies have given rise to societal transformation. For the purposes of this discussion, however, the time frame will not go back beyond the period just before contact with Western colonialism. Just prior to this disastrous event, the social condition which explains the pre-colonial underdevelopment could be identified.

Of course, the period of contact with Europeans prior to colonialism contributed elements to the underdevelopment of the area. The slave trade and the 'legitimate' trade both took a deadly toll of the capacity of the Nigerian peoples for a rapid transformation of themselves and their environments. By incorporating the pre-colonial societies into the world capitalist economy in a subjugated position, they caused the destruction of their rich and varied political systems and social structures, and the creation of new productive economic activities based on the needs of the foreign capitalist countries. In addition, they diverted attention away from local creative potentials and resources by focussing on the procurement of slaves or the production of primary resources needed by Europeans. More particularly, the slave trade caused the loss of many able-bodied men from the local economies, with a consequent lowering of economic activities and potential. It initiated slave wars among the various societies, which led to a great deal of bloodshed and loss of property, and destroyed trust, friendship, and co-operation among Nigerian peoples. Social and economic progress suffered. This required political security. Imported European goods also ruined certain local industries that produced similar commodities or substitutes for them.

It is a mistake to explain pre-colonial underdevelopment of these periods essentially in terms of these phenomena. This would ignore the fact that the external transactions involved in the slave trade and 'legitimate' trade did not in any direct way affect the investible surplus in the local economies. In fact, these external transactions never penetrated the local economies; they were not integrated into the local trade. Furthermore, the local ruling groups who were the only ones engaged in such foreign trade were not looking for profits which could be reinvested, but for certain conspicuous consumption merchandise such as weapons, alcohol, and textiles. These goods were significant for maintaining their social and political influence. They were essentially prestige goods which circulated among the elite and, although in some cases they took the place of locally-produced goods such as blacksmith's crafts and raffia loincloths, they did not enter the realm of subsistence production which constituted the dominant part of the economy. Surplus prestige products were either hoarded or destroyed in ostentatious ceremonies such as burial and coronation ceremonies.

Thus, two economic systems coexisted within the same society but were situated in spheres apparently impervious to each other. These were the village subsistence economy on the one hand, and the economy based on international and even transcontinental commerce on the other hand. For its livelihood, the society depended on the subsistence sector punctuated by the local markets that traded exclusively in foodstuffs within and among the villages. But these transactions had no connection with the external commercial trade serving only the ruling group. Herein lies the fundamental basis for pre-colonial underdevelopment. And this pattern of activities antedated the slave trade and 'legitimate' trade.

The societies stagnated essentially because there were no new inputs of ideas or investible surplus from the external sector into the subsistence sector adequate enough to transform production in a self-sustaining manner. And the subsistence sector yielded only a very insignificant surplus. Only in the North, among the Hausa-Fulani, was any significant surplus forthcoming from this sector. Here, comparatively elaborate and often highly-skilled agricultural techniques were employed to produce a reasonable surplus over the subsistence needs of the population, including the urban aristocracy, merchants, artisans, and petty officials. Although they affected a small proportion of the population, landed estates existed that were farmed by slave labor, introducing an element into the Hausa-Fulani economy quite different in scale and character from the dominant system of the autonomous household economic activity prevalent eleswhere. Such estates enabled experimentation with new crops and techniques on a large scale.

In their desire to perpetuate their authority, the ruling groups placed an excessive emphasis on their control over people, to the neglect of their control over things. The transfer of objects operated according to a system of reciprocal obligations linked to the social situation of those in the kinship or patron-client relationships. For example, in most areas of the South, the young men rendered goods and services to their elders while the latter in turn redistributed goods and favours to the former. The authority of the elders was not founded on their ownership of property, but rather on their knowledge of customs, genealogy and history associated with age. It was reinforced by such techniques as divination and cultural rites such as initiation ceremonies and medicine. Hence, the dowry (before it was contaminated by the capitalist economy) reflected neither the purchase of women, nor even an exchange for women, but the need to respect the authority and social prestige of the elders. Also, the elders' redistribution of foodstuffs to the young men did not represent a remuneration for their work but was the manifestation of the authority of the elders. To accept without reciprocity is to be subordinate.[1] This social situation was reinforced by the stabilizing effects of the egalitarian nature of the land tenure system that prevailed in most parts of the country.

Thus, the pre-colonial societies while carrying on intensive and extensive external transactions were able to preserve their social structures for a very long time. The goods resulting from these transactions were not utilized to catalyze the expansion of the local economy. Instead, they were converted into prestige goods accessible mainly to the elders, or the Hausa-Fulani aristocracy, which used it for winning friends and influencing people, or merely hoarded it. But unless new inputs of ideas and/or investible surplus were introduced into the subsistence economy, it was difficult to generate an increased level of production and the consequent division of labour and its accompanying social differentiation characteristic of more advanced economies.

Colonialism and Precolonial Pattern of Destruction

Colonialism did not reproduce this stultifying pre-colonial social condition. It destroyed it. And it set up an economic system dominated by the use of external inputs of ideas and investible surplus in the organization of local production. Yet underdevelopment is still with us. But it cannot be the same underdevelopment that plagued the pre-colonial societies. This is obvious. The social condition that reproduced that lack of economic progress was negated by the colonial economy. Some other social conditions, in the colonial society, must now account for the state of underdevelopment attendant on the colonial situation. In order to fully appreciate these social conditions, it is necessary to adequately understand the impact of colonialism on the pre-colonial pattern of economic activities. In this regard the period 1900–46 was crucial.

The most significant consequences of colonialism on social and economic progress in Nigeria lay in the impact on the production system. It replaced the subsistence economies of the pre-colonial societies with a capitalist one motivated and dominated by foreign private capital, and responding to and serving the needs of this external capital rather than the needs of the local population. By so doing it caused a sharp and dramatic break with the past history of the Nigerian people and drastically altered the dynamics and direction of their future. It charted a new historical course for the people. And hardly any links were created between these two historical processes, particularly their economic systems.

In the new colonial scheme of things, the local population lost control of its production process. Of course, much of the subsistence economic activities of the pre-colonial order persisted, but these were now subordinated to those productive ventures that were of interest to the colonialists and that now dominated the economy and engaged most of the attention, efforts, and resources of the new leadership. These dominant economic activities were no less powerful because they were limited in size during the early colonial period. They were confined to a zone (not geographical in nature) producing for the world market. Export crop production, mining of minerals for export and the importation of manufactured goods from Europe predominated. The major crops were palm oil and palm kernels, cocoa, groundnuts, and cotton. Minerals included tin, columbite, wolfram, and gold, which were exported, and coal, which was used domestically. Textile goods constituted the most important import item, but motor vehicles, bicycles, cement, other building materials, and various other consumer goods were also imported.

In fact, prior to the end of the Second World War, most of the country's resources were devoted to the expansion and improvement of this very diminutive zone. As far back as 1887 the government of the Colony of Lagos encouraged cocoa production introduced from outside the country. It established a botanical garden for cocoa seedlings. From here they were distributed free by the colonial government to farmers in Lagos, and by Christian missionaries in Western Nigeria. Hence, while 25cwt. of cocoa was exported in 1886, over 70 tons were exported in 1897.[2] In May 1901 Elder Dempster and Co. distributed tons of cotton seeds to farmers in the country. It also offered a large reward to the first person to ship 100 tons of cotton. Also, it attempted to use American cotton-growing experts to instruct Nigerians on how to grow the crop.[3] But it was the British Cotton Growing Association (BCGA) which more than any other group actively encouraged cotton production; It frequently distributed cotton seeds to farmers. Cash loans were also made to cotton farmers by the Bank of West Africa. In 1903 cotton seeds and ginning machines were introduced into the Ibadan area, and the Ibadan Council was persuaded to grant a lease on approximately four square miles of land to the BCGA for fifty years. But cotton never became an important export crop of that area. Similarly, the rubber crop failed to take root in the Ibadan area, and the Malayan rubber boom of 1913 destroyed the fledgling rubber economy.

Before 1946 schemes to encourage oil palm production were many and varied. The government subsidized any loss sustained by oil mill owners arising from inadequate supplies of fruits. The Cultivated Oil Palm Ordinance of 1935 provided that if a grower registered his plot with the government and the oil produced by him met the required quality, he would receive the full rebate of the export duty in force.[4] In 1923, following keen competition in the world oil palm market by the Belgian Congo and the Far East, the Joint West Africa Committees of the Liverpool, London and Manchester Chambers of Commerce pressured the British government to appoint a committee to consider the best means of securing an improved and increased production of oil palm in Nigeria and elsewhere in British West Africa.[5] Although the report of the committee was not implemented by the

British government, in 1928 the Agricultural Department in Nigeria took the initiative in drawing up the Produce Export Regulations to control and standardize the purity of the palm oil, palm kernels, and cocoa that were exported. It also initiated experiments in improving the cultivation of the oil palm, and by 1927 was able to distribute to growers seedlings of the best types from its station at Calabar. Also, the UAC distributed seeds free from its plantation at N'dian in the Cameroons.

In 1939 the Nigerian colonial government established an oil palm research station in Benin, which embraced over 1,000 acres of land. A subsidiary station was also set up at Onitsha. The government also created a number of other institutions for the general advancement of cash crop production. Between 1912 and 1916 the Moore Plantation was built; in 1923 agricultural experimental stations were built in Zaria and Umuahia; in 1925 an agricultural research station was set up at Vom; two years later, the school of agriculture at Ibadan was opened. In 1934 two other institutions were built: the agricultural station at Samaru and the veterinary school in Kano. In 1942 the veterinary school at Vom was created with the aid of the Colonial Development and Welfare Fund. As regards palm oil extraction, the Agricultural Department experimented with a number of small hand presses before deciding in 1932 that the Duchscher press was the most satisfactory. In addition, the UAC donated 250 palm oil hand press machines for use by farmers.

Other agricultural products which the colonial government tried to promote and improve included groundnuts, rice, and citrus fruits. The Agricultural Department experimented with improved strains of groundnuts. The resultant high-yielding seeds were distributed to the farmers. In 1933 the Department invited an agricultural officer from the Sierra Leone to introduce rice-growing to the mangrove swamps of Nigeria. He chose Warri as his experimental station, and encouraged some farmers in the area to grow rice. But very little surplus for export materialized, and therefore, the government abandoned its efforts. There was no official interest in encouraging production for local consumption, only for export. The production of citrus fruits also did not succeed beyond meeting local needs. Official efforts on its behalf were equally abandoned. Also, in the early 1930s, the Government encouraged kolanut cultivation but only to help farmers whose cocoa trees had been ruined by the black pod disease and to reduce imports of the fruit. The production of tobacco was also encouraged by the British American Tobacco Company in collaboration with the Agricultural Department. It did not initially succeed. Later, however, the company succeeded in introducing improved tobacco for local production.

An industry due mainly to the initiative of the Agricultural Department was the production and preparation for export of peeled and sunbleached ginger. The experiment did not catch on. Other trials included the planting of Japanese chillies, and the manufacture of tapioca and cassava starch. None progressed beyond the initial stages. The Veterinary Department explored the possibility of developing an export trade in dried and salted meat, but failed. But it developed one in clarified butter fat (ghee). Hides and skins, comprising one of Nigeria's most remunerative export, gained much in value as a result of the work of the Veterinary Department. In 1934 a veterinary school was set up at Kano to train veterinary staff. In 1937 a stockfarm was created at Ilorin with funds from the Colonial Development Fund to improve the breed of tsetse fly-resistant dwarf cattle in the South. Also, the Forestry Department worked to foster new export products such as gum arabic, Niger gutta (an ingredient of chewing gum) and an extract of mangrove used for tanning.

In the extractive industries, government aid, support, and encouragement were equally evident. The growth of these industries was stimulated by foreign capitalist interests in tin, gold, diamonds, salt, petroleum, and iron ore. The Government made several geological surveys to determine the availability and extent of the deposits of these and other minerals. And it intervened strongly in various ways to ensure their survival. For example, the tin mining industry had very little hope of survival until the extension of the railway to the mining areas in 1911. By 1914 a number of good roads had been built by the government in the area to further lower transport costs for the mining companies. Again in 1942, when the tin mining industry was expanding following the fall of Malaya to the Japanese during the Second World War, the companies pressured the government to conscript labour for the mines. Therefore, in February 1942, the government made an effort to conscript 10,000 men under the Nigeria Defence (Compulsory National Service Essential Mines Northern Provinces) Regulations No. 23 of 1942.[6]

In the international market the government intervened actively to promote the sale of export products. In 1934 the British government intervened to increase Nigeria's quota for tin in the world market, despite the worldwide restriction of tin production. When in the early 1930s nationalistic policies in Denmark, Germany, France, and the Netherlands threatened vegetable oil production in Nigeria and elsewhere in the British Empire, Britain abandoned her free trade policy, concluded the Ottawa Agreement and as a result pre-empted any decline in vegetable oil production in Nigeria.[7] Similarly, the British–American trade agreement of 1938 prevented the U.S. restriction of foreign palm oil and palm kernel oil from dampening the production and export of these commodities in and from Nigeria.[8]

The colonial government even promoted new colonial economic activities at the expense of the pre-colonial ones. This was more glaring on the import side. The British Government set out to destroy all local substitutes or competitors for imported goods.[9] It restricted locally competitive manufactures, particularly cotton goods whose industry was very highly developed in Northern Nigeria.[10] In the mining industry colonial policy enabled European monopolization of tin deposits in the tin mining areas. Consequently, by 1923, the local tin industry for tinning brassware, which had flourished in the Naraguta district, had completely disappeared.[11] Similarly, galena which was mined for use as a cosmetic both at Arafu, south of the Benue, and at Abakaliki in the East, ceased with colonialism.[12] Also, the salt-making industry in Bida and other districts, iron smithing, leather industry, and the glass, brass, copper, soap, brewing, silver, pot, mat, and wood-carving industries decayed and were virtually eliminated as a result of colonial policy.

In another respect the government deliberately promoted the new colonial pattern of production by building an elaborate system of infrastructure to support it. A railway system was constructed from the coasts, on the South-East and South-West, to the major centers of colonial economic activities inland, enabling an easy evacuation of export products. Thus, the 1910-20 extension of the railway from Baro on the Niger to Kano made it possible to develop an export trade in groundnuts to help diversify the then monocultural economy of palm produce. As a result, palm products fell from 82 per cent of total exports in 1900 to 31 per cent in 1937, and the groundnut trade expanded from a few hundred tons during the first five years of the century to over 300,000 tons in 1937, while its value increased from less than 1 per cent of total exports to as much as 24 per cent in 1933. Exports of cotton lint increased by 100 per cent between 1913 and 1921, with their value comprising 5 per cent of total exports in 1921.[13] In 1908 a mere 10,000 untanned hides and skins reached the ports from the North. By 1913 it was 473,000, and in 1937, over six million were exported. Cocoa exports increased steadily, reaching 19 per cent of total exports in 1937. Timber reached 3 per cent in 1920.[14]

Meanwhile, district commissioners constructed every type of roads, from the metalled highway to the dusty laterite track, to facilitate both administrative communication and the movement of goods and services. Telegraph and postal services were added to this infrastructure. Also, by 1913, deep water berths had been opened in Lagos. Thirteen years later, another was opened in Apapa. During the Second World War air transport services were expanded; thirty aerodromes were built and the existing landing grounds were considerably lengthened. As in the case of the railway system, the respective paths of this web of communication ran from the centers of colonial production, distribution, and exchange to the ships that carried the colony's trade to and from the advanced capitalist countries.

In addition, as a result of these colonial economic activities, the colonial government needed centres for co-ordinating them, as well as for the governmental administration and effective political control of the country. If the economic conditions demanded them, new urban centers were created. This was the case with Enugu following the discovery of coal nearby, Port Harcourt to provide harbour facilities, and Sapele to serve the timber industry. Others, such as Kaduna, owed their origin to colonial administrative needs, as well as the idiosyncratic urges of colonial administrators. In 1917 a Township Ordinance came into force for the creation, control, and administration of urban areas. First, second, and third-class townships were delineated. All were either situated along the railway, providing refuelling facilities for the railways, or were large centers of colonial economic activities. In other words, they were neither distinguished by the largeness of their population nor by their importance in pre-colonial times.[15]

The colonialists concentrated all their incentives for participation in colonial activities in these townships. Wage employment, small-scale business, hospitals, water supply, electricity and education, although severely limited, were concentrated there. In fact, township status guided the distribution of these amenities even among the townships themselves since the more prestigious ones represented the largest concentration of colonial economic activities. Some of these amenities, such as education and wage employment, were first and foremost a necessity for the introduction and consolidation of colonial production. Only later did they act as an incentive for urban life.

Colonial education was designed to prepare Nigerians for meaningful participation in colonial economic and administrative activities. The latter were clearly unknown in the pre-colonial societies. Therefore, the pre-colonial systems of education could not train people in them. A new educational system serving the interests of foreign capital in the production of cash crops, minerals, and the sale of foreign goods and services was needed and introduced. Initially, educated Nigerians were needed essentially as clerks and artisans in the foreign commercial firms and the colonial civil service. Later, a beginning was made in training them for high positions in these enterprises. Typical of colonial activity, this education was confined to the colonial urban centers, first in Lagos and Calabar, and later in the inland centers. Hence, in 1921 about 40 per cent of those who had received such an education in Southern Nigeria lived in thirteen urban centers with a population of less than 2 per cent of the total Southern population. In 1953 about 34 per cent of those with four or more years of colonial education in Onitsha province lived in Enugu and Onitsha, 60 per cent of those in Rivers province lived in Port Harcourt, 61 per cent in Ibadan province lived in Ibadan, and 89 per cent of those in Kano province who had completed six or more years of colonial education lived in Kano.[16]

Similarly, wage employment of the local population was a necessity of the new colonial order. Due to the hostility of climatic conditions and the local population, foreign European personnel could not migrate in sufficient numbers to fully man the various colonial enterprises. Local labour was required. Four British colonial policies – forced labour, the introduction of alien currency, taxation, and artificial scarcity – forced many Nigerians to seek wage employment in the new system of production. Increasingly, fewer of them could subsist without working or trading for longer or shorter periods of time in the colonial zones. Some of the colonial government's positive responses to labour's demands for better wages, housing, health, and other social services were motivated by the desire to retain this labour which, as time passed, acquired more and more experience and skills useful for the colonial scheme of things.

This intensive, extensive, and sustained governmental intervention on behalf of the colonial pattern of production contrasts very sharply with the colonial government's utter neglect of the pre-colonial pattern of production. While it did everything possible to promote and encourage the new import-export economy based on cash crops, minerals, and imported manufactured goods, it did virtually nothing to sustain, much less encourage, the pre-colonial economic activities. During the period between the colonization of Lagos in 1851 and the end of the Second World War in 1945, the only time that the colonial government made any effort on behalf of pre-colonial economic activities was during the war. In its desire to cut down the imports of food by 75 per cent, the colonial government stimulated the production of local foodstuffs and the revival of pre-colonial industries. But this gesture was only an emergency short-term measure which was discontinued soon after the war. In any case, it was only a very small part of a series of official actions to enable the colonial economy and Britain to withstand the hardships of the war. The other programs concerned the stimulation of the colonial economic zone.[17]

Such a downright neglect by the colonialists of the pre-colonial pattern of production cannot be the result of any adherence to the principle of non-governmental intervention in economic activities mythically associated with capitalist systems. In the light of the aggressive intervention on behalf of colonial production, it could not be. And it cannot be, as the colonial propaganda would want us to believe, out of the desire of the colonial government not to interfere with the indigenous pattern of life as a mark of respect for its uniqueness. In fact, in its desire to promote the new colonial activities, the colonial government acted to disrupt, disorganize, and destroy the pre-colonial system of production, subordinating it to the needs of the colonial economic zone.

The colonialists employed forced labour – in the building of the railways, for work in the tin mines and in the construction of the Benue bridge – to move Nigerians out of the pre-colonial into the colonial system of production very much against their will. In addition, specific distortions of the pre-colonial society were forced through by the colonial authority which compelled the people to go to the colonial zones in search of money, thereby causing them to be cash-crop producers or to sell their labour power. Among these distortions were the enforcement of British currency as the only means of economic exchange, and the introduction of fixed recurrent taxes whose equivalent was hitherto unknown in the country, except in the northern emirates. British money was introduced in 1900. Without it, payment for goods and services in the new order was impossible. More important, it was the only medium for paying the newly-established taxes, the non-payment of which incurred severe punitive measures from the Government. In order to raise money for these taxes the indigenous population had to enter colonial production. In addition, the reactionary colonial administration relied on artificial scarcity to compel Nigerians into colonial activities. It paid such low wages that more than one worker was needed to feed the extended family. At the same time, it maintained huge surpluses every year whenever possible, even during the severe economic depression of the early thirties, withholding earnings that were due to cash-crop growers. And foreign firms were permitted to make monopolistic profits.

The result was an inevitable disorganization and castration of the pre-colonial system of production. In the South, where socio-economic privileges accrued to the elders, the young and most productive elements in the society migrated to the colonial zone, causing a severe drop in the productivity of the pre-colonial zones. Similarly, in the North, the non-aristocratic segment of the population, the major tillers of the soil, migrated, disrupting local production. With this exodus of the young, the social and, eventually, cultural life of the villages began to decay. Life in the villages began to be seen as tedious, degrading, and unrewarding. As the economic, social, and cultural equilibrium of the pre-colonial societies was thus disrupted, they lost their ethos, dynamism, and collective self-confidence. The process of total decay began, and by the 1970s virtually only the old and retired Nigerians were left to carry on productive village activities. The ability of the villages to resist the encroachment of the colonial production process became weaker, enabling them to be further subordinated, exploited, and disrupted by the economic activities of colonial and neo-colonial life.

Two zones could be distinguished from this rapidly disintegrating pre-colonial system of production. There was the zone of labour reserve, usually proximal to the colonial zone or in areas of very low pre-colonial production. It essentially supplied wage labour to the colonial zone and was quite early penetrated by colonial capitalism. The labour which it supplied was largely migratory in character, helping to keep the cost of labour in the colonial zone low in terms of world scales and, therefore, ensuring abnormally huge profits for the foreign firms operating in the colony. Then, there was the zone of subsistence production, virtually isolated from the colonial zone but directly subordinated to it and supplying its needs for food. Here the local population was able to pay its taxes and fulfil its other financial obligations in the colonial society from surpluses emanating from the continuation of its pre-colonial economic activities. Such areas were usually regarded by the colonialists as being more primitive than the rest of the country. Examples include Abakaliki division and the Middle Belt region.

As Claude Meillassoux has correctly noted, capitalism acts in two ways: 'On [the] one hand it elicits a sector of production built up in its own image through the presence of capital and its corollaries – private control of the means of production and wage earning. On the other hand it feeds off the precapitalist sectors through the mechanism of primitive accumulation – with the contradictory results of both perpetuating and destroying them at the same time.'[18] The relationship between the colonial zone and the other two zones was dialectical, not static. The colonial and the pre-colonial systems constituted a dialectical dualism. The growth of the imperialist-oriented export-import sector required the destruction of the pre-colonial economies. Growth of the export-import enclave gave rise to a totally asymmetrical urbanization, over-urbanization, and the parasitism of the urban force, as well as the subsequent deterioration of the pre-colonial system, to the benefit of the commercial and industrial capitalist sector dominated by foreign capital.[19]

Obviously, therefore, the intention of the colonialists was not to build a system of production based on the reformation of the pre-colonial pattern of production. Instead, they sought to break completely and radically with the old system, create a totally different one, and utilize the resources of the old whenever and wherever possible. Herein lies a major difference between the history of Nigerian production and that of the often-quoted model of Japan. In the Japanese experience Western ideas and technology were used to reform the pre-Western pattern of production, and not to achieve a total break with that pattern. The new was fashioned out of the old, discarding obsolete ideas and obsolescent technology and replacing them with new ones. The emphasis was on the improvement in the skills with which the local population performed their traditional pre-Western production tasks, and not the wholesale abandonment of those tasks. Later, new tasks based on the Western production model but serving the specific needs and wants of the local population were added to the system of local production. Under the circumstances development was possible. In the Nigerian case, underdevelopment was inevitable. But Nigerian leaders now deem a total break with the inherited colonial system of production unrealistic. Underdevelopment is to become a way of life.

In fact, in Nigeria the colonialists were not interested in making their system of production serve the basic needs of the local population. Mention has already been made of the abandonment of efforts on behalf of rice and citrus production merely because only local needs were served. When service to the local population was brought into the productive equation it was thought of in negative and pejorative terms, to absorb that part of the output of colonial production which was not of sufficiently high standard or was otherwise unsuitable for export, to reduce cost and the waste of an industry, and allow a better utilization of the natural resources.[20] For example, the establishment of sawmills in colonial Nigeria to supply the domestic market was undertaken in order to use logs which were too 'inferior' to be exported and were usually left to rot in the forest; the industry then opened up the exploitation of secondary timbers for which again there were no overseas markets.[21] A similar case is that of oranges, pineapples, and ginger. It was found expedient to offer the 'inferior' fruits for sale in the internal market, and also to start the manufacture of fruit juices for domestic use.[22]

Thus, the loss of local control over the new production process marked the beginning of the loss of self-reliance by the Nigerian economy. This loss was exacerbated and reinforced by the external orientation of the colonial economy. In sharp contrast to their pre-colonial production of goods and services for their own use, Nigerian participants in the colonial economy produced excessively for the world market, about 34 per cent of the national income during the period 1929–37.[23] Comparable figures for other countries were Britain – 14 per cent, the United States – 3 per cent, and the Soviet Union – 2 per cent.

Of course, the new Nigerian colonial economy owed its existence mainly to external factors favourable to its cash crops. For example, the vegetable oil trade was motivated by the increasing need of Europe for machine lubricants, the increase in the European population and in the consequent demand for soaps and candles, and the augmented carrying capacity of the steamships. Between 1866 and 1945 palm oil and groundnut oil had an important place in Europe's industrial production, principally in the manufacture of soap, candles, and in the case of palm oil as a flux in the tin-plate industry. Some vegetable oilseeds, such as groundnuts, palm kernels, and cottonseed yielded a very valuable by-product in the form of cattle cake demanded overseas.[24] The demand for vegetable oils and oilseeds alone grew in Europe from 1,500,000 metric tons per year before 1914 to 2,300,000 metric tons a year during the interwar years. In North America it rose from an annual average of about 60,000 metric tons in 1909–14 to 600,000 in 1924–28 and in 1935 and 1937 to 1,000,000 metric tons.[25] Palm oil and groundnut were produced during the pre-colonial times wholly for local use. For example, before the coming of the railway, groundnuts were cultivated only for local consumption, and in 1924 about 37,000 tons were still consumed locally. But this local production dynamic played no role whatever in the creation of the externally-oriented colonial trade in groundnuts.[26]

This sudden intensive and extensive thrust into the world market caused serious adverse effects on productivity within the country. The nation entered the world market well before it had developed its internal capacity to absorb the effects of the fluctuations and uncertainty of external market conditions and to compete worldwide. It entered in a very weak position as primary producer. For the tropical producer of a primary product for the world market there were three major sources of insecurity: the notoriously variable world prices for primary commodities, the vagaries of climate and weather which affected the physical volume, and competition either from the same commodity produced in a similar but cheaper way elsewhere or from a synthetic substitute. And the country's production system could not easily adapt to alternative lines of production in order to offset the adverse effects of these sources of insecurity. There was also the problem created by an inevitable worsening of the country's terms of trade.

Herein lies another major difference with the Japanese experience. It was the rapid economic growth, dynamism, and growing adaptability to economic changes which followed the Meiji Restoration of 1868 in Japan that necessitated the country's venture into the world market in order to procure the resources needed to maintain, reinforce, and accelerate the growing internal momentum of the Japanese economy. Therefore, the Japanese entrance into the world market was a carefully planned and structured one. As much, if not a greater, value was placed on the control of the external conditions as was placed on the control of the internal environment. External factors were seriously, consciously, and directly integrated into the overall planning for national development.

This contrasts very sharply with the haphazard, uncontrolled, and unstructured participation of the Nigerian colonial economy in the capitalist world market. External forces were permitted, even encouraged, to find their own limits within the colonial economy, and to exploit it as much as they liked. For example, there was no attempt by the metalliferous industry controlled by foreign forces to conserve the mineral resources of the country.[27] There was no attempt to provide a national framework of values, structures, and procedures for resource mobilization and allocation into which external activities could be integrated. In addition, there was no co-ordination of the various types of external resources designed to build up a self-sufficient Nigerian capacity, nor any choice of them based on a rank order of priorities. The harmonization of the interests of the colony and those of foreign forces was non-existent, and there was no harmonization among a number of the various external forces. Consequently, the local will to reject any external transaction was emasculated.

Under these circumstances, the cost of external transactions increased. Dependence on external conditions and vulnerability to political pressures, as well as the manipulation of major local decisions by a coalition of external forces or the carving out of different territorial, functional, and institutional spheres of influence by competing external forces, characterized national life. Also, it became difficult to weed out inefficient and inappropriate external resources.

The dependence of national activities on external centres frustrated any attempt to transform the pattern of national and international economic life in a way consonant with the full and effective mobilization of internal resources. It imposed a straightjacket on the type and quantity of the factors of production and distribution to be utilized. In addition, by increasing external influence in the country it imposed exorbitant costs on national independence. Such a situation was objectively in the interest of the colonialists. As competitors in the capitalist world market they had no objective interest in increasing the bargaining power of the colony relative to that of their own country. This would severely limit their power and prestige in international transactions. On the other hand, this power and prestige would increase if the metropolitan country had unrestricted access to the resources of the colony. Hence, decolonization has not occurred without an intense and protracted struggle by the colonized.

Thus, colonial Nigeria's public, commercial, and economic policy was decided and its economic transformation conducted mainly by agencies outside the country and not subject to control by its population. Market prices of the exports on which colonial Nigeria depended so heavily were fixed in the outside world by forces beyond local control. Hence, they were buffeted by fluctuations in the external conditions. For example, soon after the First World War economic conditions in Europe improved, industrial activity increased, and the prices of Nigerian exports soared. Then in 1920 and 1921 the short boom collapsed and the export prices of Nigerian products fell quickly. Uncertainty was introduced into the production process. Mention has already been made of the effects of changes in the world market conditions for tin and vegetable oils on Nigerian exports in the 1930s. The most dramatic deleterious effects of external conditions in Nigerian life were felt during the Great Depression and the Second World War, both originating in Europe and America.

An expansion of the governmental sector of the colonial economy was halted by the Depression. The government depended largely on revenues from external trade, but customs revenues fell from ₦6.8 million in 1929 to ₦4.2 million in 1931.[28] Nigerian exports dropped in value from ₦35.6 million in 1928 to ₦17.6 million in 1931. During the same period the purchasing power of exports fell by 38 per cent from ₦26.4 million to ₦16 million.[29] The unit values of the major export crops fell by 53 per cent in the case of cotton and 78 per cent for rubber, with the others in between. Most severely hit in terms of total export value were the least important crops, rubber and cotton, whose value fell by 90 per cent and 88 per cent respectively. Palm oil came next with a 77 per cent decline. The least affected was groundnut export whose value fell by only 39 per cent.[30] As a result of the Depression, there was severe retrenchment in both the colonial government and colonial private enterprise.

Following the outbreak of the Second World War in 1939, Nigerian agricultural producers, middlemen, importers, traders, and wage earners were confronted with price controls and wage ceilings. As the British government sought to protect British consumer prices and control the direction of the trade in raw materials following the cutting-off of important British overseas markets by the war, export prices were set by agreement between the Nigerian colonial government and the British Ministry of Food. Prices paid to peasant producers were regulated in such a way as to allow the buying foreign firms to make enormous profits. And although the war led to increased urbanization, especially in areas of military and industrial activity, inflation later escalated. Between 1939 and 1942 the cost of living rose by 50 per cent in the urban centers.[31]

This external orientation of the colonial economy was initially caused and subsequently reinforced by an international division of labour dictated and controlled from outside the country and in which the local area remained passive. This had a disastrous effect on economic transformation within the colony. Nigeria was consistently assigned an inferior role in this division of labour, a role that was governed exclusively by the economic needs and developments of the Euro-American world. Initially, the country was assigned the role of the raw materials production for export, the importation of manufactured consumer goods, and a market for the investment of foreign capital and the exploitation of cheap labour. This period coincided with that in Europe when, as a result of the more rapid progress in manufacturing than in agriculture, the European countries needed external raw materials for the rapidly increasing industries and food to feed the growing industrial population. As consumer goods were created faster than the population could buy them, there was also a need for foreign markets for these goods. In time, because of the low wages of the industrial population, the rate of profit outstripped the rate of investment of capital, causing capital under-utilization, and creating the need for external markets for capital, particularly in areas of cheaper labour and, therefore, higher profit. Hence, prior to 1946, the manufacturing industry was virtually non-existent in colonial Nigeria. Industrial production never exceeded 1 per cent of total colonial production, and most of the industries that existed emphasized the processing of raw materials for export.

The year 1946 is regarded as marking the beginning of industrial progress in Nigeria, but it was an industrialization dictated by the changes that had taken place in the international division of labour within the world capitalist economy to which Nigeria was now firmly integrated as a peripheral appendage. Following the war the United States replaced Britain as the leader of the capitalist world and the pace-setter of economic life within the system. And in the United States progress in agriculture had gone hand in hand with progress in industry. Also, the country was rich in natural resources. Developments during the war had galvanized a new petrochemical industry, enabling the production of various synthetic substitutes for the pre-existing raw materials like rubber, cotton, and vegetable oils. The war also brought to the fore of industrial life the heavy machinery industry. The significance of traditional raw materials and manufactured consumer goods in the international economic scheme of things was radically curtailed. They were replaced by the capital goods industry and the strategic minerals such as petroleum, copper, chromium, cobalt, and uranium useful for this industry. Foreign markets were needed for the sale of the capital goods. Import-substitution manufacturing industry producing the now insignificant consumer goods in Nigerian-type economies provided one of the best opportunities for the emergence of these foreign markets. Nigeria was thus assigned additional roles in the international division of labour – import-substitution industrialization – and the production of the strategic raw material, petroleum. The present petroleum-dominated economy in Nigeria emphasizing import-substitution industrial activities is the direct outcome of this changed international division of labour.

As Tomas Szentes has correctly observed, another change in this division of labour is now occurring, giving rise to centers of scientific and technological innovation in Europe and America and their peripheries, such as Nigeria, which rely on regular imports of the technical achievements and scientific results of the former. This may even enable the capital goods industry to be possible in Nigerian-type societies provided they import the technology to establish, sustain, and refurbish the industry. But the result will be increased underdevelopment because the whole process would still be part of the division of labour imposed from outside in which the local population would be passive. Increased dependency would be the direct and immediate result, with its peripheral capitalist concomitant, underdevelopment.[32]

One of the major adverse effects of this unequal division of labour was its tendency to restrict the capitalist mode of production from fully acting out its inherent dynamics. When it is unrestricted, capitalism tends progressively and systematically to disintegrate the pre-capitalist forms of production and spread capitalist relations, thereby improving the productive forces. In this way it played a revolutionary role in transforming the primitive pre-capitalist economies of Europe and Japan into very sophisticated modern productive capitalist systems. In Nigeria, the restrictive international division of labour does not allow capitalism the independence necessary to repeat this its historic role. For example, capital could not move to areas of cheap labour for the production of local pre-colonial goods and services, or modernize the pre-colonial system of production. It could not even engage in agriculture for local consumption. And it would not permit lateral transactions with other Third World countries, or vertical transactions with the socialist economies.

Colonialism and Loss of Self-Reliance

In essence, this triple phenomenon of loss of control over production to foreigners, external orientation of the economy, and the governance of the production process by a restrictive and unequal international division of labour controlled from outside, practically destroyed the self-reliance which characterized the pre-colonial economies of Nigeria. As a result, the local economy's production was beset by alienation and a consequent slide into contemporary underdevelopment. The more intensive the penetration of capital and the higher the level of commodity production and the accumulation of GNP per capita have become on the one hand, the more marked the disastrous socio-economic consequences have been on the other. Economic change following the rise of externally-induced capitalist relations in the colonial zone resulted in a miscarriage. The old production relations were built not on the ruins but among the remnants of the old. They became structurally associated with pre-colonial conditions because the steps of economic change were taken in forms, under conditions, and with consequences that erected obstacles to further change. The result was a pervasive alienation of the local population. Extraction and distribution rather than the creative production of new goods and services were instituted. Underdevelopment became the end product of national economic life, both in the short term and long term.

By self-reliance is meant an outlook or strategy of production which focusses attention primarily, but not exclusively, on domestic resources and priorities for the accomplishment of national objectives. It insists on the internal environment as the major source of the resources for economic life. By so doing, it forces the members of society to provide incentives for mobilizing local resources that otherwise would have lain idle, and to organize or reorganize domestic social, economic, and political relations in ways that are commensurate with local values and changes in them. It relates the needs of the members to their local physical and human environment and the means available in the society for accomplishing them; and it enables them to live co-operatively while simultaneously operating to change their surroundings for the greater welfare of the members. Critical to such an outlook are social commitment, fervour, and participation by the members of the society on a basis broader than a narrow ruling elite. These values arise because the economy is perceived to address itself to the everyday economic needs, resources, and problems of the vast majority of the population. The strategy emphasizes the maximum possible mobilization and improvement of existing local resources, needs, habitual consumption and production patterns, the minimization of waste in the extraction and allocation of these resources, the harnessing of all resources to the satisfaction of these needs and demands, and the activation of most of the country's potential wealth.

In addition, self-reliance provides the necessary criteria for insuring that local independence is maximized in spite of the country's need for some external resources. And it emphasizes a low-cost and high-benefit procurement of these resources, enjoining national planners to seek only mutually rewarding interdependent external transactions. This implies that a nation ought to avoid those interactions likely to jeopardize independence, distort the local pattern of socio-economic organization, or frustrate the development of a local capacity for innovative technology. Such a discriminatory approach to international transactions would minimize the traumas of external economic relations in a world of vested interests dominated by power.

When the pattern of production is foreign and strange in its ideas and practice it never sinks into the hearts and systems of the people. To them it becomes simply a brutality. The effort to fit them into its mould merely either causes natural growth to break the mould, or causes the mould to prevent natural growth. Therefore, no matter how good in theory a national production system may be, if it is the product of foreigners and demands their control, external orientation, and the predominant use of foreign resources, the local population cannot be psychologically and emotionally attuned to it. Consequently, it will evoke little or no enthusiasm on the part of the majority of the people, and will be largely irrelevant as a significant source of change in the society. Alienation at all levels of the production process would prevail.

The colonial production process, by destroying the self-reliance of Nigeria's pre-colonial economies, introduced for the first time pervasive alienation in the people's economic relations. Prior to this, alienation was limited to man's interaction with the physical environment. This was reflected in widespread superstition and pre-occupation with religious rituals. The first major source of alienation in the colonial economy arose from the divorce between what was consumed in the colonial economy and the local resources. In pre-colonial Nigeria, most of the items of consumption were created from local resources. Cotton which was grown in the local area with local seedlings, spun, handwoven, and dyed with colours obtained from local plants provided most of the clothing of the people. Virtually all the ginning, spinning, and weaving equipment was made of local wood. The iron rods used as pedals, and the iron bar upon which the finished strips of cloth were wound, were manufactured locally by the local blacksmiths using locally-mined iron ore.

In the pre-colonial economies, iron, gold, salt, and other minerals were mined locally and used directly in various manufacturing industries. Iron manufacturing industries existed in various areas, including the famous ones at Awka, Bida, Ilorin, and Ijebuode. They serviced other local industries which forged spears and arrows used for hunting and war, household tools, and tools of husbandry. Penelope Bower observes that the locally-manufactured iron used in the local hoes was of better quality than that later imported from Germany and sold very cheaply to undercut the local industry. Even then the Nigerian farmers continued to prefer the indigenous hoe.[33] Today, the industry has disappeared. No effort was made to modernize it. Other local manufacturing industries enabled the thriving of various specialized crafts such as the terracotta figures found in the tin fields around Nok as well as in the middle Benue valley, the brass figures and ornaments of Bida and Ife, and the bronze heads of Benin. Also, there was a well-developed glass manufacturing industry at Bida. And Bida again had a prosperous bead-manufacturing industry, as well as brass and copper industries.[34]

The timbers of Southern Nigeria were utilized in a very highly sophisticated wood industry which encouraged woodcarving for doors and other purposes. In the North a long-established leather industry was based on the hides of domesticated animals. Many of the resultant leather goods were marketed in notable centers such as Sokoto and Kano. They included saddlery, slippers, and handbags. Closely associated with the leather industry was the hide and skin industry which had a separate market of its own. The soap industry found in many areas, particularly in the South, used local resources. Similarly, local resources predominated in the making of alcoholic beverages. Palm wine was simply tapped from the readily available palm trees in the South. In the North beer was brewed from local corn and millet. Stronger beverages were brewed from palm wine and kolanuts. Basket-making, mat weaving, pottery, and the production of calabashes, beehives, and rope also emphasized the use of local resources.

Again, in the house-building industry, local resources were the only material input. As in the other areas of production, Nigerians did not have to wait for imported foreign materials in order to secure shelter. They used their own ingenuity to harness local materials to their own benefit. In many areas mud from the immediate surroundings was used to build the foundations and walls of houses. Dried palm leaves and other grasses were variously treated to serve as roofs for these houses. Decorative materials from plant parts were used to paint the walls and draw pictures on them. Doors, windows, and some of the roofing materials were made of local wood and timber. The semi-permanent rainy season settlements of the nomadic Fulani were a collection of beehive huts made of light poles and grass. Their temporary houses, occupied during migrations, were conical shelters quickly made of millet sticks. Progress required the modernization of these resources – not their abandonment.

In various other fields of life the total commitment to local resources was very clear. The various means of communication made use of local resources to serve local needs. This is most dramatically reflected by the talking drums made of local wood and animal skins and used to send messages to nearby villages on important occasions. The flute was similarly made and used. Even in the area of food production the immediate environment was made serviceable. Outstanding among the wild plant products used for food were palm oil, palm kernels, palm wine, shea butter, tigernuts, and locust beans. In addition, fish, wild animals, honey, wax, gum arabic, firewood, and timber were collected from the local surroundings. In addition, by-products of some field crops were converted into useful products: guinea cornstalks, used for fencing, building, or fuel; the tops of groundnuts and beans, and their husks, were used for fodder, or for composting; and livestock milk as well as the dung were useful.

To dismiss these resources and their use by our forefathers during pre-colonial times as primitive is to display a deep-seated colonial mentality and to ignore the lessons which can, and should, be learned from the experiences of our ancestors. Their use of local resources brought them into direct and relevant contact with nature, and gave them some collective and individual confidence that they could deal with it successfully and independently, no matter how limited their capacity to do this may seem from the present perspective. By organically relating these resources to their needs and creative energies they acquired a clear direction to life so crucial for human progress. In any case, their achievements have remained the only known products of the creative utilization of local resources to serve local needs. In spite of our so-called civilization and modern technology, we are not able to even duplicate these achievements. We cannot convert unmined raw iron ore into a hoe as our forefathers did without using one external resource or the other. Therefore, the question of transcending this pre-colonial Nigerian genius and creativity cannot arise. Instead of the path of creative improvements of what our forefathers achieved, we have taken the path of borrowing and showing off, or imitating, what foreigners have achieved in the use of their creative energies to harness their local resources to their local needs and consumption habits.

This imitation of foreign achievements led inevitably to the continued importation of the foreign needs and consumption habits which motivated them, and whose importation was initiated by the colonialists. The result was a neglect of the local needs and habitual consumption pattern of Nigerians. Local alienation from production followed. The colonialists encouraged this massive importation of goods and services in order 'to promote the commerce and industry of Great Britain.'[35] In fact, the secondary motive for the introduction of cash crops was to enable Nigerians to raise the money with which to purchase imports. Nigerian farmers regarded the major agricultural export products as 'cash crops', crops that were produced solely for making money. They developed such a casual attitude to production for export that very few of them ever regarded it as a business. Income from it was lavished on ostentatious imported consumer goods, and ceremonies.

Prior to 1946 Nigerian imports from Europe consisted of a large number of luxury items for which the local population gradually cultivated tastes. These included mirrors, beads, scissors, combs and bracelets. Some were substitutes for locally produced goods: gin, rum, cutlery, matches, salt, lamp oil, medicines, boats, needles, guns, gunpowder, and textile goods. The increasing importation of these foreign goods brought with it new tastes for goods from Europe and America. New colonial economic and social changes also led to the growth of imports. For example, the building of more Christian churches caused the importation of European building materials such as cement, corrugated iron sheets, steel rods, nails, hinges, and bolts. Musical instruments such as organs were brought in, as were books, bibles, encyclopedias, and dictionaries for church schools. Railway materials, motorcars, steam launches, soap, sewing machines and thread, and some electrical goods also featured.

At the same time Nigerians in the colonial zone began to produce, not for the satisfaction of their own needs and taste patterns, but for those of people in Europe. Of course, the production of food and other items for the satisfaction of basic needs and the traditional taste patterns continued in the colonial society. However, this took place not because of, but in spite of, the colonial economy. The colonialists would have preferred that all the palm produce and groundnuts of the country be exported, and that all labour should be directed toward production for export. In any event, they did nothing to encourage local consumption of palm produce and groundnuts, or the use of local labour for other than production for export.

Nigerians began to produce what they did not consume, and to consume what they did not produce. During the pre-colonial times Nigerian exports were essentially the excess of products consumed locally. Manufactured knives, cutlasses, and hoes constituted the farm implements. A system of markets linked various political units, with each acting as the host market in rotation. In these markets, what amounted to international trade took place. The level of such trade was low because most households produced what they consumed, with only the very limited surplus being available for sale. Trade with non-Nigerians was confined to the caravan trade, the slave trade with Europe, and trade in a few non-human commodities with Europeans. In all these cases, such trade affected only a very small percentage of the total trade, and exports were mostly surpluses of what were consumed locally. In many areas almost all the basic needs for food and shelter were met by household production, while the greater part of the other goods and services consumed were produced within a small circle of nearby villages. A very large proportion of the total economic effort was geared toward production for direct consumption within the household or political unit.

In many parts of the country, particularly in the South, the premier root crop – yam – but also cassava and cocoa yam which demanded less soil and yielded more abundantly and continuously, dominated farm production. But also an array of secondary crops was produced, including legumes, cereals, bush and tree fruits, varieties of beans, gourds, maize, groundnuts, bananas, coconuts, kola, local pears, raffia palms and peppers. Wild vegetable products were also collected from the surrounding bush. They included green leafy vegetables, as well as palm oil and palm wine. The production of non-agricultural food commodities was very minor, with goats, chickens, and trapped game as occasional products. In other areas, particularly the North, the staple crops of guinea corn and millet normally occupied about two-thirds to three-quarters of farm land. Other farm products included beans, groundnuts, cotton, sesame, ginger, indigo, sugar, calabashes, cassava, sweet potatoes, and onions. Guinea-corn and millet, together with beans and cassava, were the most essential household supplies, and most farms yielded at least small surpluses of these for marketing. Again, most of these products were consumed either within the household or the political unit, and exports were merely a small fraction of what was consumed locally. Thus in pre-colonial Nigeria, just as consumption was never divorced from the use of local resources, it was never divorced from the needs of the local population.

The divorce between consumption and need in the colonial economy created alienation in the new colonial society. The local population could not understand what production was for, and whom it was for. Above all, they could not comprehend why production had nothing to do with or say about their immediate needs. Together with the divorce between local resource use and consumption, this divorce between need and consumption created self-doubt, lack of confidence, and uncertainty in the production process. Production was carried on with resources and by some dynamics which were totally strange to the local population. And the motive for production was equally strange. Under the circumstances, Nigerians participated in production but gave no loyalty or made no deep commitment to the production process. They were in it, but not of it. Their relationship to the process was mechanical, not organic. What they needed from it was merely cash with which to pay their taxes and procure what to them could only be regarded as the luxuries emanating from the production system. There could not be, and was not, any patriotic identification with the production system, the national economy. The 'I–thou' relationship prevailed between the Nigerian and his economy.

Herein lies the origin and basis of the contemporary ills of unpatriotism, indiscipline, corruption, and tax evasion. The economy and socio-political relations built around it became merely sources of material benefits, and nothing more. The Nigerian would only put in enough labour to obtain the necessary rewards. And if he could obtain these benefits without having to exert himself, the better. As J. Mars correctly observes, the Nigerian was 'capable of a strict working discipline only in case of work of which his community approves. For all other work he needs what Americans contemptuously call a "speed boss".'[36] The idea of making any sacrifice for the society as a whole was to him as strange as the production system itself. Loyalty, patriotism, and social sacrifice were values to be associated with the village community or ethnic group which had relevance for his basic needs, and therefore his life. Hence, a Nigerian would be willing, if his means permitted, to donate ₦10,000 to a project in his village community but evade the payment of income tax amounting to only ₦500.

In the appropriation of resources from the state there could be no morality. By its abdication of any responsibility to serve the basic needs of the population, the state had lost any claims to moral action by the people in dealings with it. The relevant relationship was one of struggle between the individual and the state for who will get more out of the other. Anything official became a means of making money, morally or immorally. Politics, the civil service, the army, corporations, university, schools – all made sense only in terms of how much money one could make out of them in the short run.

Such political sermons as the so-called Jaji Declaration by General Obasanjo about the need for morality and discipline in social life can only fall on deaf ears. They do not, and probably cannot, address themselves to the causes of the problems. Corruption, indiscipline, ostentatious display of wealth earned in the colonial and neo-colonial economy, tax evasion, circumvention of national laws, and the unpatriotic undermining of national goals in the interest of foreigners are social, rather than biological or psychological, problems. Their answers must be sought in creating the social conditions that will attract the loyalty, commitment and fervour of the population. to their local resources, needs, and traditional consumption habits in a modern and satisfactory manner.

Quite apart from this alienating aspect of colonial production, there is also the whole question of the negative consequences for development arising from the essential character and pattern of organization of colonial production. Since profit maximization and the satisfaction of foreign needs and consumption patterns were the motive forces of colonial production, colonial investments tended to be concentrated in a very small sector of the economy where the incomes were high. This involved primarily economic activities that fed the world market with primary products and those which catered for the high income market for imported manufactured consumer goods. This pattern of economic activities led to the progressive stagnation of income-earning opportunities in food production and to a continuing decrease in the capacity of the industrial sector to provide in part its own needs for intermediate and capital goods in order to process the nation's primary products to a more valuable stage before exportation.

Above all, it severely limited the size of the local colonial market. One of the effects of colonial foreign private investment was the absence of a moderate income internal market of the kind which stimulated economic growth in the rich capitalist countries during their pre-industrial stage. On the production side, only the proportionately few peasant cash crop farmers, some middlemen, and foreign managers and technicians of mining enterprises participated. In relation to consumer goods, the wealthiest and most prestigious segment of the local and foreign population provided the major participants. The very few that were included were expatriate officials and entrepreneurs, the local large-scale cash crop farmers, the big local traders, senior civil servants, the higher levels of the foreign firms who were Nigerians, and secondary schoolteachers. Since they enjoyed a disproportionate share of the economic surplus in the country, they were financially able to participate. The limited income of the middle-income civil servants and semi-skilled labour force significantly constrained the type and amount of the imported goods they could consume.

Consisting of the unskilled labour force, the urban unemployed and underemployed, and the mass of subsistence farmers, the majority of the population could only marginally afford these consumer items. Consequently, the size of the local colonial market was severely restricted. The colonialists could afford to ignore the negative effects of this limited size because the foreign firms operated in a global network which guaranteed them an economy of scale, and of which the Nigerian market was a very insignificant fraction. The answer to this problem of market size is not regional integration, as we are meant to believe, even though this is itself a positive development. Only by a radical transformation of the structures of supply and demand away from the external to the domestic environment, in a manner relevant to the basic needs and traditional taste patterns of Nigerians, can this distortion of economic life be arrested and the foundation laid for genuine economic growth.

Foreigh investment dominated colonial economic activities. But the foreign owners and directors of enterprises did not feel any attachment or patriotic duty to the country. They operated only when the risks did not exceed a certain maximum likely in their home country, and when the profit prospects were much larger than in their home country. The desire for a higher degree of capital security was also much stronger in the colony than in the metropole because of the much greater severity of economic fluctuations in the former.[37] Few foreign investors are likely to be interested in investing in the exporting activities of a poor country which faces inelastic world demand for food, increasing substitution of chemical for primary products, and competition from protected producers in the rich countries. Hence, although between 1870 and 1936 foreign private capital supplied about 53½ per cent of all external funds in Nigeria, considering that there was no restriction on, and every encouragement for, private investment, this was a small percentage.[38]

An example of the high profits which attracted foreign firms to the Nigerian colonial economy was the cocoa trade in the 1930s: they made a profit of 6.3 per cent on turnover eacy year. This was an excessive profit, bearing in mind that a profit of 2½ per cent on turnover was considered quite good, and firms were not dissatisfied with a profit of 1 per cent.[39] Such firms usually had a monopsonistic position in the demand for labour; they were usually the sole buyers of labour in their areas of operation. But even where several firms operated, they often had a tacit or explicit agreement as to wages for local labour. And the wages were usually poor.[40]

This excessive emphasis on profits by the foreign firms also had its corollary, the drainage of investable funds from Nigeria. As subsidiaries of giant business empires whose overall investment programs were planned at the headquarters in the advanced capitalist countries, the foreign enterprises transferred their net surpluses to the headquarters for allocation in the worldwide network of activities within the parent firms' financial empires. Hence in 1936, the total estimated fixed assets of the Nigerian mining firms amounted to ₦312,000 which was less than their estimated total transfer abroad of ₦370,000.[41] Capital invested in tin mining, for example, decreased gradually until in 1936 it was less than its level in 1929.[42] The process of this reduction was voluntary liquidation of companies followed generally by the purchase of their assets by other companies at a reduced rate, or occasionally by the formation of a new company in the same name but with less capital.[43]

All the business profits of the foreign firms, their creditorial interests and their surplus liquid assets, such as reserve capital, depreciation reserves, and surplus cash were immediately transferred abroad, without any attempt to find some use for them inside the country.[44] Such transfers were particularly damaging because, although between 1934 and 1938 about 25 per cent of national capital came from these firms, only between 11 per cent and 13.8 per cent of the domestic income was generated by them.[45]

In addition, an unjustifiably large part of the tax on the incomes of foreign enterprise was transferred to Britain or other parts of the British empire as a result of the income tax relief provisions. For example, in 1943, the standard profits of these firms were taxed at the rate of ₦1 in the pound, of which Nigeria received 50k and Britain got 50k. The excess profits were taxed at the rate of ₦2 in the pound, of which Nigeria received only 50k while Britain got ₦1.50k.[46] Similarly, their expatriate employees transferred parts of their salary abroad. A large part of this salary, 40–50 per cent, was transferred during the early colonial period. And the larger part of the tax on this salary was appropriated by the British government.[47] Also, the rigid currency system of the country compelled national loans to be raised in the London money market instead of from the currency authority. This increased the country's cost of borrowing which, from 1919 to 1935, varied between 2.7 per cent and 17.4 per cent. Again, it compelled contributions to a sinking fund even when the loan was merely used as a fiduciary cover for the permanently localized currency circulation, thus increasing the annual burden of the loan.[48] In addition to this outflow of funds, which was usually reflected in the balance of payments figures of the country, the foreign firms also repatriated funds through profits on the importation of machinery, over-invoicing of other imports bought from or through affiliated companies and branches, under-invoicing of exports sold to or through affiliated companies or branches, remittances of payments to overseas head offices for management fees, royalties, and agency fees.

This massive drainage of funds from Nigeria together with the country's very high propensity to import arising from its external orientation and its governance by an externally-directed international division of labour, rendered its self-sustained economic growth virtually impossible. In fact, it promoted self-sustained economic underdevelopment. Profits derived from business activities in Nigeria were invested elsewhere and hardly in the local economy. In other words, the multiplier effect of such profits occurred outside the country. The dynamic element of the local economy was inoperative. Similarly, the high propensity to import and the transfer of part of expatriate incomes abroad meant that incomes generated locally were spent on goods produced abroad. As a result, incomes and profits were generated abroad for foreign industries and not locally, causing further investment and growth to take effect abroad and not locally. The accelerator effect occurred abroad.

Then there is the adverse effect of the economy on managerial skills and innovative technology within the country. The shareholders, boards of directors, and head officers of the foreign firms were jealous of their power and, therefore, were unwilling to share it. Hence, they appointed agents in the colony who had much less authority than area managers. Their functions were purely administrative and rarely entrepreneurial in character, centered around the routine tasks of the monthly stocktaking, prevention of fraud, and supervision of clerks. They were provided with fixed prices for buying and for selling their goods and services. This emphasis on low-level manpower restricted the value which the services of first-rate managers could bring to the local art of management and entrepreneurship. The country was, therefore, exposed only to middle-range ideas and information, and to routine business processes. Consequently, it tended to acquire a middle-range and imitative attitude to problems of management.

Similarly, it acquired an imitative rather than innovative attitude to technology. The headquarters of the foreign firms were the first to innovate products, techniques, and equipment. Thereafter, these innovations were spread as widely and quickly as possible through the network of enterprises extending to the periphery. This was a profitable exercise because in the short run the overall cost of production was well below its sale if the product were spread widely. Therefore, the foreign firms had an interest in forestalling and preventing new, different, and independent centers of technological innovation which might hamper the acceptance and spread of their products. The only reasonable long-term solution to this problem of promoting technological innovation is a relevant scientific education which focuses on the local environment, is motivated by the needs of a self-reliant production process, and emphasizes the acquisition of innovative attitudes and skills by the masses in order to enable them to change their immediate environment through the production process and with means available in the society.

Again, the colonial economy was fragmented. In fact, there was no national economy in the sense of an internally interdependent, integrated, co-ordinated, and cohesive system of economic activities. Instead, the economy was characterized by a series of activities carried on by foreign firms and closely co-ordinated and interdependent with activities in the advanced capitalist societies. National economic integration in Nigeria was never part of this foreign economic calculus. The cocoa produced in the West, the groundnuts and tin in the North, and the palm produce of the East were not used in factories situated anywhere in Nigeria. There were no serious economic links across the various geographical and economic regions of the country. These areas remained isolated from one another without any salient economic exchanges among them.

Such a false, disarticulated, and non-cohesive economy impeded the development of equitable and mutually-rewarding economic exchanges among the various regions and population of the country. But such interactions were critical for fostering a beneficial internal division of labour, adequate and extensive resource mobilization, and the promotion of mutual economic interests and understanding among Nigerians so necessary for generating momentum in the economy. Under the circumstances, it was very difficult to lay a firm foundation for promoting increased employment, higher living standards and more rapid economic progress. In addition, the fragmented colonial economy created opportunities for microeconomic and political nationalism destructive of national integration and balanced economic growth of the country. The area interested in the export-import economy had no need of the rest of the country, which may indeed have seemed a burden upon it. It could, therefore, contemplate a micro-independence, or prevent more efficient labour and other resources from other parts of the country from being utilized in its activities.

The colonial process of urbanization in Nigeria also adversely affected economic growth. In a self-reliant and progressive economy, urban centers are organically related to economic activities in the rural areas. For example, the various pre-colonial cities of Nigeria such as Ibadan, Kano, and Sokoto arose as a result of growth in production above the needs and wants of the local population. The resultant surplus enabled a veritable division of labour in which individuals specialized in trade, crafts, and administration, in addition to agriculture. The urban areas provided the necessary infrastructure to the practitioners of the specialized activities. These specialized urban professional groups were organically related to the food producers, providing them with the necessary implements for improved agricultural production in exchange for food and other farm produce. On the contrary, the colonial cities were not similarly organically related to the growth of food production and the irrelevance of some individuals in that process, or to the emergence of locally relevant specialization of functions. This abnormal and distorted pattern of urbanization failed to uproot the urbanite from his rural base. He was in the city but not of it. He worked there but diverted his savings to his village.[49] More importantly, it adversely affected food production, the integrity of village life, and employment in the country. Those who migrated to the colonial urban centers, far from being those who had become irrelevant in food production, were the young men who were essential for its productivity. Their exodus marked the beginning of, and set the pace for, the decline of local food production and the decay of village life, with nothing yet to replace its functions for the local population. Similarly, the growth of unemployment later became a persistent feature of colonial and neo-colonial economic life. Since the pre-colonial skills could not be used in the colonial scheme of things, massive unemployment was inevitable and more and more people migrated to the cities. At the same time colonial propaganda painted a much rosier picture of life in the colonial zone than in the pre-colonial setting, causing people to enter colonial life much faster than the economy could provide them with jobs. These effects were reinforced by the colonial tailoring of employment to the profit motive. Just sufficient employment was given as was deemed suitable to maintain the enormous profits reaped by the foreign enterprises. And the interest of the foreign firms in using equipment and services from their home countries also contributed to unemployment. Such equipments were developed where labour was relatively costly, and capital was relatively abundant. Therefore, they tended to be more capital-intensive and labour-saving than was warranted by the resource condition of Nigeria, where there was very little capital and a desperate desire for employment.

In another respect the colonial economy adversely affected economic growth in Nigeria because it led to the dominance of tertiary over the more productive primary and secondary economic activities. The major engines of economic development are primary economic activities such as agriculture for basic needs and, especially, manufacturing for basic needs. But in early colonial Nigeria economic activities tended to concentrate in the tertiary sector of the economy – import-export trade, insurance, banking, wholesale and retail trade, contract and professional work – where it was easy to make huge profits in a very short time. Thus, for example, during the 1930s about 72 per cent of the total foreign capital expended in Nigeria was invested in the produce business.[50] During this period hardly any foreign capital was invested in agriculture or manufacturing. Up till today the foreign banks have refused to give loans to agriculture for food production.

There was also the negative consequence for economic growth of the intersectoral inequality introduced by the role of foreign private capital. By concentrating wealth in the colonial economic zone, it hampered domestic savings. The empirical study of an international sample of poor countries indicates that the rate of savings is negatively correlated with income inequality. It shows that under the circumstances, it is extremely difficult to mobilize the rural areas for national economic development.[51] In fact, the bulk of the incomes of the wealthy elements in a colonial society, especially of the trading, usurious, finance, and banking sectors, landowners, feudal and semi-feudal elements, is utilized for non-productive consumption. This enables the upper classes to live in luxury at the level of ultra-modern Western standards. But this pattern of life sharply reduces the potential accumulation fund and creates a home market that is extremely unfavourable for economic growth.

Finally, of course, the colonial economy destroyed the independence of the local population, rendering the people powerless to reorganize their internal and external economic activities in ways they deemed necessary for their material and spiritual welfare. As a result, the pride, self-esteem, and sense of dignity of the population were lowered, thereby reducing national morale, confidence, and the desire to participate positively in national affairs. This made it difficult to mobilize enough human energy for economic development. Hardly any trade existed between Nigeria and the Soviet Union, the only socialist state during the early colonial period. And only very minor economic relations existed between Nigeria and the other African countries. The trade between Africa and Nigeria never exceeded 2 per cent of total trade. The colonialists encouraged only economic relations with the advanced capitalist nations and discouraged others.

At the foreign exchange level the rigid exchange system imposed by colonialism did not permit the increase and decrease of the local currency to be determined by the internal currency needs. The local currency was automatically tied to the balance of payments, and issued and redeemed in pound sterling at a 100 per cent exchange standard. This caused deflationary effects in the country. Thus, for example, during the 1921–1930 period the average amount of the localized state money decreased by 29.56 per cent while the average annual exports decreased by 20.4 per cent.[52] This dependence of the volume of the local currency upon the balance of payments was also particularly harmful to Nigeria because of the high propensity to consume imported consumer goods, which aggravated the deflationary effects on the domestic prices whenever there was a depression in the world market for Nigerian exports. Such a monetary system, which kept its monetary reserves in London, also precluded any central banking activity so crucial for varying at will the volume of the localized currency in order to promote full employment, a high real income, and prosperity as a whole. And the rigid exchange system did not permit the use of Nigerian government loans as cover for permanently localized currency and did not allow any variation of the exchange rate if the purchasing power of the London pound was manipulated to the detriment of Nigeria or if the Nigerian balance of payment was fundamentally disequilibrated for other reasons.

All these constraints hampered local economic development. Therefore, even the colonial system of production imposed on the country was itself very defective and restricted. This fact has motivated both the later colonial and neo-colonial political administrators of the economy to propose and, in cases carry out, reforms designed to remedy these defects and remove the restrictions. They have acted and continue to act as if these were the major problems of the country's production process. And the academic apologists of the colonial and neo-colonial system of production encourage this attitude by devoting all of their creative energies to the struggle against these defects. But their successful elimination will leave unsolved the larger and more critical problems – the alienation of the total population from production, the consequent spiritual crisis of confidence, and the crisis of self and group identity so damaging to self-sustained growth in production – which arise from the very nature and existence of the colonial production process. The resolution of these crises cannot, therefore, be a matter of reform, but of revolution.

Consolidation and Expansion, 1946–60

In the light of the above discussion, it is obvious that the question of underdevelopment and development in colonial and neo-colonial Nigeria is not one that can be decided on the basis of statistical indices such as Gross Domestic Product (GDP), income per capita, level of capital formation, and the relationship of all these to the rate of increase of population. It is a spiritual (not in the religious sense) question of the relationship of the population to the production process. The closest that one can probably come to its indicators would be (a) the degree of divergence between the use of local resources in production and foods consumed within the economy, and (b) the degree of divergence between consumption and the needs of the vast majority of the population. The greater these divergences are, the greater the underdevelopment. And the less the divergences, the greater the development.[53] Convergence is best achieved by the application of modern scientific knowledge by the indigenous population to the transformation of local resources in the direction of providing the equipment, secondary and tertiary resources, and the food needed by the vast majority of the population.

During the post-Second World War period, colonialism did nothing to promote such a convergence. Instead, it intensified the early colonial pattern of economic activities, thereby increasing divergence and, therefore, underdevelopment. The export-import character of the economy was consolidated; the propensity to import increased; exports continued to be divorced from the local consumption of the vast majority rather than the surplus of what was consumed locally; imports still bore no relation to local needs or traditional taste patterns; and imports continued to be a high rather than a marginal percentage of the local consumption that was motivated by the colonial economy. In addition, external rather than internal conditions continued to determine major activities, and the external control of local economic activities persisted in spite of changes in the international division of labour.

Thus, for example, the volume of Nigerian exports increased by 45 per cent from 1948 to 1954, and by 56 per cent from 1954 to 1962.[54] The revenue of the country hinged on export and import taxes. In 1951 about 55.4 per cent of total federal government revenue (74.7 per cent in 1956 and 70.1 per cent in 1960) were made up of customs and excise taxes. Import and export taxes made up the bulk of these.[55] 'Improvements in agriculture were confined largely to export crops, which doubled in value from 1950 to 1960, while food crops increased by about 50 per cent from 1950 to 1957.'[56] In support of export crop production, there emerged various credit and marketing mechanisms. The most notable of these were the marketing boards. But agricultural marketing co-operatives, as well as co-operative banks, were also formed.

On the import side there was even a much greater increase. Between 1948 and 1954 imports increased by 258 per cent, and between 1950 and 1960 they increased by 192 per cent.[57] As usual, the emphasis was on manufactured consumer goods, which accounted for about 60 per cent of the total imports. As social projects proliferated, the Nigerian petty bourgeoisie increased in size and its appetite for Western goods expanded rapidly. An increase in imports became inevitable. Apart from its effect on the consolidation of the colonial pattern of production, this increase in imports also helped to drastically diminish the nation's foreign reserves and create a balance-of-payments problem for the country. With some efforts at import-substitution manufacturing, the import of capital equipment for the factories also increased, accounting for about 30 per cent of the total imports.

As was the case during the early colonial period, external conditions continued to exert the dominant influence on internal economic life. The needs of Europe and America for post-Second World War reconstruction increased the export trade of Nigeria, and consequently the income of its cash crop farmers, and governmental revenue from export taxes. Export values increased from ₦47.4 million in 1946 to ₦259.6 million in 1955 and ₦331.2 million in 1960.[58] This export boom was reinforced by the need for resources with which to prosecute the Korean War (1950–1953). As the United States stockpiled columbite for the war, Nigerian export of columbite increased. (The United States offered a 100 per cent bonus for all purchases.) In addition, both export and import prices increased as a result of the devaluation of the pound sterling in 1949.

Soon, however, the export bubble of the late 1940s and early 1950s burst. Beginning from 1955 economic recession in Europe caused the world demand for Nigerian products to be weakened. At the same time synthetics were developed in these countries as substitutes for some of the primary products, notably cotton, rubber, and vegetable oils. There was also a rapid world-wide expansion of primary products, most of whose supply is inelastic. Consequently, when demand fell, prices had to fall. Therefore, the period 1955–60 was characterized by wide fluctuations of Nigeria's export prices. Thus, for example, in 1955, although Nigerian exports and re-exports increased in volume by 7,000 tons, their value fell by ₦34 million.[59]

The declining receipts from exports occurred at a time of an increasing import bill. First, with increased social services, more imports came into the country. And second, the prices of imports were generally higher than those of exports, with a consequent deterioration of the terms of trade. The country began to run deficits in its balance of payments and to draw down the reserves it had built up during the boom period. Nigeria moved from the strong financial position of the pre-1955 period to one of greater dependence on foreign sources of investment funds. Hence, the 1955/56–1961/62 Development Plan expected 22 per cent of all investment funds to come from foreign sources, the highest percentage at any time.[60]

The colonialists also encouraged the dominance of external forces, as is reflected in the encouragement which they gave to foreign investors in the country. Such incentives were contained in the Aid to Pioneer Industries Ordinance of 1952, which relieved 'pioneer industries' from the payment of company tax during the first two years of their operation and for a further one or three years depending on the size of their fixed capital expenditure; the Income Tax (Amendment) Ordinance of 1952, which exempted part of their profits and fixed capital assets from taxation; the Industrial Development Ordinance of 1957, which made the government subsidize the purchase of some of the imported inputs into manufacturing industries; the Industrial Development Ordinance of 1958, which extended the length of the tax holidays of new industries; the Customs Duties Ordinance of 1958, which protected industries from the effects of dumping from outside the country; and the Customs Regulation of 1958, which exempted certain imports of industries from import duties. In fact, in 1959 the Investment Company of Nigeria was created in part to attract more foreign investment to the private sector. Above all, the government gave a guarantee that dividends and profits could be freely repatriated.

Consequently, foreign investment in the colonial economy of Nigeria grew from ₦23.4 million in 1954 to ₦41 million in 1959/60.[61] Such investment inevitably reinforced external control of the production process established during the early colonial period and, therefore, the adverse effects on national self-reliance arising from that control, notably the divergence between local resource use and consumption, and the divergence between consumption and local needs. Both the colonial governments and foreign firms invested generally in small-scale, export-oriented, consumption-oriented activities, and import-substitution manufacturing requiring large foreign inputs and motivated by foreign needs and taste patterns.

The infrastructural support for the export-import economy was also expanded. Various export product research institutes were created. In 1951 the West African Research Institute was formed as an expansion to Nigeria of the Cocoa Research Institute formed in Ghana in 1938. Also the Benin Oil Palm Research Station created in 1939 was transformed into the West African Oil Palm Research Institute. And the West African Maize Research Unit was established. Others included the Central Research Organization at Ibadan and Samaru, the Northern Regional Stock Farm at Shika, the Agricultural Research Station at Samaru, and the Institute of Applied Technical Research. In addition, the government established a Council of National Resources of Nigeria to co-ordinate the research programs of these establishments.

Water supplies, transport, and communications were improved to help foreign enterprises. In order to solve the land tenure problem, the colonial governments created a number of industrial estates which were rented to foreign industrialists. The industrial estates at Enugu, Port Harcourt, Kano, Kaduna, Zaria, and Ikeja near Lagos are good examples. The Bornu railway extension was initiated. Nigerian Airways was created, leading to the improvement of aerodromes and airports. The port facilities at Lagos, Port Harcourt, and Koko were improved or expanded. And a great deal of funds was invested in social services, including free primary education, expanded secondary and university education, and health and other social welfare services.

By far the most important development of this period concerned the emergence of a sizeable Nigerian petty bourgeoisie and comprador bourgeoisie with an objective interest in the consolidation and reproduction of this colonial pattern of economic life, the growth in size and power of these classes, and their assumption of the political leadership of the Nigerian masses. In these classes the colonialists found an instrument for the reproduction of the colonial pattern of economic life. Their members had acquired, were acquiring, and were encouraged to acquire, vested interests and privileges in this alienating colonial economy. The petty bourgeoisie comprised essentially those in the professions, teaching, petty trading, the middle and upper echelons of the African section of the civil service, the middle and upper ranks of the army, and the petty contractors, businessmen, and independent artisans. The comprador elements consisted of those in the export-import business, wholesale trade, produce merchants, and large-scale cash crop farmers.

These classes were pemitted by the colonialists to use the regional governments, which they controlled, to build up considerable vested interests in the colonial economy. Through the public purse they made loans for business ventures to themselves and members of their class, exploited business and contract opportunities and facilities available in the country to their own advantage, acquired considerable landed resources and property, and enjoyed immense privileges and advantages in the distribution of social welfare services such as housing, scholarships, education, health, and cultural facilities. They soon moved into the colonialists' housing quarters, adopted the colonialists' consumption habits, particularly for imported consumer goods, and enjoyed the colonialists' salary scales and innumerable fringe benefits. Even the colonialists' habit of transfering and banking their savings abroad was emulated. Their new life-style, pattern of income, social prestige, consumption habits, social and economic privileges, and even political power, became closely linked to the continuation and reproduction of the colonial economy. Inevitably, they became the greatest local apologists and advocates of the colonial pattern of economic activities. To do otherwise, of course, would have clearly undercut the basis of their social prestige and political power, and exposed their parasitic and dependent role in the economy and the total irrelevance of the economy to the needs of the majority of the population and local resources.

In addition, the demonstration effect of the life-style of the petty bourgeoisie and comprador bourgeoisie helped to spread the colonialists' propaganda on behalf of the colonial economy. As the new men of wealth in a society which had come to worship wealth, members of these classes became the leaders of the nation. As such they were well-placed to become the objects of emulation by the rest of the population. In this way the pattern of consumption which could only be satisfied by the prevailing pattern of colonial economic life was legitimized. Attention was thus diverted from the search for a more viable alternative economic system to ways and means of attaining petty bourgeois and comprador bourgeois fortunes within the colonial economic system. This was reinforced by the continuing propaganda of the colonialists on behalf of the colonial economy. Groups and movements, such as the Zikist National Vanguard, desirous of an alternative production process were ruthlessly suppressed by the colonial authorities. Contact with the socialist countries was virtually banned, an intensive communist witchhunt was mounted, the educational system dripped with anti-communist literature and theoretical frameworks, the intelligence apparatus and the army were geared and trained to hunt down and eliminate all those opposed to the colonial economic system. Only reforms rather than revolutionary transformation would be tolerated.

The major reform of the economy during this period of colonialism concerned the manufacturing sector. Between 1950 and 1960 manufacturing production increased 398 per cent.[62] And it came in the wake of a shift in the international division of labour which assigned import-substitution industrialization to the country and which required the importation of capital equipment from the advanced capitalist countries. For the first time manufacturing began to be taken seriously. As already indicated, various incentives were created to attract and promote manufacturing in the country. As a result the industrial sector grew rapidly during this period. The value-added in manufacturing establishments employing ten or more people increased by more than 25-fold from ₦5.4 million in 1950 to ₦137.2 million in 1964.[63] Again, foreign firms predominated in this new and growing area of colonial economic life. For example, in 1963, of the 321 limited companies in this field, 68 per cent of the paid-up share capital was foreign.[64]

Nevertheless, the new manufacturing activity further reduced self-reliance and the use of local resources, and increased external dependence and the propensity to import. For example, in 1949 the Kano Citizens Trading Company's textile mill in Kano purchased reconditioned British looms and equipment at a time when the Lancashire industry in Britain was discarding old equipment and re-equipping itself with newer and more modern machinery. Similarly, in 1955, the Kaduna Textiles Ltd., imported all of its machinery from the United Kingdom, the United States, and Switzerland. And the 'Star' beer of the Nigerian Brewery Company founded in 1949 was manufactured from imported hops and malt.[65] All the import-substitution industries for the manufacture of cement, metal window frames, asbestos, cement products, aluminium products, pre-stressed concrete, textiles and textile beddings, cigarettes, soap, margarine, and plastics similarly imported virtually all their equipment and some of their raw materials from the advanced capitalist countries.

Another important reform of the colonial economy was initiated in the monetary sphere. In 1959 a new Central Bank of Nigeria took over the activities of the West African Currency Board. It began to make fiduciary issue of currency. And it also began to remedy some of the other deficiencies of the Currency Board indicated earlier. However, like the reform in manufacturing, this reform of the currency system was motivated by the desire to eliminate some of the obvious and crude defects of the colonial economic system in order to improve its value to the foreign firms and their local beneficiaries. It did not address itself to the question of narrowing the ever-widening gap between local resource use and consumption on the one hand and between consumption and local needs on the other, and the consequent alienation and immobilization of the creative energies of the bulk of the population. Instead, as the gap widened further and further, underdevelopment not only became consolidated but intensified. Most of the problems of the early colonial economy either persisted or worsened.

Neo-colonialism and Underdevelopment: 1960–80

The attainment of political independence in 1960 constituted a landmark in the history of Nigeria. The foreign control of the national apparatus of state was ended, and with it the indignity, degradation, and national humiliation that accompanied that control. The forces of national self-assertiveness and emancipation achieved an important victory. But success was confined to the political realm. The battle for economic emancipation, dignity, and progress was yet to be waged. In spite of political independence the pattern of production and economic activities forcibly instituted by colonialism survived unscathed. In fact, it grew stronger and more formidable than before. The nationalist movement made no significant effort to question the colonial export-import economy. Therefore, they neglected the consequences of that economy for the marginalization of the vast majority of the Nigerian population, distortion of the consumption pattern, neglect of local needs and resources, restriction of the capitalist mode of production from disintegrating the pre-capitalist modes and increasing production in accordance with its own internal dynamics, predominance of tertiary activities over the more productive primary and secondary sectors, the expatriation of profits to foreign countries and, therefore, the loss of the benefits accruing from investments made with them, the high propensity to import and, consequently, the loss of benefits that would accrue from the use of the relevant income to purchase goods and services within the country, and the confinement of the nation to the realm of imitative, rather than innovative, technology.

The inherited pattern of production has not only persisted, it has been reinforced and strengthened by the expansion of its activities, greater orientation to the external environment, and growing divergence between local resource use and consumption on the one hand and consumption and local needs on the other. With the increased activities in the fields of manufacturing, importation, and construction industry occasioned by the growth in oil wealth, the country is more than ever before integrated into the world capitalist system in a manner which destroys self-reliance, increases external dependence, and leads to the external control of local economic life. Underdevelopment has intensified.

This intensification has been possible largely because of the class character of the leadership of the nationalist movement. The economic motivations ot the petty bourgeoisie and comprador bourgeoisie which led the struggle did not seek to make a break with the colonial production process. Members of these classes merely sought promotion within the hierarchical system of distributing the benefits of that process, particularly between them and the foreign bourgeoisie which controlled production. They had no objective interests in abandoning an economic system which guaranteed their economic provileges, social prestige, and political power. In order to improve their benefits from it they were, of course, willing to make those reforms which did not threaten their privileged position. Hence, the production relations arising from the colonial and neo-colonial system of production have not been tampered with; they are hardly ever mentioned.

Thus, one of the most significant developments of the neo-colonial period is the growth in the size and power of those local classes with vested interests in the reproduction of the inherited colonial production process. Over the years increased urbanization, greater opportunities for education, particularly at the post-secondary level, proliferation of public projects, and increased economic opportunities at the supervisory level of the economy have produced an increased and increasing number of people who have joined the ranks of the privileged classes. Many more people now than before have joined the public service at the senior service level; there are many more indigenous contractors, doctors, engineers, and members of other professions; the number of people in petty trading, small-scale industries, import-export trade, wholesale trade, and in the teaching and nursing professions has grown tremendously.

These privileged classes have increased their power through the use of public funds to build private financial empires. This practice, which first came to light during the late colonial period, became more widespread during the neo-colonial period. Politicians seized on their control of public funds to provide themselves, their friends, and relatives with much-needed investible capital funds. Additionally, they used governmental power and resources to create investment opportunities for themselves. Public funds provided investment and loan capital to private firms and individuals. Commercial contracts were awarded by the governments and their statutory corporations, making it good business to have the right political connections. Commercial patronage such as government loans, licensing, and contracting were channelled through public agencies that were political in character. The Coker Commission of 1962 exposed the elaborate program for this embourgeoisement of the petty bourgeoisie and comprador elements.

Such practices reached alarming proportions during the 1970s when top civil servants turned contracts awarded by their Ministries into avenues for amassing wealth, either by setting up private companies to obtain the contract, or receiving commissions for awarding the contract to other companies. The 10 per cent commission institutionalized by the politicians pervaded all segments of public life. Contractors receiving public contracts (virtually all) inflated their costs as a means of making fabulous profits. Consequently, contract work became a very lucrative enterprise. Many ventured into it. They invaded the public sector and emptied it of its content, initiating the practive whereby public enterprises now operate essentially through private contracting firms.

Hence, the malpractices and malfeasance of public officers revealed by the numerous public inquiries which came in the wake of the coup of July 1975 have been more widespread, brazen, and callous than those revealed by the preceding Foster-Sutton Tribunal of 1957 and the Coker inquiries of 1962. And just as the advent of military rule forced the ex-politicians to turn into very successful businessmen, the retirement exercises of 1975–77 arising from these inquiries have led to a new crop of successful businessmen constituted by the ex-public servants. With their vastly increased wealth, both the ex-politicians and ex-civil servants have once again imposed their political leadership on the people. This flexibility, versatility, and resillience of our corrupt elite reflect their increased and increasing power in the society. And underlying this power is their successful acquisition of vested interests in the inherited colonial production process.

An increasingly important method of acquiring vested interests and wealth in the economy has been the comprador elements' practice of inviting and joining foreign firms as junior partners, field representatives, or high executives. In this way they join the foreigners in their exploitation of national resources. Such practices reached their most perfidious extremes in the cement scandal of 1974–75, when Nigerian businessmen colluded with foreigners to exploit the port congestion for the purposes of defrauding the country of large sums of money. But on a much lesser scale, through the receipt of commissions and the acceptance of positions in foreign firms, Nigerian compradors are carrying on the same practice legitimately.

Indigenization is the latest instrument of the privileged classes for acquiring more vested interests in the neo-colonial economy and increasing their power and wealth.[66] With the indigenization of the public services now virtually complete, these classes have turned toward the indigenization of foreign economic activities for the improvement of their financial position, but under the cloak of economic nationalism. However, even within the indigenized enterprises, foreign influence has persisted because the enterprises' ethos, symbols, values, life-styles, relations of production, and modes of operation have all continued to derive from the imperative of exploiting local resources for the benefit of metropolitan capital. Such factors constitute strong built-in pressures on local entrepreneurs to conform to the wishes of foreign interests. Therefore, instead of the enterprises becoming more and more national in the use of local resources and the satisfaction of the needs of the vast majority of the population, it is in fact the new local owners of the firms who become de-nationalized. They abdicate their patriotism and carry on the same pattern of activities as before indigenization. In fact, the interests of the privileged classes in indigenization lie merely in their share of the profits of these enterprises. Thus, the most powerful segment of the Nigerian population has acquired enormous vested economic interests in the reproduction of the inherited colonial pattern of production and, therefore, in the reproduction of underdevelopment.

Another major development of the post-colonial economic system has been the dominant position of petroleum in the export posture of the country. The importance of this product in the country's Gross Domestic Product (GDP) has grown from 0.9 per cent in 1960 to 45.5 per cent in 1975. Petroleum now accounts for about 98 per cent of total export earnings. In 1974/5 it accounted for 94 per cent of these earnings. The growth rate of GDP in 1972/3 was 12 per cent with petroleum accounting for 5 per cent and the rest of the economy for 7 per cent. But in 1975 petroleum and other mining industries employed only 0.39 per cent of the population compared with 63.99 per cent by agriculture. Today, petroleum is the mainstay of the Nigerian economy. And its value lies essentially in its character as an export product, earning enormous revenues and foreign exchange. Between 1973 and 1975 the country's balance of payments would have been in deficit both in the current and capital accounts without oil. The upturns and downturns in petroleum production now decide the health of the neo-colonial economy. In 1974/5 the oil sector grew by 36 per cent, while the economy grew by 14 per cent and agriculture and manufacturing grew by a mere 1.2 per cent and 2 per cent respectively from the previous year's level. And when during the following year there was a cutback in petroleum production the economy slumped to a shameful growth rate of 2.8 per cent in 1976. In 1977 and 1978 severe austerity was imposed throughout the economy because of the sluggishness in the sale of petroleum.

Thus, the Nigerian economy deteriorated rapidly to that characteristic of a typical colonial economy – total dependence on one export product. The high world market rate for petroleum and the enormous revenue derived from it have tended to obscure the obvious danger of such a monocultural economy. And they have prevented the full effects of the growing underdevelopment of the country from being felt. But the experience of Ghana, which once flourished in a monocultural cocoa economy, is unmistakable. Nevertheless, the oil boom has not been able to cover up one major symptom of increasing underdevelopment: growing severe shortage of food. The country now invests a great deal of money to import food. Food production has decayed. Operation Feed the Nation has come too late in the history of production to make an impact. And given the continued export-import orientation of the economy and the distribution of incentives in favour of the export-import enclaves, the new orientation to food production is inevitably quagmired in the realm of rhetoric. It simply does not pay to go into food production compared to import trade. The foreign interests which control the production process are still not oriented toward it.

Meanwhile, the oil boom mentality, together with the vastly increased size of the privileged classes, with their characteristic conspicuous consumption of imported consumer goods, has greatly increased the propensity to import.

In fact, by the end of 1977, imports so outstripped exports that foreign reserves has been drained to a mere ₦1.6 billion from a 1974 level of ₦4.06 billion. One of the obvious deleterious consequences was the ports' congestion of 1974–7, as well as the consequent shortages of consumer goods in the country. With the newly-found oil wealth the leaders felt they achieve whatever goals they deemed financially realistic. Th fact that in their neo-colonial economy, most of th projects had to come from outside the co local resources to their goals. Th the ports needed forei

This relia aff

leadership whose power and prestige

interests of the colonialists. Therefore, it is unpatriotic for Nigerians to defend and operate that economy, even if with drastic reforms. Second, the task of creating a new economy cannot be left in the hands of groups whose interests are fundamentally opposed to those which motivate the new system. And, third, a new economy cannot be organized on the basis of the old social, cultural, and political patterns and values. This was why the colonialists had to set up new educational, political, legal, and cultural systems to train and induct people into the various roles in the new econor

Thus, the neo-colonial economy of Nigeria, which was motivated by an founded on foreign interests, must give way to an alternative economy motivated by and founded on Nigerian interests. But the present Nigerian ruling classes have acquired vested interests in this neo-colonial economy. They have, therefore, become its political and socio-cultural guardians. They cannot be expected to support, much less promote, a new economy in w their power and prestige would be severely damaged. Salvation must, the fore, lie with those classes which have antagonistic interests to those on the neo-colonial economy was founded, who have not acquired vested interests in it, and who have objective interests in a new system of pro ion. The question of Nigerian development becomes first and foremos of power, of tilting the balance of power in favour of the latter group and economics must go hand in hand.

References

1. Catherine Coquery-Vidrovitch, 'The Political Economy of the Peasantry and Modes of Production' in P.C.W. Gutkind and I Wallerstein (eds.), *The Political Economy of Contemporary A* (Beverly Hills; Sage, 1976), pp. 95–6.
2. R.O. Ekundare, *An Economic History of Nigeria 1860–196* Methuen, 1973), p. 47.
3. *Ibid*., p. 169.
4. In *ibid*., p. 164.
5. United Kingdom, *West Africa Palm Oil and Palm Kernels. a Committee Appointed by the Secretary of State for the September 1923, to Consider the Best Means of Securing Increased Production*. (London: Colonial No. 10, 1952).
6. Penelope Bower, 'The Mining Industry' in Margery Perh

o an fo had rese libra and c marke cannot universi economy in produc

In conc that the fir an alternati inherited by system which

Commerce, and Finance in Nigeria (London: Faber and Faber, 1947), p. 25.
7. Richenda Scott, 'Production for Trade' in Margery Perham (ed.), *The Native Economies of Nigeria* (London: Faber and Faber, 1945), p. 220.
8. Charlotte Leubuscher, 'The Policy Governing External Trade' in Perham, *Mining*, p. 142.
9. *West Africa*, 31 March 1917: A report from the Nigerian Legislative Council.
10. U.K., *Colonial Annual Reports, No. 476, Northern Nigeria 1904* (London: HMSO, 1905), pp. 88–9.
11. Bower, *op. cit.*, p. 4.
12. *Ibid.*
13. Margery Perham, 'General Introduction: The Country' in Perham, *Native Economies*, p. 7.
14. *Ibid.*, p. 10.
15. Akin Mabogunje, *Urbanization in Nigeria* (London: University of London Press, 1968), pp. 112–13.
16. Nigeria, *Annual Report, Department of Education, 1953* (Lagos: Government Printer, 1954), pp. 5–6.
17. Perham, *Native Economies*, pp. 12–13.
18. C. Meillassoux (ed.), *The Development of Indigenous Trade and Markets in West Africa* (London: Oxford University Press, 1971), p. 76.
19. Peter C.W. Gutkind and Immanuel Wallerstein, 'Editors' Introduction' in Gutkind and Wallerstein, *Political Economy*, pp. 12–13.
20. Leubuscher, *op. cit.*, pp. 149–150.
21. *Ibid.*
22. *Ibid.*
23. A.J. Brown, 'Conclusion: Economic Problems of a Tropical Dependency' in Perham, *Mining*, pp. 334–5.
24. Scott, *op. cit.*, pp. 217–19.
25. *Ibid.*
26. *Ibid.*, p. 238.
27. Bower, *op. cit.*, p. 14.
28. G.K. Helleiner, *Peasant Agriculture, Government and Economic Growth in Nigeria* (Homewood, Illinois: Irwin, 1966), pp. 17–20.
29. *Ibid.*
30. *Ibid.*
31. J.S. Coleman, *Nigeria: Background to Nationalism* (Berkeley and Los Angeles, California: University of California Press, 1958), pp. 256–8.
32. Tomas Szentes, quoted in Gutkind and Wallerstein, 'Editors' Introduction', pp. 22–3.
33. Bower, *op. cit.*, p. 41.
34. Ekundare, *op. cit.*, pp. 42–3.
35. *West Africa*, 31 March 1917: a report from the Nigerian Legislative Council.
36. J. Mars, 'Extra-Territorial Enterprises' in Perham, *Mining*, p. 96.
37. *Ibid.*, pp. 70–1.
38. *Ibid.*, p. 54.
39. *Ibid.*, p. 92.
40. *Ibid.*, p. 95.

41. P.A. Bower, 'The Balance of Payments in 1936' in Perham, *Mining*, p. 304.
42. Bower, 'The Mining Industry', p. 22.
43. *Ibid.*
44. Mars, *op. cit.*, p. 67.
45. *Ibid.*, p. 58.
46. *Ibid.*, p. 67.
47. *Ibid.*
48. J. Mars, 'The Monetary and Banking System and the Loan Market of Nigeria' in Perham, *Mining*, p. 203.
49. Akin Mabogunje, 'The Economic Implications of the Pattern of Urbanization in Nigeria' in *Nigerian Journal of Economic and Social Studies*, 7, 1 (1965), pp. 16–17.
50. Mars, 'Extra-Territorial Enterprises', p. 54.
51. Jerry Cromwell, 'Income Distribution, Consumption, and Economic Growth', mimeo, Department of Economics, Harvard University, January 1960.
52. Mars, 'The Monetary and Banking System and the Loan Market of Nigeria', pp. 177.
53. Clive Thomas, *Dependence and Transformation* (New York: Monthly Review Press, 1974), chapter 1.
54. Victor P. Diejomaoh, *Economic Development in Nigeria* (Princeton, New Jersey: Princeton University Industrial Relations, 1965), p. 28.
55. *Ibid.*, p. 17.
56. *Ibid.*, p. 39.
57. *Ibid.*, p. 56.
58. Ekundare, *op. cit.*, p. 225.
59. Diejomoh, *op. cit.*, p.21.1.
60. *Ibid.*, p. 23.
61. Ekundare, *op. cit.*, p. 252.
62. Diejomoh, *op. cit.*, pp. 9–10.
63. Peter Kilby, *Industrialization in An Open Economy: Nigeria, 1945–1966* (Cambridge: Cambridge University Press, 1969), pp. 16–17.
64. *Ibid.*, p. 20.
65. Ekundare, *op. cit.*, pp. 299–311.
66. Indigenization is discussed in greater detail in a separate chapter of this book.

6. Planning for Under-development in Nigeria

Bade Onimode

> For the generation of structural under-development, more important still than the drain of economic surplus from the satellite after its incorporation as such into the world capitalist system is the impregnation of the satellite's domestic economy with the same capitalist structure and its fundamental contradictions [which] organize and dominate the domestic, economic, political and social life of that people.[1] (A.G. Frank)

Introduction

After the Second World War the imperialist countries formulated economic plans for several colonies in the Third World. These plans varied from high centralization and government ownership to token government stimulation of the private sector. In spite of various differences all plans shared an underlying belief that positive government action is necessary for economic management and growth. Nigeria experienced this colonial planning, involving modest stimuli to private enterprise. Except for a two-year interruption after flag independence, development planning has been a permanent exercise in the country since. In spite of three decades of planning, however, underdevelopment has also persisted as the enduring dominant feature of the Nigeria economy. This long coexistence between development planning and underdevelopment has generated the appellation, 'planning for underdevelopment in Nigeria'.

But could not this deductive conclusion be superficial and misleading? This chapter maintains that it is not. But is it not too early to judge, since independent planning started in 1962 while planning for the country by Nigerians dates back to only 1970? Since we understand what constitutes underdevelopment and its basic generating cause, we do not even need three decades of planning to assess its structural relationship with underdevelopment. This is because the planning institutions and procedures that define the essential conception of planning, as well as the orientation, objectives, policies and implementation machinery of even one plan document, offer critical insights into the possibilities of liquidating or sustaining underdevelopment through development planning.

Colonial Planning for Underdevelopment in Nigeria, 1946–60

By 1946 the British colonial bourgeoisie in Nigeria had succeeded in establishing a colonial economy in the country as a framework for consolidating and maintaining underdevelopment.[2] This involved systematic appropriation of economic surplus for Britain's development, discouragement of manufacturing, stagnation of agriculture, as well as maintenance of mass illiteracy and sustained technological backwardness. After the Second World War, increased nationalist struggles, the weakened capacity of Britain to contain any colonial unrest and her moral obligation to show gratitude for Nigeria's military support during the war led the colonial state to initiate economic planning in the general context of socio-economic management. This led to the formulation of the 1946–56 plan which was implemented in three phases: the 1946–50 plan, 1951–56 revised plan and 1954/55 interim plan.[3]

The critical features of the 1946–56 plan may be examined with respect to its conception of development, general orientation, policy measures, technical style and implementation mechanisms. The plan's conception of development was up till 1949 the improvement of the colonial economy as a version of the traditional mode of production. After that, modernization in terms of raising the level of performance and increasing infrastructural facilities like roads, schools, and hospitals was pursued. Such a conception aggravated and perpetuated the basic features of underdevelopment. With a total expenditure of barely £55 million, or £5.5 million annually, the plan was clearly not meant to mobilize the country's surplus for any structural transformation.

The general orientation of the plan is best appreciated in terms of its objectives, attitudes to govvernment, private enterprise and metropolitan interests, as well as the planning environment and mass participation. In spite of its grandiose title, the plan's objectives were essentially to promote strict accountability and control of government expenditure, especially during 1951–56 when the Nigerian petty bourgeoisie were running the three regional governments, and to provide some modest stimulation to the economy for export promotion and amelioration of the effects of the dollar shortage on Britain. The role of government was merely the classical one of providing physical and social infrastructure or overhead capital as the foundation of the economy. Private enterprise was entrusted with the major job of developing the economy. The government role was merely to create favourable conditions for this through loans, subsidies, and technical assistance. As this private enterprise was essentially British, this meant mobilizing Nigerian resources for British capital accumulation. The metropolitan interests of Britain, especially her dollar shortage, took precedence over the needs of the colonial economy. Consequently, the planning environment was taken as given in the planning exercise. This fitted the logic of marginalist neo-classical economics beautifully. Moreover, since planning was conceived of as a purely bureaucratic and technical exercise, no conscious effort was made to ensure mass involvement, even after the Nigerian petty bourgeoisie came to power in 1952. Therefore, the orientation of colonial planning was predictably the same as the ideology of British colonialism.

The policies of colonial planners were dominated by financial conservatism, under-utilization of resources, discouragement of industrialization, and characteristic lack of urgency.[4] Fiscal orthodoxy was applied to reduce the growth rate and to plan projects in order to secure a budget surplus for British capital accumulation. Open unemployment, under-employment, low level of planned expenditure, and a general failure to mobilize the people implied that available open and 'hidden' reserves of the country were not tapped for development. The ban on industrialization also meant that available resources of raw materials, entrepreneurship, labour, etc. could not be utilized for raising value-added in manufacturing. The lack of urgency reflected in these policies was aggravated by deliberate delay of development decisions. For example, although a livestock mission was appointed by the Colonial Secretary in 1948, its conference of local experts met only in 1952, and there was yet another delay before the project was executed.[5] In terms of technical style, the colonial plans were experiments in what has been dubbed 'GDP planning'. This underlined the technical and bureaucratic character of the plans. Their targets and performance were conceived in financial terms in spite of unstable price levels. Even at this superficial level, there was no evidence of any hard data for the plans, which were at best based on informed guesses.

Finally, colonial planning was highly undisciplined, unco-ordinated and largely irrelevant to the priority requirements of the country. Though designed for strict accountability, some planned expenditures were not incurred, some development expenditures were not planned, while some expenditures were neither developmental nor planned. Thus in the federal development budget there were differences between listed and actual expenditures. When regionalism was introduced after 1950, the plan was revised for 1951–56 and during 1955/56 there was yet another interim plan. By the time the ten-year plan was half-way through, actual expenditure was only one-quarter of planned expenditure. Moreover, the development plan itself covered less than half of the planned expenditure of government; individual ministry's projects were simply compiled into a patchwork plan. The introduction of the National Economic Council (NEC) in 1955 did not make much difference. In spite of a manpower shortage, such flexibility meant that the plan had failed. It might as well, because it was not addressed to the priority requirements of industrialization, agricultural development and internal utilization of surplus, which were critical for liquidating underdevelopment.

During 1956–60, new federal economic programmes[6] improved slightly on the 1946–56 experiment in technical details. They could, however, not help but perpetuate underdevelopment because the planning environment consisting of the colonial economy and its umbilical link to Britain's exploitative capitalism remained as strong as ever. The main changes in the new programmes included administrative improvements, especially in Western Nigeria, after the World Bank mission to the country in 1955. Production development boards were reorganized and budgetary procedures were improved in the East and North with the separation of capital from recurrent expenditures in 1957/8 in the North and in 1959/60 in the East. Some of these improvements, however, were offset by the unsettling effects of administrative reshuffling involved in regional reorganization, the damaging effects of regionalization on integrated planning as well as difficulties of co-ordination. These meant that federal planning had to rely on *ad hoc* consultations, conferences for specific topics and the introduction of a Joint Planning Committee in 1958 to improve plan co-ordination.

The effects of one and a half decades of colonial planning on the underdeveloped colonial economy can be approximated dialectically by the state of productive forces and social relations of production which together constitute the mode of production. The first point to emphasize here is that after 1949 colonial planning effectively rejected the traditional economy and proceeded to endorse and consolidate the emergence of capitalist relations in the country. In particular, the export enclave got a boost which meant that Nigeria was more bilaterally integrated with Britain. Commercial agriculture and colonial commerce facilitated the transfer of economic surplus from the colonial economy for the development of Britain. Thus, by 1955, Nigeria had accumulated sterling reserves in London, which were lent out at low interest rate to Britain while Nigeria borrowed at a higher rate to finance investment at home.[7].

The establishment of a university college in 1948 together with the growth of education increased the size of the Nigerian petty bourgeoisie, which gained control of regional governments in 1952. Their power over regional planning was an opportunity to mobilize part of the colonial surplus for expanding their economic base and class strength.[8] Some of the surplus also trickled down to people through the bribing of constituencies with scholarships, schools and clinics in preparation for future elections. Another significant effect of colonial planning was its investment in physical and social infrastructure. Apart from schools and health facilities, roads, some parts, urban electricity and water supplies were also marginally improved. Such investment also meant increased demand for imperialist products, higher British profits and greater dependence.

In spite of these effects, however, colonial planning really perpetuated underdevelopment in the sense that the capitalist relations which it fostered merely streamlined the imperialist exploitation of the country. Its embargo on manufacturing intensified colonial dependence on British manufactured imports, prevented the technological development of the country while it stifled the growth of Nigerian entrepreneurship, which was restricted to petty trading, sawmilling and speculative real estate transactions. Banking and insurance remained imperialist monopolies which operated to decapitalize Nigeria while at the same time facilitating British capitalist accumulation.

Moreover, the colonial state itself was largely unresponsive to colonial planning. The divide-and-rule tactic of 'indirect rule' in local administration continued in the northern parts of the country, the incompetent colonial civil service with its British officer corps perpetuated its sluggish bureaucratic methods while the terror of the district officers persisted over savagely repressed peasants and workers. Apart from grudging pensions for a few, social security was unknown for the vast majority of Nigerians.

Consequently, at nominal independence in 1960, as per capita income hovered precariously around an abysmal £80, the 'development and welfare for Nigeria', which was the grand title of the first colonial plan, remained a pathetic perversion and sad illusion as underdevelopment, grinding poverty, mass illiteracy, debilitating disease and savage exploitation constituted the lot of the majority of Nigerians in the working class.[9] This was the challenge for the next phase of planning in the country.

The Era of Neo-colonial Capitalist Planning

The challenge of flag independence was, perhaps, too unsettling for the new Nigerian ruling group to be able to initiate any economic plan until 1962 when Nigeria launched what is popularly called the First National Development Plan (1962–68). But like its colonial predecessors, this plan was neither national nor developmental. The basic features of this and the subsequent neo-colonial capitalist plans of 1970–74 and 1975–80 will now be examined to demonstrate this.

The basic features of neo-colonial capitalist planning in Nigeria since 1962 are fairly familiar.[10] They are basically similar to those of colonial planning in broad terms, but with important differences of detail. Thus the conception of underdevelopment in neo-colonial capitalist planning is summarized in the crude 'vicious cycle' of bourgeois apologetic writers, who insist tautologically that 'a country is poor because it is poor'. This poverty is traced abstractly to shortages of capital, labour, know-how and to overpopulation. Consequently, development is seen in terms of GDP, as a growth-number game involving modernization of attitudes and methods. The orientation of neo-colonial capitalist planning is probably the most decisive in its perpetuation of underdevelopment. First, the neo-colonial environment, which essentially defines the problem of underdevelopment, is taken as the earlier colonial environment. The task, therefore, is how to manipulate plan apparatus to increase GDP, consumption and efficiency within this infinitely inhibiting environment. No serious effort is made, for example, to terminate the stifling neo-colonial domination and exploitation that is the basic generating force of contemporary underdevelopment in the country. Even in the 1970–74 plan, when indigenization[11] was introduced, this was not addressed to changing the structure of the neo-colonial capitalist economy as such.

The persistent capitalist orientation of these plans is reflected in their petty bourgeois ideology. This has been stated most clearly in the national objectives of the Second Plan (1970–74),[12] which include a self-reliant notion, 'a just and egalitarian society', 'full opportunities for all citizens' and 'a free and democratic society'. All these are to be achieved in a neo-colonial capitalist country with a mixed-economy whose foreign-controlled private sector is dominant. These objectives underline the nature of bourgeois ideology as the 'illusion of the epoch' for masking true bourgeois class interests. Within this ideological framework the public sector programme is essentially to provide the physical and social infrastructural base for the private sector to lead the development process, since it dominates the critical and fastest growing sectors like manufacturing, petroleum, construction, distribution and agriculture. Though governments have been investing increasingly in these sectors, especially in joint ventures with foreign and domestic enterprises, they are still predominantly vested in the private sector.

Moreover, metropolitan interests that featured prominently in the first neo-colonial plan are still very much part of Nigerian planning, if only less directly. The two 'expert' planners for the First Plan, W.F. Stolper and L.M. Hansen, are Americans, and they required 50 per cent of the planned expenditure to be met by foreign capital.[13] Since then, reliance on the private sector, fiscal incentives like tax and tariff relief to that sector, and huge plan projects (especially in civil engineering construction and manufacturing contracted to foreign firms) have all increased neo-colonial dependence on imperialists. The ₦45.7 billion Third Plan (1975–80) has been generating millions of naira for imperialists through contracts and fiscal incentives.

One significant aspect of neo-colonial planning in Nigeria is the persistent conflict between objectives and policies. Even though these plans claim to be 'internally consistent', this conflict betrays the contradictions of neo-colonial class struggles. What is responsible for such inconsistencies is the need to placate working class and imperialist aspirations (which are basically inconsistent) and at the same time satisfy the class interests of the bureaucratic bourgeoisie which elaborates these plans. Thus while preaching 'self-reliance', all the plans insist on a vital role for foreign assistance and a foreign-dominated private sector; they announce egalitarian objectives to mollify the working class while encouraging capitalist accumulation, elitist education and urban-biased locational measures, all of which are the basic generating forces of inequality in the country. While the plans insist that worthwhile projects are limited by available resources, the same governments embark endlessly on wasteful and counter-productive projects like stadia, FESTAC, the International Trade Fair (at which Nigeria has nothing to sell but everything to buy) and sports jamborees for the entertainment of the privileged classes.

The investment policies in these plans also intensify the contradictions of underdevelopment. The First Plan, for example, required only a projected 5 per cent net domestic investment of net domestic product.[14] This was based on the financial conservatism of bourgeois budgeting. The Third Plan jumped from this conservatism to a grandoise utopia in which its capital programme of over ₦45 billion succeeded the Second Plan's budget of barely ₦3.2 billion. Even though the Third Plan was revised in 1976, its current planned expenditure of over ₦30 billion represents an over 900 per cent increase on the previous plan, and it is difficult to see the evidence of new absorptive capacity to support such a flamboyant projection.

Like the colonial ones, the policies of the neo-colonial plans also exhibit a basic lack of urgency. The most egregious example of this is the proposed integrated iron and steel industry that was in the First and Second Plans and was only recently initiated for projected completion during the Fourth Plan. This represents a lag of some 20 years; yet this project is repeatedly acclaimed the cornerstone of the country's industrialization and Nigeria is said to be in a hurry. Similar examples include petrochemicals, fertilizers, the petroleum refinery, liquefied petroleum gas and other heavy industries.[15] While this leisurely pace persisted, the country completed such counter-productive projects like the National Stadium and Trade Fair Complex in Lagos, the FESTAC Durbar hotel at Kaduna, and staged the multi-million naira FESTAC itself in 1977.

Moreover, neo-colonial plan policies typically under-utilize national resources. The capital-intensive methods of production they adopt exacerbates this problem through open unemployment and under-employment. The small investment programme of the First Plan, as well as the unproductive projects of the Second and Third Plans, also indicate this under-utilization of potential and actual surplus. The persistent indifference of these plans to the enormous export of surplus by imperialists is also evidence of failure to tap the country's resources fully in effective combat against neo-colonial underdevelopment. This same problem arises with the persistent inability of neo-colonial planning to mobilize the masses and with the 'hidden reserves' of labour-power and potential savings dissipated on festivities in rural and urban areas.

The bureaucratic bourgeoisie that has been ruling Nigeria in collaboration with its imperialist mentors since 1960 is addicted to bureaucratic and technocratic planning. This is being faithful to its class character. The process starts with the conception of planning as a technical exercise requiring the expert skills of petty bourgeois economists, capitalist-oriented bureaucrats and similar elitist elements. This excludes other professional groups like sociologists, geographers, agronomists, political scientists, and engineers in what should be a multidisciplinary process at the technical level. Next, 'internal consistency' based on macro-economic projections is seen as the most critical test of the operational utility of neo-colonial plans. Consequently, the fundamental character of planning as a *social process*, involving all social and political forces in the country, is ignored.[16] The critical mass base to ensure the democratic character of planning through popular participation is, therefore, not available to the fragile legitimacy of neo-colonialism.

The formulation of plan targets purely in financial terms is a related feature. In progress reports plan performance is stated in terms of how much

Table 1
Sectoral Performance in Transport (£ millions)

Government	*Planned Expenditure 1970/71*	*Actual Expenditure 1970/71*	*Performance Ratio (%)*	*Pro Rata Planned Expenditure April–Sept. 1971*	*Pro Rata Actual Expenditure April–Sept. 1971*	*Performance Ratio (%)*
Federal	48.833	20.815	42.6	26.660	11.648	43.7
Benue-Plateau	0.655	1.830	279.4	0.622	0.639	102.7
East-Central	1.286	0.050	3.9	0.725	1.363	188.0
Kano	0.800	0.952	119.0	1.015	0.562	55.4
Kwara	0.980	0.195	19.9	0.450	0.396	88.0
Lagos	0.506	1.040	20.8	0.375	0.598	159.5
Mid-West	2.223	1.004	45.2	0.969	1.372	141.6
North-Central	0.603	0.274	45.4	0.725	–	–
North-East	1.125	2.213	196.7	1.036	0.917	88.5
North-West	0.600	0.327	54.5	0.385	0.051	13.2
Rivers	0.900	0.260	28.9	1.425	1.055	74.0
South-East	1.485	1.374	92.5	0.735	0.674	91.7
Western	2.772	6.691	241.4	1.214	0.364	29.9
Total	62.762	37.025	59.0	36.336	19.549	53.8
Expenditure (%) in all sectors	33.0	30.9	–	34.3	25.6	–

Source: Federal Republic of Nigeria, *Second National Development Plan, 1970–74: First Progress Report* (Lagos: CPO), pp. 59–96, Table 32.

of budgeted funds have been spent. Under inflationary conditions and rampant corruption, this makes nonesense of plan implementation, as Table 1 shows. Yet stating physical units like kilometers of road to be constructed, kilograms of rice, groundnuts, and cotton to be grown, number of classrooms to be built or students to be enrolled would have ensured better plan compliance.

Finally, the technical style of neo-colonial planning is anchored to bourgeois economics of the neo-classical and Keynesian brands. Consequently, the objects of plans are stated in terms of GDP growth rate with associated capital output ratios and proportions of GDP to be saved and invested within the Harod-Domar model of economic growth. Such static planning methodology involves rather abstract and unrealistic assumptions. For example, the First Plan insisted on gross fixed investment of 15 per cent of GDP, 5–6% capital consumption with a net capital-output ratio of 2.6 and concluded that with an annual GDP growth rate of 4.4% and an annual population growth rate of 2–2½%, the planned annual per capita increase in output would be 1½–2%.[17] Even if the data exists to validate this approach, the structure of a neo-colonial economy may not really generate development according to these rules. The persistence of underdevelopment in spite of these GDP games should be enough warning. A missing part of such calculations in neo-colonial planning in Nigeria is intersectoral input-output tables, whose supply orientation in spite of its limitations should be more useful against the supply constraints of underdevelopment.

The patent lack of plan discipline is one of the greatest similarities between colonial and neo-colonial capitalist planning. Though plan projects acquired priorities since 1962, these are invariably ignored by the bureaucratic bourgeoisie in a blatant demonstration of the superiority of its selfish class interests over avowed national objectives and in constant reflection of the mounting contradictions of class struggles and neo-colonial underdevelopment in the country.

To take most recent examples, FESTAC, which cost hundreds of millions of naira, is nowhere in any plan document. The Universal Primary Education (UPE) programme, which is the most expensive educational programme in the entire history of the country, was not in the Second Plan; its implementation started during that plan though its critical phase commenced during the Third Plan.[18] Similarly, while Gowon's corrupt regime ignored vital projects like a petroleum refinery and iron and steel plants in the Second Plan, it executed interminable cultural and sports festivals for the narcissistic entertainment of the ruling class and its allies. Frequent changes of regime, manifesting volatile class struggles, also render plan priorities extremely flexible. Thus the Third Plan was revised after the overthrow in July 1975 of the decadent and shamelessly pro-imperialist regime of Gowon.

The absence of central control vested in an appropriately powerful national agency to dish out rewards to those who implement a plan and punishment to those who violate its priorities has been a persistent failure since 1962. Though the second and third plans have a few pages[19] at the end on plan implementation and control, the Central Planning Office of the Federal Ministry of Economic Development and the Ministry of Finance charged with this responsibility have so far not been able to restrain the respective heads of government and other functionaries from distorting plan priorities. This same lack of control has rendered plan co-ordination difficult in spite of the increasing concentration of power in the federal government (e.g. over education at all levels and development financing). Indeed, in the First Plan, four capital programmes were merely patched together so that this was not an integrated plan at all. This loose control and lack of co-ordination in neo-colonial planning also reflects the intra-elite struggles within the privileged classes and the heterogeneous class interests served by these bourgeois plans.

Underdevelopment and Neo-colonial Capitalist Planning

Some of the consequences of neo-colonial capitalist planning for development in the country are implicit in the foregoing. It is necessary, however, to emphasize five of them. First, in spite of about two decades of neo-colonial capitalist planning, the basic neo-colonial structure of the economy persists in terms of its dependence on international capitalism. Indeed, by the industrialization strategy of these plans, which is anchored to import-substitution and consequently dominated by the multinationals owned by erstwhile exporters to Nigeria, post-1960 planning has criticially integrated the economy more tightly and multilaterally into the orbit of imperialism. The capital-intensive techniques of this neo-colonial industrialization together with the orientation towards consumer-goods manufacturing in the country, particularly the domestic production of former imports of manufactured goods, both imply increased reliance on imperialists for imports of capital-goods. The ports congestion of the early post-war years and the drastic shortages that resulted underlined that point. This is also why most of the civil engineering constructions like roads, harbours, monstrous bridges in Lagos, and even housing, rely so helplessly on Julius Berger, Dumez and other imperialist multinationals. The export of national economic surplus to imperialist countries in Western Europe, North America and Japan, together with the stifling of domestic entrepreneurship, have been decapitalizing and sustaining the industrial and technological backwardness of the country. These are among the forces sustaining the underdevelopment of the country. Thus by 1975 manufacturing only accounted for 4.7 per cent of GDP even though it is one of the fastest-growing sectors (see Table 2).

Second, the sectoral distribution indicated in the table shows that in fifteen years manufacturing increased its share in GDP from 3.6 per cent to 4.7 per cent. Agriculture's share fell from 63.4 per cent to 23.4 per cent in the same period while mining (petroleum) rose from 0.9 per cent to 45.5 per cent. This indicates a perverse pattern of increasing dependence on petroleum, a wasting asset. The failure so far to use petroleum funds to trans-

Table 2
Major Components of GNP in Nigeria (Percentages)

Years	*Total GNP (₦ million)*	*Agricultural*	*Mining and Quarrying*	*Manufactu-ring*	*Electricity and Water*	*Building and Construction*	*Distribution*	*Transport and Communi-cations*
1960	2,244.6	63.4	0.9	3.6	0.3	3.0	9.1	4.4
1961	2,373.4	61.7	1.4	3.9	0.3	3.3	9.8	4.6
1962	2,630.8	61.2	1.7	3.6	0.4	3.4	9.6	4.3
1963	2,806.4	59.7	2.1	5.8	0.5	4.4	12.2	4.6
1964	2,914.0	57.6	2.0	5.6	0.5	4.4	13.6	5.0
1965	3,080.6	54.9	2.8	5.6	0.6	4.3	14.3	4.9
1966	3,210.0	55.6	4.8	6.2	0.6	5.2	14.0	4.4
1967	3,051.8	56.1	5.1	6.1	0.6	5.1	13.5	4.0
1968	3,140.8	55.0	2.7	9.6	0.6	4.9	13.7	3.9
1969	3,278.2	53.2	2.9	8.6	0.6	4.9	13.5	3.9
1970	3,485.8	51.3	3.7	9.5	0.6	5.0	13.2	3.7
1971	9,442.1	36.0	33.1	5.0	0.3	3.5	9.1	1.8
1972	11,177.9	32.0	39.3	4.1	0.3	4.1	8.1	1.9
1973	11,993.1	27.9	43.4	4.8	0.4	4.7	7.4	2.1
1974	13,135.5	24.7	45.1	4.8	0.4	4.4	6.9	2.1
1975	44,410.7	23.4	45.5	4.7	0.4	4.7	6.7	2.3

Sources: Federal Office of Statistics, *Annual Abstracts of Statistics* (Lagos); Federal Ministry of Information, *Second National Development plan, 1970–1974* (Lagos, 1970); Central Planning Office, *Third National Development Plan, 1975–80*, (Lagos, 1975).

form other sectors of the economy is a potential source of increasing weakness for the economy; government revenue and foreign exchange earnings from this export commodity leave worsened foreign dependence.

Third, the continuing stagnation of agriculture, which still comprised 63.99 per cent of total gainful occupation in 1975 while petroleum and other mining and quarrying accounted for only 0.39 per cent,[20] is a serious drag on the structural transformation of the economy. In the post civil-war period, particularly, food shortages and land problems have emerged. This not only makes life increasingly precarious for the toiling peasant majority, but constitutes a potential constraint on the supply of food and raw materials necessary for even sustaining current underdevelopment. There is nothing in the neo-colonial capitalist plans, besides flirting with bourgeois co-operatives, farm settlements and mechanization (which also imply greater dependence on imperialism), to indicate any real strategy for resolving agricultural stagnation and rural decay.

Fourth, the implications of these perverse effects of neo-colonial planning for liquidating underdevelopment even in the first half of the next century are clearly dim. This is particularly disturbing as the vital resources of the country like petroleum and other wasting primary products are being rapidly depleted. If current trends in the international capitalist system continue, increasing contradictions within it (e.g. between Japan and Britain, and the U.S.A. and West Germany, over trade) will mean intensified imperialist exploitation of countries like Nigeria and the exacerbation of underdevelopment. The masses, as usual, will be called to bear the brunt of such hardship, if neo-colonialism survives it.

Finally, the human dimensions of neo-colonial capitalist planning require special mention. Rather than reducing inequality, planning since 1960 has actually exacerbated it in terms of creating opportunities for the emergence of a few millionaires through the manipulation of lucrative contracts or outright looting of public treasuries within the planning context. The democratic aspirations of the masses of peasants, workers and petty artisans who have not been directly involved in plan formulation have so far been largely ignored. This is true in spite of token concessions like low-cost housing and rural electrification, which increase the contract earnings of the urbanized domestic and foreign capitalists. Thus, by 1969/70, 56.07 per cent of the population were still earning less than ₦400 annually or 23.53 per cent of gross income. The corresponding shares for 1971/72 were 39.9 per cent and 14.84 per cent respectively. Conversely, the highest income group, with ₦6,000 and above, constituted 1.28 per cent of the total population and got 21.55 per cent of total income. In 1971/72 their percentage shares were 1.87 per cent and 24.7 per cent respectively.[21] In terms of general social welfare Nigeria in 1971 had 23,000 people per registered medical practitioner and 15,000 per hospital bed.[22]

Conclusion

This brief survey of development planning in Nigeria has tried to show the critical sense in which both colonial and neo-colonial capitalist planning have been intensifying the contradictions of underdevelopment in the country. It has argued that both types of planning are similar in their essential character and that their basic role in perpetuating underdevelopment arises from their continuing failure to grapple with its basic generating force, which is the imperialist domination and exploitation of the country within the framework of its increasing multilateral integration into the international capitalist system. This is what has stagnated agriculture, retarded manufacturing, blocked technological advancement, crippled education and decapitalized the country generally, with consequent pauperization of the toiling masses in the dialectical process.

The associated increase in the prosperity of the privileged classes with the surging development of the imperialist countries logically suggests that planning in Nigeria has been inseparable as a class category from colonial and neo-colonial policies of underdevelopment. Therefore, the conversion of planning from an instrument of class domination and exploitation into a powerful organizational principle for liquidating underdevelopment and generating genuine development with the liberation of the masses requires continuing class struggles.

References

1. Quoted in A.G. Frank, *Lumpen-Bourgeoisie and Lumpen-Development: Dependence, Class and Politics in Latin America:* (London: Monthly Review Press, 1974).
2. For other case studies of colonial underdevelopment, see A.G. Frank, *Capitalism and Underdevelopment in Latin America* (London: Monthly Review Press, 1969); Colin Leys, *Underdevelopment in Kenya* (Ibadan: Heinemann 1976), chapters 2 and 3; Walter Rodney, *How Europe Underdeveloped Africa* (Dar es Salaam: Tanzania Publishing House, 1972).
3. This was the *Ten Year Plan of Development and Welfare for Nigeria, 1946 to 1956* (Lagos: Government Printer, 1946).
4. See S.P. Schatz, 'The Influence of Planning on Development: the Nigerian Experience', *Social Research*, 27, 4 (1960).
5. *Ibid.*
6. See *ibid*.
7. For a graphic account of this colonial mechanism of underdevelopment, see K. Awosika, 'The Role of Fiscal and Monetary Policy in Nigeria's Industrialisation, 1956–66' (Ph.D. thesis in Economics, Oxford University, 1975).
8. See S. Osoba, 'The Nigerian Power Elite, 1952–65' in C.W. Gutkind and P. Waterman (eds.), *African Social Studies – A Radical Reader* (London: Monthly Review Press, 1977), pp. 368–83.
9. See Federal Government of Nigeria, *Economic Suvery of Nigeria* (Lagos:

Federal Ministry of Information, 1959).
10. They have been described in a critique by O. Oni and B. Onimode, *Economic Development of Nigeria: The Socialist Alternative* (Ibadan: The Nigerian Academy of Arts, Sciences and Technology, 1975), chapter 4.
11. *Second National Development Plan, 1970–74* (Lagos: Federal Ministry of Information, 1970), pp. 288–9.
12. *Ibid*, p. 32.
13. *First National Development Plan, 1962–68* (Lagos: Federal Ministry of Information).
14. See S.P. Schatz, 'Appraisal of Nigeria's First Development Plan, 1962–68', *Nigerian Journal of Economic and Social Studies*, 5, 2 (1963).
15. See *Second Plan*, pp. 148–9 and *Third National Development Plan 1975–80*, pp. 157–64.
16. See Josef Pajestka, 'Planning Methods and Procedures and Plan Implementation' in *Planning and Plan Implementation*, papers submitted to the Committee for Development Planning, Second Session (New York: United Nations, 1967), p.8.
17. See Schatz, *op. cit*; *Second Plan*, chapters 5–75; *Third Plan*, chapter 5.
18. See *Third Plan*, p. 246.
19. *Second Plan*, pp. 333–9; *Third Plan*, pp. 397–404.
20. See S.O. Olayide, *Economic Survey of Nigeria, 1960–75* (Ibadan: Aromolaram, 1976), p. 22, Table 2.
21. B.A. Etim & F.N. Eronini, 'Personal Income Distribution in Nigeria, 1969/70–1971/72', paper presented to the 1975 Annual Conference of the Nigerian Economic Society at Kano,
22. Quoted in Oni and Onimode, *op. cit.*, p. 134.

7. The Poverty of Ideology in Nigerian Development

Uzodinma Nwala

The discussion of ideology in the context of development strategies raises a fundamental philosophical question as to the relation between ideas and the socio-material processes that go on in any given society. It also calls for a more adequate theoretical formulation of the very concept of ideology and socio-political action.

Idealism, especially Hegel's dialectical idealism, seems to put the whole weight of causal influence on ideas, consciousness or reason. In the famous Socratic dictum, 'knowledge is virtue'; what is required for ethical excellence and moral rectitude (i.e. the 'good' man) or even for a good society is knowledge of the good or of the most fundamental ethical values. In the realm of contemporary socio-political action it is generally said that what is required are 'leaders' who know what the society needs and in whose hands the welfare of the society is to be entrusted. Such leaders are to formulate and equip themselves with a body of ideas or a system of ideology that ideally expresses the goals which the society *ought* to pursue. And then they should embark on a programme of education to teach the rest of the citizens these ideals. When the leaders and the led share knowledge of this ideology and the leaders at the same time sincerely implement this ideology, then such a society is assured of political and social stability and progress.

This theoretical perspective often goes with the assumption that the interest of the society as a whole and those of the various strata of its members are identical. For example, the interest of the multinationals who do business in the society are believed to be identical with the interests of the society. The same assumption is also made in respect of the interest of the workers and their employers. Unity of action is thus conceived as a necessary guarantee for realization of this unity of purpose. This idealist perspective gives us one definition of ideology, which we here refer to as 'ideology as utopia'.

Ideology as Utopia

This, as we have indicated, is simply an ideal system of ideas defining a 'hoped-for' and 'not-yet-realized' state of affairs. Such a state of affairs carries certain fundamental goals and the means for achieving them, as well as the ideal relation which should prevail in such a state of affairs. It is often adumbrated independent of any actual social and historical process. It assumes that the historical process is absolutely determinable in terms of ideas or reason.

Plato's *Republic* is a classic example of this type of ideology. In its ideal expression it is a speculative product of the thinker. However, often such an ideology may in fact be a rationalization of the existing conditions. Plato's *Republic* appears in fact to be an attempt to construct an ideal socio-political order based on the existing elements in the Greek society of his time. For example, the class character of the Greek society is preserved and given a harmonious expression in *Republic*. This harmony is expressed in the supreme law which requires everyone to maintain his place in the scheme of things. In our day, Chief Obafemi Awolowo, a leading Nigerian politician, adopted the same Platonic position in his book *The Peoples Republic*.[1] The key to harmony in his ideal Nigerian society is love. All classes and strata in our society are to love one another. With that, Nigeria's socio-political problems will be solved and development assured.

Political parties in Nigeria often present this utopian ideology in their party manifestos and programmes. In such programmes both the general ideals and needs of the society as well as the specific ideals of each strata and every individual are theoretically reflected. In the 1979 political exercise in Nigeria, each of the five parties officially recognized by the Federal Electoral Commission aimed at achieving the ideals of national unity, peace, solidarity, progress, egalitarianism, freedom of private enterprise, socialism, justice, etc. At the same time the interests of the worker and the employers, the nation as a whole and the multinationals, the chiefs and the masses, women and youth, all religions, all tribes and all ideologies are provided for. The eclecticism of these claims is unsurpassable.

At other times this idealist perspective expresses itself in constitutional struggles. Here attempts are made to make the Constitution 'better' as a guarantee for creating a more equitable and progressive social order. The nationalist struggle in Nigeria often took the form of constitutional struggle. And to many a participant it was seen as the way to end colonialism. It is not surprising, therefore, that many people regarded constitutional guarantees as the solution to the contradictions posed by colonialism. Similarly, the contradictions in Nigeria's First Republic were seen to be just as amenable to constitutional resolution. Thus General Murtala Ramat Mohammed in his address to the opening session of the 1975 Constitutional Drafting Committee said that the Constitutional Drafting Committee had the responsibility 'to produce an initial draft of a Constitutional arrangement which would provide a social basis for a continuing existence of a United Nigeria'. Furthermore, he declared that his administration believed strongly that 'the provisions of the Constitution can be used for removing or minimizing some of our basic problems'.[2] The Constitutional Drafting Committee echoed this view when in its report it criticized past Nigerian leaders for their 'preoccupation with power and its material benefits that political ideologies as to how a society can be organized and ruled to the best advantage of all hardly entered into the calculation'. However, they blamed the constitution for this state of affairs because it failed to provide the adequate rules and ideological directives.[3]

Many people in contemporary Nigerian society share this false perspective of socio-political development, namely the view that mere knowledge, ideas in idealic systematic expression or as a utopian ideology, can, on their own, be an instrument of serious transformation of society. Such a view lacks a correct understanding of the laws of social change and the dialectics of ideas and reality. Nevertheless, it was this perspective that guided the Nigerian nationalist leaders who inherited the colonial society intact and who believed it would produce an ideal constitution or political ideology for the evolution of an ideal society.

The Concept of Ideology: A Marxist Perspective

Ideology is a form of social consciousness, the perspective of reality. It expresses the way a people perceive the world around them as well as the goals and ideals which they cherish. Ideology also provides explanation for their actions. This perception of reality may be an *ideal* perception, or an *actual* perception which reflects the objective processes in the society. As ideal perception, it is utopian because it adumbrates goals and ideals not yet realized. As we have tried to demonstrate above, utopia expresses *what ought to be* in relation to *what is*. As an actual perception it is an expression of the actual historical processes which go on in any socio-historical context. Such an actual ideology, as an objective process, has its basis in the mode of production of society, namely the way men create and recreate the material basis of their existence as well as the relations which emerge within the given mode of production. It is thus the sum total of the political, economic, legal, religious, artistic and philosophical expressions that correspond to the mode of social production in any given society.

Karl Marx put the relationship between ideology and production quite succinctly in the following words: '. . . in the social production of their life, men enter into definite relations that are indispensable and independent of their will, relations of production which correspond to a definite stage of development of their material productive forces. The sum total of these relations constitutes the economic structure of society, the real foundation of which rises a legal and political superstructure and to which correspond definite forms of social consciousness.'[4]

The ideology of a society and the material foundations of that society have a dialectical relationship. There is a continuous reciprocal, contradictory, and many-sided relationship between the material conditions of production and the relationship of the productive forces on the one hand and the ideological expression on the other. The material foundations of every ideology in any given society are lodged in the production process. Each society is unique in terms of its socio-historical conditions. And the way it conceives of its socio-historical practice reinforces this practice. Not every idea in a society can immediately be traced to the production process. Human thought is subject to the laws of the dialectics and in a sense has its partial independent course of development according to which, having derived its ideas from the material foundations of reality, the mind has the capacity to weave these ideas into all types of forms and structures. Its capacity for doing this is limitless. But thought comes back to its good sense when it has to test its fantastic creations on reality. It is thus only in practice that we know what is realistic or not.[5]

This is a major contribution of Marxism to philosophy, that the test of the truth of ideas is ultimately practice. It is only in practice that the antinomies of thought can be resolved. The ability of ideas or thought to influence practice depends on the objective conditions. For example, no legal provision, no religion, philosophical doctrine or ideology can eliminate corruption, inflation or unemployment in a capitalist economy which at the same time leaves the structures of that society intact. The situation is even worse with a neo-colonial and dependent economy as we have in Nigeria.

The concept of society in relation to ideology need not be understood in a holistic sense. Each society is a congerie (mass) of conflicting ideologies and forms of socio-economic and historical practice. But there is always a dominant socio-economic and historical practice, with its corresponding ideological expression, which practically and theoretically dominates this society and all the existing minor forms and their ideological expressions. This dominant ideology for all practical purposes becomes the ideology of the society and its socio-economic system.

In a feudal society, for example, the feudal mode of production, with its ideology, is dominant. However, within the same society there exist subordinate elements of communalism (relics of the past) and also the aspirations of the serfs and some independent artisans and self-employed persons, which point beyond the logic of the existing dominant system of feudalism. Similarly, within a capitalist society, there exist non-capitalist sectors which bow to the dominant influence of capitalism.[6] And the accompanying dominant bourgeois ideology is the ideology of the ruling bourgeois class which dominates the ideological aspirations of the proletariat. This state of ideological plurality is the pre-condition for the existence of class struggle. The intensity of the class struggle however mirrors the degree of class consciousness, as well as the intensity of the contradictions in the society.

Society is not static. Both its material foundations and the corresponding consciousness or ideology are in a constant process of transformation. There is a struggle between the ideologies of the various classes in relation to the concurrent transformations going on in the objective dimension. There are congeries of contradictions in society. As a matter of fact, there is constant struggle between the dominant mode of production and its ideological expression. The ideas of the ruling class often outstrip their present productive techniques. In which case their ideas influence their practice. But the degree to which it does this is conditioned by the realities of the socio-historical process. Thus development programmes (a set of ideas meant to express and guide practice) may go beyond existing practice, but how far its stipulations are carried into effect depends on the practical realities that prevail in the society.

The decisive forces that influence the direction and course of development in society are social forces. Social forces are defined as the power of the various groups of people in society defined in terms of their relation to the production process. And this in turn involves their relations and place in the whole nexus of production and distribution. Thus, social forces have both economic and social roles. In modern capitalist society the two fundamental social forces that determine the nature and direction of social, economic and political development are the bourgeoisie or capitalist class (made up of the property-owning members of the society who are at the same time employers of labour) and the proletariat or the working class. The division into these classes corresponds to the relation which each has to the means of production. The capitalists have a relation of ownership and control of the means, factors, or instruments of labour (or production), including labour power and the products of labour. The working class, who are the real producers in society, have no such control over the instruments of labour or production (including themselves), nor over the products of their labour. Consequently, they are the objects of exploitation by the capitalists and suffer alienation in the production process.

The total production process involving the instruments of labour (or production) and these relations of the social forces constitute the mode of production. Each mode of production has a corresponding dominant ideological expression. Thus capitalism is the mode of production in which capital dominates labour. Therefore, in discussing the ideology and development of any society, we have to examine the system of production of that society which forms its material foundation, the social consciousness which corresponds to this system, and the relationship between the two.[7] Both the material foundation as well as its corresponding forms of consciousness have to be grasped historically.

The above analysis implicitly rejects the bourgeois approach to the concept of ideology, which treats ideology as a form of human consciousness that seems to exist independently of its environment and social practice, and which does not reveal the contradiction between ideology and its material foundation, or between social consciousness and social being. This perspective also emphasizes the class character of ideology as a reflection of the dominant socio-economic system in any given society. The ruling class in a capitalist society advertises the ideals of all humanity. They also provide a systematic rationalized body of ideas which ideally express a harmonious and 'potentially' progressive social order. But in fact such an ideology remains essentially utopian, incapable of being realized because of the prevailing realities. Some of the ideals such as freedom of expression, equality before the law, etc. are realizable by only members of the ruling class who possess the economic power necessary for achieving these political rights or ideals.

Material Foundations of the Ideological Struggle

Nigeria, as a political and economic entity, is a creation of British imperialism. The prime motive force for British imperialism was to seek new sources of raw material and new markets for her manufactures. Hence, all the social and political activities of the British in Nigeria were geared towards creating a convenient administrative structure for maximum exploitation of the human and material resources of the country.

Colonialism, as a form of imperialism, bred its own contradictions. One such contradiction was the resistance of Nigerians as a result of increasing alienation from their society and its natural resources, in addition to racial oppression. In the early twenties, African political parties had emerged with the objective of organizing the people in constitutional struggles for independence. The Peoples' Union, the Nigerian National Democratic Party (1922), the Lagos Youth Movement (1933), which later became the Nigerian Youth Movement, and the National Council of Nigeria and the Cameroons (1944) emerged to promote national identity and mobilize the people towards achieving independence. The resolution of the contradictions in the colonial order were seen in terms of the achievement of political freedom. The economic and political institutions established by Britain were accepted as a basis for the social and political transformation of Nigeria. Only minor constitutional and economic reforms were, therefore, advocated. The winning of political power was the ultimate objective around which all nationalist strategies and tactics were organized. Western capitalism and bourgeois parliamentary democracy formed the framework for economic and political transformations.

In the course of time contradictions arose in the nationalist movement. First, there was the contradiction between the interests of the leaders of this movement and the movement itself. This led to the emergence of parties around personalities. The N.C.N.C. gravitated around Dr. Nnamdi Azikiwe, the Action Group (A.G.) around Chief Obafemi Awolowo, and Northern People's Congress (N.P.C.) around the Sardauna of Sokoto. Each leader sought a political base within his nationality or tribe. In this way another form of contradiction emerged, that between Nigerian nationalism and the tribal movements. With this trend there also emerged the increasing gap between the North and the South in regard to the rate at which they were being absorbed into the main stream of the capitalist system. The National Council of Nigeria and the Cameroons (N.C.N.C.), which began as a national party, soon came under the domination of the Igbo and the Igbo State Union led by Dr. Nnamdi Azikiwe. The Action Group Party, which emerged in 1951, sprang from a Yoruba tribal organisation, the *Egbe Omo Oduduwa* – founded by Chief Obafemi Awolowo. This party advocated rigid regionalism with the slogan: 'West for the Westerners, East for the Easterners, North for the Northerners, and Nigeria for all of us'. In the North, the Northern Peoples Congress was founded in 1951 with the motto: 'One North, one People, irrespective of religion, rank or tribe'.

The British, whose strategy was to 'divide and rule', encouraged this backward trend in Nigerian nationalism and institutionalized it in the regionalization of 1954 when Nigeria was split into three major regions: West, East and North, and the Federal territory of Lagos. With these developments, little empires emerged ruled by sub-groups of bourgeois-cum-feudal alliances. All national action became a question of compromise among the ruling class in the nationalist movement. It soon became obvious that this ethnic chauvinism was that of just three dominant ethnic groups within Nigeria, namely the Hausa-Fulani, Yoruba and the Igbo. They dominated the economy and politics of the country and suppressed the aspirations of the minorities within each Region.

By 1960, when Nigeria attained political independence from Britain, the country had no clearly charted course of political and economic development. What existed were only the inherited colonial institutions and vague political and economic theories such as parliamentary democracy and a self-reliant economy. Strategies for development were based on the imperatives of a dependent and peripheral capitalist economy. Attention and efforts were concentrated on sharing the national wealth among the elite class. In politics it meant the replacement of British colonial authorities with local ones; it meant Nigerianization of the public service to make room for the emerging local bureaucrats, and appointment of Nigerian judges, police, and army commanders. The strategies never attempted to alter the existing social structures and relations. Before independence the working-class movement had been a major instrument for political and economic mobilization and agitation, but after independence the class cleavage became obvious. The interests of the emerging bourgeois class became glaringly antithetical to that of the working-class in Nigeria. Just as the Nigerian Trade Union Movement had to embark on a strike action in 1945 to force the colonial authorities to make certain political and economic concessions, it also had to embark on strike action in 1964 in its struggle against the corrupt and impotent neo-colonial regime of Balewa and Azikiwe. In short, the exploitative system of the colonial order was still intact after independence.

Party Ideologies

Some attempts were made by some of the political parties to articulate the ideological basis of their political, social and economic programmes. Let us examine two of these very briefly: first, the so-called *Pragmatic Socialism* of the National Council of Nigerian Citizens (N.C.N.C.), led by Dr. Michael Okpara, and second, the *Democratic Socialism* of the Action Group led by Chief Obafemi Awolowo. The motivation for advertizing social and political programmes that have a socialist label was due mainly to the realization by these parties that the Nigerian masses were becoming increasingly restless over the decadence of the existing order. Afraid of the discontent felt by the masses and its possible consequences for those in power, the later quickly resorted to deceptive phrase-mongering.

Pragmatic Socialism

The invention of the term Pragmatic Socialism was an act of desperation. And no wonder! The authors failed to realize that pragmatism is the philosophy of capitalism rather than that of socialism. Pragmatism is taken from the Greek word *pragma*, which means business, a thing done. It was a philosophy developed in the United States to express the spirit and practice of Big Business. As a philosophical doctrine, pragmatism is based on the contradictory assumption that the world is both unknowable and irrational. But the pragmatic sceptic could not deny one thing, namely human productive activity, which he discovers through a process not unlike the Cartesian argument 'I think, therefore I am' (*Cogito ego sum*). In the case of the pragmatic sceptic, the human productive activity is beyond all doubt and so he concludes: 'I produce, therefore I am'. And he goes further to argue: 'Whatever I produce, I produce'.

The exponents of pragmatism account for human action on the basis of their experience of the ethics and logic of Big Business. Consequently, they project a philosophy of action based on sheer egoism: 'The useful or advantageous is good'. The logic of its ideology was 'instrumental' or 'experimental' which proceeds 'through trial and error for the type of behaviour most advantageous in particular situations'. The sum total of pragmatic philosophy is best expressed by the Machiavellian principle, 'The end justifies the means', which is the motto of exploitative socio-economic systems. Pragmatism exaggerates the active, volitional character of human activity and makes it the basis of reality by its assertion that the world is what we make it. And by ignoring objective facts, the idealist philosophy of pragmatism fosters adventurist, aggressive tendencies, as well as unprincipled opportunism in political life.

In the 1962 election campaign for the then Eastern House of Assembly controlled by the N.C.N.C., Dr. Michael Okpara's stand was 'No vote for N.C.N.C., no amenities', which he vigorously carried into effect in Ibeku, Umuahia and the minority areas of Calabar, Ogoja and Rivers Provinces. This is typical of a pragmatic political approach. There was nothing socialist in the explicit expression of this theory nor in the actual practice of the N.C.N.C.

Democratic Socialism

The doctrine of socialism that the Action Group advocated is based on the idea that contradictions in the Nigerian society can be resolved through a mechanical unity of all the contending forces in Nigeria, notably the unity of the feudal lords (Obas, Obis, Emirs, and Chiefs), the bourgeoisie and petty bourgeoisie, the workers and peasants. It denies the reality of the class struggle in Nigeria and fails to grasp the nature of the dialectical resolution of social contradictions which is advocated by the more perceptive scientific socialism.

Resolution of contradictions in society, according to Chief Awolowo in his *The Peoples Republic*, is achieved through *love* and *unity* of all the classes.[8] Such an appeal to subjective feeling (love) ignores objective conditions such as the fact that love has nothing to do with resolving inflation, corruption, crime, and the exploitation of the working class. It further ignores the fact that love is compatible with nepotism and tribalism. Democratic socialists ask the Nigerian workers to resign themselves to the awful realities in which they live and work because the essence of love is forgiveness. Hence, the exploited should forgive and live in harmony with the exploiters.

Nigerian Social Democrats were influenced by the British Social Democrats. For the Nigerians, Social Democracy was a populist and nationalist doctrine for welding together all the different strata of society. However, their comprehension of Nigerian society in its relation to imperialist domination was very shallow. Thus the Manifesto of the Action Group opens with the declaration: 'Nigeria has entered a new era. The battle with imperialism has been fought and won'. In the same Manifesto, the party programme makes provision to enable the 'employer class to expand their economic activities in a way to contribute to the welfare of the society'. No socialist programme would encourage the expansion of the property-owning class. Those who believe in the magnanimity of the rich and, therefore, would allow them to accumulate enormous wealth, build financial empires and in turn set up welfare programmes and foundations to help the toilers in society are proved wrong by the experiences of the exploited class in the United States as well as here in Nigeria. Even if the welfarism advocated by the Action Group were a viable proposition, the productive capacity of the dependent Nigerian economy would be incapable of sustaining any meaningful welfare programme.

The Northern Peoples Congress (NPC), the dominant political party in the North and in the Federal coalition government of 1959–66 had a more reactionary ideology and a stronger pro-British attitude. It was a party of feudal-cum-bourgeois elements interested only in itself and expressing an arrogant paternalistic attitude to the Nigerian masses, especially those in the North.

Nigeria was never destitute of radical forces. Their inability, however, to forge a strong front and provide an alternative leadership to the parties of the ruling class is explicable in terms of the anti-communist sentiment created and sustained by British imperialism and their neo-colonial agents. For purposes of security, many radical elements were forced to operate within the reactionary political parties. Only the trade union movement afforded some of them a more progressive front. These radical elements were responsible for whatever progressive programmes that existed in the conservative parties. They were also influential in such progressive organisations as the Zikist Movement, the Nigerian Youth Congress, the Socialist Workers and Farmers Party, in several small socialist parties, and in the students unions. Some of them were champions of the rights of the minority peoples in Nigeria. Through their unrelenting propaganda and agitation, they helped to undermine the corrupt regime of Abubakar and Azikiwe.

During the early days of the nationalist struggle and up to the beginning of independence many nationalist leaders, irrespective of their ideological stance, were aware of the exploitative nature of the colonial rule; they knew also that the very social, political and economic system introduced in the colonies, and which was inherited at independence, was designed to sustain this system of exploitation. The question is why did those nationalists refuse to destroy this system when they achieved political power? Several answers can be given but they all relate to the very character of the nationalist struggles as well as the realities of the colonial forces. But the strongest reason is that at some later stage the material interest of the nationalist leaders coincided with the status quo, with the neo-colonial and dependent economic and social system. Having become the most important sector of the ruling class, their social being was enhanced by the existing social order. They themselves became the exploiters and sought theoretical justification for the status quo. No effort was therefore made to question the economic ideas of the so-called foreign experts. Foreign investment, foreign aid, capitalism in general, or the so-called mixed economy and profit-oriented activities, became, for them, the only true expressions of economic life.

The above observation is confirmed when we contrast the views about the economic system expressed in 1961 by Mallam Waziri Ibrahim, the former Minister of Economic Development, with the views expressed by members of the Constitutional Drafting Committee in 1976. The views of Mallam Ibrahim were expressed in a Ministerial statement on Nigeria's economic planning policy.[9] According to him, the policy of the Nigerian Federal Government as a whole was 'one of encouraging private investment – both indigenous and foreign' – in order to develop 'our resources'. The Minister went on to justify the need for foreign investment and declared, 'But foreign investment comes in to make profit. We must accept that and allow them to repatriate their profits.'[10] Questioned by the Honourable Members about the danger of foreign economic domination and exploitation, the Minister argued that both are inevitable and natural. He argued that, '. . . much as we appreciate the good intention of Honourable Members, we must also not overlook the fact that we shall continue to be under the control of imperialists and capitalists who have taken the lead in this world in economic development.'[11] Then the Minister cynically advised that a break with imperialism could not be radical, if it was possible at all.

He appeared fully aware of the difficulties in actually winning economic freedom, even though there was empty talk of freedom of economic action. Hence the Minister asked: 'What do members think is the reason for the assassination of Patrice Lumumba?'[12] – and he went on to state: 'Imperialists saw that he [Lumumba] was a real nationalist, that he was out to see that the resources of the Congo were used to improve the welfare of the Congolese people as a whole. When imperialists are in economic control of any country, it is not easy to free that country. For this reason, we do appreciate all the excellent ideas advocated by Honourable Members, but a complete turn-about of the economic system is not an easy thing.'[13]

It is therefore obvious that by 1961 the Nigerian leaders were fully aware of the neo-colonial character of our economic and social system. But because of the impotence of the nationalist ideology aimed at just nominal transfer of political control and emasculated political will, it could not free the country from the foreign economic stranglehold. The refusal to try other alternative social and economic systems such as scientific socialism was not the result of political, logical considerations. It was initially the result of political expediency, namely to strike a compromise with imperialism. Thus Mallam Ibrahim, in that statement, admitted that the refusal to accept a true socialist philosophy in Nigeria was because it would offend the imperialists and thus endanger the physical and political survival of the nationalist leaders. According to him,

> Certain measures have been taken to introduce a socialist philosophy of economic planning in certain neighbouring countries and this has resulted in the imperialists sabotaging the country. Imperialists have got various means of defending their monopoly. They have got their newspapers and television, and they go to any extent to tell lies. They can say or write any amount of untruths to discredit us. If we want really to set about improving our economy in any particular ways, they may say we are communists. They can make our countrymen to suspect our moves. If they do not succeed by false propaganda, by calling us all sorts of names, if they fail to make us unpopular in order to win their case, they can arrange assassination. They can do it by poison or by setting our own people against us. They can go to any extent without discrimination.[14]

In this statement is demonstrated the awful political realities of imperialism, which are not abated even when a dependent country has political independence. This type of information is totally missing in the contents of development programmes, trade agreements and all types of political and economic ties between the centre of world capitalism and its peripheral regions. What we find in formal documents are nice theoretical justifications for aid, investment, loan, savings, profit and the myth of 'world market'.

The Age of National Reformism

The contradictions within the neo-colonial Nigerian state with its inherited bourgeois institutions led to various economic, political and social crises soon after independence. Among the ruling class there was a fierce struggle for political hegemony. Several strategies were adopted to build a dependable political basis. Ethnic unions, which had been in existence before independence, flourished and took on a direct political role, and this was called 'tribalism' to emphasize its ethnic-oriented strategies. Employment, promotion, scholarships, award of contracts were influenced by attempts by those in power to patronize their tribesmen with a view to securing their support in the political battle. There was general corruption and nepotism in social and political life.

There was fierce competition to amass wealth by the ruling class. Most of them played a comprador role to foreign capital. Foreign trade missions, financed by the state and undertaken on behalf of the country, were often occasions for contracting private business relationships. Unviable government agencies were created to provide jobs for political allies and clients. While these developments were going on the lot of the working class deteriorated owing to inflation, unemployment and breakdown in morale. This was compounded by an austerity programme by the government in which workers were called upon to make sacrifices. Workers embarked on a general strike in 1964 which rocked the very foundation of the state. Crisis followed upon crisis. The government was unable to conduct a national census or even an election. In the Western region tribal strategies reached such dangerous proportions that the masses took the laws into their hands in order to protect themselves against the manipulation of the bourgeoisie, especially within their own tribe.

Eventually, some army officers, motivated by the desire to reform the social and political systems carried out a *coup d'etat* which toppled the civilian regime of Azikiwe/Balewa. A wave of political and social reforms were introduced by the successive military regimes of Aguiyi Ironsi and Yakubu Gowon. In spite of such reforms, the deterioration in the system continued and led to one of the most destructive civil wars in African history.[15] It was thought that the Gowon regime which was in power from 1967 to 1975 was responsible for the continued crisis in the system. With its overthrow by Murtala and his men, one of the most far-reaching set of reforms was introduced. Prominent among these were the creation of more states to diffuse tribalism and encourage even development, the removal and trial of some corrupt public officers, new agricultural (Operation Feed the Nation) and educational (Universal Free Primary Education) programmes, anti-inflation and anti-corruption bodies, and foreign exchange tribunals[16] introduced in order to cleanse the society. Years after these measures were introduced Nigerian society still faces those basic contradictions. And, in fact, the contradictions have intensified. Corruption has never been higher, there is staggering inflation, the working class and the masses of Nigeria have never had it so bad. In spite of the oil boom, the country is broke and is now borrowing from Britain and other Western sources.

The last army Head of State, General Obasanjo, who previously rejected the idea of any ideological commitment by Nigeria, later made a fervent appeal for a national ideology as a way of saving the system from collapsing. General Obasanjo was in effect re-echoing Gowon when he said in 1970 that 'Nigeria is suffering a serious social malady and the nation has never had it so bad'. In spite of the disappointing lessons in the history of reformism in Nigeria, the ruling class is unable to learn that reforms within the capitalist system can only bring about temporary changes. In spite of the lessons of the thirteen and half years of military regime marked by radical reforms that have proved futile, Nigeria has returned to another civilian regime while maintaining intact the same neo-colonial social structures. The hope for resolving the contradictions facing the country is now placed on the new Constitution and the new parties with their party programmes and manifestos.

The new constitution has recommended a 'mixed economy' as the ideology of the new society. The five registered political parties have tacitly endorsed the mixed economy ideology. This ideology is put forward as an ideological expression of the historical and social realities in Nigeria. The majority of the members of the 1975 Nigerian Constitutional Drafting Committee argued that, 'Nigeria has always had its ideology, namely, Mixed Economy, and that there are no compelling reasons for abandoning that ideology in favour of one conceived in a foreign political and social climate. In point of fact Nigerian Economy is "socialist" in certain areas of the economy whilst in other areas individual initiative and ownership is permissible.' The objective realities clearly show that 'mixed economy' is another name for capitalism. 'The State or public sector which is regarded by the mixed economy theoreticians as the socialist sector is in fact established to promote private accumulation of the capitalist class. It is not run on socialist principles. Thus the so-called "state enterprises" and institutions such as the railway, the telecommunication, the airways, mining, civil service, the army, the police, the public works, etc., do not serve the interest of labour but rather serve the interest of capital. Furthermore they are operated mainly by private contractors and managed by members and clients of the bourgeois class.'[17]

An examination of the programme of the five political parties reveals the same populist and idealist perspective, which ignores the objective realities, in particular the class character of our society. Two of the parties, the Unity Party of Nigeria (UPN) and the Redemption Peoples Party (PRP), make the greatest showing of being socialist. The UPN has declared that it would not nationalise any private enterprise. The PRP has said almost the same and promises freedom to private enterprise as well as a 'mixed economy'.

We have seen the weaknesses of the ideological perspective of the ruling class in Nigeria. Their utopian perspective on the question of development ignores the realities of the society. Every society mirrors an ideology. And each ideological framework allows a possible range of development and change within it. This defines the limit or boundary of the efficacy of reforms. Beyond that, certain changes are only possible given a radical and revolutionary transformation of the society. Thus inflation, corruption and unemployment can be resolved only beyond the limits of the capitalist system. The basis of this radical transformation is the economic structure of the society.

The efficacy of ideas for development is also circumscribed by the prevailing socio-economic realities. The class character of the Nigerian society is, however, totally ignored. Instead, a manipulative populism is popularized in order to rationalize the exploitative capitalist system and to avoid revolutionary transformation of the society. It is obvious that for a nation to embark on the course of a meaningful and authentic development that will unleash its creative potential with respect to the material, cultural and spiritual spheres, it must run a self-reliant economy. No self-reliant economy is possible if the structure of the economy makes the society dependent on external manipulation as is the case in Nigeria. But a neo-colonial economy serves the interest of the ruling class while negating the interest of the working class and the masses in the society. For a meaningful development therefore we need a radical and revolutionary departure from the existing social and economic order and its corresponding bourgeois ideology.

References

1. Chief Obafemi Awolowo, *The Peoples Republic*. (Ibadan: Oxford University Press, 1968).
2. *Draft Constitution of the Federal Republic of Nigeria*, vol. 1 (Lagos, 1976), pp.xli.
3. *Ibid.*, vol. 11, p. 35.
4. K. Marx, 'Preface to *A Contribution to the Critique of Political Economy*', in Karl Marx and Frederick Engels, *Selected Works*, vol. 1 (Moscow: Progress Publishers, 1969).
5. In the absence of practice, and still on the level of pure theory, science (as theory) endeavours to expunge the human mind of some of its absurd creations substituting it, as Engels observed, with less absurd creations. F. Engels to Conrad Schmidt (1890), cited in *Marx and Engels: Selected Correspondence*, p.4.
6. In contemporary Nigeria, capitalist social formations exist together with feudal and communal social formations. But the rest bow to the dominant influence of capital.
7. The relationship between the economic structure of society and the ideological expressions is not a one-to-one correspondence in which there is economic cause for each idea. Engels emphasises this point when he wrote: 'The basis of the law of inheritance – assuming that the stages reached in the development of the family would be difficult to prove, for instance, that the absolute liberty of the testator in England,

and the severe restrictions imposed upon him in France are only due in every detail to economic causes. Both react however on the economic sphere to a very considerable extent, because they influence the division of property'. Engels, *op. cit.*

8. Awolowo, *op. cit.*, pp. 188–9.
9. Mallam Waziri Ibrahim, Hon. Minister of Economic Development, *Ministerial Statement on Nigeria's Economic Planning Policy and its relationship to Distributive Trades and Road Transportation*, made in the House of Representatives during the Supplementary Budget Session, 22 November 1961.
10. *Ibid.*
11. *Ibid.*
12. *Ibid.*
13. *Ibid.*
14. *Ibid.*
15. On 30 May 1967, as a result of breakdown in the political and social framework of Nigeria, a section of the country declared itself the independent state of Biafra. The session was called off in 1970 as a result of military defeat.
16. According to Col. Mohammadu Jega, those measures, such as Price Control Board, Corrupt Practices Investigation Bureau, and the Public Complaints Bureau, which were introduced to clean up the society of certain social vices, have failed. But Col. Jega wrongly blames Nigerians as human beings for this failure, forgetting that it is as Nigerians living in a capitalist society that they should be blamed. *New Nigeria* 12 January 1978.
17. T. Uzodinma Nwala, 'Ideological Dependency and the Problem of Autonomy in Nigeria,' paper read during the *Workshop on Dependency and Underdevelopment in West Africa*, organized by the Institute of African Studies, University of Nigeria, Nsukka, April, 1978.

8. Class Struggle as a Reality of Nigerian Development

Bade Onimode

> Economic development has always been propelled by classes and groups interested in a new economic and social order,has always been opposed and obstructed by these interested in the preservation of the *status quo*, rooted in and deriving innumerable benefits and habits of thought from the existing fabric of society, the prevailing mores, customs, and institutions. It has always been marked by more or less violent clashes, has proceded by starts and spurts, suffered setbacks and gained new terrain – it has never been a smooth, harmonious process unfolding placidly over time and space (Paul A. Baran, 1967)

A perspective on class struggle as a reality of the development of Nigeria derives directly from a general conceptualization of development and class struggle. Briefly, development means fundamental structural transformation from an outmoded social system to a new one through a determined struggle against the conservative retrograde forces of the *status quo*. It requires a basic reorganization of the economic, political and social structure of the stagnant society through an all-out mobilization of all its creative resources. This is required in Nigeria to liquidate imperialist domination, terminate capitalist exploitation, transcend technological rigidities, and raise the consciousness of the masses.

These processes involve class struggle – defined as the inevitable conflict between the forces of social transformation and the reactionary forces of the old society. This confrontation between the class demanding a social order and the conservative ruling class defending and imposing the outmoded system is essentially a political struggle to control the determination of social policies, especially the allocation of national resources. The inevitability of struggle arises from the fact that: 'Since a social organization, however inadequate, never disappears by itself, since a ruling class, however parasitic, never yields power unless compelled to do so by overwhelming pressure, development and progress can only be attained if all the energies and abilities of a people that was politically, socially and economically disfranchised under the old system are thrown into battle against the forces of the *ancien regime*.'[1]

Class struggle as a social *reality* of Nigeria's development is here construed from three points of view. First, the past transformation of

Nigeria from pre-capitalist modes to the present neo-colonial capitalist system has, in fact, empirically involved class struggles. Second, the current demands in the country for genuine development, as opposed to the prevailing policies of underdevelopment that the ruling class has been pursuing in active collaboration with foreign capitalist forces, is manifest class struggle. The outcome of the current struggle and its future character will determine the course of Nigeria's development. Third, the nature of class struggles outlined above is not merely incidental and epiphenomenal to economic development in Nigeria, but central and decisive both to its best understanding and dialectical path.

The rest of this essay will elaborate these viewpoints. The first part examines the nature of social classes and class formations in Nigeria from the colonial period to the present. This is followed by an investigation of class struggles and economic development under the colonial system. The subsequent section discusses the class struggle in neo-colonial Nigeria. In the final section, there is a brief examination of the possible trend of class relations and economic development in the future.

Classes and Class Formation in Nigeria

The discussion of class struggle in the development process hinges critically on the demonstration of the existence of social classes and the nature of class formations. This is particularly important in Africa where obscurantism and ideological distortions becloud the rational analysis of classes. To deal with these issues, this section demonstrates the applicability of class analysis to Nigeria and indicates the general outlines of class formation in the country since the pre-capitalist era.

The concept of class is anchored to the ownership of the means of production. Accordingly, social classes are based on the division of social groups with respect to ownership of the means of production, where ownership includes both control and appropriation of surplus value by one social group from another. This emphasizes that it is not merely juridical property relations but *social* relations of production between persons that are critical.[2] Lenin underlined the same point when he defined social classes as 'large groups of people differing from each other by the place they occupy in the historically determined system of social production, by their relation (in some cases fixed and formulated in law) to the means of production; by their role in the social organization of labour, and, consequently by the dimensions and mode of acquiring the share of social wealth of which they dispose.'[3] One other feature of social classes emphasized by this conception is their dynamic nature. This arises both from the fact that the relations of social production that define classes are basically dynamic and changing phenomena; moreover, the process of class formation involves structural changes.

These observations lead directly to the two theoretical distortions of class concept. First, it is argued that in some sense classes cannot be identified with respect to certain criteria. These include education, occupation, income, power and life-style. In particular, social mobility is advanced as invalidating the existence of classes. In spite of their static character, it will be demonstrated below that these criteria are typically correlated with the control of productive forces and appropriation of surplus value. Moreover, social mobility in social stratification studies underlines the process of class formation and class differentiation as discussed below. Second, it is argued that members of a social class do not always demonstrate consciousness of class membership. The point, however, is that complete class solidarity is not necessary for all situations involving conflict of class interest while class consciousness may not be fully manifest to individuals until they are actually involved in class conflict. As Shivji argues, this makes it methodologically wrong to interview people in order to determine their class consciousness.[4]

In application to Nigeria and other African countries, class analysis encounters the bogus assertion that we have ethnic, and not class, relations. This argument is based on the ethnic relations inherited from the colonial past and nurtured by contemporary bourgeois politicians who want power based in communal hegemony. But what is required is to make the place occupied by individuals in the historically determined system of social production the basis of analysis. 'The importance attributed by ethnologists to cultural elements of . . . populations has long concealed the nature of the socio-economic structures into which these populations are integrated.'[5] While ethnic consciousness is not denied, it has to be recognized rightly as 'part of the ideological rationalisation that reinforces and in turn reflects relations of production'. Our classes may be embryonic, but they exist. Thus, while ambitious petty bourgeois politicians and others are busy preaching the deadly parochialism of ethnic chauvinism, they actively form alliances with other petty bourgeois elements in various ethnic groups to consolidate their repressive domination of the masses. In periods of conflict between the ruling class and the working people, solidarity is underlined by identity of class interest, which is the motive for whipping up ethnic sentiment.

This 'communal or ethnic strategy' of class struggle is revealed with respect to the 'role of emergent classes in Nigeria' and the 'communal basis of democracy' when Sklar wrote: 'Rising class interests were found to have motivated the organisation and activities of the principal pan-tribal or nationality movements; they were fundamental to the momentous controversy over the African Continental Bank; they have produced intense conflict within the dominant party in the Eastern Region, altered a traditional class structure in the Northern Region, generated political opposition within communities in areas of traditional habitation, and mobilised that opposition effectively for nationalistic purposes[6] . . . In Nigeria, the power exercised by leaders of the major political parties would appear to derive mainly from the class and communal foundations of these parties and their unofficial ancillary structures. Communal interest groups generally accept the leadership of emergent and dominant class-interest groups.[7]

The development of social classes reflects changing modes of production. In Nigeria, these processes can be divided broadly into the pre-independence period (embracing the pre-colonial and colonial era) and the post-independent or neo-colonial capitalist period. In broad terms, the pre-independent class formations in Nigeria corresponded to the colonial and the mixed feudal-communal-slave modes of production. The separation of the colonial mode is necessary to focus on the salient features of the colonial economy and the impact of colonialism on class formations, which also reflect the production relations of the traditional society.

Pre-colonial Nigeria exhibited two broad societal and ideological types, the centralized and non-centralized.[8] The former included the Habe and Fulani dynasties, Yoruba and Benin kingdoms, as well as some Igbo chiefdoms. These were governed by ruling classes based on the divinity of kinship. In the non-centralized societies, the ruling classes were based on age and religious status. In both types of societies, the non-ruling classes consisted of hunters, peasants, warriors and sometimes slaves. Though the classes were differentiated customarily by lineage, age and religion, these criteria also conferred advantages with respect to control over productive forces (such as labour under communalism, and slavery and land under feudalism) and the relative appropriation of surplus which supported the superior life-style or consumption level of the ruling classes. In the colonial epoch the British imperialists superimposed their capitalist mode of production and ideology on the traditional ones. Hence the colonial economy of Nigeria could be characterized with respect to its mechanisms of integration into the international capitalist system, the predominant form of exchange activity, ownership structure, and surplus appropriation.[9]

The major economic links between the colony and international capitalism included import-export trade, foreign investment, shipping, air transport, foreign 'aid' and technical assistance. In addition, specific institutional mechanisms like central banking (initiated as the West African Currency Board for British West African colonies), marketing boards and West African Airways constituted the other bilateral colonial links between Nigeria and Britain.

The main exchange activity of the colonial economy was export production to meet the colonizing motives of securing cheap sources of raw materials for British industrialization and a profitable outlet for imperialist monopoly capital and British export manufactures. Consequently, colonial capital, infrastructural investment and economic management were geared to cheap production of cocoa, cotton, tin, groundnuts, rubber, palm oil and kernel, timber, and hides and skins for export. Domestic manufacturing was actively banned or discouraged to protect Britain's export market in Nigeria, while food production for domestic consumption was left to haphazard peasant endeavours. Agriculture was the mainstay of the economy.

Commercial agriculture for so-called 'cash crops', mining, commerce (import-export trade and wholesale distribution of imports) and finance (banking and insurance to finance the colonialists' transactions) were the main sectors of the colonial economy. The imports consisted of machinery, equipment, beverages and drinks as well as other manufactured consumer goods.

The ownership of these sectors, except agriculture, was vested mainly in the British, since other imperialists were excluded from the Nigerian colony as much as possible. The appropriation of economic surplus corresponding to this economic structure was monopolised by the British. It involved taxation of income from agriculture and other sources, appropriation of marketing board surpluses generated from underpaying peasants for their agricultural exports, underpaid labour, rents and royalties from mining, underpricing of exports, and overpricing of imports.[10]

The social classes corresponding to the colonial modes of pre-capitalist and capitalist production consisted of the imperialist ruling class, an emergent petty bourgeoisie, and the peasantry and the working class.[11] The imperialist ruling class consisted of the Nigerian representatives of the British national bourgeoisie or ruling class. They included the colonial governors, residents, district officers, other administrators, military and police officers, merchants and financers. This upper class was assisted in its exploitative activities by other foreign merchants. The British imperialist ruling class monopolized political power, controlled the state apparatus and dominated the economy with their foreign allies.

The Nigerian (or domestic) petty bourgeoisie initially consisted of clerks in the public and private sectors, teachers, local government administrators, small merchants engaging mainly in retail distribution from the imperialist mercantile houses, and produce traders or licensed buying agents who were middlemen between peasant producers and the marketing boards. Later, they were joined by land speculators, lawyers, doctors, engineers and other professionals, big farmers (or kulaks producing cocoa, cotton, groundnuts, and rubber on a large scale with hired labour) and students. The leadership of the nationalist movement, political parties and trade unions emerged from this class. The working class consisted of workers, peasants, petty artisans, petty market-women and jobless primary school-leavers whose numbers increased in the 1950s. The workers were initially migrant labourers from the rural peasantry. This class constituted the mass base of the nationalist movement in Nigeria.

After the Second World War, the numbers and strength of the petty bourgeoisie and the influence of the working class grew rapidly with the expansion of the economy, increasing economic opportunities for Africans and the intensified nationalist struggle which involved formation of political parties, mass political recruitment, and African participation in government at the regional level. The petty bourgeois class gained quantitatively and qualitatively at the expense of the masses in this period, especially after the introduction of regional governments run by Nigerians in the North, East and West in 1951. These new regional administrations used state machinery to expand and consolidate the petty bourgeois class economically and politically.[12]

After nominal or 'flag' independence in 1960, Nigeria was transformed from a classical colony into a neo-colonial capitalist system. The process involved two critical changes: state power was now formally vested in the leaders of the nationalist struggle, and the institutional as well as economic links that tied Nigeria to Britain bilaterally were increasingly becoming multilateral so that Nigeria was more effectively integrated into the international capitalist system. These changes meant that in structural terms the neo-colonial economy was essentially the same as the colonial economy. Both exhibited similar division of labour with agriculture remaining the predominant sector of the economy.[13] There was a persistent export orientation within the erroneous bourgeois conception of 'exports as the engine of growth', domination of the economy by British and other imperialists and appropriation of economic surplus by them for foreign development and Nigeria's underdevelopment. With a new 'open door' policy that exposed Nigeria to the unbridled exploitation of any interested imperialist country, American capital has steadily displaced British monopoly capital while Germans, French, Japanese and others have increasingly exploited the economy, especially with the increasing importance of the Nigerian petroleum sector since the mid-sixties. (See Table 1 for the main sectors of the neo-colonial economy).

Table 1
Sectors of the Nigerian Economy, 1962–8 (%)

Sector	*1962–3*	*1963–4*	*1964–5*	*1965–6*	*1966–7*	*1967–8*
Agriculture, Livestock, Forestry and Fishing	61.2	61.1	59.2	56.4	54.9	55.9
Mining	2.0	2.2	3.2	5.3	7.2	3.5
Manufacturing & Crafts	5.8	5.4	5.4	5.9	5.9	7.4
Electricity & Water Supply	0.5	0.5	0.6	0.6	0.7	0.7
Building & Construction	4.4	4.6	4.4	5.2	5.1	4.9
Distribution	12.2	12.7	13.3	13.1	12.7	13.3
Transport	4.2	4.3	4.0	3.6	3.4	3.4
Communications	0.4	0.5	0.5	0.6	0.6	0.5
General Government	3.9	3.6	3.6	3.3	3.3	3.3
Education	2.7	2.6	2.9	2.8	3.0	3.2
Health	0.5	0.5	0.6	0.6	0.6	0.6
Other Services	2.1	2.0	2.1	2.3	2.6	3.2
Total	100.0	100.0	100.0	100.0	100.0	100.0

Source: *Second National Development Plan, 1970–74* (Lagos; Federal Ministry of Information, 1970), p. 51, Table 4.

The most significant feature of this economy is its independence on foreign capital and the consequent persistent export of much of its surplus by imperialists. These developments were based on the active collaboration of the new Nigerian ruling class. Another feature of the post-independent economy is the increasing participation of the Nigerian petty bourgeoisie, especially through the manipulation of the state apparatus. Nigerianization increased lucrative job opportunities while politics and kleptocracy became the most important mechanisms of capital accumulation by this spineless, corrupt and parasitic elite.[14] Since 1972 the ambivalent indigenization programme[15] has opened up new avenues for Nigerian petty bourgeois incursions into Levantine-controlled small-scale businesses and equity participation in other imperialist enterprises without real control over the productive forces of the country.

These developments in the neo-colonial system produced significant changes in class formations, especially at the upper levels. First, a country-wide bourgeois class with foreign and domestic components emerged more clearly. It is not a national bourgeoisie because of its dependent character, but its domestic branch has a ruling group that monopolizes state power. It consists of a foreign bourgeoisie, which has increasingly added an industrial arm to its predominantly commercial structure, and a domestic petty bourgeoisie. The members of the foreign commercial bourgeoisie include imperialist merchants dominating the import-export trade, shipping, banking and insurance, as well as Lebanese and Syrian merchants. The foreign industrial bourgeoisie comprises the local representatives of the imperialist industrial establishment in the petroleum and manufacturing sectors. Together, the foreign commercial and industrial bourgeoisie are the patrons of Nigeria's petty bourgeoisie. The Nigerian petty bourgeoisie, which acquired state power in 1960, may be sub-divided into four branches. First, there is what has been called the 'bureaucratic' bourgeoisie, the ruling group and executive committee of the bourgeoisie as a whole, foreign and domestic. The bureaucratic bourgeoisie is identified with the state bureaucracy, with top decision-makers in government ministries, corporations and other parastatals, as well as in the private sector. They include ministers (commissioners under military rule since 1966), state governors and their secretaries, permanent secretaries, and other higher civil servants, corporation chairmen and directors, Nigerian chairmen and directors in the private sector, higher military and police officers, as well as higher academics and administrators in universities and polytechnics. Most of them are characterized, as Shivji puts it, by bureaucratic rather than democratic decision-making ethics and by technocratic rather than political behaviour. Their style of economic planning in Nigeria reveals this most clearly.

Second, there is the comprador bourgeoisie, which is identified by its intermediary role between foreign capitalists and Nigeria; they are the local conduits for imperialist exploitation. Generally identified as merchant distributors, they are 'factors' or agents of imperialist importers and mercantile firms peddling electronics, building materials, textiles and similar goods. Some of the bureaucratic bourgeoisie accumulate savings and/or manipulate their positions to acquire capital for participation in these lucrative comprador enterprises. These commercial petty bourgeois elements are most dependent on imperialists for supplies and capital. Big capitalist farmers should also be included in this group because they share control over some capital and labour and depend on foreign supplies (fertilizers feeds, and machinery).

Third, the professional bourgeoisie consists of the burgeoning group of academics, doctors, lawyers, engineers, accountants, management executives, teachers (with degrees or a National Certificate of Education), and other professionals. They share the common features of specialized expertise, an urban base, and service under either the foreign bourgeoisie, the state apparatus, the private sector, or engagement in self-employment as consultants. The rapid expansion of university education in the post-independent era as well as the increasing division of labour in social production account for their rapid increase. Some of these professionals also engage in comprador enterprises like the bureaucratic bourgeoisie.

Fourth, there are the middle and lower-salaried sector in the public and private sectors, including primary school teachers, the rank and file of the army and police, shop-keepers and students. This petty bourgeois group is also largely urban-based, but they are less homogeneous than other groups in the petty bourgeoisie. Indeed, many of them, like the lower salaried clerks, share the same sub-culture with workers, except that the career ambitions and job security of the former lead them more towards the petty bourgeoisie than the working class.

Below the petty bourgeoisie are the toiling masses, Fanon's 'wretched of the earth', who are the worst exploited and most insecure members of Nigeria's population. They are the truly dispossessed, consisting of workers, peasants, petty artisans and petty market-women. These are the classes that have retained their social identity most since the pre-independence period. They are also the classes that have experienced most frequent and most violent confrontations with the ruling group. Though the workers are urban-based, the peasants are widely dispersed throughout the rural areas on small private plots from which they eke out an uncertain existence. More recently, with increasing land speculation by the petty bourgeoisie and population pressure in the south-eastern region, land hunger has been driving more of these peasants into paid employment. Indeed, the peasantry is the genesis of the African workers, some of whom still retain their rural agricultural links.

Class Struggle in Colonial Nigeria

Colonial Nigeria has been selected as the first scenario of class struggle in the country, not because it is historically the earliest example, but because it provides the best empirical data and the sharpest, longest and most intense class antagonisms in the pre-independence era. But to clarify the discussion, it is necessary to present a brief statement of the conception of class struggle.[16]

Class struggle is in fact one of the defining features of social classes. As Marx puts it: 'The separate individuals form a class only in so far as they have to carry on a *common battle against another class;* otherwise they are on hostile terms with each other as competitors'.[17] This again underlines the dynamic nature of social classes; they are not just static, placid social collections. Moreover, though class struggle constitutes the motive force in history, it may not always be immediately clear and pure as class struggle. It can also take different forms depending on the concrete historical conditions. Except in periods of overt confrontation or revolutionary situations, it may be latent and unidentifiable. However, since the colonial environment was established by violent confrontation and continuously juxtaposed the Africans against the imperialists, its class struggle was manifest most of the time, even though it might not be seen in class perspective.

The third point about class struggle is its essentially political character. This arises because the social relations that underlie classes also embrace political relations. And since these political relations are most clearly defined around the state, it follows that the state is central to class struggle. *Class struggle is, therefore, political struggle against the apparatus of political power of one class over another*: this political power is centralized in the state and its apparatus, which then constitute the seat of political power and class domination. Hence the state is a class category. 'Since the power of the ruling class is always concentrated in the organization of the state, the oppressed class must aim directly against the mechanism of the state. Every class struggle is thus a *political struggle* which in its objective aims at the abolition of the existing social order and at the establishment of a new social order.'[18]

Given the nature of the colonial state and economy as symbolizing the collective oppression and exploitation of the total Nigerian population by the imperialist British bourgeois class, the struggle against it was nationalist. The nationalist movement was a class struggle because it was inspired, led and co-ordinated by members of the domestic petty bourgeoisie in an alliance of patriotism with the Nigerian working class and students against the state power of the British colonial bourgeoisie. The Nigerian Youth Movement (NYM) and, later, the three major political parties – National Council of Nigeria and the Cameroons (NCNC), Action Group (AG) and Northern People's Congress (NPC) – that spearheaded the anti-colonial struggle were all led by the Nigerian petty bourgeoisie and allied directly to the working class and students through trade unions and student unions, which were led by the lower segment of the petty bourgeoisie. There was also mass recruitment from the peasantry, petty artisans and petty market-women.[19]

In particular, Sklar shows that the formation of the emergent petty bourgeois class and the development of the nationalist parties corresponds to the 'intermixture' of elites. He states that all the three major parties were created and periodically revitalized by professionals, journalists, educators, businessmen and students. These groups later united with less radical elements like chiefs, local government functionaries, and traders to form the privileged class of petty bourgeoisie which mobilized workers and peasants. For example, in 1958, 80 per cent of the top leadership of the NCNC were in the ranks of professionals, educators, merchants and senior civil servants; the corresponding percentages for the AG and NPC were 74 and 97 per cent respectively. For all three parties, 84 per cent of the top 211 executive members were in the occupational categories of the upper layer of the petty bourgeoisie.[20]

Beyond demanding national autonomy or control of state power, the class struggle against the British bourgeoisie was critical for the economic development of Nigeria. This can be appreciated from four basic considerations: the colonial economic policies of the British, specific demands of Nigerians in the struggle, the overall ideology of the nationalists, and the major concessions of the imperialist bourgeoisie during the struggle.

On the first point, the British bourgeoisie in Nigeria sought to exploit the colony through the imposition of capitalist social relations of production. The specific policies addressed to this objective included control over land. Thus in 1937 the British colonial government awarded Shell and British Petroleum the total land area of Nigeria as an oil concession. Some of the land was also alienated as British plantations. This struck at the root of the traditional feudal and communal land relations as it introduced private property in land. Partly to ensure labour supply on plantations, mines, commercial and other imperialist enterprises, poll and other taxes were imposed on the peasantry to drive them into wage slavery. Forced labour was also used. These workers were then systematically exploited to raise surplus value, and when trade unionism was allowed, it was based on the British single-company union system. This labour policy was only part of the systematic introduction of capitalist commodity exchange in which labour itself is just another commodity. The commercialization of agriculture was part of this process. To crown these new capitalist relations, the appropriation and utilization of national economic surplus was centralized in the imperialist bourgeoisie as government revenue from taxes, marketing board surpluses, and the profits of British enterprises.[21]

Against the systematic transformation of the social, political, and economic organization of the pre-colonial mixed mode of production, its dominant interests represented by chiefs, merchants and other petty bourgeois elements mounted resistance against specific grievances. These included land ownership, mineral rights, forced labour, oppressive taxes, and employment conditions; these were initially addressed directly or indirectly against the prevailing capitalist accumulation by the British bourgeoisie. After the Second World War more sophisticated nationalists from overseas military service and universities eventually accepted the increasing capitalist transformation but demanded national control of the new capitalist relations and economic surplus. This was the point where the three major political parties emerged. Confrontations over land, forced labour and traditional social relations were replaced by better-organized conflicts centred around control of state power, workers welfare and appropriation of surplus. Trade union struggles in this period resulted in the appointment of various commissions to review wages and salaries in the 1940s and 1950s.[22] The businessmen in the Nigerian petty bourgeoisie also had a protracted struggle for the survival of their small enterprises, especially in banking. This was monopolized by the British imperialist banks like Barclays, which used their huge capital resources for ruinous competition with the weak indigenous banks.[23]

The third feature of the colonial class struggle centres on the ideology of contending classes. While the British bourgeoisie were still aggressively imperialist, the Nigerian petty bourgeoisie, most of whose leaders (merchants, professionals and educators) had been cultivated by the British and nurtured with capitalist values during their education in Nigeria and overseas, even became defenders of the capitalist order.[24] It is, therefore, not surprising that the dominant ideologies of all the three major political parties were implicitly petty bourgeois; none of them explicitly adopted a specific coherent ideology. While a radical youth wing of the NCNC, the Zikists, opted for mild socialism embracing pragmatism and liberal democracy between 1946 and 1950, the party itself never endorsed socialism; in the AG, 'principled welfare statism' was the central tendency, while in the NPC, which was the most reactionary of the three parties, 'feudal and islamic conservatism' was the dominant ideological inclination. As all the parties were preoccupied with liberal democracy and political freedom, their petty bourgeois nationalism only resulted in the betrayal of the bourgeois democratic revolution at independence in 1960, because it failed decisively to wrest economic independence for Nigeria from the British imperialist bourgeoisie.

In terms of the colonial class struggles, five results were critical for economic development in colonial Nigeria. First, the agitation of Nigerian nationalists over land partly helped to preserve traditional land tenure systems of communal and family holdings in many parts of the country and checked imperialist alienation of land. This also accounted for the survival of the mixed pre-capitalist modes of production into the post-independence era. The ensuing mixed land tenure systems in the country have certainly contributed to problems of agricultural transformation. On the other hand, the imperialist strength in the land struggles accounts for the development of private property relations in land which have now exploded into capitalist land speculation and the proletarianization of the peasantry.

Second, class struggle over the control of labour, nevertheless, conceded the institution of wage-slavery and contributed to some proletarianization of the peasantry by the imperialist bourgeoisie. The Nigerian victory consisted of the check on the use of forced labour and the development of trade unionism among Nigerian workers. Though the unions were weakened by their organizational fragmentation into single enterprise bodies and by their largely economic demands, they nevertheless provided political support for the nationalist parties. For example, by 1949 when the focus of nationalist struggle shifted to trade unionism, the split in the Nigerian Trades Union

Congress over affiliation to the NCNC resulted in a leftist faction which formed the Nigerian National Federation of Labour and linked up with the NCNC. It was in the course of this effort to mobilize the trade unions for political struggle that the famous Iva Valley Coal miners tragedy occurred in which 2 were murdered and 51 others injured while striking for redress of industrial grievances. This police brutality on the order of an European officer has been credited to have 'first proved the subjective reality of a Nigerian nation'[25] on account of the spontaneous anti-imperialist solidarity it evoked among Nigerians throughout the country.

Third, conflicts over taxation were really centred around the appropriation of surplus. This issue led to the famous Aba women's riot of 1929. The persistent inability to mobilize local surpluses for national development partly accounts for the observed stagnation of the colonial economy and the development of Britain. In particular, these surpluses were generated by the peasantry whose oppression through multiple taxation meant that they bore the brunt of much of whatever capital accumulation occurred under colonialism and even neo-colonialism,[26] in spite of the notorious failure of these systems to stabilize produce prices or peasant incomes.

Fourth, after the Second World War, the intensification of the cumulative contradictions of the colonial system forced the British bourgeoisie to embark on colonial economic planning in 1946.[27] In spite of the small amount, the fact that the imperialists had to commit some resources to the ostensible development of the colony at all was in reality a refinement of the colonial policy of underdevelopment. After some thirty years of such planning in Nigeria, it is now fairly clear that it is part of the strategy of underdevelopment by capitalist ruling classes in the Third World.

Finally, by 1947 the Richards Constitution created three regions preparatory to the institution of regional self-government in 1952. This was the greatest victory of the nationalist struggle before 1960. For the first time, Nigerians were given a share of state power with the British bourgeoisie. The petty bourgeois leadership of the three major parties quickly seized the opportunity to increase primitive capital accumulation by their supporters and to plunge the country into vicious ethnic regionalism which has been one of the signal betrayals of the anti-colonial struggle. The Lyttleton Constitution of 1954 then ushered in a federal structure to institutionalize the British imperialist policy of 'divide and rule'. After regional self-government in 1957/58, flag independence was granted in 1960, when formal state power was relinquished by the British bourgeoisie to the ruling group within the Nigerian petty bourgeoisie.[28]

Class Struggle in Neo-Colonial Nigeria

The euphoria of nominal independence from British oppression under the nationalist slogan of 'freedom, equality and fraternity' might lead to the illusion that class struggles had ended in Nigeria. This was buttressed by propoganda by the new indigenous ruling class on the need for national integration and development for the welfare of all Nigerians, which suggested a homogeneous national population of 'one people, one destiny'. However, even in the jubilant mood of independence celetrations, it soon dawned on people that even to displace the British bourgeoisie from sensitive positions within the state apparatus and from lucrative civil service posts would involve conflict of interest. When, in addition, the Nigerian ruling class had Nigerianized colonial privileges with better jobs, housing, big cars and immense political power without corresponding improvements in the conditions of the workers and peasants, it was clear that independence was the landmark of a new era of intensive class struggles between the new ruling class and the imperialist bourgeoisie on one hand and between the Nigerian petty bourgeoisie generally and the masses on the other. The new class struggles over neo-colonial development centred around both ownership and control of the means of production and the appropriation of national economic surplus. They defined the framework for changing the economic, social and political organization of the country.

Ambivalence Towards the Imperialist Bourgeoisie

The Nigerian petty bourgeoisie has historically been ambivalent towards the imperialist bourgeoisie because of the former's divided loyalty towards the national state. On account of its material class interests and 'dual mandate' (from the national population and the imperialist bourgeoisie), the petty bourgeoisie has to fight the imperialists in order to expand its economic base in the domestic economy. But because this economy is neo-colonial under imperialist domination, the petty bourgeois class is at the same time economically subordinate to, and dependent on, the imperialists with whom it has to collaborate in order to maintain its political power through foreign 'aid', foreign investment and military/technical assistance, as well as to secure local credit from the imperialist banks and distribution agencies from foreign mercantile firms and manufacturing companies. The formation of a British-Nigerian Chamber of Commerce and an American-Nigerian Chamber of Commerce underline this imperialist collaboration. This has led to greater integration of the neo-colonial economy into the international capitalist system over time. It is the foreign appropriation of domestic economic surplus involved in this neo-colonial nexus that perpetuates underdevelopment in the country.

This ambivalence towards the British imperialists is best illustrated with respect to Nigerianization/indigenization and such pro-imperialist policies as the 'open door' policy on foreign investment, foreign trade links with capitalist countries, reliance on capitalist 'aid', cultural subservience to imperialism, and the general choice of capitalist development strategy in spite of its empirical disaster in Latin America, South-East Asia and Africa. With respect to the confrontations between the Nigerian petty bourgeoisie and the imperialist bourgeoisie, these were initiated immediately after independence by the Nigerian bureaucratic bourgeoisie (the ruling group within the petty bourgeoisie) over Nigerianization. This policy opened up vast job opportunities for the ruling group and its other petty bourgeois allies in the government, the private sector, the corporations, the armed forces, the police, and the universities. The Nigerian Enterprises Promotion Decrees, 1972 and 1976,[29] broadened Nigerianization into indigenization. Both were aimed essentially at increasing the participation of the petty bourgeoisie in the economy through total takeover of small-scale enterprises (mainly Levantine) and equity participation in others. As expected, indigenization has been celebrated by the petty bourgeois Nigerian chambers of commerce, industry, mines and agriculture as a major breakthrough.[30] The indigenization exercises were financed by the state's Bank for Commerce and Industry and the Nigerian Development Bank, as well as other public and imperialist banks. The ambivalence towards the imperialist bourgeoisie emerges clearly in these indigenization programmes, which in 1972 were to exclude the imperialist monopoly firms in the crucial sectors of the economy; these were half-heartedly implemented[39] and even in 1976 consistently fell short of a total take-over of the major foreign enterprises. Another class angle to indigenization is the virtual exclusion of the majority of the Nigerian population, since the government refused to socialize or undertake the purchase of foreign enterprises on behalf of the total population. The indigenization compromise has also intensified contradictions between the comprador state and the multinational oil corporations since the 1973 energy crisis.

Another ambivalence towards the imperialist bourgeoisie involved the commitment to free inflow of foreign capital under fiscal incentives and the export of national surplus overseas. Together with the imperialist orientation of Nigeria's import-export trade, such policies have collectively intensified the foreign domination of virtually all sectors of the neo-colonial economy to the exploitative advantages of the domestic petty bourgeoisie and their imperialist mentors. Lucrative construction contracts go to imperialist firms like Julius Berger and Dumez; educational, health care, mass media, economic planning and other programmes are tied to imperialist models and supplies. Within the domestic petty bourgeoisie itself, intra-elite struggles have been manifested in clashes over tariffs, rents, revenue allocation, the census and other policies. The civil war of 1967–70 was the traumatic climax of these class struggles among the various segments of the domestic petty bourgeoisie and the imperialists. The Land Use Decree of April 1978, which has been opposed by the landed aristocracy, has added a new angle to these intra-elite struggles.

National economic planning is another arena of class struggle in neo-colonial Nigeria. Planning personnel and decision-making, plan objectives and policies, plan projects and the results of planning have all reflected class antagonism in the country. The petty bourgeois conception of planning as a purely bureaucratic and technocratic exercise has meant that petty bourgeois bureaucrats and economists have dominated the planning apparatus at all levels. The same bureaucratic and professional bourgeoisie monopolize planning decisions at federal and state levels. The working people are only exhorted to regard the plans as theirs and make sacrifices for their execution.[32] Moreover, the objectives of these plans reflect the class interests of the petty bourgeoisie. In particular, such objectives are typically articulated as slogans to coincide with the aspirations of the masses, but the policies elaborated for their realization are generally either inconsistent with, or inadequate to realize, them.[33] For example, the plans enunciate social equality and self-reliance as basic objectives and proceed to ask for foreign resources, but leave the foreign-dominated private sector intact and concentrate most facilities in urban areas where the petty bourgeoisie live. In such situations it is well to recognize that not only will such plans do nothing to remove inequalities but that they will exacerbate them. This is because a capitalist system necessarily generates inegalitarian social structures. This reality has been activating the working class into demanding such concrete egalitarian measures as free education at all levels, free medical services, guarantee of full employment and more equitable distribution of income. Since 1960, however, apart from the Socialist Workers' and Farmers' Party, which articulated these demands on a national party basis, the ban on politics since 1966 has fossilized this urgent working-class struggle.

Table 2
Lagos Daily Wage Rate (in Kobo)

Year	*Government Rate*	*Private Firms' Rate*
1938	10	12
1945	20	19
1950	28	35
1957	48	–
1960	58	61
1964	58	68
1965	78	79

Source: P. Kilby, *Industrialization in an Open Economy: Nigeria, 1945–66* (Cambridge University Press, 1969).

The projects listed in the development plans make inequality inevitable. Most of them are urban-based, capital-intensive, and obscenely elitist, like specialist hospitals, car assembly plants, expressways, monstrous overhead bridges in Lagos, and the manufacture of ostentatious luxuries like lace, carpets and similar frivolities for the petty bourgeoisie. Rural feeder roads, pipe-borne water, electricity and health centres for the masses are of a second order priority.[34] In 1977 alone, the Second African and World Black Festival of Arts and Culture (FESTAC) and an International Trade Fair were hosted at a cost of hundreds of million of naira. Increasingly, various mass organizations such as the trade unions, farmers' associations and student' unions have been condemning the distorted priorities and inegalitarian distribution of projects in these neo-colonial capitalist plans.

Finally, the collective consequences of these plans only intensify the class contradictions of underdevelopment in the country. They have succeeded very well in generating highly lucrative contracts for both foreign and domestic capitalists, especially since the oil boom started in 1973. This has vastly expanded the ranks of the petty bourgeoisie, increased their primitive accumulation (especially by 'mandarin millionaires') and scandalous life-style. At the other extreme, it has produced an unprecedented rate of inflation and land speculation since 1970 which have pauperized the masses and increased the proletarianization of the peasantry to the point of raising serious doubts about the capacity of Nigerian agriculture to feed the population. These disastrous consequences of neo-colonial capitalist planning have intensified class struggles by workers and peasants on several broad fronts.

Table 3
Minimum Daily Wage Rate for Unskilled Labour (in Kobo)

Year	*Western Region*	*Eastern Region*	*Northern Region*	*Lagos*
1945	–	–	–	22
1946	15	15	15	27
1947	15	15	15	27
1948	15	15	15	27
1949	15	15	15	27
1950	15	17	15	28
1951	19	17	15	30
1952	23	23	15	34
1953	19	23	16	35
1954	50	27	18	39
1955	50	32	21	48
1956	50	32	21	48
1957	50	32	24	48
1958	50	32	28	48
1959	50	50	28	48
1960	50	50	30	60
1961	50	50	30	60
1962	50	50	30	60
1963	50	50	30	60
1964	63	63	50	78
1965	63	63	50	78

Source: Helleiner, *op. cit*., p. 446.

After independence the economic crises of the colonial era persisted.

To deal with them and avert serious social crisis, the Balewa regime (1960–66) and the various military administrations resorted to the economic management policies of the British colonialists. In particular, with the new affluence of the petty bourgeoisie, and the rising cost of living associated with neo-colonial planning, workers entered a new phase of economic hardship and embarked on various industrial actions to back up their demands for pay increase and more equitable distribution of income. This culminated in the June 1964 general strike which virtually paralysed the whole country for about two weeks. The government was forced to capitulate, and it appointed the Morgan Commission[35] for the review of wages and salaries. The minimum awards of the Commission were as usual tied to the cost of living with the customary inflationary consequences. By 1966 workers were again feeling the pinch under Ironsi's military regime (see Table 2). This was carried into Gowon's military rule, where contradictions within the petty bourgeoisie led to civil war (July 1967 to January 1970) over the attempted secession of the former Eastern Region. These contradictions arose with respect to control of the federal state apparatus, oil revenue, and the ethnicity of regional intra-elite rivalry, all of which were viciously exploited by the greedy British, American and other imperialists in the context of imperialist 'oil politics'. The workers and peasants bore the brunt of the war destruction, shortages and unprecedented inflation, especially with Gowon's coercive decree of 1969 which banned strikes and froze wages.

By the end of the war, the antagonistic relations between the petty bourgeoisie and the workers had been so intensified that work-to-rule actions were mounted in open defiance of the 1969 ban on strikes. Another round of welfarist management was adopted with the appointment of the Adèbo Commission to review wages and salaries. The Commission's First Report offered an interim award in 1970 to match increases of about 34–50 per cent in cost of living, and proceeded to a detailed Second Report which tied wage increases to productivity in order to avoid inflation.[36] It, therefore, recommended a machinery for periodic review of wages and salaries which culminated in the Udoji Public Service Review Commission of 1974.[37] The implementation of the Report of this most comprehensive of all commissions, however, failed to harmonize private and public sector remunerations and widened inequalities. Hence it led to a spate of wildcat strikes which thoroughly shook Gowon's corrupt regime. Some of the strikes must also have been inspired by Gowon's 1974 October broadcast which betrayed his earlier promise to restore civilian rule by 1976. The culmulative effect of these contradictions led to the overthrow of Gowon's dictatorial regime in July 1975. Since the beginning of the Second Plan in 1970, bureaucratic planners have been pushing an *incomes policy* which has persistently clamped down on wages and strikes while allowing profits and dividends to rise astronomically. As a result, during the indigenization exercise, the published accounts of many of the foreign enterprises showed over 100 per cent profit rates.[38] By contrast, Table 3 depicts the persistently low level of wages.

After an initial period of vigorous revitalization of the state with mass support, the new regime relapsed after the assassination of its leader, General Murtala Ramat Muhammed, in February 1976. By mid-1976 pernicious inflation and persistent shortages were again imposing serious hardship on workers. This led to fresh labour agitations with strikes and work-to-rule actions which culminated in the coercive 1976 decree proscribing trade unions which engage in 'industrial unrest' in 'essential services'.[39] Moreover, the central labour organizations were dissolved, the assets of their officers probed,[40] and an administrator of trade unions appointed to restructure them into industrial unions with a government code of conduct for their officials. The workers rejected various aspects of these reforms, which created the Nigerian Labour Congress (NLC) as the sole central Labour organization, with some 70 industrial unions according to the Labour Amendment Decree of August 1978. In spite of the progressive features of the decree, the ban on strikes and the wage freeze in effect subordinated the welfare of workers to industrial peace and the huge profits of the Nigerian and imperialist bourgeoisie. Nigerian students have increasingly overcome their middle-class inhibitions and progressively identified themselves with the workers' struggles.

One persistent aberration of workers' struggles in Nigeria has been the failure so far to form any real political alliance with the peasantry whose scattered locations, relative illiteracy and generally placid existence have rendered them the most viciously exploited and repressed group. Moreover, the labour aristocracy, consisting of many of the older trade union leaders, has shown less willingness to organize and mobilize the workers for genuine class struggle than to manage their own personal survival under the guise of spurious ideological differences.

As the most traditionally passive groups in Nigeria, peasants have persistently been the worst oppressed. The colonial marketing board system, which was the dominant institution for this, persisted from the 1940s until 1976. This perpetuated multiple taxation of peasants and the appropriation of their surplus as marketing board surpluses for the elitist projects of the petty bourgeoisie. As cocoa was traditionally the most important export crop handled by this marketing system, and as the commodity was produced by the cocoa peasants of Western Nigeria who have been among the most enlightened peasants in the country, peasant struggles against the petty bourgeoisie have been most prolonged, best organized and most violent in Western Nigeria.[41] The most decisive battles in these confrontations were fought in the *Agbekoya* ('peasants resist oppression') riots of 1968/69, characterized by resistance against government tax extortions, police repression, grinding poverty and the generally marginalized existence of the peasantry. This resulted in the withdrawal of government repressive agents from the rural areas and the proscription of the Agbekoya Farmers' Association.[42]

In other parts of the country peasants have also been resisting the low prices and surplus appropriation of the marketing boards, tenement rates which fall regressively on the working class, land speculation by the urban petty bourgeoisie, oppression by local courts and police, as well as the virtual neglect of the peasant majority in the allocation of infrastructural facilities like roads, health centres, schools, electricity and pipe-borne water. In these struggles, socialist forces in the country have persistently articulated the desperate plight of the peasantry. The continuing neglect of these pressures has culminated in the recent stagnation of the country's agriculture. Table 4 indicates the relative distributive share of farmers in 1970/71.

Table 4
Relative Size and Income of Socio-Economic Groups in Western Nigeria, 1970/71

Socio-Economic Group	*Percentage Shares* *Income Units*	*Total Income*	*Average Group Income*
Farmers	68.98	55.62	81
Craftsmen	5.50	3.71	68
Traders	5.91	8.42	143
Wage-Earners	17.66	31.14	177
Others	1.95	1.11	57

Source: O. Fajana, 'The Distribution of Personal Income in Nigeria', paper presented at the 1975 Annual Conference of the Nigerian Economic Society.

The current Operation Feed the Nation (OFN) and farm settlement schemes, with their elitist orientation and studied neglect of the toiling peasantry, cannot arrest this agricultural decay. Indeed, such reformist bourgeois programmes merely redistribute income in favour of big capitalist farmers and bureaucrats responsible for distributing credit, fertilizers, new seeds, and tractors, which hardly ever get to the peasants. A recent study of the farm settlement schemes shows their negligible effects on surrounding peasants.[43] Moreover, the Agricultural Development Bank and various Co-operative Banks, which are supposed to offer credit to peasants, have only succeeded too well in diverting state funds into the development of capitalist farmers among the petty bourgeois. For the same elitist reasons, capitalist co-operatives have only made the peasants more amenable to bourgeois electoral manipulation.[44] The government appointed a panel[45] in 1977 to study the land tenure systems in the country in view of persistent problems of land racketeering and the proletarianization of dispossessed peasants. This has recently metamorphosed into the Land Use Decree of April 1978, which aims at rationalizing land utilization without abolishing landlordism. With all these, the peasants struggle has still exhibited less organization and co-ordination than the workers' struggle, largely because of the greater relative social deprivation and inertia of the peasantry. On this count, students have been manifesting growing support for the peasants.

The spillover effects of the main class struggles outlined above resulted in demands by the working class for state control of exploitative rents and prices, the eradication of corruption, and introduction of more equitable educational and health services. In particular, exhorbitant rents and prices as well as corruption have developed since the colonial period into standard mechanisms of primitive capital accumulation by members of the Nigerian petty bourgeoisie and the imperialists. Together with the bourgeois monopoly of the educational and health services, these mechanisms have resulted in inhuman suffering for the masses, who have been the helpless victims of the mindless oppression of Nigeria's 'new rich' and their elitist allies.

With increasing urbanization, persistent underdevelopment, and rapid population growth, there has been an acute shortage of accommodation in the urban areas. As houses there are largely owned by indigenous capitalist landlords, this has resulted in the sky-rocketing of rents for poor tenants and the lower layer of the petty bourgeoisie, some of whom are summarily ejected from their quarters. This provoked the formation of tenant associations in various urban centres to agitate for rent control. The result has been various rent control decrees and edicts, the most famous being that of 1976.[46] The ambivalence of the programme is revealed by the facts that some of the edicts (in Oyo, Kaduna and Bendel states) initially raised rather than lowered rents, while their rent tribunals were loaded with the very landlords whose exploitation was to be curbed. Consequently, many of the decrees and edicts have not really checked capitalist rent extortion; they could not, because the same petty bourgeois class that were being tried have been the judges.

Similarly, price control to check the inflationary spiral of the post-war era has resulted from the restive agitation of the working class and the professional and lower petty bourgeoisie who own no enterprises. This makes the struggle a confrontation between the foreign bourgeoisie, Nigerian businessmen and women and the other members of the petty bourgeoisie who earn profits and dividends on the one hand and the rest of the national population on the other. In particular, bourgeois development economics which recommends mild inflation as a source of growth has been the implicit rationalization for the profiteering in post-independent Nigeria, a process which became alarming after 1970. The Price Control decrees of 1974/75 and 1976, which attempted to deal with this problem, have had minimal effects. This is because they have not sufficiently addressed the structural distortions of neo-colonial capitalism that result in supply shortages; they tolerate imperialist imports that also involve the importation of the inflation of imperialist countries, as well as fail to understand the inevitable financial crisis of capitalist development. Moreover, the restriction of price control to beer, soft drinks, petrol, and similar non-essential commodities up till April 1978 also testifies to the basic superficiality of the whole exercise.

In the face of these hardships of the Nigerian majority, the different groups of the petty bourgeoisie have persistently resorted to kleptocracy as a major source of capital accumulation in the country. In the colonial period, the Foster-Sutton Tribunal of Inquiry into the African Continental Bank in

1956 probed the allegation of corruption in that bank, while similar inquiries[47] were instituted after independence into the former Electricity Corporation of Nigeria (ECN, now NEPA), and the Nigerian Railway Corporation. More recently, the Gowon military regime descended to the rock-bottom of corruption in the country with governors converting their states into virtual personal estates.[48] Members of the lower petty bourgeoisie and the working class have constituted themselves into informal anti-corruption crusaders as reflected in the anti-corruption affidavits against members of the ruling group.

Finally, working class and student agitation for better education and health services have resulted in the Universal Primary Education (UPE) programme of 1975/76, free tuition in universities and polytechnics (1976), and the launching of the new multi-million National Health Programme in December 1977. The student struggles for more democratic education, elimination of inequalities, better style of public life, and re-orientation of the economy have led to the Kazeem Commission of Inquiry of 1971 and the Mohammed Commission of Inquiry of 1978. These national responses demonstrate the intensity of mass struggle in the social service sector. The ruling group has continued to resist really egalitarian welfare programmes for all social services, but the contradictions posed by the existing reforms offer a good basis for intensifying class struggle on this front. It is important to emphasize the critical importance of these programmes in the transformation of the mode of production. Marx himself insists that welfare exists at the centre of capitalist production and emphasizes the importance of class action around the issue of welfare.[49]

Future Class Struggle and Development

The future of class struggles and economic development in Nigeria was orchestrated in the debate on Nigeria's Draft Constitution.[50] The petty bourgeois composition of its Drafting Committee, the unabashedly capitalist character of the Draft masked under the ideology of 'mixed-economy', the suppression of the more progressive Minority Draft Constitution, Section 36 of the accepted Draft which makes the 'right to property' a fundamental human right, the provision for an executive president with sweeping powers as the leader of the executive committee of the petty bourgeoisie, the refusal to make the provisions of chapter II, which enunciates 'fundamental objectives and directive principles of state policy' justicable, point to its capitalist class character. The undemocratic composition of the Constituent Assembly called to ratify the Draft, most of whose members were elected by electoral colleges of local councils, about 50 per cent of which were elected by indirect election, and the bourgeois character of the nominated members reveal a deliberate insistence on the exclusion of the working people from any real participation in the making of the new constitution for civil rule.[51] This truly reveals the Nigerian state as a class category.

In spite of this, the limited debates (by the educated elite) on the Draft between November 1976 and October 1977 clearly revealed strong and persistent demands for the socialist transformation of the country. This significant left swing even among the middle and lower layers of the petty bourgeoisie is indicative of a sharpening of class divisions and the increasing consciousness of the masses whose aspirations are being eloquently articulated by the progressive members of the petty bourgeoisie.

Moreover, military rule in Nigeria has since 1966 endorsed neo-colonial capitalism and decisively intervened on the side of the foreign and domestic capitalist interests in the major class conflicts. It has merely thinly veiled this class intervention on the side of property by repeated insistence that the military has no intention of imposing any ideology on the country,[52] as if Nigerians in fact ever voted on the wage-system, Barclays Bank, UAC and other capitalist institutions in the country. In future it is likely to be more difficult for the military to maintain this position; its real choice is to define its own class character and enunciate its developmental ideology.

Finally, the rising consciousness of the workers and students under the impact of their grinding oppression, as well as the de-mystifying mass education of socialist forces, should rapidly materialize into an alliance of workers, peasants, students and other progressives. The prospects for this should be particularly real in the light of the resumption of political activities in 1978. Together with progressive ideological tendencies within the petty bourgeoisie itself, these developments indicate a sharpening of class divisions over the direction of national development. One thing is clear, the existing contradictions in the country, which reflect the increasing frustrations of underdevelopment, together with the very negligible prospects of any breakthrough under the present neo-colonial capitalist system imply that class struggles are likely to be intensified in the future.

The real alternative results of the confrontations hover uneasily between temporary gains for the petty bourgeoisie and their imperialist allies under increasing fascist tendencies, and the ultimate victory of the toiling masses in socialist transformation. Much of the outcome and its timing will depend on the relative strength of the international capitalist system which bolsters up every tottering regime in its exploitative orbit. However, since the people are ultimately the heroes of history, it is inconceivable that they will lose in the long run.

Conclusion

Class struggles have been an integral part of the process of economic development in Nigeria as elsewhere since the pre-capitalist era. Though the social classes are embryonic relative to the classical ones of Western Europe and North America, their main formations are, nevertheless, clearly visible with respect to the usual criteria of Marxist class analysis. Bourgeois distortions of this objective reality reflect the unscientific methodology of imperialist social science generally and the specific political utility of emasculating concepts in order to obscure their social reality and historical implications.

In Nigeria's recent history, three dominant classes have waged dialectical struggles that were often overt and visible, and sometimes latent and imperceptible. These are the imperialist bourgeoisie centred around the British in Nigeria, the Nigerian petty bourgeoisie which emerged as a ruling group after 1960, and the toiling class of workers, peasants, petty artisans, petty market-women and others. In the colonial era, the petty bourgeoisie allied with the masses in a joint nationalist struggle to wrest political power from the British imperialist bourgeoisie. Ethnicity was freely used by the rival elites in the three regions to buttress their class interests. No real social transformation was intended by this nationalism and so no development ushered in flag independence, apart from the British imposition of capitalist relations on the traditional pre-capitalist modes of production.

After 1960 a two-cornered struggle emerged essentially between the now multilateral imperialist bourgeoisie and the Nigerian petty bourgeoisie (led by the bureaucratic bourgeoisie), and between this petty bourgeoisie and the working class. Both struggles were fought simultaneously, while there were also ancillary intra-class conflicts, especially within the petty bourgeoisie. In the foreign-versus indigenous bourgeois conflicts, the latter typically appealed to the patriotic sentiments of the masses for alliance. This has been the case with Nigerianization and indigenization. In conflicts with the working class, however, the domestic petty bourgeoisie, after winning nominal independence, allied with the imperialist bourgeoisie to emphasize that they share stronger exploitative class interests with imperialists than nationalist interests with the masses. This best betrays the prostitute nature of the domestic petty bourgeoisie. In these struggles, moreover, complete class solidarity was neither necessary nor possible. Thus, when the struggle was over wages and salaries, the position of the professional and lower petty bourgeoisie was closer to that of the workers than to the bureaucratic bourgeoisie. Similarly, in the struggles of the peasants, though the workers psychologically identified with them, they did not necessarily join in the actual battles. Over time students have, since their patriotic and successful agitation against the notorious Anglo-Nigerian Defence Act of 1959, identified increasingly with the progressive struggles of the working people.

Moreover, these class struggles have dialectically resulted in changing patterns of ownership of productive forces (e.g. capital and land) and changes in the distribution of surplus. But because such reforms have fallen short of revolutionary or complete structural transformation, they preserved the pattern of imperialist domination of surplus appropriation and, therefore, they have sustained the underdevelopment of the country. In this process, the consistent and dominant role of military regimes as ruling groups within the petty bourgeoisie has been implicit alliance with, and overt defence of, the interests of the domestic and foreign capitalists. To sustain such a role they have had to institute populist reforms which preserve the critical nature of neo-colonial capitalism and underdevelopment. For the future, the possibilities of a class alliance of workers, peasants, students and others, the increasing weakening of the international capitalist system as well as the growing consciousness of the masses, are going to be critical for the direction of national economic development in Nigeria.

References

1. Paul A. Baran, *The Political Economy of Growth* (London: Monthly Review Press, 1967), p.14.
2. For detailed discussion of the nature of social classes and their relevance to Africa, see Issa G. Shivji, *Class Struggles in Tanzania* (Dar es Salaam: Tanzania Publishing House, 1975).
3. Quoted in *ibid*, p.19.
4. *Ibid*.
5. Quoted in *ibid*, p.41.
6. R.L. Sklar, *Nigerian Political Parties: Power in an Emergent African Nation* (Princeton, N.J.: Princeton University Press, 1963), pp.487 and 494.
7. *Ibid*, p.501.
8. See I. Nzimiro, 'Ideology and Directive Principles of State Policy', paper presented at the National Conference on the Draft Constitution, NISER, University of Ibadan, April, 1977.
9. See L.H. Gann and P. Duignan (eds.), *Colonialism in Africa, 1870–1960*, 5 vols. (C.U.P., 1969–75); V. Perlo, *The Empire of High Finance* (N.Y.: International Publishers, 1957).
10. See W. Smith *Slaves and Palm Oil, Economic Transition Politics on the Western Slave Coast, 1870–94* (Chicago, 1969); M. Crowder, *The Story of Nigeria* (London: Faber, 1962); G.K. Helleiner, *Peasant Agriculture, Government and Economic Growth in Nigeria* (Homewood, Ill.: Richard D. Irwin, 1966).
11. Sklar, *op. cit.*, chapter 11; Nzimiro, *op. cit.*
12. S. Osoba, 'The Nigerian Power Elite, 1952–65', in P. Gutkind and P. Waterman (eds.), *African Social Studies – A Radical Reader* (London: Monthly Review Press, 1977).
13. By 1962/63 agriculture still accounted for 61.2 per cent of GDP. See *Second National Development Plan, 1970/74* (Lagos: Federal Ministry of Information, 1970), p.51. However, in the 1970s and, especially after 1973, the oil boom in Nigeria has made the petroleum sector the dominant contributor to government revenue and foreign exchange earnings.

    For the main features of the neo-colonial capitalist economy, see O. Oni and B. Onimode, *Economic Development of Nigeria: The Socialist Alternative* (Ibadan: The Nigerian Academy of Arts, Sciences and Technology, 1975).
14. See Osoba, *op. cit.*, for the details of this development.
15. This will be discussed later.
16. See Shivji, *op. cit.*, chapter 1.
17. Karl Marx, 'The German Ideology' in K. Marx and F. Engels, *Selected Works*, Vol. I (Moscow: Progress Publishers, 1969) p.65. My

emphasis.

18. Lewis L. Lorwin, 'Class struggle' in *Encyclopedia of the Social Sciences*, quoted in Shivji, *op. cit.*, pp. 7–8. Emphasis in original.
19. See J.S. Coleman, *Nigeria: Background to Nationalism* (Berkeley and Los Angeles: University of California Press, 1958).
20. See Sklar, *op. cit.*, chapter 11.
21. See Smith, *op. cit.*, Helleiner, *op. cit.*
22. These include the Bridges Committee (1941), Tudor Davies Commission (1945), Harragin Commission (1946), Miller Commission (1947). Fitzgerald Commission (1949), Gorsuch Commission (1954), as well as the Mbanefo and Morgan Commissions of 1959. See Ola Oni, 'Wages and salaries Review: Tight Rope of Bourgeois Economic Reformism in Nigeria, Part I', *Theory and Practice*, 1,1 (1974), pp. 110–132.
23. For this banking competition, see W.T. Newlyn and D.C. Rowan, *Money and Banking in British Colonial Africa* (Oxford: Clarendon Press, 1954).
24. Thus the leadership of the NCNC denounced the Zikists after their conviction over their 'Call for Revolution' and 'Youth internationalism' in Lagos on 27 October, 1948. See Sklar, *op. cit.*, pp.75–6.
25. Sklar, *op. cit.*, pp.76.
26. See Helleiner, *op. cit.*
27. This was the Ten-year Programme for Economic Development and Welfare. See Coleman, *op. cit.*
28. See *Ibid*.
29. Consider Nigerian Enterprises Promotion Board, *Nigerian Enterprises Promotion Decree, 1972* (Lagos, 1972); and Federal Republic of Nigeria, *Federal Military Government's Views on the Report of the Industrial Enterprises Panel* (Lagos: Federal Ministry of Information, 1976).
30. This reaction is best summarized in *Theory and Practice*, 1.1 (1974), which states the position of the chambers and of the working class.
31. *Ibid*, p..4.
32. See *Nigerian Journal of Economic and Social Studies (NJESS)* 4,2 (1962).
33. For a critique of these plans, see Oni and Onimode, *op. cit.*
34. See Federal Republic of Nigeria, *Second National Development Plan 1970–74* and *Third National Development Plan, 1975–80* for some of these prestige projects.
35. See the *Report of the Wages and Salaries Review Commission, 1964* (Lagos: Federal Ministry of Information, 1964).
36. See *First Report of the Wages and Salaries Review Commission, 1970* and the *Second and Final Report, 1970/71* (Lagos: Federal Ministry of Information).
37. *Public Service Review Commission – Report on Grading and Pay, Vol. I–IV*. (Lagos: Federal Ministry of Information, 1974).
38. See Oni and Onimode, *op. cit.*, chapter 2.
39. *Trade Disputes (Essential Services) Decree, 1976* (Lagos: Federal Ministry of Information).
40. See *Report of the Tribunal of Inquiry into the Activities of the Trade Unions* (Lagos: Federal Ministry of Information, 1977).
41. Helleiner, *op. cit.*, C.F. Beer, *The Politics of Peasant Groups in Western*

Nigeria (Ibadan University Press, 1975).

42. See Tafa Adeoye, *Agbe-ko-ya: Farmers Against Oppression* (Lagos: International Press, 1970).
43. See R.O. Adegboye *et al* 'Impact of Western Nigerian Farm Settlements on Surrounding Farmers', *NJESS*, 2,2 (1964), pp. 229–40.
44. See Oni and Onimode, *op. cit.*, chapter 11.
45. The report of this Panel has been submitted to the Federal Military Government, which enacted the Land Use Decree, 1978.
46. See *Federal Military Governments Views on the Report of the Rent Panel* (Lagos: Federal Ministry of Information, 1976).
47. See *Report of the Coker Commission of Inquiry into the Affairs of Certain Statutory Corporations* (Lagos: Federal Ministry of Information 1962); *Report of the Electricity Corporation of Nigeria, Tribunal of Inquiry* (Lagos: Federal Ministry of Information, 1967); *Federal Military Government's Views on the Report of the Tribunal of Inquiry into the Importation of Cement* (Lagos:: Federal Ministry of Information, 1976), pp. 7–12. *Federal Military Government's Views on the Investigations of the Farms owned by Mr. S.O. Ogebemudia & Alhadji Audu Bako* (Lagos: Federal Ministry of Information, 1976).
48. Part of the gory details of this era in the *Report of the Special Panel on the Farms of Alhaji Audu Bako & Mr. S.O. Ogbemudia* (Lagos: Federal Ministry of Information, 1976). These were the former governors of Kano and Mid-West (now Bendel) states. Other governors, commissioners, permanent secretaries, etc. were affected by the asset probes and confiscation.
49. Paul Corrigan, 'The Welfare State as an Arena of Class Struggle', *Marxism Today* (March, 1977), pp.87–93.
50. See *Reports of the Constitution Drafting Committee*, Vols. I & II (Lagos: Federal Ministry of Information, 1976).
51. Consider Nzimiro, *op. cit.*; O. Nnoli, 'The Ideological Foundations of the CDC's Draft Constitution' (mimeo, 1977); B. Onimode and E. Osagie, 'An Economic Interpretation of Nigeria's Draft Constitution' (mimeo, 1977).
52. For the response of Nigerian socialists to this illusion, see *Nigerian Vanguard*, 14 November 1975, p.4.

9. Progress Versus Reaction in Nigerian Development

Okwudiba Nnoli

Progress, Reaction, and the Dialectics of Development

Progress and reaction are integral, but contradictory, aspects of the dialectics of development. They are two sides of the same coin, but they are dialectically related. In other words, any social situation contains forces that struggle to bring out some of the best qualities of humanity embodied in it, and other forces which oppose this struggle because of one reason or the other, but usually in the interest of one group or another. As this conflict is resolved a new situation emerges, which is itself the unity of a new set of contending opposites. Therefore, the nature and direction of social movement at any historical point in time is determined by the balance of power between these two forces. When the progressive forces prevail, there is a forward movement. However, stagnation or retrogression accompanies the triumph of reactionary forces.

Since life in a society is a composite of numerous social situations, many confrontations between progressive and reactionary forces go on at the same time. Even within the same social situation various contradictions between them may exist simultaneously. But while the outcome of each of these contradictions affects the nature and direction of social change in the society as a whole, their impacts vary greatly in importance. Some are of major significance, while others are relatively insignificant in their overall contribution to social praxis. Therefore, a distinction must be made between the principal contradiction whose impact is the greatest, and which virtually determines the character and direction of a society's development, and the minor contradictions that are closely interdependent with the principal one and that either reinforce its impact or tend to dilute it.

Thus, one of the most critical aspects of development is to correctly identify the principal contradiction in a society, concentrate the attention of the population on it, and resolve it in the direction of greater progress for humanity. In this respect, the principal contradiction, like all contradictions, has an objective character. The members of the society may or may not recognize it as such. In fact, they may even identify a different and minor contradiction as the most significant, and devote most of their energies toward solving it. In Nigeria this has been the case with contradictions in ethnic relations. Such subjectivism only serves to obscure the principal contradiction and consequently postpone its resolution, usually to the detriment of the development of the society. The first major task of any developmental process, after correctly identifying the principal contradiction as well as the progressive and reactionary forces associated with it, is to tilt the balance of power between them in favour of the progressive forces in order to resolve the conflict in the direction of greater development. To do otherwise is to equivocate, or mystify and obscure the developmental process itself, thereby serving the cause of reaction.

It is also important to keep in check the various minor contradictions in a society in order to prevent them from escalating beyond their proper position in the scheme of things. Such an escalation creates the risk of a subjective interpretation of one of the minor contradictions as the principal one, and the focussing of attention, energy, and resources on it to the detriment of the efforts on behalf of the principal contradiction. In fact, a special effort must be made in this regard because of the tendency of reactionary forces associated with the principal contradiction to divert attention away from their reactionary and inhuman policies to other real but less important social situations. For example, the notorious British colonial policy of 'divide and rule' served in this way to delay and temporarily diffuse the nationalist drive toward independence in many British colonies.

As one principal contradiction is resolved a new one takes its place. Usually the latter merely assumes greater prominence and significance, having been in existence when attention was focussed on the former principal contradiction. This fact sometimes creates problems for social praxis. Confusion may arise regarding the nature of the principal contradiction at a period in time because of the coexistence of the earlier and later principal contradictions. Unless such difficulties are properly cleared up the tasks of development would be made more difficult. For example, contradictions exist in the neo-colonial economy between national and external interests, and between the interests of the local privileged and underprivileged classes. Which of these is the principal contradiction in the society?

Often one hears about progressive groups, parties, movements, and ideas. Some of these only masquerade as progressive while their essential character is reactionary. But how is one able to identify a truly progressive force from its counterfeit? A genuinely progressive regime, group, or movement is characterized not solely by what it says on behalf of the interest of the underprivileged majority of a society in particular and mankind in general, but, more importantly, by what it does or suggests to be done to tilt the balance of power between the privileged minority and the underprivileged majority in favour of the latter. The underprivileged majority represent the interests of human progress because their socio-economic and political conditions are usually so intolerable that any movement out of them constitutes an achievement, not only for them but for humanity at large. Contrariwise, the privileged minority usually have vested socio-economic and political interests in the existing pattern of life that constrain them from acting in the interest of the underprivileged majority and indeed compel them to act against the latter in defense of their vested interests. Historically, therefore, the privileged elements of a society have constituted its major reactionary force.

Of course, privileged classes change with time. Consequently, a previously underprivileged class may later attain the position of power and privileges, as the national bourgeoisie in Europe did after the French Revolution of 1789. Therefore, at one point in history a class may be progressive in character, but at another time it may be quite reactionary. Thus, the Nigerian petty bourgeoisie which led the nationalist movement was quite progressive at the time of the struggle for independence. At that time the principal contradiction in the society was a political one between Nigerians and foreign rule. This contradiction obscured that between the local petty bourgeoisie and the peasants and workers. However, with the attainment of political independence in 1960 the latter contradiction assumed greater prominence. It is still masked by the more significant conflict between national economic interest and foreign economic domination but not to the degree that prevailed during the struggle for independence.

These changes arise essentially from the shifting power positions of the various classes. And the shifts themselves result from the differential acquisition of power resources. Initially, the vital resources may be political, organizational, or economic. In the case of the emergence of the European bourgeoisie it was economic. As it became more and more powerful, it began to assert itself more and more politically until it achieved predominance in the bourgeois revolution. In Nigeria on the other hand, the power resource of the petty bourgeoisie was initially political in character. Through its mobilization of the masses of the people and world opinion, prolonged agitation for political reforms, protests, demonstrations, and sometimes violent resistance as in bloody labour strikes, it imposed severe political costs on the colonial regime, forcing the latter to grant independence. But with its control of the political resources it began to acquire economic resources and to transform one set of resources into the other as the need demanded. Therefore, further changes in the relationship between the progressive and reactionary forces must be sought in, and envisaged from, the power resources that each side is mobilizing and its skills and capabilities in this mobilization effort. Progress on the part of the underprivileged classes, who control very little economic resources, depends on their organizational skills in mobilizing the masses. They cannot rely on the same economic resources that the dominant classes monopolize and depend on.

Thus far the question of progress and reaction in national development has been discussed at the level of abstraction, the principal and minor contradictions in the society together with the alignment of progressive and reactionary forces in them. However, in reality, it is human labour that builds and destroys civilizations. It is responsible for the creation of new products, including the means for their production. The physical, biological, and inter-human environments cannot be transformed to the benefit of man without the creative application of human labour. Even capital and other means of production such as technology that play a crucial role in the production process of the advanced modern societies owe their origin to creative human labour.

In fact, social relations arose from the needs of human labour to improve its effectiveness and creativity. Man needed to unite his labour with that of other men in order to improve his creative achievements. In the process, various forms of social life emerged, first in the realm of production but later in other fields such as economics, politics, culture, and social life generally. In the final analysis, all were designed to make labour relations satisfactory to all involved in them and, therefore, to increase production and further development. In other words, man extends himself socially through his labour. He regenerates, renews, and reproduces himself socially and eventually culturally, economically, and politically through his labour activities. In turn, social, economic, cultural, and political life make sense only in the extent to which they contribute to the improvement of the quality of labour. Through such improvements man liberates himself from the insecurity of the non-human environment, asserting his freedom, confidence, and pre-eminence in the universal scheme of things.

This central determining role of human labour explains why throughout history progressive forces have been identified with policies and activities that tend to release human labour and its creative energy from those forces that shackle them. More specifically, they struggle to prevent labour from being alienated. When labour is alienated, it ceases to be a liberating force and turns into a monstrosity which destroys man's humanity. Reactionary forces on the other hand recognize the importance of human labour but subordinate it to such non-human factors as capital, per capita income and technology, or attempt to limit its improvement to a small segment of the population. However, the more widespread this liberating effect of improved labour is in the human population, the more the progress of humanity.

Obstacles to the qualitative transformation of human labour arise from two major sectors of human existence, the hostility of the non-human environment, particularly the physical environment, and the relations of man with other men. In capitalist societies, including the peripheral capitalist societies of the Nigerian type, emphasis has been concentrated on the conquest of the hostile non-human obstacles, to the utter neglect of those constraints arising from social, political, economic, and cultural relations. Hence, progressive forces in these societies have focussed their efforts on inter-human relations in order to eliminate, or at least ameliorate, their deleterious effects on the improvement of the quality of labour of the vast majority of mankind. Their programmes include demands for radical land reforms that release the tiller of the soil from the oppression of the big land-owners, exploitative merchants, money lenders, and the monopolies. They also agitate for the implementation of progressive labour legislation such as worker participation in industrial decision-making, a fair system of wage and salary distribution according to work done, an enormous increase in the funds for the improvement of the social forms of the worker's personal consumption (such as state social insurance, free medical services, pensions, free education at all levels), an extensive and free system of mother and child welfare, and full employment.

The reactionary forces usually counter with the argument that in the first place there are not enough funds in the society to implement these social programs. Of course they cannot accomplish these goals and at the same time leave intact the enormous privileged wealth which accrues to the limited minority ruling classes. Secondly, they argue that such social progress runs counter to economic progress because an attempt to divert funds from the rich to these social services for the majority will reduce the potential funds for investment. But the experience of all the socialist countries has exploded this myth, exposing it as a reactionary defense of the vested interests and privileges of the minority ruling classes.

Progressive forces are also positively oriented toward the national independence of peoples, their right to self-determination, the political and social equality of citizens, and the freedom of the individual. These values are important for human labour because in their absence man suffers a severe crisis of confidence and identity which adversely affects his creativity, capacity to solve problems and, therefore, his labour power. Loss of national independence creates a collective crisis of confidence and identity, which has the same effect on the labour power of the population. Under these conditions labour becomes alienated and constitutes a fetter on human progress instead of a catalytic and liberating agent. Therefore, all forces which mutilate the full personality of a people, perpetuate inequality in social, economic, or political life, and deny the human freedom of the population to make all the decisions that affect their lives are reactionary forces.

Thus, the progressive reorganization of the social, cultural, and vocational standards of the working people is among the principal prerequisites for development. An emphasis on social progress demands that special attention be paid to the socio-economic factors that hold back major improvements in the working people's welfare. It means that for the progressive forces of Nigeria the goal of development must be conceived broadly as the improvement of the labour of the population, at least its vast majority, the workers and peasants who are quagmired in poverty, ignorance, and disease. A crucial part of their task is to identify those factors which cause labour alienation for them, and to determine ways and means of eliminating them, or at least ameliorating their adverse effects on the population. This will involve programmes for ending the present unsalutary international division of labour, and replacing the unhealthy peripheral capitalist relations, norms, and system of work with more humane and less alienating ones. Also, it will involve a restructuring of property relations and the accompanying pattern of appropriation of the surplus from production in favour of the broad masses of the working people.

However, in order to fully grasp the principal area of confrontation of progressive and reactionary forces in Nigeria today, the roles of the local privileged and underprivileged classes in the resolution of this contradiction, the nature of the resources involved in this resolution, and the direction of the outcome, it is necessary to examine how this contradiction emerged in the past and assumed its present form and importance. A historical analysis is imperative. And in this regard it is necessary to resist the temptation to treat Nigerian history in terms of the pre-colonial, colonial, and post-colonial period. The critical area of focus must be the phenomenon whose history is being recreated, rather than the historical periods through which Nigeria has passed irrespective of whether or not the phenomenon existed in all of these periods. This is particularly important because the contradictions of the colonial period were not all the result of the resolution of contradictions of the pre-colonial societies. In fact, many of these contradictions, especially the principal ones, did not even exist during pre-colonial times.

Today, the principal contradiction of Nigerian development is that between foreign domination of local production and the national interest in eliminating that domination and asserting national sovereignty over the national production process. In its most significant form this conflict did not exist during the pre-colonial times. Similarly, its precursor, the contradiction between foreign political domination and the nationalist demand for independence, was of colonial vintage, and a prospective contradiction, that between the national bourgeoisie and the working class, could not have been anticipated by the pre-colonial system. Therefore, any serious discussion of the contradiction between progress and reaction in Nigerian development must have its historical starting point as the colonial intervention.

Colonialism as a Reactionary Force

Colonialism, like all forms of imperialism, is a very reactionary force. It mutilates the full collective personality of its victims, humiliates them in various ways, exploits them viciously, takes undue advantage of their weaknesses, and inhumanly disorients them, thereby distorting their lives. In fact, it denies them any claim to full human existence, using its power to reduce them to a subhuman standard of living. In the process, it destroys their individual and collective creative genius, rendering them subject to the whims and caprices of the creative genius of other peoples in a way totally alien to man's humanity. In its singleminded pursuit of colonial interests it throws all caution and morality to the wind, and does not hesitate to use devious devices such as the celebrated British policy of divide and rule, as well as the alienation of the victims from their past and traditional culture without allowing them full access into the new colonial culture.

Thus, British colonialism in Nigeria shamelessly and unscrupulously seized control of the apparatus of state and exercised political power without integrating itself into the local population, particularly the latter's needs and interests. The British colonialists were in the country but not of it. They developed no loyalty to Nigeria and had no sense of belonging to the country. Their loyalty and sense of belonging were channelled to Britain, the metropolitan power. Hence their dealings with Nigerians were not governed by any sensitivity on their part to humane principles of a higher order but by cold and brutal calculations about the interests of Britain and Britons. However, in order to be able to justify their inhuman colonial policies and actions to themselves and the rest of mankind, they created the myth of the inferiority, indeed subhumanity, of the victims. The latter were presented as having no history and no culture worthy of humanity. Their past life was one of bestiality, brutishness, and war of one against all and all against one. Their state of being had remained at the subhuman level of infantilism and congenital anarchy.

By thus emptying the pre-colonial lives of Nigerians of any human substance, the colonialists set the stage for justifying the non-application of human principles to these 'savages'. The colonial mission was white-washed as that of civilization – not exploitation – to raise the state of being of the colonized to the level of humanity. Therefore, in the name of humanity, any action taken to accomplish this task was justifiable, a crude 'end-justifies-means' attitude. Hence, the Christian missionaries were presented as working, sometimes against all odds, to save Nigerian souls for God and humanity, rather than preparing them spiritually to accept colonial and neo-colonial exploitation. Similarly, the foreign capitalist was presented not as an exploiter but as a businessman operating to eliminate the country's state of backwardness. Western education, a means of socializing Nigerians into the acceptance of, or at least acquiescence in, the inhuman and exploitative colonial and neo-colonial pattern of life detrimental to the material and spiritual interests of Nigerians, was presented as a means of bringing modernity to Nigeria and propelling the country into the mainstream of modern civilization. And the illegal foreign seizure of the local state apparatus was not a British acquisition of power for unchecked exploitation and repression of the Nigerian people in the promotion of British interests, but a part of the British duty to humanity to teach Nigerians how to establish and run a civilized government and society.

The colonialists sought to perpetuate this myth of the white man's burden by a strict adherence to it in both theory and practice. They were the first real champions of what later became Goebel's thesis on propaganda: 'tell the same lie over and over again and it will in time become a truth'. But in order to be consistent, colonial policy had to reduce Nigerians to a subhuman existence first. This was accomplished by alienating them from various aspects of life.

In the economic realm alienation of the Nigerian population was achieved in various ways. By organizing a pattern of production totally alien to the population, that had nothing whatsoever to say or do about their basic needs, traditional consumption tastes and habits, and the local resources, the colonialists thoroughly alienated Nigerians from the colonial and later neo-colonial production process. Also, the labour of Nigerians was completely alienated by the colonially-induced complex national and international division of labour in which the working man was a mere statistical unit, mechanically, rather than organically, related to the production system. He played no role whatever in deciding what to produce, when to do so, how to produce, or why and how the products were to be marketed.

Nigerians did not even have the choice regarding how to dispose of their labour power. They were either forcibly conscripted for work under inhuman conditions in the colonial order or were otherwise compelled to take up employment there by the need to raise the colonial currency with which to pay the colonially-imposed taxes and eke out a meager existence under conditions of severe scarcity and hardship imposed by the colonial order. When they resisted these measures, they were ruthlessly repressed. Thus the Dancing Women's Movement in Eastern Nigeria in 1925 against the colonial order was repressed, as were the uprisings against taxation in Egbaland in 1918, Calabar in 1925, Warri in 1927, and in Owerri, Calabar and Rivers provinces (the Aba Riots) in 1929.

Taxation of the local population under colonialism represented the exploitation of Nigerians above and beyond that exploitation which took place at the place of work. They were made to pay for the upkeep of an order which the British officials in their many unguarded moments declared to be operating in the interest of Britons rather than Nigerians. Even those who took no direct part in colonial activities, such as the majority of the rural population, were still subject to this burden. And it further reduced the already very low receipts of the working population from the surplus product of colonial production, even though most of the colonial services paid for by the taxes, such as public administration and infrastructural facilities, benefited the colonialists and the foreign firms. The same taxes paid for the maintenance of defence and police forces whose *raison d'etre* was the repression and pacification of the local population in the interest of the profits of foreign capitalist enterprises, which demanded law and order as essential for their success. Furthermore, taxes on incomes above ₦1,000 were more regressive in Nigeria than in Britain, the metropolitan country. And such incomes were the privilege of the foreigners working in Nigeria. Those who benefited most from the colonial order were exempted from an equitable contribution for its maintenance.

At the place of work colonial exploitation was starkly intolerable. Labour conditions and wages were monopsonically set by the foreign capitalist firms. Hardly any labour legislation existed during the early periods to protect workers from the unscrupulous labour policies of these firms. The working population toiled like slaves without the least regard being shown by foreign firms and the authorities for their comfort and welfare, without any provision for them when they were old or incapacitated. Not only were strikes illegal for a long time, but the brutal and punitive reactions of the employers and colonial officials were symptomatic of the degree of exploitation envisaged for the workers by the colonialists. On 21 June 1947 defenceless United Africa Company (UAC) employees in Buruti were shot down by the police simply because they went on strike in furtherance of a wage demand. But by far the bloodiest of these strikes was that of 18 November 1949 at the

Enugu colliery following unrest and dissatisfaction among the coal miners over claims for a wage increase, the payment of daily allowances for certain categories or workers, and for arrears which the colliery management was withholding. Only the long struggle of the workers in alliance with the nationalist movements against colonial reaction enabled the former to make some gains in terms of wages, conditions of work, and trade union rights.

The situation was equally unsalutary for the peasant producers of the cash crops that sustained the colonial order financially. Colonial policy enabled the foreign firms to set prices at which farmers sold their crops, usually well below the world market prices, enabling the firms to amass huge profits at the expense of the peasant producers. In this way the Nigerian farmers were forced to sell the products of their labour power at prices well below its real value, even by market standards. This system of unbridled exploitation of the peasant producer for the monopoly profits of the foreign firms was later institutionalized in the activities of the public marketing boards. The latter had been established ostensibly to protect the producer from the adverse effects of the vagaries of the world market and climatic conditions. In reality, they turned out to be an instrument for their systematic exploitation. They were expected to build up a surplus during boom years to be used during the lean years to maintain prices at stable levels. Instead, they maintained a surplus at all times, even during the lean periods, thereby further exploiting the producers by denying them what was due to them. In effect these surpluses were another form of taxation imposed by the state on the farmers, and the proceeds were used not to develop their factors of production but to develop the services and facilities which benefited foreign capital.

While the colonialists utilized the peasants' wealth to improve the facilities of the urban zones which were considered more significant for the profitability of foreign capital than the rural zones, the peasants who produced the wealth were themselves encouraged to improve their own lives through community development. This became another form of exploitation of the rural areas and was widely implemented under the guise that governmental resources were not enough and that it was morally healthy for the population to learn to fend for itself without depending on others. Why community development was never advocated for the urban centers was never explained. Nor was there an explanation for not spending most of the meagre public resources on the rural zones where the vast majority lived. Therefore, when it is shorn of all propaganda, rhetoric, moralizing, and perfidious diversion of frustration, community development remains starkly what it has always been, a form of exploitation of the rural population, a different form of taxation to raise resources for social tasks which rightly belonged to the government but which the latter had shamelessly and inhumanly abandoned.

In the social realm, colonial alienation and dehumanization of Nigerians were equally pervasive. First, although they were compelled to enter colonial activities they nevertheless found that within the colonial enclaves the doors to the glorified world of the white man were securely fastened by racial barriers. They were subjected to inhuman humiliation in the fields of employment, remuneration, education, medical services and housing by a system of racial classification that consistently relegated them to virtually inhuman levels. The British colonialists put as much social distance between Europeans and Nigerians as was possible and prevented as much contact between the two races as they could. Hence sporting facilities and burial grounds were racially segregated. This systematic dehumanization of the Nigerian was reinforced by the pervasive colonial racist myth of his inferiority to the European, his powerlessness to redress this injustice, his deep-seated alienation, and his crisis of personal and national identity. Self-confidence gave way to self-doubt. Consequently, creative labour gave way to subservience, slavish imitation, and alienated labour.

Second, while pretending to be carrying out a mission of uniting incorrigibly warring tribes, British reactionary colonial policy consciously and systematically separated the various Nigerian peoples, creating conflict and ill-will among them where none existed in pre-colonial times. Hence, although no precolonial history of hostility and conflict existed between the Igbo and Yoruba, Igbo and Hausa, Igbo and Ijaw, and Igbo and Efik, deep-seated antagonisms have emerged in these relationships which in some cases have given rise to genocidal massacres. In this way the colonialists were able to channel the aggression against the colonial order and the colonial white racists, arising from the frustrations and humiliations of colonialism, away from its rightful victims onto fellow Nigerians.

By categorizing all the various linguistic groups of Nigeria as tribes the colonialists began to create parochial consciousness and exclusiveness where none existed. All official forms required information on the ethnic origin of the individual and so did all the other official means of identification. Feeling that he was regarded as a member of an ethnic group by others, and that they would act toward him accordingly, the individual began to feel the need to identify with this group and to feather its nest relative to the other ethnic groups whenever and wherever he could. Thus, for example, during the precolonial period although theYoruba shared the same language and myths of common ancestry, they were organized into various kingdoms that fought disastrous wars among themselves and certainly shared no common consciousness. Such consciousness emerged in the colonial order in part as a result of this official policy of ethnic identification. Similarly, the Igbo who shared no common consciousness in the past, but in fact were self-consciously divided into Olu and Igbo, began to acquire this consciousness.

In Northern Nigeria the colonialists pursued an active policy of segregating northerners from southerners. Initially, the indigenous residents of a town in the North got along very well with migrants from the other parts of the North and also from the South. This was embarrassing to the colonialists whose racist ideology had assumed that only conflict characterized such interactions. In order to avoid this embarrassment they invented the policy of *Sabon Gari*. Migrants were forced to live apart from the indigenous populations in areas designated as *Sabon Gari* or 'strangers'' quarters. At first the northern and southern migrants lived together there. Later, however, the two were further segregated, with the northern migrants moving to a different section of town, Tudun Wada. Only in those cities such as Katsina and Gwandu where the emirs successfully resisted this policy of *Sabon Gari* did the three groups continue their harmonious interaction until the socio-political crises of 1966. In fact, official intelligence reports in the North often contained information on which emirs were not to be trusted on the policy of *Sabon Gari*.

Colonialism effectively interrupted the mixing of peoples that had taken place in Nigeria for many centuries. The history of the area is replete with wholesale migrations of peoples to and from the region. In each case the migrants and hosts worked out a mutually rewarding and acceptable relationship; in many cases the groups blended together to form one group. This had been the experience of the Hausa-Fulani interaction and the assimilation between the Igbo, Ijaw, Ibibio, and Efik in the Niger Delta. By freezing ethnic group boundaries, encouraging ethnic exclusiveness and consciousness, and exploiting ethnic differences to create and inflame inter-ethnic hostility, colonialism strongly discouraged these assimilationist processes and tendencies.

Third, colonialism thrives on the policy of divide and rule. During the 1945 general strike, which the colonialists blamed on the nationalist activities of Azikiwe and the Igbo, colonial officials in the North exploited the hardships caused by the strike to life in the North to incite northerners against the Igbo. This led to the Jos riots of that year in which Hausa residents killed and wounded a number of their Igbo compatriots. The same policy was reflected in the divergent patterns of social policy in the different parts of the country, which created antipathies among the various regions of the country but particularly between the North and South, and which caused immense difficulties for the nationalist struggle for independence. Not only was a different system of administration and judiciary designed for the North, a different system of education and cultural life also prevailed there. As a result, the North has lagged behind the South in the development of manpower to run the colonial and neo-colonial administrative bureaucracies, to play an adequate part in the professional life of the country, and to compete effectively in the colonial and neo-colonial job market. This caused fears of domination of the North by the South, which made northern leaders oppose an earlier independence for the country and which compelled them always to want to keep federal political power in their hands.

And fourth, the colonial policy of divide-and-rule ensured that the various parts of the country did not share a common political experience for a long time. In fact, from the time of the amalgamation of the North and South of Nigeria in 1914 until 1946 when the Richard's Constitution was introduced, the two sections of the nation were only tenuously linked in law. They maintained distinct political identifies and separate administrations. Even the Richard's Constitution provided for a House of Assembly and a House of Chiefs in the North, but only a House of Assembly in each of the two regions of the South. Similarly, under the 1951 Constitution, while in the East and West three stages of indirect elections prevailed, there were four stages in the North. And in the South universal adult suffrage was first introduced into the electoral process in the Lagos Town Council election of 1950, then in 1954 in the Eastern Region, and in 1956 in the West. In the North on the other hand, it was introduced for the first time in the federal elections of 1959. Even then, only male persons were eligible to vote, in contrast to the South where both men and women could vote.

As a political line the colonialists manipulated sectional sentiments as a means of dividing the nationalist movement and maintaining colonial power. In 1920 Sir Hugh Clifford employed it against the National Congress of West Africa to torpedo the move toward a pan-West African nation. Again, the colonialists used it to check the march of Nigerian nationalism by sponsoring reactionary regional interests in the North and preying on northern sectional sentiments and animosities. Consequently, they manipulated northern elections in the interest of the North and against the South. This was particularly so with the 1951 Kano elections. British officials were very sympathetic to the northern Native Administration and together with it set out to destroy all northern political parties allied with southern parties. In the process they poisoned the relations between the two parts of the country.

In another respect colonial policy was alienating and dehumanizing because it subordinated the human welfare interests of Nigerians to the demands for profit by the foreign firms. For example, education, employment, medical services, and welfare benefits such as old age pensions were tailored in such a way as not to diminish in any way the enormous profits carted away by the foreign firms. The colonial argument about the scarcity of resources was never allowed to intrude into the sphere of the profits to be amassed by the foreign firms. On the question of a choice between increased profits for the firms and increased social welfare for Nigerians, the colonialists chose profits. Therefore, while children in the metropolitan country, Britain, enjoyed free education at the primary and secondary levels, their Nigerian counterparts were made to pay for these services even though colonial education totally alienated them from their past and immediate surroundings, and only mechanically prepared them for service to foreign capital. The colonialists and their neo-colonial successors cannot conceive of any reduction of the profit margins of capitalist enterprises in order to raise the resources for these services. This is dehumanizing.

Colonial capitalism also introduced new forms of debilitating socio-economic inequality previously unknown in most parts of the country. While creating anomic conditions of fierce socio-economic competition among Nigerians, it did so under conditions of extreme inequality which alienated and dehumanized those, usually the vast majority of the population, at the bottom end of the ladder of inequality. Thus, for example, economic power was concentrated in the hands of a few expatriate firms, the most prominent of which was the UAC. In the 1930s it controlled about 40 per cent of the import and export trade; in the 1940s it handled over 34 per cent of all imported merchandise, and 43 per cent of all of Nigeria's non-mineral exports. In a monopolistic association with a few other foreign firms the UAC controlled import agreements, allocated export quotas, and handled about 66 per cent of Nigeria's exports and nearly 70 per cent of its imports.

In other spheres the predominance of foreigners in the hierarchical scheme of things was ensured by the racially discriminatory pattern of income distribution and the provision of social welfare services. There existed separate salary scales for Europeans and Africans, with the African scale being inferior to the European one. This gap between the European and Nigerian was further widened by the more favourable service conditions and fringe benefits of the former. Racial inequality was further entrenched in the decision process of the public service. It was not until 1941 that a Nigerian was named as a member of the provincial committees created to advise on the wages of public employees. Despite the comparatively large number of Nigerian lawyers, the country's judiciary remained predominantly European until the late 1940s. In the racially-segregated African Civil Service only 3 per cent of the positions were classified as 'senior'. By 1939 there were only 23 Africans in the 'Senior Service' of the Government.

Even in relationships among Nigerians inequality prevailed. This could not be otherwise since inequality was accepted as an inevitable, even natural, aspect of human existence, the acquisition of wealth was worshipped, and the goods and services of the nation were deplorably scarce. The few Nigerian middlemen in the import and export business depended on their skill in taking advantage of price changes, as well as the ignorance and illiteracy of the primary producer, to amass excessive profits. This gave rise to a wide socio-economic gulf between the producers and their middlemen exploiters. Inequality also existed in the distribution of both food farm land and cash crop farm land, with a tiny minority of the wealthy farmers holding most of the land in several parts of the country, notably in the cotton, cocoa, and groundnut belts.

However, human equality, the acceptance in practice of the absolute and fundamental equality of all individuals, is central to justice and human dignity, man's humanity. There must be equality because only on that basis will men work together co-operatively. A man develops himself by making his own decisions and increasing his knowledge and ability in conjunction with others in the community on terms of equality. Socio-economic inequality between members undermines their mutual respect. And it emerged in colonial Nigeria as a result of the encouragement of acquisitive instincts in the population through the use of wealth as the basis for social status and political power. Inequality leads to economic and political oppression, and sets off a spiral of interpersonal competition whose effect is anti-social.

Thus, the values that British colonialism implemented in Nigeria, and the pattern of life that it established, sharply contradicted its professed objective of *mission civilisatrice*. Far from improving the quality of life and humanity of Nigerians, exploitation, racial segregation in housing, education and political participation, together with the creation of socio-economic imbalance among Nigerians, the encouragement of disunity and hostility among them in housing, education, and politics, the promotion of inequality in socio-economic relations, the worship of wealth, and the limitation of social welfare services alienated, degraded and dehumanized them. On the other hand, however, these values and pattern of life greatly helped the colonialists to maintain domination over Nigeria, exploit its human and material resources, and cart away its exploited wealth to the metropolitan country. Fanon has observed that colonialism thrived only in areas where the people were so alienated from their society and dehumanized that they had no alternative but to be subservient and docile in relations with the colonizer. The colonial myth of inferiority, its practical expression in racial segregation and socio-economic domination, periodic repression, and political domination served to generate this subservience and docility. The various policies of divide and rule served to divert the attention of Nigerians away from colonial political domination and economic exploitation, weaken the anti-colonial struggle, and channel hostility generated by the alienating colonial system away from the colonialists themselves. Under the circumstances, the professed moral objective of colonialism can only be interpreted as a white mask over black political domination and economic exploitation.

Ethnicity as a Counter-revolutionary Force

Locally, colonial reaction found allies in the traditional rulers who, in the first place, surrendered local sovereignty to the colonialists after collaborating with their predecessors in the inhuman and obnoxious slave trade. Given to selfish self-indulgence in luxurious consumption to the neglect of the economic development of their subjects, and selfish interest in maintaining some form of social power over the local population, the traditional rulers found it very easy to accept the role of clients in the colonial order. They proved so useful in the North, where ironically they had put up the fiercest resistance against colonial penetration, that the colonialists set about trying to create them elsewhere where they had not existed in pre-colonial times. Hence, the Warrant Chiefs of Igboland were commissioned. In return for services to colonialism in the collection of taxes, pacification of the population, and the spread of colonial patterns of economic activities, the colonialists strengthened the local power and privileges of the traditional rulers, especially in spheres such as religion, customs and traditions, which were not particularly important to the metropolitan country. The main function of the chiefs for colonialism was to ensure a very peaceful colonial penetration of all areas of the country and all segments of the Nigerian population. For this they were well rewarded in various ways. Of course, when they fell out of step they were severely punished with either banishment or dethronement.

The nationalist movement for independence constituted the main progressive force pitted against this reactionary alliance of colonialism and traditional rulers. Composed essentially of the emergent classes of the colonial order and their organizations, such as trade unions and ethnic associations, it was led by the petty bourgeoisie and drew its physical support from the peasantry, the rural majority. Although it started out as a movement for the reform of the obvious injustices of the colonial order, such as arbitrary taxation, land acquisition by the colonial government, the colour bar, and the denial of political rights, it later developed into a movement for the unity and independence of the British West African colonies and finally matured into a force for national independence. But it is in this its last phase of activity that the movement assumes a historical importance.

The father of that movement was Herbert Macaulay whose party, the Nigerian National Democratic Party (NNDP), arose out of the need to counteract the collaborationist activities of the Lagos traditional aristocracy, arbitrary colonial taxes, official seizure of land, and the harrassment of the Lagos market women. As a protest and reform movement it condemned colonial acts of injustice and argued for fair play and equality in the treatment of the African population, for reform of the Legislative Council to include more Nigerian representatives, and for the democratization of national deliberations. In its activities it was supported largely by the emergent Lagos urban middle class, notably the Lagos market women, the lawyers and doctors who were the major victims of the colour bar and the denial of political rights, and the working population of the capital city. Macaulay accomplished a great deal in exposing the arbitrariness and injustices of colonial rule and in mobilizing Lagosians to struggle against them, thereby increasing their political consciousness and improving their organizational skills and resources. Unfortunately, his party and movement were limited to the capital city and therefore were unable to embrace the broadest section of the total population. Nevertheless, his ideas, technique of protests, and pattern of struggle spread to other parts of the country, helping to galvanize them into anti-colonial nationalist activities.

Thus, by 1936, his activities had been supplemented or complemented by those of many other vibrant nationalists, including Nnamdi Azikiwe whose fiery and militant press did more than anything else to spread nationalist sentiments across the literate reading public and whose public speeches helped to galvanize many nationalistic organizations and associations into militant nationalistic activities; Ernest Ikoli of the *Daily Service*, a doyen of the fearless nationalistic press corps; and Obafemi Awolowo, who at this time was instrumental in galvanizing nationalistic consciousness in the trade union movement. The institutional expression of this burgeoning nationalistic fervour and activity was the formation during that year of the Nigerian Youth Movement (NYM). It embodied the national spirit of the drive for emancipation, aspiring to extend nationalistic activities, organizationally and in terms of the scope of its activities and the spread of its ideas, to all the nooks and crevices of the country.

The Second World War served to quicken the tempo of nationalistic activities and increase the strength and number of nationalist activists. It showed how glaringly the colony was organized for the benefit of Britain.

Local resources and behaviour were rigorously organized to enable the metropole to achieve its war objectives. Nigerians were made to fight in a war which had little or nothing to do with them and their interests, and in fact created cost-of-living difficulties for them. Nigerians who fought in the war came home with new ideas and experiences about liberty, equality, fraternity, anti-racism, self-determination, and the hollowness of the invincibility of the white man. These developments at the local level were reinforced by the ascendancy of progressive anti-colonial forces in the world community. The two superpowers to emerge from the war, the Soviet Union and the United States, were committed to anti-colonialism, the former on a revolutionary basis, and the latter on a reformist basis. The Atlantic Charter which they signed during the war denounced colonialism and looked forward to its demise and the granting of self-determination to the colonized peoples. The United Nations, which they were instrumental in creating, championed the cause of the colonized nations.

Further external stimuli for local nationalism included the emergence to independence of the former colonies of India, Pakistan, and the nations of Indochina. In addition, the Labour Party's assumption of governmental powers in Britain encouraged the movement. The party, famous for its more progressive views on decolonization than the Conservative, was committed to self-determination and the encouragement of trade unionism. At about the same time as this growth of anti-colonial sentiments in the world community, the movement for pan-African unity was picking up momentum. Its 1945 Manchester Conference was instrumental in bringing together many Pan-African nationalists who, although they were committed to some form of African continental union, were nevertheless fiercely opposed to colonialism and its oppression, humiliation, and balkanization of the African peoples. Such meetings served to keep alive the ideas of self-determination, equality, and freedom so crucial in the propaganda of the nationalist activities.

The rapidly growing momentum of Nigerian nationalism, arising from these favourable internal and external circumstances, soon began to be dampened by the reactionary influence of ethnicity. Mention has already been made of the manipulation of ethnic sentiments by the colonialists as a means to divide and rule the people. This, as well as the adverse effects of that phenomenon on the anti-colonial movements that became significant from the 1940s, was possible because of the counter-revolutionary character of ethnicity. Contrary to Euro-American propaganda, contemporary ethnicity in Nigerian is not the result of some primitive mystigue of the African causing one linguistic group to fight another, but the result of the need for the local population to adapt to the colonial and neo-colonial society.

Thus, for example, the ethnic problem was a phenomenon of the colonial and the neo-colonial urban areas. Here contact between different ethnic groups was possible. Rural inhabitants of different groups did not make contact and therefore could not be a source of conflict. But contact alone was not enough for ethnic problems to arise. Individual and group socio-economic insecurity was another crucial factor, and the colonial and neo-colonial urban centers engendered such insecurity. During the early colonial period the urban dweller not only had to look for employment, he had to pay for the education of his children, provide for his and his parents' old age, and take care of funeral expenses. The need to find an effective instrument for performing these functions led to the formation of ethnic associations. The colonial government had abdicated its roles in these respects, concentrating on the protection of the enormous profits of the foreign firms. Its reprehensible withdrawal from the realm of social services created a void which was filled by the ethnic associations. Hence, the period of the Depression of 1928–34, corresponding to the period of the government's most extensive withdrawal from social welfare services, witnessed the unrivaled growth in the number and membership of these associations. In this way ethnicity emerged and has persisted as a mechanism for the individual to overcome the insecurity of the colonial order and, therefore, for adaptation to colonialism. In other words, it served the interests of colonialism to have the local population enter and remain in the colonial society. Thus it was and has continued to be the instrument of reaction, serving to prop up the reactionary systems of colonialism and neo-colonialism.

Apart from this reactionary adaptive role, ethnicity was also a counter-revolutionary force because it diverted attention away from colonial oppression and injustice. For example, ever since ethnicity intruded into Nigerian politics in the Ikoli-Akinsanya affair of 1941, which split the NYM nationalist movement along sectional grounds, the nationalists have devoted more of their efforts to the struggle for ethnic ascendancy rather than to the exposure of the repressive colonial system. In fact, by the late 1950s when the prospect of independence was around the corner, hardly any struggle had been waged against colonialism. Instead, the various factions of the movement concentrated on how to ensure monolithic electoral support in the ethnic homeland, widen the political base from that area, win elections in the region of ethnic supremacy in order to control its government, use governmental power to eliminate the influence of its ethnic opponents in the area, encourage minority ethnic agitations in regions controlled by rival ethnic groups, and use federal power to channel national resources to the ethnic homeland. Under these circumstances, the constitutional conferences degenerated to the mere adjustment of ethnic demands, with the crucial issues of ending foreign economic exploitation of local labour resources, the need to replace the colonial army and police designed to protect foreign interests with a people's army and police serving the local population, the whole question of changing the production process, and the shortcomings of the cabinet and regional systems of government being either ignored or neglected.

In addition, as a counter-revolutionary force ethnicity split the anti-colonial movement, thereby weakening it. The 1941 division within the NYM in which ethnic prejudice was charged was reproduced in the late 1940s and the 1950s in the conflict and competition between the Action Group (AG) and the National Council of Nigeria and the Cameroons (NCNC). This division progressively destroyed mutual trust, goodwill, solidarity, and the will to co-operate among the leaders of the nationalist movement. Thus after the 1959 elections the natural alliance for anti-colonial progress between the NCNC and the AG against the local conservative wing of the nationalist movement represented by the Northern Peoples Congress (NPC) was sacrificed on the altar of fear, mistrust, and ethnic advantages. Similarly, the NPC government was so consumed by its leaders' fear of the South that it preferred colonial domination to national independence under conditions advantageous to the southerners. Hence, the Northernization policy of the NPC government in the North gave job and social preferences to foreigners over their southern compatriots. That same government also delayed its acceptance of self-government to a time later than the other regions and violently opposed an early independence date of 1956 for the country, inspiring riots in 1953 against the Igbo living in the North in protest. In this atmosphere of fear, suspicion, and mistrust the Nigerian leaders were so disunited that they could not muster enough strength to successfully oppose the colonialists' imposition of an obnoxious defence pact and an intolerable burden of paying the pensions of the expatriate ex-colonial civil servants on the country.

Ethnicity was able to divide the nationalist movement because as a reactionary force it does not accept the common humanity of all peoples. It is exclusive in character, focussing on differences among them to the utter neglect of similarities. Hence, it ignored the fact that the Nigerian peoples shared a common heritage of colonial oppression and colonially-induced capitalist exploitation with its consequent poverty, ignorance, disease, and poor diet. Similarly, they shared a common alienation from the colonial production process which neglected local resources, consumption habits, and needs; and an alienation from that complex system of local, national, and international division of labour which governed colonial production. Associated with this exclusiveness has been the tendency of the members of an ethnic group to regard other groups as inferior. They have imitated the racist colonialists who operated on the basis of an hierarchy of cultures in which theirs was at the apex and acted as the yardstick for deciding the superiority and inferiority of other cultures. Those cultures that approximated that of the colonialists were deemed more civilized than those less suitable to it. As products of the colonial process of socialization Nigerians uncritically imbibed this reactionary racist categorization of peoples and cultures. Those groups which had made progress in the acquisition of petty bourgeois fortunes in the colonial order tended to regard their other compatriots as inferior, to be discriminated against socially. Such an attitude not only created a barrier between Nigerians but undermined their capacity to struggle effectively against colonialism. If the colonialists' society was the ideal to which all aspired, then what was the moral basis for challenging the domination of the colonialists? Why should Nigerians be expected to build this society better than those to whom it belonged? Such implicitly nagging questions, by engendering and perpetuating inferiority complex, sapped the will of the nationalists to fundamentally challenge the colonial order and thereby militated against the anti-colonial struggle. At the same time, the inter-ethnic struggle for superiority, or at least to avoid the stigma of inferiority, dissipated much of the energy of the nationalist movement.

In addition, ethnicity is counter-revolutionary because it generates aggressive anti-social competition and hostility, which dehumanized those involved. In order to emancipate their members from the socio-economic and political scarcity, and the adverse effects of the system of inequality imposed by the colonial order, the various ethnic groups engaged in vicious competition with one another which severely strained the social fabric of the nation. In such an atmosphere it became easy to relax the constraints against hostility toward others, permitting it to be expressed against members of rival ethnic groups as a means of limiting competition. But such hostility distorts and undermines the humanity of all those caught up in it and hampers their capacity for creative life, including the creation of a progressive anti-colonial order. Violence sometimes attends such hostility and not only saps human energy but leads to the destruction of human life. Mention has already been made of the riot in 1945 in Jos. However, during the colonial period the most violent ethnic riot occurred in Kano in 1953 in which 36 were reported dead and 241 wounded. But the full effects of this hostility were to be felt later in the ethnic massacres and consequent civil war of the late 1960s.

Nevertheless, in spite of the impediments imposed by the ethnic phenomenon and the collaboration of certain traditional authorities with colonialism, the progressive anti-colonial forces were triumphant, ushering in on 1 October 1960 a new era of sovereignty and national political independence. In the face of the increasing costs for maintaining law and order, the increasing denunciation of colonialism, the isolation of colonialists in the comity of nations, the moral crisis of conscience about colonialism in the metropole, and the weakening of the colonizing power by the Second World War, Britain was forced to embark on decolonization, and to attempt to pursue its colonial objectives by other means than direct colonization. With this accession to independence the Nigerian people had won a great victory, and a new principal contradiction emerged in the society.

Neo-colonialism and the Indigenization of Reaction

The sovereign and independent Nigeria that joined the comity of nations was a neo-colonial society. By this is meant that the major contradiction between the foreign control of the Nigerian apparatus of state and the right of Nigerians to regain that control was resolved in the direction of greater human progress, the victory of the rights of all nations to self-determination, independence, and equality, but the fundamental elements of the colonial system of production – characterized by foreign domination of the production process through foreign private ownership, control over the governing division of labour, and domination of access to markets, production ethics, what is produced, how it is produced, and when it is produced – continued to prevail. Herein lies the principal contradiction of the post-colonial neo-colonial society. The colonial production process served essentially the interests of foreigners and not those of the local population who were thoroughly alienated by it. Therefore, a major determining contradiction exists between the foreign interests in the continuation of this inherited pattern of production and the interests of the vast majority of Nigerians for a totally different pattern of production attuned to their interests and controlled by them. Of course, this contradiction existed within the colonial society but it was subordinated to the political struggle for the control of the state. Without resolving the latter contradiction it would have been extremely difficult to tackle the former. However, both were related because without much progress toward economic independence political independence would be emptied of all substance.

This close link between political independence and economic independence has led some to deride the achievement of national independence as empty, an event orchestrated by the local petty bourgeoisie and the colonialists as a means of preserving foreign interests and privileges while advancing the interests of the local privileged classes. Although it is true that the pattern of production and the rewards from production did not change significantly, and that since independence the petty bourgeoisie has improved its economic position at the expense of the masses and sometimes the foreigners, it is very unscientific to dismiss the attainment of independence as making little or no impact in the lives of the people as a whole. Such a view ignores the national humiliation, degradation, dehumanization, alienation, loss of confidence, inferiority complex, and crisis of identity attendant on foreign control of the political activities of the country, which the attainment of independence eliminated. Colonialism attacked and conquered the Nigerian people at two interrelated levels – the politico-psychological level and the material-economic level. The people waged their struggle at both levels. That victory was achieved first at the political level does not diminish its importance and value to the people but only indicates that the struggle must continue until total victory is attained at both levels. That view wrongly implies that the opportunity provided for the seizure of political independence should not have been grasped until it was also possible to achieve economic independence. The people's heroic struggle for progress is a historical and multifaceted one in which victories are won in stages. It has never been and can never be the result of a single apocalyptic stroke leading to an utopia in which victory is attained simultaneously in all spheres of life. Instead, it is everywhere determined by the balance of forces among the different contending interests on various issues, with each issue being resolved as its contradictory forces reach the stage of maximum maturity.

The nationalist struggle for independence was a truly people's struggle against foreign control that united all the local classes in the pursuit of a common cause. Therefore, it masked the differences among these classes regarding the kind of society that should emerge at independence and, more relevantly for our present discussion, it masked the differences among them regarding the colonial pattern of production and what should be done about it. Although anti-colonial nationalism benefitted all classes in the local society, it did so differentially. Therefore, these classes expected different socio-economic benefits from the elimination of colonialism, which became much clearer with the attainment of independence. It is this fact which makes it very crucial to observe the class leading the nationalist movement. The pattern of distribution of the benefits of the nationalism during the immediate post-colonial period is decided by this class, first and foremost in its interest. It cannot be otherwise. It is unscientific and, therefore, utopian to expect it to be otherwise. And it has nothing to do with the ignorance or gullibility of the other classes.

For example, in Nigeria the petty bourgeoisie led the nationalist movement but the latter also consisted of the various other classes thrown up by colonial capitalism. This leadership by the petty bourgeoisie meant that its interests determined not only the values, strategies, and tactics of the nationalist movement, but also the character of the emergent independent society. Unlike the national bourgeoisie or the proletariat the petty bourgeoisie has not played any significant revolutionary role in history. Its role in production is not a central or creative one and as a shifting class its members aspire to the role and privileges of the bourgeoisie proper but may be reduced by objective circumstances to the proletariat. In colonial Nigeria the petty bourgeoisie was a spineless, uncreative, unprincipled, and largely opportunistic class, whose role in production was as dependent on foreign control as the colonial economy itself. The anti-colonial objectives of its members were, therefore, characteristically selfish and oriented to the distribution of the benefits of production rather than to the creative transformation of the productive forces.

Members of this class were the hardest hit by the colonial racist colour bar in employment, job remuneration, business, housing, and sports. Their anti-colonial activities were motivated by the objective of eliminating this colour bar and acquiring the privileges previously reserved for the whites. Hence, for example, just before and after independence they succeeded in moving into the residential areas previously reserved for whites, where they have segregated themselves from their less-privileged compatriots of other classes. During the independence struggle they presented such selfish class interests as the interests of the nation at large. They gave little or no thought at all to the character of the production process and its consequences for productivity and development within the country. Similarly, very little concern was shown for, or thought given to, the specific interests and problems of the vast majority of the population. It was merely suggested that once independence was attained the concrete problems of the people would be solved. But this was a lie.

The various slogans, values, and moral posturing of the petty bourgeoisie during the period of anti-colonial struggle were blatantly self-serving. The democratic value of freedom, equality, and fraternity exploited the prevailing world democratic atmosphere of the period to mobilize internal and external support against colonialism. This view is supported by the actions of this class when it attained political power at independence. It set about to undermine and frustrate these same values. Political opponents were harassed and practically eliminated in the regions and, to a less degree, at the federal level. Soon even the political ritual of periodic elections was abandoned as a result of the intervention of the military wing of this class. The leaders closed their eyes to the incidence of inequality in the society and even began to rationalize them as an inherent aspect of human existence. Ethnic exclusiveness and segregation, as well as segregation on class lines in residential areas, quickly took the place of the value of fraternity. Justice was sacrificed at the altar of expediency and selfish class and personal interests. Under the circumstances, the unity of the people, which was founded on the demands for justice during the era of nationalist struggle for independence, was disrupted, and replaced by unity founded on the leaders' demand for blind loyalty to their concept of national interest; law and order clearly prevailed over justice in the affairs of the nation.

The petty bourgeois character of the leaders was most glaringly exposed by their use of the political machinery to amass wealth and privileges for themselves at the expense of the interests of the majority of the country who had created the wealth; they were oblivious of the conditions of their people and the inherent injustice of their actions. Their selfish actitivies showed that they were more desirous of imbibing the life-style and privileges of colonialism that in abolishing its injustice and oppression of the Nigerian masses. But they were not interested in the creative production that characterized the metropolitan bourgeoisie that controlled colonial production, only in the perquisites of the colonial political stratum. Their interest was petty bourgeois in nature, focussed on relations of distribution, the traditional area of focus of the petty bourgeoisie. Unable historically to increase production because of their remoteness from the directly productive functions and because of their uncreative role in production, the petty bourgeoisie relies on the manipulation of the distributive forces for whatever benefits its members derive from the production process. Consequently, they have ignored the relations of production, thereby perpetuating the colonial pattern of production characterized by foreign domination and its intolerable exploitation of the peasantry and working classs. This neglect militates against the mobilization of the creative energies of the population toward growth in production through the transformation of the productive forces.

Another consequence of this orientation toward distribution is the exacerbation of ethnicity and its counter-revolutionary role. Since the colonial economy was fragmented along regional lines the petty bourgeoisie became regionalized, with each regional faction quagmired in the economic activities of its regional colonial enclave. The members of each faction exploited the local advantages accruing from colonial production and the colonial bureaucracies. In the process they acquired a regional economic outlook which limited their horizon and encouraged them to exclude members of other regional factions from sharing in the benefits of their region's economic activities. Since each region was dominated by an ethnic group this regional chauvinism coincided with ethnic chauvinism, which played a crucial role in the 1966 political crisis and the consequent civil war (1967–70).

Thus, the emergence of the petty bourgeoisie to power explains the unsalutary state of affairs of the post-colonial society for the vast majority. Part of the blame for this must be borne by the leaders of the underprivileged classes for allowing the petty bourgeoisie to get into positions of dominance in the nationalist movement and through it the emergent neo-colonial society. Hardly any political party of the poor classes emerged during the colonial period to champion their causes. And the Zikist National Vanguard, which operated as an arm of one of the petty bourgeois parties but articulated some of the interests of the underprivileged peasants, workers, and unemployed in favour of a new system of production, proved ineffective. It was theoretically barren, strategically adventurist, politically tactless, and organizationally incapable of establishing structural links with the vast majority of the poor. It relied on the same populist slogans as the petty bourgeois parties and was quagmired in personal loyalty to an individual petty bourgeois leader, becoming disillusioned and immobilized as the selfish class character of its idol became more and more apparent.

The petty bourgeoisie of independent Nigeria did not only fail to change the colonial production process which, with the clipping of the political wings of imperialism, became a neo-colonial economy with imperialist forces exercising indirect control of the economy and society; it in fact transformed itself into the major local guardian of this system of production as a means of guaranteeing its economic, social, and political privileges. As a result of this development, imperialism was able to indigenize its reaction to the progressive aspiration of the people to control their production process and employ it in the service of their own interests. The petty bourgeoisie thus entered an informal reactionary alliance with the forces of imperialism in which in return for the pacification of the underprivileged classes, particularly the working class, it would be given more of the benefits of neo-colonial production, such as those that have accrued as a result of the indigenization of the personnel of the foreign firms, the establishment of public corporations, the award of contracts, the granting of licences, joint partnership with foreign firms and, most recently, the purchase of some foreign firms. In return the petty bourgeoisie and its comprador bedfellows threw the economic door wide open to capitalist investors in a manner reflective of the multilateral character of contemporary imperialism. Dependence was multilateralized, under the guise of diversifying trade and investment, from Britain to the major capitalist powers and institutions such as the International Monetary Fund (IMF) and the International Bank for Reconstruction and Development (IBRD). Such dependence paved the way for informal access to, and control of, the economy and society by the new mode of operation of imperialism in the changed international environment.

Of course, contradictions exist between the petty bourgeoisie and the comprador elements and the imperialist forces, but these are subordinated to and secondary to the principal contradiction of neo-colonialism, that between imperialist economic domination and local economic nationalism. Similarly, the contradictions between the progressive forces, consisting of the emergent national bourgeoisie, the working class, and the peasantry must be dominated by the demand for struggle against the common enemy. In this regard it is necessary to point out that although the national bourgeoisie is presently small in size it nonetheless exists, and contrary to common assumptions has objective interests in ending foreign economic domination, not in the interest of the underprivileged classes, but in the pursuit of its own objective of national capitalist exploitation and power.

The struggle between these informal and objective alliances of the progressive and reactionary forces over the question of economic independence promises to be a very protracted one. Obviously, the poor majority is unlikely to acquiesce in its intolerable economic situation arising from national economic dependence on the advanced capitalist countries and will eventually bring about the desirable change. However, the present balance of power between the two groups tilts so heavily on the side of reaction that, barring a pro-people's military *coup d'etat*, such a change is not possible in the immediate future. While the majority has remained without the economic and political resources necessary to wage a successful struggle, and have remained organizationally weak and disunited, the reactionary forces have grown steadily in wealth and power.

The local elements of reaction have utilized their control of the newly-independent state apparatus to accelerate the process of increasing their share of the local component of the national wealth and through it to strengthen their political grip on the country. It is not accidental that the old politicians of the first civilian regime dominated the political activities leading to the return to civil rule in 1979. By hook and crook they have succeeded in confining the national share of Nigerian resources to themselves. At the same time the importance of petroleum in the national and world economy has heightened the interests of the advanced capitalist countries in maintaining in power an indigenous regime that protects their economic interests. And their competition with the Soviet Union over influence in the world and the latter's recent successes in Africa makes them more dedicated to keeping Nigeria, the largest and potentially the most powerful country in Africa, within their camp. Therefore, they will be quite willing to support their local allies economically, politically, militarily, and in the area of intelligence and diplomacy, in any struggle with their progressive underprivileged majority.

On the other hand, the progressive forces are beset with intractable problems. There has been a rapid increase in the number and political consciousness of this camp. Its members and representatives, especially the revolutionary wing of the petty bourgeoisie such as students and radical intellectuals, have become more articulate and rhetorically combative. But very little progress has been made organizationally. Although the trade union movement has achieved greater unity, enabling it to successfully resist governmental control, it has remained essentially economistic in its activities. At the same time the counter-revolutionary force of ethnicity, theoretical confusion, and tactical mistakes continue to plague the efforts of the anti-neocolonial movement. Mutual suspicion and intolerance make the relationship between the national bourgeoisie on the one hand and the workers and peasants on the other still a hope rather than the reality of revolutionary thinking and efforts. The more conservative wing of the movement prefers to use the same populist slogans, strategies, and resources as the parties of the reactionary forces, rather than establishing structural links with the poor majority. Lacking in the wealth of the reactionaries, they are unable to make political progress. Meanwhile they disenchant the masses.

The problems of the progressive forces are further compounded because the lines of struggle are not clearly demarcated. Unlike the nationalist struggle for independence, the enemy is not clearly visible. Associated closely with the foreign-controlled production system are various Nigerians who have grown to depend on it for their livelihood, and some of whom have become its guardians. These in turn have close blood and other putative kinship ties with members of the underprivileged classes, which make it difficult to wage a struggle against class privileges. Such situations are clearly favourable to the reactionary forces of the status quo.

However, until the progressive forces are able to overcome these problems, the struggle for economic independence cannot be resolved in the direction of greater progress for humanity. And unless the working class, the most progressive and revolutionary wing of the anti-neocolonial camp, leads the struggle, the progressive forces are likely to commit a similar error as during the independence struggle. The national bourgeoisie would lead the struggle and when successful would create a society in which the contradiction between it and the other progressive classes would form the principal contradiction, and the majority would still be exploited and pauperized. Under the leadership of the proletariat, victory would mean the immediate ascendancy of the majority because that class not only represents the majority of the future as industrialization spreads, but constitutes the most exploited class of the neo-colonial society and, therefore, the most representative of the best aspirations of humanity. But until the victory of the progressive forces is achieved the struggle for economic independence will continue to be waged. Meanwhile, underdevelopment persists.

10. Indigenization for Lumpen-Bourgeois Development in Nigeria

Inyang Eteng

The Problem

Our present but increasing level of knowledge of the inner laws of the capitalist mode of production in general and their operation in the present Nigerian neo-colonial political economy in particular calls for a straightforward analysis of the celebrated indigenization policy of the country. We view that policy as consistently underscoring the country's lumpen-bourgeois development efforts. In this essay we hope to examine the following propositions:

(1) Current indigenization policy is historically subsumed in the British colonial process, which is directly related to the growth and development of capitalism in Nigeria.

(2) More clearly and purposefully articulated in the Second and Third National Development Plans (1970–80), indigenization proper is basically both a modern reactionary policy consistently pursued by an historically ill-equipped Nigerian lumpen-bourgeoisie against persistent foreign economic domination and control of the 'commanding heights' of the country's economy, and an extension of the civil libertarian policy of accommodation and 'assimilation' within the imperial colonial system evolved by the first breed of African aristocratic elites who were propped up by merchant and colonial capitalism itself, especially during the era of the trans-Atlantic slave trade.

(3) Contemporary indigenization process is not only predicated on Nigeria's traditional 'open door' socio-economic policy; it is also essentially diffusionist in orientation and, therefore, wholly dependent for its effectiveness on foreign monopoly capital and its operative institutions and machinery within and outside Nigeria.

(4) Also indigenization as enunciated in these national development plans practically reflects the prevailing petty bourgeois nationalism and externally-motivated entrepreneurship among the Nigerian ruling class and its pro-capitalist allies; as such, it amounts to what Andre Gunder Frank calls 'lumpen-development'.[1] In other words, rather than promoting authentic development and progress for the benefit of the majority of the Nigerian producing masses, indigenization intensifies, often quite covertly, the pre-

vailing multinational control of the Nigerian political economy and, hence, the country's persistent underdevelopment.

The foregoing propositions, which will be examined below, together constitute some of the corollaries of the central thesis which posits that indigenization as systematically spelt out in the Second and Third National Development Plans covering the 1970–80 decade is fundamentally a national bourgeois mechanism deliberately devised to enthrone national capitalism in Nigeria within the general framework of the world capitalist hegemony. It cannot, therefore, realistically offer the country any way out of underdevelopment. In the first place, indigenization cannot usher in national capitalism primarily because it is in the historical and structural nature of metropolitan capitalism to preclude and arrest the growth and development of indigenous capitalism. In the second place, the Nigerian state, as Gavin Williams has aptly noted, has generally been inclined to wilfully promote through indigenization programmes the development of foreign capitalism essentially 'by shifting resources from competitive to less competitive [and one would add, uncreative, exploitative and parasitic] producers, from craft to factory [and manufacturing] production, from agriculture to industry, from rural to urban areas, from the poor to the rich, and from Nigerians to foreigners.'[2] Thus, by hardly ever guaranteeing free rein to the ability of the bulk of Nigerians to produce goods and services that satisfy their basic needs, the Nigerian state has tended to promote the 'wealth of the nation' as it were, but only by the progressive and cumulative decapitalization and impoverishment of the country's producing masses.

In the current but fruitless liberal bourgeois search for 'communalistic' and other supposedly indigenous bases for re-ordering Nigeria's present political economy, there is a general tendency among state functionaries,[3] liberal-bourgeois intellectuals and Nigerian businessmen to refrain from diffusing altogether the impact of Western colonial and capitalist forces that directly militate against authentic national development. Rather, the main strategy and orientation have been, particularly since the end of the Nigerian civil war, to verbally castigate these external forces, and thereafter to present the economic and political interests of foreign and indigenous capitalists as sharply contradictory. On the basis of this, minimal and gradual curtailment of the exclusive control of the country's economy by foreign interests is proclaimed as an appropriate national policy, in terms of which some areas of easy maneuverability are created for indigenous capitalists but still within the confines of monopoly capitalism. In these terms, indigenization creates an erroneous impression that the only constraints on Nigeria's development are provided by foreign interests which must gradually yield place to the Nigerian capitalists, who are normally presented to Nigerians as the country's true economic and political emancipators.[4]

The following analysis will assume, among other things, both historical and holistic perspectives. It will be shown (a) that current indigenization policy as elaborated in the post-civil war development plans basically constitutes the culmination of politico-economic reactions of the local petty bourgeoisie against colonial and capitalist impositions; (b) that indigenization, which essentially seeks to guarantee to the Nigerian ruling class and its allies a modicum of indigenous control of, and participation in, the local economy currently under stringent foreign control, has taken various forms over the decades in reaction to the growth of capitalism from its mercantilist to its advanced monopoly capitalist stage; and (c) that because indigenization in whatever form is merely an accommodative reaction to the logic of capitalism and neo-colonialism, it is at best a lumpen-bourgeois development palliative, not an authentic national development praxis. This analysis will generally cover the pre-colonial, colonial and post-independence eras, with particular attention to national development efforts under the Nigerian military regimes, especially during the seventies.

Background and Objectives of Indigenization

Promulgated in a more systematic and comprehensive manner on 28 February 1972 as the Nigerian Enterprises Promotion Decree No. 4 under the Second Plan, the indigenization policy is essentially the historical culmination of previous attempts by the Nigerian ruling classes since colonial times to create within the capitalist system elbow-room for themselves and other Nigerian petty bourgeois aspirants. This 'gradual movement toward the acquisition by Nigerians of more active and increasing entrepreneurial role in the economic life of the country' apparently began in the forties with the legislative establishment of produce marketing boards for the purposes of transferring control over the marketing of the country's export commodities from expatriate firms to Nigerians and to the Nigerian governments. It took another eight years after independence to promulgate the Companies Decree of 1968 that 'compelled all alien enterprises to register as Nigerian entities' for purposes of bringing these local subsidiaries of multinational corporations under more efficient control, and another twelve years to consider promulgating the indigenization policy which virtually came into force on 31 March 1974.

The philosophy of the 'open private enterprise economy' was officially upheld in the 1962–68 Plan. Even then official interest in increasing local control of the economy was quite discernible. According to Akeredolu-Ale,[5] certain historical constraints tended to direct government orientation in the new direction. These antecedents included Nigeria's economic difficulties since the mid-1950s and the way they were explained, and the lesson in self-reliance forced upon Nigeria's political class by several national experiences and events, especially during the 1960–70 decade.

In this regard Nigeria has since 1955 been subject to unfavourable balance of payments and progressively worsening terms of trade caused by the cessation of the export boom induced by the Korean war; the escalation of imports explained partly by the 1955–1960/61 Development Plan; the general rise in the cost of private foreign investment especially through the repatriation of profits, capital and capital gains; the decline in the inflow of private foreign capital; and the dwindling and progressive tightening of conditions of official aid flows into Nigeria. Aside from these, government's efforts to stimulate indigenous entrepreneurship since the 1950s had similarly achieved very little because of capital shortage, inadequate managerial expertise, 'negative socio-cultural and motivational characteristics' of the world of private indigenous entrepreneurs, and the dominant presence and restrictive practices of private foreign-owned commercial banks which dominated the credit system and had hitherto demonstrated their aversion to aid indigenous businesses.[6]

Enlightened radical opinion had also capitalized on the country's post-civil war economic difficulties and relentlessly pressured the military government to tighten its control over the economy and to curb the excesses of foreign monopoly capital in the country. Some of the factors which galvanized public resentment against foreign control of the economy, and which apparently forced the policy of self-reliance on the Nigerian political and bureaucratic classes, included, among others, the substantial shortfall in the anticipated foreign contributions in the 1962–68 Development Plan, the increasing cost to Nigeria of her continued dependence on foreign capital, the escalation of restrictions on migration from the poor to the rich nations, the anxiety to avoid the political embarrassment to Nigeria which would apparently result from the crystallization of foreign economic dominance in the country, and the war-time austerity which Nigeria experienced between 1967 and 1970.[7]

The Nigerian government's reaction to these historical antecedents was to create an erroneous impression of an existing fundamental conflict of interest between foreign monopoly capitalists and the Nigerian lumpen-bourgeoisie. By further regarding the class interests of the national 'capitalists' as consistent with those of the majority of the exploited Nigerian producers, the government generally couched the country's development problem as primarily that of limiting the dominant role of expatriate interests. From this standpoint, the government presumed (again erroneously) that by promoting indigeneous entrepreneurship in the country, national capitalism, economic development, and social progress were simultaneously advanced, and monopoly capitalist control of the country's political economy correspondingly minimized. Judged from expanded government expenditures – ₦3,192 million for the 1970–74 Plan and ₦43.3 billion for the 1975–80 Plan respectively – and from the structural pattern of sectoral distribution of plan appropriations, it was evident that the government expected the private sector to carry the brunt of the country's present and future socio-economic development.

In the main, the indigenization policy was purportedly designed to (a) effect a process of transferring control over small-scale industries and the service sector of the economy to Nigerian entrepreneurs; (b) reduce the incidence of profit repatriation by foreign investors operating in the country; (c) effect a gradual and effective transfer of technology and managerial expertise to the emergent entrepreneurial and managerial classes in Nigeria;

(d) cut down considerably the existing and future expatriate quota at the highest echelons of the Nigerian labour force; and (e) raise the level of intermediate capital goods production.

To these ends, twenty-two business concerns under Schedule I were exclusively reserved for Nigerians, while thirty-three others under schedule II were open to aliens with the guarantee of 40 per cent indigenous participation if such activities had a capital of over ₦400,000 or an annual turnover exceeding ₦1 million. To ensure effective implementation of the policy, elaborate machineries were set up by the Federal Military Government under the decree 'to accelerate and smoothen the process of ownership transfers'; these included the Nigerian Enterprises Promotion Board (NEPB) to co-ordinate activities of states' Enterprise Promotion Committees; the Nigerian Bank for Commerce and Industry (NBCI) to provide loan and finance to 'a few deserving Nigerians' who seek to assume full or partial ownership of existing foreign enterprises, or who wish to establish new ones; the Capital Issues Commission (CIC) established in 1973 to regulate the issuing and sale of shares or debentures to the public; and the Center for Management Education and Training (CMD) and a number of polytechnics located in various states ' to furnish the new entrepreneurs with management and technical advice.' Government's euphoria over the successful launching of the policy is reflected by Ayida's reference to the programme as one principal indicator of the revolutionary transformation of Nigeria into a 'New Political Economy' under a decade of the country's military leadership.[8] V.I. Bello, one-time Secretary to the Nigerian Enterprises Promotion Board, emphatically indicated that the policy will be regarded as one of the boldest achievements of the military regime.[9]

While some sympathetic petty bourgeois elements regard the indigenization decree as the country's 'Economic Magna Carta', others describe it as the purveyor of 'the People's Capitalism'. Let us briefly examine the extent to which these encouraging remarks are justified by empirical data.

Two years after the promulgation of the decree, government and official representatives had cause to express satisfaction over a high degree of compliance of all concerned. According to A.E. Ekukinam, a top government official in the Economic Development Ministry and one-time President of the Nigerian Economic Society, of some 306 businesses under Schedule I, about 237 worth nearly ₦20 million had complied and exchanged hands.[10] Similarly, of the 628 concerns under Schedule II, an estimated 503, with an aggregate investment of some ₦60 million, were reported to have complied. This gave a total of 954 organizations in both schedules out of which 740, or 77.5 per cent, had presumably complied. Additionally, between May 1973 and October 1974, over 54 million ordinary shares of 50k each were purportedly transferred to Nigerian citizens and associations. Also, within the first year of its operation, the Nigerian Bank for Commerce and Industry approved ₦15 million in loans and equity capital to facilitate the indigenization process. With about ₦83 million (or ₦103 million allowing for probable over-valuation by something like 20 per cent) thus far spent in the acquisition by Nigerians of Schedule I enterprises, and the indigenization of 40 per cent of activities under Schedule II with the aid of private commercial banks, it was apparent that the private sector was perceived as being increasingly controlled by Nigerians as envisioned by the indigenization policy.

By 1975, however, fresh evidence clearly showed that government's initial claims of an appreciable degree of compliance were exaggerated. As several discrepancies turned up, the government was forced to appoint a high-powered Industrial Enterprises Panel on 17 November 1975, led by Justice Adeosun, whose Panel confirmed that the 1972–4 indigenization exercise succeeded only in a limited way while failing woefully with regard to wider national policies and objectives.[11] From available statistics it was found that of a total of 950 existing organizations affected by the decree, 357 fell under the total indigenization of Schedule I, while 593 came under the 40 per cent indigenization of Schedule II. It was further shown that as of 30 June 1975 only 58 per cent of Schedule I enterprises and 89 per cent of Schedule II organizations had *provisionally* complied, and that confirmed cases of *actual compliance* numbered only 314, or 33 per cent. It was additionally noted that 81 enterprises were exempted on very flimsy and questionable grounds, while known defaulters were never brought to book two years after the decree came into effect.

The Panel particularly noted that, aside from many in-built structural defects in the decree, several devices were frequently employed by expatriates and Nigerians alike to circumvent the provisions of the decree. Such devices included fronting by Nigerian businessmen, application for naturalization by foreign investors, extended use of the definition of Nigerian citizenship, interpretational problems of classification of enterprises, the 'gentle approach' to implementation of the decree, and frequent amendments on the part of government officials providing for exemptions on dubious grounds. Onosode's observations regarding the acquisition of shares is even more dramatic and revealing. According to him, 'From the upsurge in the demand for shares a new breed of 'professional shareholders' has emerged. In the bid to secure maximum allotment, varying tactics, all of a dubious and representative character, were employed, such as changing the profession as well as the order of one's names to produce incredible permutations and combinations, and using the names of pet animals, and procuring domestic servants, nightwatchmen and secretaries as applicants with a view to consolidating holdings through private transfers which, though strictly legal are, in my view, contrary to public policy.'[12]

Surprisingly, the government expressed disappointment over its realization that in almost all instances the subversive devices employed by foreigners could not have materialized without the active support and connivance of those it described as 'some disgruntled Nigerian citizens', a description which belied the fact that the so-called 'disgruntled Nigerian citizens' were the very prime beneficiaries of the provisions of the indigenization decree. Among the 'deserving Nigerians were business tycoons, professionals, public servants, civil commissioners, university dons, educational administrators, and traditional chiefs. Suffice it to say, however, that the Industrial Enterprises Panel viewed the compliance gap serious enough to warrant about 58 amendments, most of which were incorporated into the 1977 revised version of the decree, which made provisions for three schedules and extended provisos.[13]

Indigenization and Egalitarianism

One of the expressed goals of Nigerian development plans is the creation of a just and egalitarian society. Available evidence, however, strongly indicates that the implementation of the indigenization policy is a far cry from this objective. Indeed, the most incisive critiques of the policy's anti-egalitarianism have come from the policy's petty bourgeois adherents.

Representative critics indicate that Nigerian participation has fallen below expectation; that enterprises under Schedule I reserved exclusively for Nigerians provide little or no sophisticated entrepreneurial challenges since these ventures have always been the traditional preserves of Nigerians;[14] that several other categories of enterprises of Schedule I activities such as blending and bottling of alcoholic drinks, newspaper publishing, municipal bus services, radio and television broadcasting, supermarket business, distribution and servicing of motor vehicles, inter-city haulage and transportation, which were initially reserved for Nigerian entrepreneurs, have been monopolized by federal and state governments which have also bought up shares sold by large foreign firms such as the UAC; that there is a strong element of government discrimination against private Nigerian interests, particularly over the question of expatriate quota restrictions; that 'the future sum of dividends and capital gains have been so thinly spread among so many Nigerians that the likely result is that this new wealth will be used for consumption rather than [for] investment'; and that meaningful investment is still outside the reach of a large number of the Nigerian citizens, mostly low-income wage-earners and peasants, even though most of the shares are being offered at rock-bottom prices of (say) 50k per share.

The government's insensitivity to the dangers of concentrating wealth in the hands of a few Nigerians resulting from the indigenization programme is reflected in the cavalier manner in which the Nigerian Enterprises Promotion Board dismissed the programme's anti-egalitarian issue. First, the Board regarded wealth concentration at the expense of the Nigerian masses as a purely social rather than an economic question, thereby implying that both are only incidentally related, with the social question assuming only tangential importance. Second, it argued that although the problem of concentration of wealth is a legitimate one, it was the Board's main task to ensure the smooth take-over of business by Nigerians no matter their states of origin or their numerical strength. Finally, it argued that if inegalitarian share ownership eventually carried the potential for dangerous class conflicts, this danger would ultimately dissipate as Nigeria became increasingly industrialized and the scope and size of businesses grew beyond the competence and capability of the family clan.[15]

In the first place, it is an historical and a holistic fallacy to assume that indigenization as an economic programme has no social and political implications, even when its consequences for entrenching class distinctions are relatively obvious. After all, the assumption of political authority by the Nigerian petty bourgeoisie since 1960, rather than eliminating social inequalities and their attendant class antagonisms, has intensified these tendencies. The Board, therefore, exhibited gross intellectual myopia by failing to acknowledge the implications for the intensification of existing capitalist social relations and social formations which the new pattern of share ownership entailed.

The Board was also exceedingly naive in believing that a smooth take-over of affected businesses by Nigerians, no matter their state of origin and regardless of their numerical strength, implies egalitarian resource distribution. Egalitarianism is simply not defined in terms of such socio-cultural commonalities as state of origin, ethnicity, religion, sex or other such characteristics, nor by the fact that the Nigerian government now owns 60 per cent equity in foreign enterprises, nor even by the fact that most Nigerian petty bourgeois elements who own shares in these foreign companies are drawn from the various ethno-linguistic nationalities that make up the federation. More appropriately, the country is a class society.

Finally, the Board was unnecessarily utopian in believing that with increasing levels of industrialization, class distinctions will correspondingly diminish in Nigeria. An analysis of the growth and development of capitalism and neo-colonialism in Nigeria, which also reflects the increasing level of capitalist industrialization in the country, generally negates this thesis. On the contrary, the Nigerian petty bourgeois who are directly linked with foreign-controlled and industrialized urban growth enclaves now constitute the dominant forces in relation to the exploited Nigerian producers. And, with the increasing investment of foreign monopoly capital in the country's economy, the gaps between the rural and urban centers, between the 'haves' and 'have-nots', and between mental and manual workers are widening not closing.

Indigenous Managerial Control

The current 'management boom' in Nigeria is partly attributable to the indigenization programme, under whose provisions government established the Center for Management Development and a number of institutes of management to supplement the efforts of the existing Administrative Staff College. In addition, it launched a crash programme for the training of middle-level technical and managerial manpower in selected foreign countries such as India, the United States, France, Bulgaria, and Yugoslavia. The government's efforts apparently reflect its recognition of the lack of executive capacity as one of the major handicaps of the implementation of development plans. These efforts also constitute an appreciation of the serious shortfalls in the number of well-trained indigenous managers and technicians required for the effective implementation of the indigenization programme.

Official manpower development and training programmes within the context of indigenization and the mixed economy are generally grounded on false premises and, hence, ill-fated. There is, first, the erroneous assumption that managerial and technical expertise are neutral and, therefore, insensitive to the given mode of production within which they are employed. Yet, it is clear from historical evidence that managerialism, rather than collective decision-making, thrives much better in a capitalist, free enterprise system, with management essentially operating as front-line exploiters of human and material resources for owners and controllers of the essential means of production. In this regard, even the managers operating in completely Nigerianized establishments have continued to be guided by capitalist 'scientific management' spiced with doses of human relations gimmicks. They have to, since operations in these enterprises are fundamentally subject to the imperative of foreign capital and technology through which monopoly capitalism dominates the country's economy.

Indeed, the same argument can be directed against the mere infusion of Nigerian managers and technicians into the existing capitalist factory system in Nigeria. Already there is so much talk about the general innocuousness of Nigerian engineers, who more or less serve as appendages to their foreign counterparts, or as conduits for the distribution and disposal of foreign engineering hardwares and know-how. At best, potential graduates of the Nigerian managerial and technical crash programmes may be content to operate in fully-indigenized or partly-owned establishments in Nigeria as glorified storekeepers, repairmen and service technicians as long as the organizational, technological, and socio-cultural inputs of these ventures are still externally controlled by monopoly capital.

There is also the erroneous presumption which regards equity transfer as simultaneously conferring on Nigerians central decision-making power within the country's political economy. This assumption is basically oblivious of the central concern of any given political economy, namely power in the allocation of resources, not managerial efficiency as such. The main issue of Nigeria's present experience centers around the distribution of economic power and public patronage among individuals, ethnic and racial groups, and socio-economic classes.[16] Professor E. Nell properly put the importance of political economics in perspective when he surmised as follows: 'Orthodox economics tries to show that markets allocate scarce resources according to relative efficiency; political economics tries to show that markets distribute income according to relative power. It is good to know about efficiency but in our world [Nigeria], it tends to be subservient to power. Power is usually enhanced by efficiency but the two are nevertheless quite distinct. Economic power ultimately rests on the ability to inflict a loss – the stick. A subsidiary form is the ability to bribe – the carrot.

If economists paid as much attention to bribery and extortion as they do to marginal utility, we should be able to develop rough quantitative indices by means of which one could sensibly discuss the distribution of economic power in society. By failing to accord the distribution of income between labour and capital, as a properly central role, orthodox economics has become cut off from the central issues of our time. . .'[17]

Share ownership in, and managerial control of, foreign enterprises open to Nigerian businessmen are, thus, two distinct variables, as indigenous equity participants in these foreign ventures are now realizing. Central issues pertaining to these foreign firms such as what technology to employ, research to be undertaken, the location and diversification of investments, manifest and subtle capitalist exploitative strategies and tactics required in a given economy, engineering and patenting of technology and equipment, and sensitive marketing strategies, are usually decided at the metropolitan headquarters of these firms, not in Nigeria, notwithstanding the fanfare and undue media publicity accorded the elevation of Nigerians to positions of managers and executive directors of such foreign companies. In the main, foreign companies require the services of Nigerian managers and company executives because they are cheaper to hire relative to their foreign counterparts, because Nigerian executives perform maximally well in exploitative operations of routine nature, because as partners in capitalist exploitation and expropriation Nigerian managers can be trusted to keep the secrets of foreign companies at the expense of the security of the Nigerian state, and because hiring Nigerian executives is a mandatory requirement of the government's Nigerianization policy. There is nothing altruistic or humanitarian in these considerations.

The government's recruitment of highly-paid foreign personnel to man its enterprises, which include state corporations, has also created a paradox which perceptive indigenous entrepreneurs have not lost sight of. Government has accordingly been criticized for controlling the supply of managerial expertise, a highly critical input without which the indigenization policy cannot succeed, and whose availability should be subject to market dynamics like any other factor of production.[18] The government usually gives the impression that expatriate quota restrictions are short-term palliatives, which will be unnecessary when Nigeria is capable of providing her own managers and technicians. But the issue is hardly whether these capitalist exploiters are foreign or indigenous. Nor could it be argued that exploitation in Nigeria is less brutal and alienative because it is perpetrated by Nigerian capitalists upon indigenous labour. Nigerian capitalism is not increasingly humanized by the recruitment of an increasing number of indigenous managers and technicians into local work organizations whose *modus operandi* are generally informed by exploitative capitalist organizational and managerial principles.

In sum, to the extent that equity transfer leaves the dominant control and ownership of the essential productive forces in the country in the hands of foreign monopoly capitalists, to that extent indigenization fails utterly to deal with the central issue in contemporary Nigerian development planning and implementation. Authentic development in Nigeria will not come about by socializing the country's middle-level manpower in the art of capitalist exploitative techniques and strategies. Finally, no alternative administrative and management techniques, however revolutionary, will survive in the country's present neo-colonized political economy unless the present mode of production and distribution are drastically transformed.

Indigenization and Technological Transfer

The governments of Nigeria firmly believe that indigenization will foster technological transfer from Western industrialized nations to Nigeria by ensuring constant contacts between industrialists and businessmen from Euro-America and their Nigerian counterparts. The official position on the issue of technological transfer was recently recapitulated by Dr. Ominiyi Adewoye, the Nigerian Commissioner for Economic Development, while addressing the Lagos Chamber of Commerce in a lecture captioned 'The Private Sector and the Wealth of the Nation'. According to him, 'There is a second reason for the preoccupation of the government with the private sector. It is the transfer of technology from the advanced industrialized nations and the development of local technology appropriate to our needs. After a number of years in government, I have come to the conclusion that private investment is a good tool for accelerating the transfer of technology from the developed to the developing countries, . . . and given the right kind of policies and incentives by government, transfers of technology can be effected in particular instances within a given time limit.[19]

Some well-worn arguments are generally adduced to justify the technological transfer thesis. For instance, it is often suggested that Nigeria would benefit from several decades of scientific and technological advances made by industrialized nations through massive technological importation, rather than establishing an autonomous science and technology base of her own. Our previous analyses of the capitalist mode of investment and capital formation in Nigeria during the colonial and post-colonial eras, as well as other studies of the role of multinational corporations in the Third World in general and in Africa in particular, however, suggest that indigenization as an instrument for engineering development-oriented technological transfer is another typical liberal bourgeois myth.[20] According to Essang, this myth apparently feeds on the absence of national science and technology policies, which in turn leads to the official tendency to view imported technology as a substitute for concerted national efforts in development of indigenous technology.[21] The assignment of a development role in Nigeria to foreign technology is also based on an erroneous assumption by the Nigerian leadership that monopoly capitalism is capable of manifesting humanistic and philanthropic tendencies. The history of the role of the multinational corporation in Nigeria and other developing countries, however, suggest that monopoly capital, which is essentially propelled by profit maximization at minimum cost, is generally extra-sensitive to the kinds of technology that are exported to developing nations, and in what particular venture they are invested. Since the international mobility of monopoly capital is primarily guided by the search for higher profits, the scientific and technological underdevelopment of non-industrialized countries normally renders them easily susceptible to capitalist manipulation and exploitation.

In this regard, technologies imported into Nigeria from Western capitalist countries have generally included obsolete and scrapped materials, often repainted and then exported as newly-manufactured equipment; machinery which is often inappropriate for the prevailing ecological, edaphic and tenurial conditions in Nigeria; equipment which perpetuates existing contradictions between the country's urban growth enclaves and impoverished rural areas; technologies which enable controlling foreign interests to take full advantage of the government's ultra-liberal incentives and concessions usually designed to safeguard foreign establishments incorporated in Nigeria against stiff external competition; foreign-patented, low-cost capital goods generally invested in high profit but low capital formation ventures (assembling, processing, packaging, distribution and other import substitution establishments), and consumer durables like radios, television sets, vehicles, etc., which are frequently subject to inelastic demand and whose increased importation, particularly since the end of the civil war, has contributed immensely to the country's present trade imbalance and foreign reserve depletion; and capital goods which facilitate the diversification of foreign investments in order to avoid or contain local competition.

There are several deleterious consequences which result from Nigeria's continued dependence on foreign, particularly Western, technology; these are often glossed over by the country's policy-makers. They include the inextricable subjection of Nigerian skilled workers to the dictates of foreign technology required by externally-oriented work organizations operating in Nigeria; the constant depletion of Nigeria's scarce resources, especially foreign reserves, partly due to the high cost of imported equipments and high interest rates on foreign loans borrowed to finance the importation of expensive mechanical equipment; the subjection of Nigeria's educational, scientific and general research and service orientations to the restrictive logic of foreign science and technology; the continued dependence of local industries, including the completely indigenized ones, on foreign material and human inputs required by foreign technology, thus creating booming markets not only for the imported technologies and spare parts but also for the foreign resources required to operate them; considerable government subsidization of Nigerian enterprises which depend solely on foreign capital equipment; high unemployment rates occasioned by capital-intensive technologies; frequent employee turn-over, and inter-factory as well as inter-sectoral transfer of workers; and the intensification of the prevailing system of clientelistic and inequitable distribution of assets, material resources and opportunities, which are generally skewed in favour of urban businessmen, rural capitalists, and the generality of the country's lumpen-bourgeoisie. Other unsavory consequences include the incessant subjection of the nation's economy to imported depression and stagflation (inflation plus unemployment), and other forms of chaotic labour mobility, such as the migration of young people and unemployed rural youths and school-leavers to urban areas, the migration of Nigerian workers from the public to the private sector, and the emigration of highly skilled Nigerian personnel to Western capitalist nations; in other words, the migration of scarce productive labour and other essential resources away from the exploited and neglected Nigerian rural peripheries that need them most to the exploiting growth centres within and outside Nigeria.

Overall, the Nigerian authorities in addressing their minds to the country's problem of technological backwardness pursued externally-oriented policies which directly negated the fundamental orientation initially and explicitly specified in the Second Plan as follows: 'The changing pattern of the world economy and the increasing concentration of the world's economic and political power poses a great challenge for Africa, which Nigeria cannot ignore. Nigeria will therefore quicken its pace of development through the use of her own resources instead of relying unduly on external aid. This is the only way for an aspiring nation like Nigeria to develop at a rapid rate and in the right direction.'[22] In pursuance of this seemingly emancipatory policy, the government declared its grim determination to 'occupy the commanding heights in the quest for purposeful national development', and recognized planning as a deliberate tool of social change and for correcting defects in various spheres of production, distribution, and exchange. But, in practice, the Nigerian Federal Military Government easily fell prey to the extremely negative prescriptions of foreign exchange 'gap' theory which gives undue pre-eminence to the role of the external sector in the country's growth process, to the neglect of the problem of low social capacity for technological problem-solving that fundamentally accounts for Nigeria's perennial trade gap and declining foreign reserves.

But Nigeria's technological dependence and its 'technological transfer' solution merely aggravated 'economics of quantitative growth without development', which dates from the First National Plan when her industry was largely still at the early stages of import-substitution in beer, cement, and textile production with resultant impressive value-added in manufacturing and craft production.[23] In attempting to deal with the persisting problem of 'low interdependence' in manufacturing by upgrading the local production of intermediate and capital goods for sale to other industries, the government, however, acted against its commitment to 'self-reliant development' when it threw open the private sector of the economy to foreign and indigenous investors, while arrogating to itself 'effective control' of the proposed iron and steel complex, petrochemicals, hydro-electric installations, fertilizers, and defence manufacturing, and simultaneously going into partnership with erstwhile multinational companies in a variety of 'turn-key' projects,[24] and the manufacturing of import substitutes with production techniques which are largely externally conditioned.

To compound its problems, the government launched a ₦43.3 billion Third National Development Plan based on the current nineteen-state framework, and geared toward the completion of, among other things, various expensive capital-intensive projects such as another oil refinery, a major electrical installation and extensive telecommunication networks and installations; iron and steel complexes, dam irrigation and hydro-electrical installations, a large-scale Operation Feed the Nation (OFN) agricultural scheme, country-wide Universal Free Primary Education (UPE) Program, military reorganization, demobilization and large-scale construction of army barracks, and the establishment of new universities. This gigantic plan, which represents a growth rate of over 2,117 per cent of the country's planned investment from the First Plan (1962–68), was being implemented under the most unfavourable socio-economic and political conditions, in which the nation's satellite economy was precariously borne by a rickety oil monoculture, in which the essential forces of production, distribution and exchange such as human and material resources, capital goods, finance capital, entrepreneurial skills, and managerial know-how were all virtually externally determined and controlled, and in which post-civil war ethnic, religious, and class antagonisms precluded the generation of a national ideology undergirded by socialized production and distribution, social justice, and a democratized socio-culture.

In the circumstances, Nigeria could not escape being trapped by two deadly aberrations which afflict most neo-colonialized Third World economies, namely 'importer' and 'contractor' syndrome, generally aggravated by technological transfer under monopoly capitalism. Here lies the historical paradox; the indigenization policy was apparently designed to enable Nigeria to gradually escape from the clutches of foreign monopoly capitalism, yet in its implementation the policy consistently immerses Nigeria deeper and deeper into the monopoly capitalist quagmire. Let us briefly consider these related 'mixed economy' syndromes.

'Importer' Syndrome

Unrestrained government spending, especially from the inception of the Third Plan period, is not uncorrelated with astronomical increases in the country's oil revenue and the Third Plan budget noted earlier. From negligible levels in the sixties, oil exports steadily increased to account for as much as 94 per cent of the country's overall 1974/75 export earnings. Thus, while the oil sector alone contributed only about one per cent of Nigeria's gross domestic product in 1967, between 1970 and 1974 this share had jumped to about 15 per cent. A sectoral breakdown of aggregate growth rate of the country's GDP in 1972/73 shows that the oil sector singly accounted for 5 per cent out of the overall GDP growth rate of 12 per cent, while agriculture and manufacturing accounted for only 1.2 and 2 per cent respectively during the same period. Furthermore, in 1974/75 the oil sector grew by 36 per cent from the previous year's level, while the economy recorded an overall growth rate of 14 per cent, but subsequently slumped to a dismal level of 2.8 per cent in 1976 following a drastic cutback of 1.5 billion barrels daily from the 1974 daily production rate of 2.33 billion barrels.

According to Okonjo,[25] the critical importance of oil as the primary export and chief foreign exchange earner is illustrated by the country's balance of payments position between 1973 and 1975, which showed that without oil Nigeria was in deficit both in the current and capital accounts. In other words, in 1975 for example, Nigeria recorded a deficit of about ₦4.026 million in current account and approximately ₦175 million in capital account if oil proceeds were excluded, while with oil revenue added, there was an overall positive balance of ₦156 million. Okonjo thus inescapably concluded that Nigeria's economy has been kept relatively buoyant by oil, which provided an estimated 44.6 per cent of the 1975 GDP of ₦15.5 billion.

With projected regular inflows of large proceeds from oil to the magnitudes of ₦4.1 billion in 1974/75, ₦3.8 billion in 1975/76, and ₦4.0 billion in 1976/77 expected to boast appropriations for the Third Plan, the country's leadership became overwhelmed by a short-lived 'oil boom' euphoria, and became equally susceptible to the 'importer' syndrome'. Nigerians went on shopping sprees overseas and quickly turned Nigeria into a junkyard for the disposal of all manner of Euro-American goods. The most immediate effect of government unrestrained spending was that Nigeria's volume of imports of foreign goods and services consistently outstripped her exports, so that by the end of 1977 the country's foreign reserve, which stood at ₦4.06 billion in 1974, had sharply declined to an intolerably shaky level of ₦1.6 billion, barely enough for two months imports, even though oil proceeds during the same year amounted to more than ₦6.5 billion.

The most significant increases in the volume of imported goods under Standard International Trade Classification (SITC) indices were recorded in heavy machinery and transportation equipment, whose value rose in 1975 by about 15.8 per cent from the 1974 figure of ₦611.8 million, thus accounting for about 42 per cent of total imports during the year compared to 35 per cent of 1974 total imports. Other items with similar increases in 1975 included food and live animals, manufactured goods and materials, chemicals, and beverages and tobacco, with recorded import values of ₦298 million, ₦1,008 million, ₦333 million, and ₦46 million respectively, representing percentage increases of 91, 93, 74 and 428 per cent respectively over 1974 figures of ₦155 million, ₦523.4 million, ₦191 million, and ₦9 million.[26]

This general trend has continued with trade deficits of approximately ₦600 million with ₦1 billion recorded for 1977 and the first half of 1978, at the end of which sudden brakes by way of orthodox import restrictions (in order to induce Nigerians to patronize foreign and indigenous producers of home-made goods, and to save the country's economy that was certainly tottering on the brink of collapse) had to be applied. By the time the 'oil boom' euphoria had subsided, analysts like Kunle Adamson drew the country's attention to the revealing fact that Nigeria's foreign reserves fell by about 38 per cent between 1962 and 1964, rose by about 50 per cent between 1972 and 1974, and fell again by 21 per cent between 1975 and 1977,[27] during which the Nigerian leadership frittered away the country's resources in prestigious, image-building, but totally irrelevant and wasteful, projects which included FESTAC '77, an international Scout Jamboree, the ECOWAS Games, Kaduna Sports Fiesta, an International Apartheid Conference, and the First Lagos Trade Fair.

Nigeria's 'importer syndrome' was eloquently reflected by the First Lagos Trade Fair (1977), whose promotion was strongly engineered by indigenous parasitic 'capitalists' drawn from the country's Chamber of Commerce, the Manufacturer's Association of Nigeria (MAN) and similar bodies. A summary classification of foreign exhibitions and sales which dominated the Fair is very revealing, and sharply contradicts the official expectation that impetus to indigenous industry and manufacturing through 'technological transfer' will be greatly aided by the exposure of Nigerian entrepreneurs to foreign capital and consumer goods and their foreign producers by organizing such fairs. In general, Western capitalist participants in the Fair displayed mainly capital goods and consumer durables ranging from electrical and electronic gadgets, agricultural machineries, various brands of vehicles and spare parts, building and construction equipment, office equipment and stationeries, telecommunication equipment, textile and welding machineries, and water treatment plants.

The thrust of foreign participation was solely in sales, not in 'technological transfer' as the Nigerian public had been programmed into believing. For instance, Britain, which fielded about 112 companies with the largest contingent of assorted goods displayed, realized ₦83.25 million from immediate sales. The United States, represented by 34 establishments, reportedly realized a total of ₦27 million from on-the-spot sales, in addition to sales totalling about ₦236 million which were expected within the next twelve months from established contacts with Nigerian distributors. Also, the American contingent secured 47 immediate agreements for joint ventures with their Nigerian appendages, while 12 companies also succeeded in establishing business contacts with indigenous agents and distributors. Austria, famous for her smuggled lace materials and electrical products, fielded 46 companies and realized about ₦2 million from immediate sales during the Fair, with other anticipated sales totalling ₦1 million from contracted supply of beer to Nigerian agents. Canada made sales during the Fair worth about ₦1 million, while France, Finland, Denmark, West Germany, Bulgaria, Yugoslavia, Holland, Italy and Spain, with undeclared on-the-spot sales, also negotiated distribution contracts with several Nigerian businessmen. A *Business Times* commentator noted the positive reaction of an official of the Netherlands embassy in Lagos, who aptly summarized the general satisfaction of foreign capitalist participants in the Fair. 'We are pleased with the Trade Fair, and the approach was good', said the official.

But good for whom? Certainly not for Nigeria whose laughable exhibitions in contrast consisted mainly of local staples (such as yam tubers); traditional export commodities including cocoa, palm produce, and of course crude petroleum that needed no further advertising; and local handicrafts which many foreign tourist may have seen and bought as souvenirs. But for all her troubles, and for spending over ₦142 million in the construction of the now underutilized Trade Fair complex (whose contract was won by Energoprojeck, a Yugoslav building and construction firm), the Nigerian government realized a paltry sum of ₦11.5 million, primarily from pavilion fees. And to further stretch Nigeria's economic lack of planning, the organizers spiced the Fair activities with hopelessly irrelevant comic side-shows and a 'Miss Nigerian Trade Fair' parade, and then brought the two-week old Fair to an inglorious close by awarding gold and silver medals to representatives of the participating foreign firms that came and drained away the country's reserves. In the end the First Lagos Trade Fair, which carefully avoided the real Nigerian producers, turned out, in the words of Lt. General Obasanjo, the Nigerian Head of State, 'to provide at the country's expense, a showroom for manufacturers from all over the world to make bigger sales which do not in any way free the country from total dependence on the industrialized economies'.[28]

The 'importer syndrome' is essentially an affliction emanating from the capitalist diffusionist path to development preferred by the Nigerian leadership. Unable to effectively exploit, mobilize, and employ available physical and human resources in order to produce in sufficient quantities goods and services needed by Nigerians, the country's ruling class has consistently resorted to mass importation of foreign commodities. And since Nigerians have been thoroughly domesticated to believe that government action in the face of scorching and unrelenting inflationary spirals is the best in the circumstances, they expect more and more imported goods distributed under government supervision. The more imported goods and services Nigerians consume, the more they come to regard the government as a benevolent and a welfarist godfather, and the more the government further reciprocates by importing more goods in order to continue to enjoy the people's goodwill. The present crisis of frivolous government over-spending which now grips Nigeria has proven conclusively the untenability of this policy.

'Contractor' Syndrome

This syndrome, which results directly from scientific and technological backwardness, has been aggravated in Nigeria by the increased oil revenues noted earlier, which induced a false sense of self-sufficiency among public officials who, while the 'oil boom' lasted, were frequently known to indicate that money was never one of Nigeria's development problems, and who therefore thought that there was nothing that Nigeria could not buy. The syndrome is also associated with the illegitimate dichotomy of the Nigerian economy into the 'public' and 'private' sectors, and the association of the latter with managerial and technical efficiency. By also assuming a natural functional interdependence and complementarity, rather than a dialectical contradiction between both sectors, it was thus popularly accepted as a fundamental 'mixed economy' postulate, that the main function of the public sector (generally regarded as the 'socialist' component of the national economy) is to provide the private (capitalist) sector with necessary infrastructures, materials, other resources, and political legitimacy. Subsequent development plans in Nigeria merely articulated and streamlined more systematically and comprehensively under a more stringent military supervision what have been the respective colonial functions of both sectors of the country's capitalist economy.

The 'contractor syndrome', to which the so-called 'public' sector is perennially addicted, is fundamentally a manifestation according to which the execution of every single government project designed within the framework of a development plan must, as a rule, be contracted out to a foreign or an indigenous contracting or consulting firm under an agreement stipulating the type of materials to be used, the quality of the completed work, the total cost of project, and the timing and method of payment of fees. In the country this practice obtains even for those projects in respect of which the government commands an adequate supply of material resources, as well as a sizeable concentration of the most qualified indigenous personnel capable of accomplishing the necessary tasks.

The planning, organization and execution of FESTAC '77 project is a typical example of resource wastage and mismanagement through contract awards. In this specific case, innumerable government contracts and subcontracts were reportedly awarded for the building and construction of permanent structures and for (a) the ordering and procurement of FESTAC vehicles (for which some prominent Nigerians received upwards of ₦50,000 commission from the overseas supplying company but incurred no government censure) and electronic equipments totalling about ₦58 million; (b) the construction of the ₦36.5 million National Theatre which has since been under-utilized; and (c) the building of the ₦8.27 million Durbar Hotel and restaurants at the Lagos Festival village, including the completion of the Kaduna Durbar camps costing about ₦5.05 million. Other contracts were similarly awarded totalling over ₦48.8 million for the procurement of hard furniture, vehicles, kitchens, laundry and sound equipment, and for the provision of ₦35 million worth of consumables, including items that could have been directly and locally produced by Nigerians on a non-contract basis.

According to articulate Nigerian public opinion, FESTAC '77 particularly epitomizes extreme official folly in inefficient mobilization and mismanagement of the country's scarce resources. A recently published Government Report and Summary Accounts, which reported a total public expenditures of ₦141 million during the festival, has been openly challenged as a gross under-estimate. Also, the *New Nigerian* editorial of 1 July 1978 strongly suspected that, '. . . from the type of extravaganza and colossal waste of resources which we witness during the festival . . . the belief exists that very many people enriched themselves, and milked the nation of several million Naira through FESTAC. [Therefore] any report which fails to dig deep into this aspect of the matter and to let us know approximately how many of our moneyed men are FESTAC millionaires is not likely to meet with public acceptance.'[29]

Apart from the foregoing, the government's addiction to the 'contract syndrome' is also graphically illustrated by the indiscriminate awards of contracts for the development of virtually all of the nation's socio-economic infrastructure, which include the construction of dams and irrigation works; intra-country and international expressways leading into the Republics of Benin, Chad, Niger and Cameroun; iron and steel complexes; government housing estates, ports and airfields; police posts and army barracks; secretariats and educational institutions; communication installations and electricity power stations; and government-owned industrial and commercial establishments. There are also contracts and sub-contracts for the repair and maintenance of these establishments and installations; for the furnishing of government quarters and secretariats; for the supply and distribution of agricultural inputs, building materials, imported food items, laboratory and allied equipments and stationeries, drugs and medical equipments, research and consultancy services, etc. to government ministries, agencies, and corporations, educational institutions, local government councils, and federal and state parastatals.

National development by contract generally tends to limit the number of direct decision-making participants in national development processes. It equally induces a shopping-list orientation to development, especially since project implementation is essentially guided by profit maximization for contracting private organizations and the 'commission' it can generate for the state officials who award contracts, rather than by the contribution of completed projects to the improvement of the quality of life of the majority of Nigerians. Evidence from several government commissions of inquiry and government White Papers and gazetted material emanating from these inquiries indicate that (a) government officials have been variously involved in graft and other untoward practices associated with contract awards; (b) contract awards are frequently influenced by political, ethnic, religious and other personal considerations not provided for by government requirements; (c) costings and evaluations of contracts have often been unduly inflated through the invocation of the inflation bogey, and the multiple supply of the same equipment and resources for which multiplicated payments are made by the government; (d) uncompleted contracts have been endorsed as completed and then actually completed from government resources at further costs to the public; (e) foreign contractors have often fled the country after being paid the initial and often substantial mobilization fee, thus necessitating the re-awarding of contracts so affected; (f) original contract documents are sometimes mutilated, or officials are hoodwinked into overlooking major conditions that ought to be included in the original contract without which the entire project for which contract is being negotiated will result in a total failure; (g) Nigerian governments have quite often been forced into awarding contracts whose completion depends solely or partly on foreign inputs, including material resources and personnel, even when these are available in large proportions within Nigeria; and (h) contracting firms have also been known to have handed over shoddily-completed projects, often with the connivance or collaboration of the Nigerian officials who re-contract these projects to the original firms either for maintenance, repair or for new construction.

It can therefore be seen from the foregoing that government's execution of its development projects through contract awards is fundamentally inimical to the spirit of the indigenization decree. Rather than engendering and fostering indigenous creativity necessary for self-sustained industrialization and self-reliant development, 'contract syndrome' fosters the growth of a class of parasitic businessmen, distributors and 'commission agents'. In the Nigerian 'mixed economy', where the so-called 'public' and 'private' sectors are both sustained and controlled by foreign monopoly capital, and in which both sectors thrive on the massive importation of capital goods and consumer durables needed by capitalist-run state corporations and privately-owned import-substitution enterprises, all are guided by the central capitalist motive of profit maximization. The expectation that contract awards will adequately contribute to self-reliant national development seems somewhat misplaced.

Conclusion

The process of indigenization is more encompassing than the limited one of Nigerianization of the country's public service. It is motivated by the central objective of localizing the capitalist mode of production and has tended to take various forms over the decades. Toward the end of the colonial era, particularly from the mid-1950s, indigenization was manifested by the traditionalization of neo-colonial monopoly capitalism on the part of the 'moderate' Nigerian petty bourgeoisie, which had hitherto successfully relegated the traditional chiefs to the background. Through intensive socialization in Western education and in Western parliamentarianism, two crucial aspects of the tortuous decolonization process, members of this class came to define themselves as the inheritors of the colonial system. Now enjoying a new socio-economic status guaranteed by the first colonial-designed Ten Year Development Program and the entrenched regional and ethnic politics of the time, the political and bureaucratic elites, in alliance with their intellectual and professional counterparts, threw open the country to more and new foreign investors, who laid the foundation of neo-colonialism and monopoly capitalism in Nigeria.

In post-independence Nigeria, dating from the First National Plan launched by the first republican civilian government, indigenization consistently took the form of defining national goals of development in petty bourgeois terms. More systematically and comprehensively articulated in subsequent national development plans of the 1970s by the country's military regimes, the policy has sought to establish domestic capitalism through state sponsorship of indigenous entrepreneurship and managerial and technical expertise. This policy is, however, grounded on false premises chief among which are that (a) the main problem of Nigerian development is the assumed dissonance of interests between foreign and indigenous capitalists; (b) the economic and political interests of the Nigerian lumpen-bourgeoisie are coincidental with those of the exploited Nigerian producers; and (c) the Nigerian petty bourgeoisie as a definable socio-economic class logically constitutes the most historically and structurally-equipped modernization catalyst in the country.

Our presentation of the Nigerian indigenization policy provides a number of observations which are summarized below.

The history and structure of Nigerian underdevelopment reflect the growth and development of capitalism from its embryonic mercantilist-colonial stage to its monopoly capitalist stage, just as Nigeria correspondingly graduated from a pre-colonial agglomeration of disparate ethno-linguistic nationalities to the status of a politically 'sovereign' state through several developmental stages, first as a colony, then as a colonially-inspired federation of partially autonomous regional governments, and then as a neo-colonized political economy under civilian and military regimes.

The history, structure, and mechanics of neo-colonialism and monopoly capitalism in Nigeria are more appropriately captured by the emergent center-periphery model of Third World underdevelopment to which a number of brilliant analysts of Third World development have subscribed. Within the context of this powerful framework a number of insights are provided as follows:

(a) The Nigerian political economy should be more properly viewed in terms of power and dependency relationships involving resource distribution and exchange, and emanating from the ongoing capitalist mode of production. As such, the country's political economy defines a special class system, and Nigeria becomes more than just the traditional homeland of antagonistic ethno-linguistic and religious groups, as the 'co-operative federalists' among the country's liberal-bourgeois writers would want us to believe.

(b) The role of the Nigerian bourgeoisie and petty bourgeoisie in the localization and indigenization of neo-colonialist monopoly capitalism is thus of special historical import, for without their acquiescence and collaboration the penetration, growth and development of capitalism in Nigeria could not have materialized.

(c) The center-periphery model also defines the *structure* of the neo-colonialist power and the dependency relationship between Nigeria and international monopoly capital. In this context, indigenization is both an attempt to establish an indigenous capitalism and an accommodative, clientelistic stratification mechanism devised by the country's bourgeois and petty bourgeois elements for sharing with foreign interests the gains of the monopoly capitalist exploitation of Nigeria. Within the country's clientelistic-feudalistic system, the processes and mechanisms of distributing inequalities and opportunities on class, ethnicity and other bases are clearly elucidated.

(d) The model also enables us to properly locate the prevailing ideological and normative predicates of the superstructural institutions of the family, law, religion, education, and polity within the existing modes of production, distribution, exchange and consumption. It is therefore possible to show that the ongoing normative system, though derivable from the structure and dynamics of the economic infrastructure of the Nigerian political economy, tends generally to reinforce the latter. And, since the capitalist value content of the prevailing normative system normally forms the basis of socialization within Nigerian society, most Nigerians have generally come to accept the existing pro-capitalist system in the country as natural. Operating thus from the standpoint of transfigured and fragmented reality, these unconscious and falsely conscious Nigerians do not, and often cannot, appreciate the capitalist basis of the values and ideologies they espouse.

(f) Since indigenization, in whatever form and at whatever developmental stage of Nigeria's socio-history, is essentially elitist and guided by externally-motivated entrepreneurship, it is decidedly not a tool for social engineering nor an instrument of real, self-reliant national development.

(g) Having linked the problems of Nigerian underdevelopment with various stages and strategies of Western capitalism and imperialism, the essay perceives that true national development in Nigeria must, by implication, come about by totally destroying the monopoly capitalist and imperialist foundation of the prevailing conditions of underdevelopment through the socialist path to national development. The socialist alternative must aim at producing a qualitatively (that is, structurally) different Nigerian policital economy characterized, among other things, by socialized modes of production, distribution, exchange, and consumption; an interactional pattern based on equality and social justice for all, and a participatory and democratized socio-culture. These should form the bases for perpetually resolving the perennial contradictions in the country between ethnic and religious groups, between educational growth and an increasing rate of unemployment, between a burgeoning GNP and a stagnating and even deteriorating per capita income, between rural and urban Nigeria, between manual and mental workers, between agriculture and industry, and between increased consumption and low productivity.

Today Nigeria is at the crossroads. Therefore, an alternative path to national development based on scientific socialist principles (rather than on what the Nigerian Hegelians call 'the ideology of scientific populism'[30]) and informed by the positive gains and experiences of advanced socialist societies must be pressed harder and harder at the Nigerian home-front. The country is presently witnessing a neo-fascist process of deliberate, 'stratocratic' stage management through which the same corrupt and thoroughly discredited politicians and their bureaucratic and intellectual collaborators, most of whom were ignominously purged, rusticated, dismissed and finally driven into political hibernation, have now been deftly reactivated and boldfacedly foisted upon the Nigerian masses through economic manipulation, political machination and constant threats of brutal physical coercion.

The ban on politics has been lifted after over twelve years of military interregnum. Out of 54 political associations that ultimately emerged, nineteen successfully registered within the dateline stipulated by the Federal Electoral Commission (FEDECO), which has been invested with transcendental and non-justiciable powers. Of these nineteen political associations, only five with populist nomenclatures and very identical, elitist and pro-capitalist manifestos were finally registered as political parties to contest the elections leading to a return to civilian rule. These were the National Party of Nigeria (NPN) led by Alhaji Shehu Shagari, the Unity Party of Nigeria (UPN) led by Chief Obafemi Awolowo, the Nigeria People's Party (NPP) under the leadership of Dr. Nnamdi Azikiwe, former Governor General of Nigeria, the Great Nigerian People's Party (GNPP) led by Alhaji Waziri Ibrahim, and the People's Redemption Party (PRP) led by Alhaji-Aminu Kano. They presumably satisfied FEDECO'S discriminatory and preclusive criteria which could only be satisfied by the country's 'naira mandarins'. In contrast, the 14 unregistered political associations which contain the cream of the country's radical and progressive elements were legally and peremptorily outlawed.

A new constitution patterned after the American presidential system, drafted by a cross-section of the Nigerian bourgeoisie and the petty bourgeoisie, and decisively elitist in its ideological and entrepreneurial orientations, has entrenched the capitalist 'mixed economy' approach to national development. Accordingly, the 'rehabilitated leaders' of the legally-sanctioned political parties, who have been flaunting their ill-gotten wealth organizing unrepresentative conventions, have declared their intention in their parties' respective manifestos to render the Nigerian economy more and more susceptible to foreign and indigenous private investment if returned to power.

Today, national universities are consistently and purposefully being stifled financially and muffled politically. The country is also presently gripped by crippling incidences of ritual murders, mob lynchings, road accidents, state and community boundary disputes occasioning homicides, armed robbery, official corruption, incurable smuggling and 'stagflation', pervasive indiscipline, army and police brutality often leading to Soweto-type shooting of agitating undergraduates and high-school students, rampages involving these law enforcement agents resulting in wanton destruction of property and civilian lives, brutal suppression of radical trade union movements, utter disregard of human lives bordering on national psychosis, and a pervasive propensity toward profligacy, ostentatiousness, and vulgar materialism. All of these are, more or less, behavioural manifestations discernible in capitalist societies.

Nigerians are increasingly less quiescent and apathetic. They are seen everywhere, in farms, market places, shops, bars, offices, campuses, and along streets, discussing, often in muffled apprehension, the ongoing political and economic turmoils. Will there be another civil war, perhaps fought this time along class lines? Will the military return sooner or later? Is Nigeria destined to be ruled and her resources continuously rampaged by known political, bureaucratic and economic brigands aided by a crop of political upstarts? Why should the Nigerian poor grow increasingly poorer and the few Nigerian rich increasingly richer? And, according to what immutable law must foreign companies annually record huge profits while Nigeria, assumedly ninth-ranked in world's oil production, yearly go borrowing? These and similar questions have long since been agitating the minds of the Nigerian masses. A popular revolutionary and emancipatory praxis must, however, be informed by a critical understanding of the historical and structural bases of the country's prevailing underdevelopment to which Nigeria's elitist indigenization strategy subscribes.

References

1. Andre Gunder Frank, *Lumpen-Bourgeoisie and Lumpen-Development*, (New York: Monthly Review Press, 1972). Frank describes the indigenous agents of neo-colonialist monopoly capitalism in Third World countries as 'lumpen-bourgeoisie', which designates the state, the nature of setting consequent on monopoly capitalist exploitation and expropriation in these societies as 'lumpen-development'. He prefers the term lumpen-negation – ideological, political, economic, social, cultural and psychological – as an accurate conception of reality in Third World societies today.
2. Gavin Williams, 'Nigeria: A Political Economy' in Gavin Williams (ed.), *Nigeria Economy and Society*, (London: Rex Collings, 1976), p. 13.
3. Welfarist inclinations of the present government and the country's lumpen-bourgeoisie are reflected in the economic provisions of the new constitutions; see for example *Reports of the Constitution Drafting Committee*, Vol. 1, Section 3.7–2, p. xii. (Lagos: Federal Ministry of Information, 1976); and Nnamdi Azikiwe, 'Re-orientation of Nigerian Ideologies', *Weekly Star*, 2 January 1977, pp. 12–13.
4. This is the main line of argument of all the legally recognized political parties, each of which has promised to intensify the present government's indigenization policy. A theoretical justification of this thesis is provided by E.O. Akeredolu-Ale in his book, the *Underdevelopment of Indigenous Entrepreneurship in Nigeria*, (Ibadan, Ibadan University Press, 1975); and his article: 'Private Foreign Investment and the Underdevelopment of Indigenous Entrepreneurship In Nigeria' in Williams, *op. cit.*, pp. 106–22.
5. Akeredolu-Ale, 'Private Foreign Investment', p. 113.
6. Among others, see S.P. Schatz, *Development Bank Lending in Nigeria: The Federal Loans Board* (Ibadan, 1964); 'Aiding Nigerian Business: The Yaba Industrial Estate', *Nigerian Journal of Economic and Social*

Studies, 6, 2 (1976); Peter Kilby, *Industrialization in an Open Economy* (Cambridge, 1969), especially p. 335 where the author observes that 'all the major government programmes to develop indigenous industry . . . achieved disappointingly modest results'.

7. Akeredolu-Ale, 'Private Foreign Investment'.
8. A.A. Ayida, 'The Nigerian Revolution, 1966–1970', Presidential Address, Proceedings of the 1973 Annual Conference of the Nigerian Economic Society on Public Enterprises in Nigeria, University of Ibadan, pp. 7–8.
9. V.I. Bello, 'The Intentions, Implementation Processes, and Problems of the Nigerian Enterprises Promotion Decree (No. 4) 1972', in *Proceedings of the 1974 Symposium Organized by the Nigerian Economic Society on the Subject: "Indigenization – What Have we Achieved*?', p. 18.
10. A.E. Ekukinam, 'Opening Address', *Proceedings on Indigenization*, pp. 1–2. The author's figures of complying foreign firms differed from those provided by S.O. Asabia in the same *Proceedings*, pp. 30–31, which reflects inefficient record-keeping by government institutions and officials directly responsible for planning and plan implementation.
11. For a sample of unfavourable but often naive newspaper reviews of the indigenization policy, see S.A. Akinsanya, 'Egalitarianism and The Sale of Shares', *Business Times*, 8 March 1977, p. 7; Editorial Comment – 'Wider Share Ownership: But How?', *Business Times*, 1 February 1977, p. 3; Editorial Comment – 'Failure of Phase I', *Business Times*, 10 August 1976, p. 3; Taju Danmole, 'New Scramble for Alien Enterprises' *Business Times*, 10 August 1977, p. 16; Editorial Comment, 'Majority without Control', *Business Times*, 19 July 1977, p. 3; and *Business Times* of 13 July 1976, pp. 5, 11 and 13; 20 July 1976, pp. 7 and 11. Indigenization has also been called several sonorous names, but none is as ridiculous as Akintunde Asalu's, 'People's Capitalism', *Business Times*, 22 February 1977, pp. 3 and 5.
12. G.O. Onosode, 'Indigenization Decree and Its Implementation – Patterns of Shares Acquisition', *Proceedings on Indigenization*, pp. 19–31.
13. The revised Indigenization Decree of 1977, among other things (a) extended the list of Schedule I activities to 40; (b) further increased both the number of economic activities under Schedule II to 56, and the percentage of indigenous equity participation in them to 60; (c) created an additional Schedule III consisting of 39 large-scale foreign business organizations requiring at least 40 per cent Nigerian equity participation; (d) granted permission to these large-scale expatriate firms to continue participating in all Schedules I, II and III operations, provided that the respective annual turnover of each firm was not less than ₦25 million, the entire business of each respective body corporate was operating in at least 10 states in the federation, and that 60 per cent of each firm's equity was extended to Nigerians; (e) guaranteed individual share-ownership at any one time of not more than 5 per cent of total equity holding of any single company, or a portion of the equity valued at not more than ₦50,000, whichever is higher; (f) extended at least 10 per cent of a company's shares to its employees, from which 5 per cent is to be reserved for non-managerial employees; and (g) transferred large-scale agricultural production from Schedule II to III with several incen-

tives for purposes of attracting foreign and indigenous investments into this sector. The foregoing notwithstanding, the 'commanding heights' of the country's economy is still largely externally controlled.

14. Some of the activities reserved exclusively for Nigerians under Schedule I include: blocks, bricks and ordinary tiles manufacture; bread and cake making, candle manufacture, hairdressing, laundry and dry cleaning, manufacture of jewellry and related articles, retail trade, rice milling, singlet manufacture and tyre treading, ordinary garment manufacture and candle production, activities in which Nigerians have hitherto shown great interest.
15. Bello, *op, cit*., p. 16.
16. Ayida, *op. cit*., p. 7.
17. R. Blackburn (ed.), *Ideology in Social Science: Readings in Critical Social Theory* (New York: Fontana/Collins, 1972).
18. Olu Akinkugbe, 'Nigerian Enterprises Promotion Decree and Its Implementation', *Proceedings on Indigenization*, pp. 38–43.
19. *Business Times*, 26 December 1978, pp. 10–11.
20. See, among others, A.Chinweizu, *The West and the Rest of Us: White Predators, Black Slavers and the African Elite* (New York: Random House, 1975); Walter Rodney, *How Europe Underdeveloped Africa* (Dar es Salaam: Tanzania Publishing House, 1972); Inya A. Eteng, *Elements of Agrarian Capitalism* (work in progress); O. Oni and Bade Onimode, *Economic Development in Nigeria: The Socialist Alternative* (Ibadan: Nigerian Academy of Arts, Science and Technology, 1975); Ikenna Nzimiro, *Class Struggles in Nigeria* (London: Monthly Review Press, forthcoming); Ikenna Nzimiro, 'The Political and Social Implications of Multinational Corporations in Nigeria', IDEP, CS/2562–7, Dakar, 1974; and Peter Kilby, *Industrialization in An Open Economy, Nigeria, 1945–1966* (Cambridge University Press, 1969).
21. S.M. Essang, 'Technology Policy and Agricultural Development', *New Nigerian*, 13 July 1978, pp. 5, 7 and 13; and Iya Abubakar, 'Science and National Development', *New Nigerian*, 5 January 1978, pp. 5, 7, 9 and 15, and *New Nigerian*, 7 January 1978, pp. 5 and 10.
22. *Second National Plan*, p. 33.
23. Anyegbunam W. Obi, 'Self-Reliance, Foreign Exchange Illusion, and Industrial Development: The Case of Nigeria', Unpublished manuscript, Department of Economics, University of Nigeria, Nsukka, p.9. The author draws attention to the fact that value-added in manufacturing and crafts, for example, grew at a compound annual rate of 10 per cent between 1963 and 1973, with manufacturing alone growing by 12.2 per cent in 1962. Even though the growth rate is ostensibly impressive, the content of the increase is another matter altogether, especially since for every naira of value-added in manufacturing, the economy spent 0.67 naira on imports, especially of non-factor inputs at a time when manufacturing output is dominated by commodities such as food, textiles, footwear and petroleum refining which are local resource-based.
24. Kilby, *op. cit*., chapter 3.
25. C. Okonjo, 'Road of Progress: Building New Society', *Academic Star*, 2, 1 (February 1977); pp. 3–10, 20–22, first delivered as an inaugural lecture titled 'Economic Science, Imperialism, and Nigerian

Development', University of Nigeria, Nsukka, 1976.

26. Table of Imports by S.I.T.C. Sections (1974–76) and first half of 1977 complied from Central Bank of Nigeria data; see also *Business Times*, 3 January 1978, p. 10.
27. Kunle Adamson, 'Away with current Development Plan', *Daily Times*, 12 January 1978, p. 32.
28. For pertinent and critical evaluations regarding the pernicious implications of the First Lagos Trade Fair, see O. Ugochukwu, 'A Fair in a Trading Post Economy', *Business Times*, 20 December 1977, p. 11 and 20; S. Egbochuku, 'First Lagos International Trade Fair: Importance of the Exhibition', *Business Times*, 6 December 1977, pp. 9 and 24; and E. Akenzua, 'Double or Quit, That's the Game', *Sunday Times*, 11 December 1977, p. 7.
29. The *New Nigerian* editorial of 1 July 1978 specifically referred to an earlier publication of *New Nigerian* of 29 June 1978, pp. 1 and 3.
30. Chuba Okadigbo, *Time For Change with the Ideology of Scientific Populism* (1979).

11. Path to Nigerian Development: Conclusions

Okwudiba Nnoli

The Poverty of the Capitalist Path

Three priorities of politico-economic action follow from the impact of foreign investment on Nigerian underdevelopment so clearly illuminated by the contributions in this book. One is to secure complete indigenous ownership of all the dominant means of production, distribution, and exchange in the country. Another is the need for nationalist forces to intervene decisively in foreign trade in order to break the monopoly of vertical links with the advanced capitalist societies in the Nigerian economy, increase interregional exchanges within the country, and establish mutually rewarding lateral communications and exchange arrangements with other African and Third World economies and with the socialist nations. The other priority is a development policy which includes the satisfaction of the needs and demands of each and every citizen for a minimum of biologically and socially reasonable standards of nutrition, health, clothing, housing, employment, education, entertainment, and effective participation in national activities – to which he should be entitled as a matter of social rights. Without such a social policy, the vast majority of the population will remain psychologically unwilling and physically unable to maximize their potential capacity for development.

The second and third priorities hinge on the first. For example, it is not possible to change the direction of trade substantially without first changing the structures and institutions which carry on such trade. The banks, insurance companies, and the monetary system, which are dominated by Western interests and which dominate foreign trade, cannot be sympathetic to trade with the East, are reluctant to venture into new and unproven areas of trade, and are unwilling to re-orient their trading activities away from traditional markets and clients. And through a system of financial linkages with one another they already dominate the trade of most of the other Third World countries. Similarly, foreign-owned enterprises cannot be expected to support national welfare services at the expense of their profits. An important prerequisite for such a support is a psychological sense of solidarity and commitment to a common and worthwhile cause. But the foreign firms share no blood or other sentimental ties with the indigenous population. Their activities in the country are both marginal to their overall activities and to the total productive endeavours of the local population. They cannot be motivated by economic considerations of the positive impact of welfare measures on their long-run profits. In any case, they have only a short-term perspective of their existence in the country.

Therefore, how best to effectively eliminate foreign control of the Nigerian production process is central to the question of overcoming national underdevelopment. Nigeria has so far adopted four basic approaches to the problem: (1) the Nigerianization of the senior management and administrative staff of foreign firms; (2) state participation in economic life through the establishment of public enterprises in competition with foreign businesses in the same area of activity; (3) state participation in the ownership structure of foreign firms through a majority share holding; and (4) the indigenization of foreign enterprises through compelling foreigners to raise a substantial part of their capital requirements from the domestic market, or to sell their enterprises to nationals. All these measures fall short of nationalization, and are intended to maximize the benefits and minimize the costs of international capitalist participation in the national economy. They are motivated by ideological attachments to 'free enterprise' or the so-called 'pragmatic' necessities of politics and economics. They are being carried out within the context of the international capitalist economy in which Nigeria was incorporated by colonialism and neo-colonialism as a peripheral and dependent appendage of the advanced capitalist economies. They reflect the decision of the Nigerian ruling classes to seek development through the capitalist path.

These measures are fairly progressive. Optimal advantages accrue to foreign firms, and therefore optimal disadvantages flow to the country, when they own completely the means of production, distribution, and exchange. Therefore, any intervention by the state which reduces their power of ownership ameliorates the worst adverse effects of foreign capital. Sometimes foreign enterprises acquiesce in, or even support, these measures. However, this is done not out of preference for these policies, but rather because in the absence of monopolized markets automatically guaranteed by colonial rule, in the light of the vastly increased risks of total nationalization, and in the presence of increasing difficulties and checks against the repatriation of profits, such measures are among their most favourable alternatives. The foreign firms do not view their advantages in terms of all or nothing, but in terms of a continum. As a group they are willing to make concessions up to a point on the continuum commensurate with their control of the production process and, therefore, the guarantee of their monopoly profits, even though the size of such profits may be reduced. Below that point they will discontinue their activities. Therefore, their continued presence in the Nigerian economy reflects their continued manipulation of the country's system of production to thieir own advantage.

In other words, for various reasons these measures are incapable of eliminating foreign control of production in Nigeria and its concomitant, national underdevelopment. As regards the first policy, much state activity is directed toward pressuring the foreign firms into allowing nationals to participate in the higher echelons of their management. The objective is to nationalize the decision-making and, therefore, operations of the companies. Often, however, progress is measured primarily in terms of the number of foreigners whose jobs have been taken over by local personnel. Hence, in 1972, the Permanent Secretary in the Nigerian Ministry of Mines and Power, P. Asiodu, indicted the Shell-BP Company as follows: 'At the end of 1970, of 12 people of management status only one was a Nigerian and he was not really involved in the technical process of producing and marketing oil. In the senior professional and technical positions, excluding accountants and medical people, there were twice as many expatriates as Nigerians. In the grade of supervisory staff the numbers were about even. The company has trained about 340 graduates during more than 25 years of activity in this country. This is for a company whose turnover last year exceeded £400 million, considerably more if values are strictly determined on the basis of posted prices, and whose declared surpluses and transferred dividends for the year were large by any standards used in evaluating returns on investments. The position in the Gulf Oil Company, Mobil, Safrap, Agip, Tenecco, Texaco, and others is even worse than the picture in Shell-BP.'[1]

There are several fundamental weaknesses of this approach. First, it underestimates the social power of the foreign firms and their capacity to control the individuals working within and for them. The foreign firm is among other things a system of rules, regulations, procedures, guidelines, and incentives, which govern not only the choice of employees but also the choice of what to produce, when, how, and how the products are marketed. They derive from the overriding imperative of exploiting local resources for the monopoly profits of the firm. This system provides a strong built-in socializing agency ensuring that those who work in the firm adhere to its ethos, values, life-style, and manner of doing things. It constitutes a strong internal pressure on indigenous personnel to conform to the wishes of the foreign enterprise. Therefore, instead of the firm becoming more national in its decisions and activities, the indigenous personnel, in fact,become more and more foreign in their attitudes towards the activities of the firm. This gives the enterprise a national image without endangering foreign control. Furthermore, the firms tend to appoint Nigerians to managerial positions with the least impact on its activities, but which are most visible to the public, such as the front office, public relations departments, and personnel positions. Second, the phenomenon of organizational substitution arising from the technological possibilities of instant communication permits the firms to nominally fill even managerial posts of immense responsibility with nationals, but at the same time empty them of any decision-making significance. They simply refer to the head office decisions that normally would have been made locally. And third, local decisions usually concern the routine, non-creative, and middle-level matters of administration that only marginally determine the nature and dynamics of the foreign firm.

The other and significant decisions are made at the head offices of the subsidiary foreign firms where the policy of indigenization cannot penetrate. Thus, as a goal, the Nigerianization of the operations of the foreign firms is clearly and cleverly defeated.

The second policy of establishing local publicly-owned companies and corporations to compete with foreign enterprises is usually little more than a token recognition of the problem. The waste it involves in duplication, and the very futility of seeking to compete peacefully with the foreign firms, indicates a genuine unwillingness or political incapacity to tackle the problem. State enterprises such as state-owned insurance companies, investment corporations, the Nigerian National Oil Corporation, and state purchasing firms do not intend to break with the pattern of activities established by the foreign firms, or the rules, regulations, and procedure for organizing and carrying them out. They merely wish to secure part of the profits accruing from such activities for the state governments. But as relatively new entrants in the fields of business they do not have the experience of the foreign firms in how to manipulate these rules and regulations; they do not have as much knowledge of their business activities as their foreign counterparts. Therefore, although they may make profits, they must depend on the latter for the interpretations of rules and procedures, and for access to both the local and world market. The state enterprises cannot match the inexorable financial power and managerial skills of the foreign firms developed over many decades of exploitative operations throughout the capitalist world. Local subsidiaries of foreign firms with which the state enterprises compete are only small parts of vast economic empires operating at the global level, some of which have been in business for centuries. Therefore, any effective competition must involve the neutralization of not only the local foreign firm but the power of its parent group which sustains it. Under these circumstances the state enterprises cannot compete effectively to change the nature and rules of the relevant business activities in order to orient them to local conditions. In addition, state enterprises suffer the adverse effects of the alienation of labour so characteristic of public enterprises in Nigeria's peripheral capitalism. No one takes government work seriously because of the past history of the government's remoteness to the population. And the state enterprises cannot buy this loyalty the way the foreign firms do because they are not as rich. Thus state enterprises do not aid national control of production.

The third approach involving the participation of the state as a majority shareholder in foreign enterprises is the most prevalent among progressively-inclined Nigerian-type countries. Usually, the state buys at least 51 per cent of the shares of the companies. The objective is to acquire legal power for the nation over the management of the activities of the foreign firms that accompanies majority share ownership. This will enable the country to appoint some of the most powerful executives of the company, and thus be able to lay down the ground rules and policies for its operation. Again several basic factors prevent this approach from engendering an effective national control of the relevant foreign enterprises. In practice it has only helped to effect a redistribution of the profits and incomes of the enterprises to the greater benefit of the country. The state lacks an adequate knowledge of the technical and managerial processes of the firms, as well as their operational experience in the manipulation of rules, regulations, procedures, resources, manpower, and market to their own advantage. Therefore, its participation in ownership usually means entering into formal or informal management agreements with foreign capital. But this does not diminish the power of foreign decision-making in, and real control of, the enterprises. And these agreements often constitute a significant source of income drain from the country.

The local foreign firm is a peripheral branch of some multinational business concern whose head office in the North Atlantic area (and increasingly Japan) makes most of the crucial decisions concerning its activities. Therefore, any significant and effective state participation must ensure that inroads are also made into the decision centers at the head office. In addition, their greater bargaining skills, control of technology, and greater access to the world market give the foreigners such a superiority in the activities of the firm that they can still effectively control it even from the position of junior partner.

Nigeria places most of its hopes for local economic control on the fourth and final approach, the indigenization or local ownership of the foreign enterprises. These hopes are reflected in the government's and public's interest in the promulgation and implementation of the indigenization decrees of 1972 and 1976. This policy also contains a number of equally fundamental limitations. When forced to sell some of their shares the firms usually do so in such quantities and in such a way as to avoid putting the real control of the enterprises in danger. This is reinforced by the tendency for these shares to be taken up by local enterprises and businessmen who wish to 'partner' foreign capital. Where the foreign business is already a going concern the issuance of local shares simply provides the firm with funds to invest elsewhere outside the country, where there is no threat of indigenization.

The local capitalists who buy shares in the foreign enterprises or who buy the enterprises themselves are not motivated by their interest in creative production, but by their desire to get rich. Hence, indigenization has created a new class of Nigerian millionaires without any significant change in the character of national production. Very often these local capitalists operate the firms in the same way as their erstwhile foreign owners. They had developed in the shadow of the latter, depending on them for goal definition, a business ethos, and mode of operation. In the final analysis, local bourgeois nationalism merely seeks promotions within the hierarchical income, status, and power structure of the capitalist world, rather than national economic independence as such. In fact, their power and privileges derive ultimately from the center of this structure, which is located in the advanced capitalist states. They cannot successfully challenge these metropolitan countries because, on the one hand, they do not command the loyalty of the vast majority of their population and, on the other hand, they cannot compete with the large and powerful aggregate capital from the center. They are prisoners of the taste pattern and consumption habits set by the advanced capitalist countries, and must depend on foreign capitalist institutions for access to international markets, technical advice, capital, political ideas and, when necessary, military support.

In Nigeria, the interests of the local capitalists and those of the working class, the peasantry, the rural notables, and the intermediate strata of intellectuals, military officers, and senior civil servants contending for control of state power are not identical or even complementary. There is an immanent struggle among them for predominance. Consequently, national private capital often shrinks back from self-reliant and independent capitalist development well before it completes the task of winding up underdevelopment. It tends instead to enter into an alliance with foreign monopoly capital through partnerships economically and military aid politically. This provides some security for, and benefits from, the system based upon private ownership, but it does not show a way out of underdevelopment or bring about the unrestricted rule of national capital over the national economy. The experiences of Latin America and, to some degree, Egypt are illustrative.

It only serves to support what is increasingly evident, namely that local capitalists of Nigerian-type societies do not have an overriding interest in ending economic dependence. They do not wish to promote a radical transformation of their inherited colonial social and economic structure, which severely constrains national development. They cannot be expected to do this unless they misjudge their interests. These are not deeply antagonistic to the interests of the foreign enterprises and, therefore, cannot generate the kind of politico-economic momentum required to break dependence and ultimately underdevelopment.

On the other hand, even if national capital is able to assert its independence of foreign capital, it is unable to transform the productive forces while maintaining its private nature. As a result of the underdevelopment of the national economy, national private capital is quite small. Under the circumstances a very high degree of co-ordination is necessary to ensure a reasonable and positive impact of capital on the economy. The state may, of course, act as the co-ordinating agency and a source of the funds to increase the size of private capital. But the degree of state control necessary to produce the desired effect would vitiate the essence of the free enterprise economic system conducive to the functioning of private capital, even under state capitalism. In fact, the difference between such a state intervention and an outright takeover of economic activities by the state would be negligible.

In addition, in order to sustain its independence, it would be necessary for private national capital to increase the size and integrity of the national market by experimentation with, and introduction of, new taste patterns relevant initially to the traditional and habitual consumption patterns of the vast majority of the population, which the foreign enterprises are not interested in or familiar with and, therefore, cannot control. Under conditions of low capital and technology this would mean immense sacrifices by the national bourgeoisie, particularly with regard to its members' expectations of immediate returns on investment. The radical transformation of the structure of demand and supply that is involved, as well as the satisfaction of the basic social needs of the population, would necessitate investments whose profits could only accrue in the very long run. It is unrealistic to expect national capitalists to operate under these conditions. For them to do so would involve a measure of altruism which is not usually associated with capitalist enterprises, national or foreign.

Furthermore, the low level of private national capital adversely affects the incentive system in capitalist enterprises. The usual capitalist incentives for increased productivity such as high wages and numerous fringe benefits of an economic nature cannot be sustained. Foreign firms are able to maintain the present level of wages and fringe benefits in spite of the overall low productivity of the national economy because of the latter's integration into the global capitalist system in which overall productivity is high and because of the much higher cost of labour in the advanced countries which enables monopoly profits to be made in Nigerian-type economies by the foreign companies. In an autonomous capitalist economy this level of wages cannot be maintained, at least in the short run, without an intolerable burden of inflation. Since the working force does not have any directly visible stake in the new enterprises except wages, it is difficult to imagine other kinds of incentives which would stimulate the workers to realize the level of productivity necessary for the economic viability of the enterprises. Private capitalists do not monopolize state power, and as such cannot use coercion and unfair labour laws as an instrument of increased productivity, as was the case in the West in the eighteenth and nineteenth centuries. Labour consciousness and capacity for industrial action have changed in such a way as to make a return to the inhuman factory conditions of the past very unlikely. Under the circumstances, it would be impossible to drastically improve the productive forces of the nation.

Finally, even assuming that independent national capitalists are able to develop the productive forces and create an independent integrated economy, there are serious obstacles to their continued success in building national wealth. The advanced capitalist countries have been able to maintain relatively high levels of sophisticated economies in part as a result of their exploitation of foreign countries, first through colonialism and now through neo-colonialism. The changed international political and economic situations makes it highly unlikely that the newly-born imperialism will get a place in the rapidly setting sun of international exploitation. And if its growth and power attempt to rely exclusively on internal sources of exploitation, it will cause unbearable internal tensions and create an extremely unstable social order.

Meanwhile, the present course of peripheral capitalist development continues to lead to a dead end. The economic development strategy of import-substitution industrialization continues to be based on the neo-colonial economic infrastructure ill-adapted to the task of industrial development. Because some increased industrial activity has already taken place in the country, the government will increase its strategic and ever-growing role in the process. It will likely intensify and expand protectionist measures, reorganize the pattern of incentives in favour of the industrial sector, invest further in infrastructure and high-level manpower, and establish some manufacturing enterprises. However, these new industries will continue to produce goods based on the imported taste patterns which only the middle- and high-income groups can afford and which adversely affect the size of the national market.

Eventually, the industrial sector will expand to produce a highly diversified system of final consumer goods of the type found in the mass markets of the advanced capitalist nations, but only for the very limited, local, privileged income groups. Such a constricted market will not permit the specialization and standardization of the industrial structure so necessary for the efficiency, flexibility, and dynamic growth of the kind that has occurred in the advanced capitalist states to take place in the country. Consequently, entrepreneurs will move from one line of production to a new one as saturation of the market quickly develops in each industry, many small-sized plants will emerge to produce a great variety of consumer goods, and manufacturers will be more interested in producing new foreign consumer products capable of yielding quick and high profits rather than expanding the existing markets. Similarly, large public investment in electricity, petroleum, transportation and communication, steel, and petrochemicals will fail to increase economic momentum and dynamism as it did in the advanced countires. In the latter countries it acted as a motive force for the development of heavy industry, the transformation of the rural sector, and the generation of innovative technology and attitude. In Nigeria, on the other hand, it will end up as a catalyst for the creation of industries manufacturing externally-induced consumer goods. For example, increased electricity will give rise to the growth in the consumption of electrical appliances, while the steel industry, which in Europe, America, and Japan gave rise to industries producing agricultural, mining, and industrial machinery, will merely supply industries producing such consumer durables as automobiles and luxury building materials. In this way the neo-colonial structure of demand will frustrate any attempt to significantly change the structure of production, thereby freezing further growth in production, particularly the construction of a foundation for self-sustained economic growth.

As long as industrialization emphasizes import-substitution, even in the short term, it will remain viable only when the number of foreign consumer items to be produced locally is large. Numerous entrepreneurs will be attracted by the huge profits to be made with each line of industrial production, leading to some expansion of national productive capacity, but as the number of substitutes decreased with increased industrialization, the attractiveness of manufacturing to entrepreneurs will tend to diminish. As a result, overcapacity will tend to emerge in one activity after another. This will occur at the same time as industrial growth will be running into structural difficulties. As industrial production approaches such areas as consumer durables, machinery and equipment, and intermediate goods, much more intractable problems will face the production process than faced it earlier at the time of the establishment of light industries. Technological problems will be more complex, the need for highly-qualified manpower much greater, and the administrative problems more complicated. In addition, industries will become more capital-intensive, causing the minimum economic size of industrial plants to become larger and larger until it exceeds their respective markets. Consequently, and because of the monopolistic market structures that will develop in such a situation, an increasing fraction of the industries will operate below capacity. Thus, industrialization will reach a point of decreasing real returns to additional amounts of invested capital.

Under the circumstances, the pace of industrial growth will tend to level off, and with it, the rate of growth of the economy as a whole. And as a result of the full protection which such markets of relatively small size will enjoy from the government, the production process will be characterized by the inefficiency, waste of resources, and high concentration of property and income so deleterious to the full mobilization of human resources. In addition, the capital-intensive nature of the industrial structure will give rise only to a limited increase in employment opportunities. Agriculture, already stagnant because of the divorce of industrialization from agricultural production, will further deteriorate, causing malnutrition and undernourishment of very large portions of the population. Mechanization, where it will have taken place, will lead to increased productivity per man rather than yields per unit area of land. Together with stagnating agricultural production it will contribute to rural decay and the influx of rural migrants into the urban areas, which will heighten urban unemployment and underemployment.

Thus, the Nigerian economy will reach the inevitable dead-end of expansion. This has been the experience of the Latin American countries, India, Egypt, and other Third World nations which have a longer history of peripheral capitalist development than Nigeria. Regional integration will only delay the time of arrival to the dead-end, but will not be able to bypass it. By expanding the size of the middle- and high-income groups benefitting from import-substitution industrialization on a wider regional basis, it will postpone the arrival of overcapacity in industries and the other adverse effects of that process which make its future bleak. Only a development strategy that is fundamentally antagonistic to economic dependence and external control will break the grip of this inevitable stagnation.

The Compelling Logic of the Socialist Path

Theory as well as the abortive attempts of the national bourgeoisie of Nigerian-type societies to eliminate foreign dominance of the local production process proves the weakness or unwillingness of this class in the struggle against economic dependence and national underdevelopment. It suggests that the only available hope lies in the control of the means of production, distribution, and exchange by the state. This is one of the ways through which the idea of socialism emerges in these societies, from the process of development and the logic of the struggle against underdevelopment. After decades of futile attempts to reform the colonial and neo-colonial system of production it begins to dawn on the underprivileged section of the population that only a revolutionary transformation of the debilitating system of production and politics will bring underdevelopment to an end.

Sometimes, socialist consciousness starts with the idea of egalitarian distribution of income, goods, and services in the society, including a number of naive illusions about altruistic sacrifices by the rich, the indirect way of regulating income distribution through a progressive tax policy, or the power of sermons and moral exhortations regarding justice, fair play, and brotherhood. But as the economic and social failures of the petty bourgeoisie, comprador bourgeoisie, and national bourgeoisie to arrest underdevelopment become increasingly evident, the forces of vested interest disperse the altruistic illusions and the need for active state intervention in economic and social life becomes obvious, the idea of distributive socialism merges into the practice of real socialism based on ownership relations and the dominance of labour over capital in production, even before adequate theoretical clarity has been attained.

Therefore, the march toward a socialist form of development on the part of Nigerian-type societies does not need to stem from any *a priori* proletarian consciousness. It can, and does, arise from a realization over time and from previous experience that it is the only general policy capable of ending national economic dependence and pulling the country out of its quagmire of national underdevelopment. As it arises from, and is supported by, the objective logic of the historical struggle for development, life and practice tend to teach all those who are dedicated to the national interest of their country, or just obliged by the objective situation to be dedicated, that this is the only feasible path to development.

The first and most dramatic step in the socialist reconstruction of Nigerian-type societies is the nationalization of the local economy. Nationalization will contribute positively to the nation's withdrawal from the global capitalist system, which distorts and hampers its development. In this regard, it is not necessary for nationalization to be total for it to be effective in the fight for economic independence. In the short term at least, only the strategic sectors, or the commanding heights of the economy through which foreign enterprises effect their domination of economic life, need to be nationalized. By focussing on the foreign firms and their major local agents, nationalization will be able to sever the significant links connecting the national economy to the international capitalist system. Certainly, those structures of the economy that tend to reinforce the nation's external economic orientation, propensity to import, and subservient and passive role in the international division of labour ought to be the first to be nationalized. Included, of course, are import-export businesses, wholesale trade, shipping, banking, insurance, petroleum, petrochemicals, steel, mining, and major manufacturing enterprises. The petty economic holdings which characterize village economic activities and the small-scale industries and trade of the urban centers need not be nationalized in the near future.

As subsidiaries of larger businesses, foreign firms organize their activities across several countries. One purpose of nationalization is to set up a system which organizes economic activities in Nigeria only. This will permit the centralization of capital, co-ordination of the various enterprises by one center within the nation, and the elimination of the meaningless product differentiation that the existence of foreign enterprises generates. Over time it will provide the country with a full complement of skills, occupations, and products. It will create a situation in which the benefits of the horizontal and vertical integration of economic activities by the headquarters of the multinational corporations will be transferred to Nigeria, and the adverse effects of the peripheral location and character of the country within the international system served by the multinational corporations can be eliminated.

The nation will then be able to control and co-ordinate the primary, secondary, and tertiary economic processes of its natural resources. This will stimulate an increased capacity to transform and adapt the structures of production to changing demands and conditions. Thus, the country can be encouraged to focus attention primarily, but not exclusively, on domestic resources and priorities for the accomplishment of national objectives. By so doing it will bring all its potential local resources into productive use and into the mainstream of economic life, enabling the society to maximize the benefits accruing from those of its resources where it enjoys a comparative advantage over others, including the benefits from scientific and technological research, the final products, and their marketing. It is under such conditions, rather than those where the more advanced stages of the products – elaboration, production, marketing, and research – take place in foreign countries that the economy can become flexible, dynamic, and capable of adapting itself to new conditions. Such an economy is a prerequisite for economic development.

This flexibility together with the accompanying dynamism arising from this centralization of capital and other productive resources in the state will be reinforced by the centralization of political resources in the state. The coincidence of economic and political power in one center will enable a ready reorganization of the production process to create an internally integrated economy based on the use of local resources to satisfy the basic needs and traditional consumption habits of the population. The task of socialist reconstruction of the economy and society is a difficult one which demands immense sacrifice from the broad spectrum of the population. Among the difficulties will be the inevitable hostile reaction of the foreign capitalists and capitalist countries to the nationalization of foreign enterprises. The centralization of both political and economic resources in the state will enable Nigerian society to marshal one type of resource in support of the other as the need arises in order to overcome these obstacles, to engender a sense of national consciousness and commitment to the restructuring of the production process, and to ensure that the new production system is organized in the interest of the population. In this way national unity and national identity will be assured, and national loyalty and fervour will galvanize the production process to the benefit of increased creative production.

Flexibility coupled with efficiency of the production process leads to a high degree of scientific and technological capacity, as well as to a certain degree of economic specialization. That is precisely what accounts for the power and success of the foreign multinational corporations. Foreign dominance of the means of production, income, and technology is largely incompatible with changes that are necessary to create flexibility and efficiency at the national level, because the multinational firms' pattern of activities tends to limit these qualities to the advanced capitalist countries where their headquarters and innovative centers are located. This adverse situation is remedied by nationalization. And by cutting the national economy from its major links with the world capitalist economy, it will offer a challenge to the population which can lead to the acquisition of innovative mentality and capacity through the process of learning-by-doing. By ensuring that there are no more foreign enterprises and resources to lean on, nationalization will induce a disciplined economic order which will encourage self-reliance in all spheres of economic and social life, thereby promoting self-confidence and self-pride so essential for the creative mobilization of resources.

An adequate strategy for achieving the twin and minimal goals of economic growth and national independence for a poor state is one which effectively relates the needs of its members to their physical and human environment and the means available in the society for accomplishing them, and which enables them to live co-operatively while simultaneously operating to change their surroundings for the greater welfare of the members. Critical to such a strategy are commitment, fervour, and participation by members of the society on a basis broader than a narrow ruling elite. National dependence on external resources cannot be such a strategy because it cannot provide any meaningful basis of fervour and commitment in the poor state. In fact, a massive importation of external resources has a negative impact on participation because it tends to give the impression that foreigners, their knowledge, and their goods and services are better than their indigenous counterparts. Its impact on local morale and participation is, therefore, negative. A nationalization policy that successfully eliminates the dominance of foreign influence and resources in the local economy will greatly promote such a strategy.

In addition, the neo-colonial economy of Nigeria is a rigid and inefficient structure which encourages the transfer of potential savings to the advanced capitalist countries. Nationalization provides an opportunity for ensuring that most of the capital generated by the economy will be available for use in the country. This will enable the full mobilization of local resources for local transformation. The multiplier and the accelerator mechanisms will make their most significant impacts in Nigeria rather than abroad. For example, one of the practices of the foreign banks is to conduct their external transactions through their headquarters. A foreign bank which wishes to make payment to a French bank first pays its head office in sterling, which is then converted into francs before payment. The result is a 'double dealer's margin' of profit which adds to the amount of money paid out from the country. By dealing directly with foreign countries the nationalized system can eliminate such losses of funds.

Similarly, in the present neo-colonial economy foreign balances of the banks are uneconomically spread among the various banks, sales to the Central Bank are sporadic, and surpluses of non-sterling currencies are sold in the form of sterling after the deduction of the dealer's margin. Although the Central Bank has the legal power to buy all foreign balances, it lacks the ability to determine for itself what is a minimum working balance when the country has a tradition of maintaining a high ratio of private foreign balances to official reserves. With nationalization, however, foreign balances in excess of working balances can now be sold on a day-to-day basis to the Central Bank and made to earn interest. Also, a nationalized bank will be unlikely to deposit its funds abroad as the foreign banks now do. Likewise, the nationalization of insurance enterprises will lead to the progressive investment of its reserves in domestic assets instead of abroad, as well as a gradual curtailment of reinsurance abroad.

Gains will also accrue from the nationalization of the import, export, and wholesale businesses. Where the export of goods is undertaken by a foreign company primarily to its head office in Europe, America, or Japan, there is an incentive to understate the value of the goods in order to avoid company taxation. Also, imports routed through foreign confirming houses may be affected by the bargaining power of the importing firm. The normal confirmation fee is 2½ per cent, but the nationalized enterprise can obtain the service for considerably less. Again, many small importers obtain unnecessarily expensive suppliers' credit because of their weak financial position. A nationalized undertaking on the other hand can calculate the relative costs of the different terms of payment and choose the cheapest in foreign exchange terms. And nationalization will pave the way for the elimination of the confirming, financing, and secret commissions paid for the over-invoicing of imports by introducing new buying methods and more competitive tendering and cross-checking.

Nevertheless, that development policy which begins and ends with nationalization cannot solve the problem of underdevelopment or legitimately claim to follow a socialist path. It may merely give rise to bureaucratic capitalism, the use of state capital by a managerial elite in a manner which conforms to the ethos, values, and dynamics of private capital. For a country that has emerged from colonial domination and whose post-colonial period has been dominated by colonial structures, attitudes, norms, and ideas, the interests of the bureaucratic elite and those of foreign capital are not necessarily incompatible. During the colonial times the bureaucracy was dependent on the metropole for ideas, expertise, and solutions. And when independence came the bureaucrats emerged as among the greatest beneficiaries of the privileges inherited from colonial times. They will, therefore, oppose any transformation of the economy likely to erode their privileged position. Their reward will be an easy access to the national surplus and the life of conspicuous consumption that goes with it.

Of course, the bureaucrats are likely to make marginal reforms of the economy to avoid its early stagnation, widen their benefits, and improve their status position in relation to their foreign counterparts. Such reforms, however, are not likely to be carried to the point where the maximization of the potentialities of nationalization will damage their privileges, even if this is necessary for sustained economic growth, national independence, and the greater welfare of the majority of the population. Therefore, the bureaucrats are likely to use the nationalized enterprises to continue in one form or the other the pattern of production inherited from colonialism for which their experience and training best prepare them and which is the basis of their power, status, and privileges in the society. But as long as they continue the neo-colonial production process they will have to depend on foreign capitalists for managerial skills, technical expertise, technology, and access to world markets. This will lead to the debilitating dependence on the advanced capitalist world that is the basis of national underdevelopment, even in the absence of foreign ownership of local economic enterprises.

On the other hand, the pressure of the vast number of underprivileged workers in the nationalized enterprises, applied through workers' supervision of management, workers' participation in management, and eventually workers' self-management of the enterprises, is capable of ensuring that the management of the nationalized enterprises remains true to the national interest of eliminating economic dependence, overcoming underdevelopment, and in general catering to the welfare interests of the vast majority of the population. This involvement of the workers in the decision-process of enterprises should take place through the instrumentality of a political movement of poor peasants, workers, petty-traders, and the underemployed and unemployed, which is motivated by the workers' interests, dominated and guided by their organizations, devoted to the implementation of progressive policies, and protected by an army that would have been transformed from an inherited colonial institution designed to safeguard foreign capital and its pattern of production to a veritable people's defense force committed to progressive change. Such a party will enable the workers to participate effectively in production at increasing levels of political consciousness of their interests and that of the social collectivity as a whole.

This revolutionary role of the workers in production is possible because the working class of Nigerian-type countries represent one of the major segments of their national societies whose interests are deeply antagonistic to those of foreign capital. The inherited colonial institutions, dominated by foreign capitalist enterprises, represent the unjust exploitation of the workers' labour and the neglect of their socio-economic needs. They have a personal and class interest in overthrowing these institutions and replacing them with others in which labour is dominant over capital and state enterprises adjust their priorities against luxurious and prestigious goods and projects that cater primarily for the high-income groups. Their interests coincide with the more dynamic, self-expanding, and industry-generating projects relevant for servicing the interests of the vast majority of the population.

Workers' control of what is produced, when it is produced, how it is produced, and for whom it is produced will help to redirect the production process to the needs of the people and away from those artifacts which only the firms can supply and which only the privileged classes can afford. This will eliminate foreign control over local consumption and, therefore, will lead to national emancipation from foreign domination. Since the major needs of the vast majority of the country, such as the production of staple food crops, the use of local resources for building houses, roads, bridges, making clothing materials, and manufacturing drugs to be used on a large scale, are not of interest to the foreign firms, it is impossible for local production organized to satisfy these needs to be controlled from abroad. The products of these activities do not have a global market to which the foreign firms are oriented, and are not of any significance in the advanced capitalist states where the firms' innovation of products takes place on the basis of the prevailing consumption habits. Thus production will be more adequately and effectively related to local conditions, and controlled by nationalist forces.

This democratic participation of the worker in the management of production together with the obvious relevance of the production process to his needs and environmental resources will go a long way toward eliminating that alienation of labour at the psychological level arising from the neo-colonial system of production, which adversely affects labour productivity. His active involvement in the organization of the production process, at the same time that he is the executor of one or more production functions in conjunction with others, uses the means of production and disposes of the product of labour collaboratively with others, and is responsible for the work of the production collective and ultimately of the entire national economy, will enable the worker to maintain mental contact with all aspects of the production process up to, and including, the end product and its distribution. Such a democratic participation at the production level, which is made possible by the elevation of the worker to the status of proprietor of the nationalized enterprise and the feeling by the workers that they are co-proprietors of the socialist economy, will stimulate them to great creativity and awaken their latent energy and desire to work to the utmost of their ability, increase productivity of labour, optimally exploit material resources and working time, and improve the production process.

Furthermore, the worker, conscious of himself as proprietor will strive not only to improve his own labour input; he will also be deeply concerned that his comrades work well too. Therefore, he will actively combat all manifestations of negligence, inefficiency, and violations of discipline by those workers around him who do not yet have the necessary social consciousness and sense of responsibility. As a true proprietor, the worker, along with his co-workers, will carry out a search for unexplored and unexploited ways to raise productivity and to improve the results of common labour.

In another respect, since the national effort for radically transforming the society and mobilizing national resources against underdevelopment entails immense sacrifices, the pattern of distributing these becomes crucial. The granting of more and more privileges to those nearer the economic, political, and military seats of power creates a very destabilizing potential for the national leadership. By creating alienation at the material level for the rest of the people, it is likely to lead to the immobilization of the human resources of the vast majority of the population. The only helpful alternative is an egalitarian democratic system of socialism based on the fairness of the system of distribution according to work done, an enormous increase in the funds for the development of the social forms of personal consumption such as state social insurance, an extensive and free system of medical services, adequate pensions, free education at all levels, an extensive and free system of mother and child welfare, and full employment.

The labour enthusiasm and the upsurge in the people's creative powers that marked the early and subsequent stages of the socio-economic development of the socialist societies are largely due to the considerable improvement in the conditions of the working people, which did not stop even during the economically disastrous periods of national economic reconstruction, and which was the result of the adoption of such a progressive social policy. The experience of these countries explodes the myth that such a policy is not economically feasible. It shows that a progressive social policy is possible provided that the living standards of all segments of the population, and the real wages of the working people, do not as a rule increase for any considerable time faster than the increase in production and the productivity of labour; and that progressive legislation is employed to ensure the maximum removal of non-productive incomes from conspicuous consumption towards more productive areas as well as social welfare services for the broad majority of the population. Since the standard of living is a result of the volume of production of both raw and final products, its growth rate, and the level and growth rate of labour productivity, it must not run ahead of the expansion of production, but must follow the latter, keeping a certain distance behind it as far as all segments of the society are concerned. Only the observance of this condition can ensure the harmony between the economic and social aspects of development, which turns social progress into a motive force for economic growth.

By making the individual's level of material well-being directly dependent not only on his own labour but also on the labour of the entire collectivity, such a social policy encourages the worker to be personally interested in attaining maximum economic efficiency and therefore the improvement of production. It also helps to eliminate poor health, ignorance, and in general the hostility of the environment which adversely affects the ability of the worker to contribute his maximum to production, and which thereby reduces his material reward from production calculated on the basis of the productivity of his labour. It gives rise to a system of material stimuli that includes wages but goes beyond them to encompass other benefits broad enough in scope to engender as wide an input on production as possible.

In another respect, the progressive social policy of socialism is useful to social life because it undermines the socio-economic insecurity of the individual that gives rise to, and exacerbates, aggressive anti-social economic competition and ethnic identity and alignments, both of which cause instability of the social order. By an active involvement in the social welfare of the individual the state preempts the crucial functions of ethnic associations and ethnic alignments, thereby transferring overriding loyalty from the ethnic group to the state. This does not mean that ethnic sentiments and identities will cease to exist, but rather that divisive inter-ethnic and socio-economic competition will have no material basis and, therefore, ethnicity will lose its social sting. Similarly, wealth will be undermined as a basis for welfare, power, and influence in society since there will no longer be any material basis for its accumulation; most of its basic material functions will be fulfilled by the state's social welfare program, and the major means of production are owned by the state. Consequently, the anti-social competition for wealth and the deleterious social effects of its conspicuous consumption will be eliminated. And the division of the society into the haves and the have-nots so inimical to a stable human order will be abolished.

Finally, in order to be true to its objectives of economic independence, self-reliance, and self-sustained economic growth, the new socialist economy must re-orient its activities to emphasize the improvement of production in the rural areas. It is here that the vast majority of the population, as well as the greatest material and human resources, are located. Therefore, production that is based on the demands and supplies of this sector is most likely to yield the widest possible market for goods and services and to be the basis for an internally integrated economy in which each region maximizes its comparative advantage relative to the other regions. The emphasis of production must be initially to utilize the resources of the nationalized industries to perform better and more easily the present economic tasks of the rural population, using essentially local resources. This will mean an emphasis on food production, the provision of housing, and the manufacture of drugs for such endemic diseases as malaria and gastro-enteritis, as well as for childbirth. All national resources must justify themselves in terms of their contribution to the success of this pattern of production rather than in terms of increases in employment, foreign exchange, primary export production, and abstract GDP. The application of the existing knowledge of agricultural farm management, architecture and civil engineering, and medicine must be supplemented by a strong emphasis on applied research and the use of local resources which are linked with technological innovations. In other words, in addition to the extension of the existing knowledge of production with local resources to the rural population every effort should be made to create and disseminate new knowledge of such production.

What is needed to make such a program successful is a long-term view of production in which the rural areas become the social and institutional framework through which indigenous science and technology are developed and applied to agricultural and other forms of production. The villages must emphasize the establishment of local links between resource ownership and use, and consumer demands. They must start with a focus on the exploitation of existing demands, particularly for food, and then move on to the satisfaction of domestic demands for high protein foods such as milk, eggs, butter and meat, which have displayed the highest income elasticities of demand as well as a universal tendency to be consumed more and more at intermediate levels of income. Another important group of products includes cereals, such as maize and millet, which can be used directly as food or indirectly through their role as feed for animals. And the villages must aim at producing surpluses which can be used as a basis for local industries, and must aspire to operate at such a level of increasing efficiency that their role in agricultural production will steadily decline as their role in industrial manufacture correspondingly increases.

On the other hand, manufacturing should be organically linked with the other aspects of production in the rural areas. Emphasis should be placed on the production of implements for farming, processing of local materials for building houses and bridges, and a petrochemical industry for the manufacture of clothes and other goods. Like all other sectors of the economy it must justify its existence by the extent of its service to the economic progress of the rural areas. Emphasis should be placed on the transformation of local raw materials into secondary products that may be the means for further production or items to be consumed. With such inputs from the manufacturing sector, the agricultural sector should be able to increase its productivity and therefore produce enough surplus food and other resources to feed the industrial population and fuel the various industries. Only under such a condition in which manufacturing transforms local resources in order to satisfy local demands and traditional consumption habits will it be an effective motive force for self-sustained economic growth.

Once the pattern of demand and supply has been transformed and the new production system effectively related to local needs, consumption habits, and resources, external resources may be permitted to play some role in the new society. Of course, only those which are capable of making a contribution in the new scheme of things will be accepted. They will be judged by their ability to serve local needs and interests rather than by the level of their scientific sophistication. Here emphasis must be placed on criticizing the shortcomings of that foreign equipment identified as relevant to the needs, aspirations, resource endowments, and the local environment of the vast majority of Nigerians, and changing it in such a way as to meet the local needs. At the same time, the basic knowledge of such equipments must be applied to the creation of new and related ones which can be more easily employed by the local population in production. The idea must be to change foreign equipment from complicated to simple, heavy to light, big to small, wasteful to economical in the consumption of materials, and low to high in efficiency with regard to the transformation of the local resources by the people for their own use. Only in such conditions will technologically innovative attitudes and capacity be engendered in the population.

Thus, nationalization for socialist development must go hand in hand with an egalitarian democratic policy in the nationalized enterprises, the political system, and in social life in general in order to reserve the existing neo-colonial relationship between labour and capital, ensure national economic independence, and engender the growth of the productive forces on a self-sustained basis. Far from being passive in this process the masses must participate actively in these national tasks, serving at least to hold the fort against any attempt by the leaders to shrink back from their accomplishment. Therefore, further discussion of Nigerian development must concentrate on the details of the strategy and tactics for bringing about the necessary socialist transformation.

Reference

1. Quoted in Owen T. Adikibi, 'Impact of U.S. Multinationals in Africa: The Case of West Africa', a paper presented at the African Regional American Studies Conference in Abidjan, Ivory Coast, 25–28 July 1976, p. 29.

Index